Anyone Can Teach In English

누구나 영어로 가르칠 수 있다

Anyone
Can Teach
In English

 누구나 영어로 가르칠 수 있다

저자 황기동   **해설** Gerry Gibson
Gregory Goguts
Diane. B. Hertberg
Katherine Spinney

황기동

Professor of English at the Korea Naval Academy, Ph.D. in Linguistics
Completed D.L.I. Advanced English Instructor's Course in Texas, U.S.A.
Research into TESL/TEFL courses at the University of Birmingham in 2007

저서
『실용 모델 영작문』
『삼위일체 기본 영문법』
『현대 교실영어와 교수법』

해설
Katherine Spinney : University of Virginia, Master in Teaching
Diane Blietz Hertberg : University of Phoenix, Master in Education
Gerry Gibson : Leicester University, Master in Applied Linguistics
Gregory Goguts : Westfield State College, B.A. in English

The purpose of this textbook is practical: its main roots lie in the problems facing many Korean EFL instructors who feel that they lack the ability to take command of their lessons and their students through the use of the English L2.

Expectations for Korean EFL instructors to demonstrate a communicative command of the English language in the EFL classroom stem in large measure from the reforms initiated by the 6th National Curriculum in 1992. It was then that the shift in emphasis from grammar-translation to communicative language teaching (CLT) was mandated. Yet, according to recent statistics, less than half of Korean EFL instructors have adopted the CLT approach and 28% of them have continued to apply grammar-translation methods (Kwon, 2003). Clearly, many Korean EFL instructors are not completely comfortable teaching through an approach that requires a command of the English language to a certain degree. More specifically, two key reasons the CLT has yet to catch on are that many Korean EFL teachers feel they lack adequate speaking skills, and the grammar-translation methodology does not require a command of spoken English.

Thus, the motivation for creating this text is to directly address this problem by developing a resource that teachers can use on a daily basis when preparing their lessons. This book will, we hope, serve as a guide or resource for Korean teachers to reference for common expressions used by English native speaking teachers during various parts of a lesson.

It is not our intention to provide Korean EFL instructors with lesson plans. Rather, we would like to equip instructors with the classroom language necessary to facilitate all manners of classroom interaction that EFL instructors face day in and day out.

In terms of the specifics of the text, it provides Korean EFL instructors with a variety of commonly used expressions compiled by Professor Hwang Ki Dong over a 10 year period working closely with English native speaking EFL instructors. The expressions address both formal and informal usage and also distinguish between American and British English expressions when necessary.

With respect to how the book facilitates a teacher's command of English in any given lesson, it provides a comprehensive collection of useful expressions that teachers commonly use during specific parts of a lesson. Parts of the lesson that are addressed in this book include the following:

— Getting the lesson started
— Taking attendance
— Introducing the lesson or topic
— Setting up pairs and groups
— Facilitating pair and group work
— Engaging students in reading activities

- Engaging students in listening activities
- Eliciting questions and answers from students
- Checking for homework
- General classroom management

These are just a few of the lesson areas that are addressed in this book. Also, the text addresses classroom situations that are not directly related to the lesson itself. Namely, it provides insight into the types of small talk that frequently occur between teacher and student before or at the end of class.

Ultimately, we hope that Korean EFL teachers will find this book and its English expressions easy to access, and with any luck it will furnish them with the support they need to enter the classroom equipped and ready to deliver their lesson completely in English. Moreover, our vision in producing this text is to motivate Korean instructors to take the initiative to teach lessons in English and to be role models for their students. We hope our book provides them with the support they need to achieve this end.

Gerry Gibson

Kwon, O. Narrowing the gap between ideals and realities in TEFL in *The First Asia TEFL International Conference*, 2003.

영어를 이용하여 수업을 진행하거나 토론을 하기 위해서는 먼저 교실에서 사용되는 영어표현은 어떤 것인가를 알아야 한다. 이를 위해 필자가 교실영어에 관계된 다양한 자료를 검토해 본 결과, 표현의 종류가 극히 한정되어 있으며, 대부분 매우 쉽고 단순하다는 사실을 알았다. 그래서 그와 같은 표현들은 영어선생님이 한 번만 읽어보면 교실에서 쉽게 응용할 수 있다는 확신을 가지고 자료를 수집 정리하게 되었다. 이 책의 자료는 부분적으로 영어교육에 대한 각종 영문 저널과 교실영어와 관련된 서적을 참고하였으나, 모든 자료는 실제 외국인 영어교수들과의 대화와 토론을 통해서 재구성하였다. 또한 엄선된 자료는 우리 환경에 맞게 편집하였으며, 특히 현장예문의 경우에는 오늘날 사용하고 있는 미국영어와 일치하는가를 확인하기 위해서 미국인 영어교수들과 하나하나 토의하여 정리하였다.

사실 몇 년 전 저자가 출판한 교실영어와 관련된 서적은 대기업의 교수용 영어 교재로 채택되고, 대학 교수, 일선 학교의 선생님에게 많은 호평을 받았다. 실제 일선에서 가르치는 영어 선생님들은 책을 읽고서 영어 강의에 많은 도움이 되었다고 했다. 그러나 출판 후 검토해 본 결과 세부적인 설명이 부족하고, 특히 현장예문에 대한 설명이 미흡하였다. 그리하여 이번에는 그 책을 사용한 분들의 논평을 참고하여 각 단원을 현장예문을 중심으로 편집하였으며, 각 단원의 마지막에는 영어교육에 이용될 수 있는 일상영어 및 영어교수법에 대한 각종 연구 자료를 첨부하였다.

이 책은 3장으로 나누어져 있다. 1장에서는 학과수업을 시작하기 전 수업 준비와 관련된 표현을 정리하고, 2장에서는 교과수업 중에 사용되는 각종 지시어 및 교과 설명에 빈번하게 사용되는 표현들을 수록하고, 3장에서는 분야별 영어 수업과 관련된 표현들을 정리하였다. 한편 각 장에 포함된 현장영어와 교수법에 대한 자료는 주로 영어교육에 관계된 저널 — English Language Teaching Journal, TESOL Quarterly 등 — 과 교실영어에 관한 최근의 서적들을 참고하여 우리 현실에 맞게 수정·정리한 것이다. 그리고 각 장의 교수법 자료 중에서 구체적인 저자 표시가 없는 자료는 『현대교실영어와 교수법』(황기동, 2014)에 포함된 저자의 교실영어에 대한 논문자료를 편집하여 정리한 내용이다. 이 자료들은 영어교육에 사용되는 각종 표현과 교수방법에 대한 지식의 습득뿐만 아니라 개인의 영어 능력 향상을 위해서도 많은 도움이 될 것이다.

이 책을 처음부터 끝까지 읽고 내용을 보충·수정한 Gerry Gibson, 부록의 상용 교실영어를 감수·수정한 Gregory Goguts, 기본표현을 용법에 따라 분류·수정한 D. B. Hertberg, 모든 문장을 미국 현지영어와 일치하도록 편집·교정한 Katherine Spinney, 수시로 자문에 응해 주신 미국인 영어 선생님들, 그리고 이 책의 출판을 즉석에서 받아들인 김수영, 윤석전 이사님에게도 사의를 표합니다.

끝으로 이 책이 일선에서 영어교육을 담당하고 있는 모든 선생님 그리고 나의 내자에게도 조금이나마 도움이 되기를 바랍니다.

2020년 6월

황기동

용법구문

이 구분은 외국인 영어선생님들이 직접 표시한 것이다. 간혹 몇 가지 문장에 대해 개인차가 있었지만 여기에서는 종합적인 의견을 바탕으로 정리하였다.

문장유형에 의한 구분
formal (공식영어, 격식영어)
informal (일상영어)
casual/colloquial (구어)
slang (속어)

사용빈도에 따른 구분
usual/common (일상적)
rare (가끔 사용)
cliché(낡은 표현)

존대에 따른 구분
polite (높임형)
impolite (낮춤형)
rude (무례한 표현)

어법에 따른 구분
correct (맞음)
awkward (어색한 표현)

표현 방법에 따른 구분
indirect (간접적 표현)
implied (함축적 표현)

해설	문장의 의미와 활용에 대한 설명	**syn**	동의어, 유의어
참고	부가적인 설명	**ant**	반의어
주의	틀리거나 구분해야 할 경우	**cf.**	관련된 유사예문
어휘	용어에 대한 설명	**A.E.**	American English
어법	문법적인 사항	**B.E.**	British English

CONTESNTS

Anyone Can Teach In English

Part 1 수업준비

Preparing for the Lesson

Unit 1 인사 및 소개

1. 현장예문(Real-life Situation)

Introduction Practice
(based on M. Helgesen(1996) & C.F. Meloni et al(1982))

아침 인사를 나눈 후에 선생님이 학생들 간에 자신을 소개하는 연습을 시키는 상황이다.

When a teacher meets his students for the very first time, he introduces himself and oftentimes will ask the students to introduce themselves as well. In the typical student self-introduction, students give their name, some basic family background information, and talk about their hobbies. They are not, however, expected to mention private personal information such as their religion and how much they earn if they are employed.

Now listen to the dialogue.

T: Good morning, everybody.

Ss: Good morning, (Ma'am).

T: Well, how are you all, today?[1]

Ss: Very good, thank you.[2] How about you?

T: Fine, thank you. Nice to see you all here. Welcome! Well, let's introduce ourselves, shall we? Now, Kim Sumi and Jung Mija, will you introduce yourselves to each other? (*Sumi and Mija stand up.*)

Sumi: Hi. I'm Sumi Kim. I saw you in my supplementary math class last year, didn't I?[3]

Mija: Right. My name is Mija Jung. Glad to meet you, Sumi.[4]

Sumi: Nice to meet you, Mija. I'm from Seoul. Where are you from?

Mija: I am from Pusan.

T: Good job! Now, will you please divide into groups of three and introduce your friends to each other? After you introduce yourselves, you should find out a little more about each other, such as where you are from, what subjects you like, etc.

(Later Kilsu, Sumi, and Mija form a group.)

Sumi: Kilsu, meet Mija. She and I were in the same class last year.

Kilsu: Hello, Mija. Nice meeting you. I don't think we've met before. I'm Kilsu Kim.

Mija: Hi. Glad to meet you, too. My name is Mija Jung.

Kilsu: Mija, do you like to study English?

Mija: I don't really like English much. I'm taking this class because I have to. By the way, have you ever taken a class with this teacher before?

Kilsu: No, I haven't. But I've heard she's good.

Sumi: I learned English from her last year. [5] She's really good.

Mija: That's good to know. [6] Then I can improve my English this year.

1 (모두 안녕하세요.) How are all of you today?

2 오늘날 미국영어에서 'How are you?'로 물으면 '(Very) Good.', 'Fine.', 'I am alright [O.K.].' 등 다양하게 답을 한다. 또한, 'How are you doing?'이라고 물으면, 문법적으로는 '(I'm doing) (very) Well.' 또는 'Fine.'이라고 답해야 한다. 그러나 이 경우에도 미국에서는 '(I'm doing) Good.', '(I'm doing) Alright.'이 널리 사용된다. 따라서 위의 두 가지 인사말에 대한 답을 할 때에는 '(I'm) Fine', '(I'm) Good', '(I'm) Alright'을 반드시 구분할 필요 없이 자유롭게 혼용해서 사용하면 훨씬 새로운 느낌을 줄 수 있다. 실제 우리나라 사람들은 'Fine.'을 너무 많이 사용해서 외국인에게 단조롭고 식상한 느낌을 주는 경우가 있다.

3 일과 외의 '(수학)보충수업'은 '(math) supplementary class'라고도 한다. 수식어 'supplementary'와 과목을 나타내는 'math'는 서로 순서가 바뀔 수 있다. 반면 결손에 대한 보강수업은 'make-up class'라고 한다.

4 (만나서 반갑습니다.) Pleased to meet you ; Nice to meet you ; Nice meeting you ; It's nice meeting you.

5 '수강'은 초등학교 또는 중등학교에서는 'class', 대학교에서는 'course'라고 한다.
   I took her English class [course] last year.
   I had her for a English class [course] last year.

6 (그거 좋은 소식이구나.) I'm glad to know that.

해석

선생님: 안녕하세요, 여러분.
학생들: 안녕하세요, 선생님.
선생님: 그래요, 오늘 기분 어때요?
학생들: 아주 좋아요. 선생님은요?
선생님: 좋아요. 여러분을 보니 반갑습니다. 자, 각자 소개를 해볼까요? 자, 김수미와 정미자, 서로 소개해 볼래?
(수미와 미자가 일어선다.)
수미: 안녕, 난 김수미야. 지난 해 보충수업에서 만났지?
미자: 맞아. 나는 정미자야. 만나서 반가워 수미야.
수미: 미자야, 나도 만나서 반가워. 난 서울 출신이야. 너는 어디 출신이니?
미자: 나는 부산 출신이야.

선생님: 잘했습니다. 자, 세 사람씩 그룹을 지어 친구에게 서로 자기소개를 해볼까요? 서로 소개한 다음에는 서로에 대해 좀 더 자세히, 이를 테면 출신이 어디인지, 어느 과목을 좋아하는지 등을 알아보세요.

(조금 뒤, 길수와 수미와 미자가 그룹을 형성한다.)

수미: 길수야, 이쪽은 미자야. 그녀와 나는 지난 해 같은 반이었어.

길수: 미자야 안녕. 만나서 반가워. 우리 처음 만나지. 나는 김길수야.

미자: 안녕, 나도 만나서 반가워. 나는 정미자야.

길수: 미자야, 영어 좋아하니?

미자: 나는 사실 영어를 별로 좋아하지 않아. 그러나 이 과목은 필수이기 때문에 듣고 있어. 그런데 넌 전에 이 선생님 수업 받은 적 있어?

길수: 아니, 없어. 그런데 그녀가 좋다는 말은 들었어.

수미: 나는 지난 해 이 선생님한테 영어를 배웠어. 그녀는 아주 좋아.

미자: 그거 좋은 소식이다. 그러면 나도 올해 영어실력이 좀 늘 수 있겠네.

2. 기본구문

여기에서는 수업을 시작하기 전에 선생님이 학생들과 나누는 간단한 대화 및 인사말을 다음과 같이 정리하였다: A. 인사 B. 감사·유감·축하 C. 소개

A. 인사

> ① T: Good morning, everybody.
>   Ss: Good morning, Mr. Baker / Ms. Baker.

해설 'Everybody' 대신 'everyone', 'class 3'[3반일 경우], 'girls and boys', 'children', 'all', 'ladies and gentlemen' 등이 대체될 수 있다. 친한 사이이거나 아랫사람에게는 간단히 'Morning.'이라고 표현하기도 한다.

주의 Title — Mr., Ms., Dr., Prof. 등 — 은 이름 앞에는 사용하지 않고, 반드시 성 앞에서만 사용한다. 예를 들어 'Julia Jones' 박사의 경우를 보자.
   e.g. Dr. Julia Jones (O), Dr. Jones (O), Ms. Jones (O), Julia (O), Dr. Julia (X), Ms. Julia (X)

> ② T: How are you (all)?
>   Ss: Fine, thank you. How about you?

해설 인사말은 매우 다양하게 표현할 수 있지만, 인사를 받은 다음에는 반드시 상대방에 대한 안부도 되묻는 것이 예의이다.

syn T: How are you doing (these days)?

How's everything (going)?

How're things?

How's life?

How have you been?

Is everything okay with you?

What have you been doing?

What have you been up to?

Are you well [O.K., alright] today?

(상대편의 건강 또는 심리적 상태를 염려한 인사말)

— 위의 인사말에 다음과 같이 다양하게 답할 수 있다.

S: Good [Alright, OK], thanks. And you? *(informal, usual)*

I'm good [alright, OK]. And you? *(usual)*

Fine, thanks. How about you? *(formal, usual)*

Pretty good, thanks. How about you?

Oh, not bad, thanks. And you?

So-so. And you?

Same old, same old. And you?

(매우 기분이 좋을 때)

Couldn't be better. How about you?

Never been better, I can't complain. How about you?

I've never been better. How about you?

Terrible. I've had a headache all morning. *(informal, between friends)*

주의   친밀한 사이가 아니라면 상대방의 인사말에 대해 "Well, I have a cold." 또는 "Not so good.", "So so.", "Not bad."와 같은 부정적인

답은 예의에 어긋난다. 반면, 서로 친밀한 관계에서는 사실대로 부정적으로 "Not so good.", 또는 "Terrible."이라고 답할 수 있다. 그러나 이 경우에는 분명한 이유를 덧붙이는 것이 좋다.

참고 위의 인사법이 가장 일반적으로 널리 통용되는 인사이다. 반면 아주 친밀한 사이에서는 다음과 같이 좀 더 구어적인 인사말도 사용할 수 있다.

A: What's up?
　What's new?
　What's going on?
　What's shaking? *(slang)*
　What's cooking? *(slang)*
　(위의 인사말은 전부 우리말로 '별일 없어?'라는 의미를 지닌다.)

위의 인사말에는 주로 다음과 같이 답을 한다.
B: Not much.
　Nothing special [new].
　Nothing (much). (그래 별일 없어.)

어법 다음 예문에서 보는 바와 같이 'fine'의 의미는 앞의 질문에 따라 다르다.

A: How are you?
　('오늘 기분이 어떠니?'(How are you feeling today?)의 의미이다.)
B: (I am) Fine [Good], thanks.
　(위의 'fine'은 형용사로 '몸이 상태가 좋은(in good health)'의 의미이다.)

반면 다음 예문을 보자.

누구나 영어로 가르칠 수 있다

A: How are you doing?

('요즘 생활은 어떠니?'(How's your life (in general)?)라는 의미이다.)

B: (I'm doing) Fine [Good, Very Well], thanks.

(이 경우 'fine'은 부사로 '잘하고 있는'(well, in a way that is satisfactory or acceptable)이라는 의미를 지닌다.)

cf. It's been a while. (오랜만입니다.)

③ A: **Say hello to your brother for me.**
B: Yes, I will.

해설   동생에게 안부 전해라 [안부 전해주세요]. 'My regards [My best wishes]'를 사용하면 정중한 표현이 된다.

syn   A: Tell your brother "Hi" for me. *(informal)*
Tell your brother I said "hi" / "hello".
Say "hi" / "hello" to your brother for me.

Tell your brother I'm thinking of him. *(formal)*
Give my regards [my best wishes] to your brother. *(very formal)*

Give your brother a pat on the back for me.
Give your brother a handshake [hug, kiss] for me.
Remember me to your brother. *(rare)*

B: Okay. / I will. / Sure.

④ T: Have a nice weekend.
  S: Thank you. **(The) same to you.**

해설   T: 주말 잘 보내세요.
      S: 네, 선생님도요.
      : 상대방의 작별인사에 대한 대답은 다음과 같이 여러 가지로
      표현할 수 있다. 작별하기 위한 여러 가지 가벼운 변명에 대한
      것은 Part 2, Unit 5의 '작별인사의 유형과 표현 방법'을 참조할
      것.

syn   S: Thank you. I hope you (will) enjoy your weekend. *(formal)*.
      Thanks. You too.

      Thanks. Take care (of yourself). *(informal)*
      Thanks. Take it easy.

      Sure. Stay out of trouble. *(casual)*
      ('말썽을 일으킬 행동은 하지 마라.'라는 의미로 주로 윗사람이
      아랫사람에게 염려해서 하는 말이다.)

      *Thank you, too. *(incorrect)*
      (학생들이 흔히 사용하는 위와 같은 응답은 잘못된 것이다.)

참고   그 외 헤어질 때 일반적으로 사용되는 작별인사는 다음과 같다.
      S: Good-bye. / Bye. / See you (later). / So long.
      Take care. / Take it easy.

      Have a good [nice] day.
      Have a good one. *(casual, slang)*
      ('One'은 막연히 시간을 나타내는 명사로, 상황에 따라 'time',
      'day', 'weekend', 'vacation' 등의 의미를 가진다.)

Don't work too hard. *(informal)*

(이 경우 'Don't work too hard'는 '잘 지내'라는 의미이다. 우리 말로 직역하여 '너무 열심히 공부하지 마라'라는 의미로 해석해서는 안 된다.)

B. 감사·유감·축하

---

① Mr. Kim: **Thank you so much for your help**, Miss Lee.
I really appreciate it.
Please let me know if I can return the favor.
Miss Lee: **Don't worry about it.**

해설   김씨: 이양, 도와주서서 고맙습니다. 진심으로 감사드립니다. 도움이 필요하면 알려주세요.
이양: 신경 쓰지 마세요.

syn   Mr. Kim:
Thank you for **your help** [your assistance]. *(formal)*
It was very kind of **you to help me. Thank you.** *(very formal, polite)*
Thank you. That was really kind of you.

Thanks. **Your help** [Your assistance] is much appreciated.
I really appreciate your help.
Thank you for your assistance.

Thanks! You've been a huge [tremendous] help.
Thanks. That was a big help. *(casual)*

— 간단히 '감사합니다'는 다음과 같이 표현한다.

Thanks a lot [a bunch, a million]. *(usual)*
Many thanks.
It's much appreciated.
I'm very grateful to you.
I really appreciate it.
It's really kind [nice] of you.

I owe you one. *(casual)*
Many thanks. *(casual)*

Thank you so much. *(usual)*

*Thank you too much. *(awkward)*
*Thank you a lot. *(awkward)*
(학생들이 종종 사용하는 위의 표현은 사용하지 않는 표현이다.)

— 감사의 표시에 대해 대개 다음과 같이 대답한다.

Mr. Lee: My pleasure.
　　　　Think nothing of it.
　　　　It's my pleasure.
　　　　Not at all.
　　　　Don't mention it.
　　　　Forget about it.
　　　　Not a problem.
　　　　Don't worry (about it).
　　　　Any time.
　　　　You're welcome.
　　　　No worries.
　　　　No problem. *(casual)*
　　　　It's the least I can do.

('별거 아닌데요' : 기꺼이 도와주고 싶었을 때 사용하는 표현이다.

로저: 시장님! 누추한 저의 집을 방문한 것을 환영합니다!

시장: 오히려 제가 기쁩니다. 로저 씨!

참고1 'My pleasure.'는 위와 같이 도움을 받은 뒤에 상대가 감사히 여길 때 응답으로 '뭘요(해드려야지요).'라는 의미도 있지만, 처음 도움을 요청할 때 '기꺼이'라는 의미로 사용할 수도 있다.

A: Could you do me a favor? (좀 도와주시겠습니까?)
B: Sure. My pleasure. What can I do for you?
　(물론. 기꺼이. 무엇이지요?)

참고2 'Don't worry (about it).'는 '(어떤 문제에 대해) 신경 쓰지 말라.'는 의미로도 사용된다. 이 경우에는 다음과 같이 표현할 수도 있다.
It's nothing to worry about.
No worries. / Not to worry.
Don't sweat it. *(casual, slang)*
No sweat. *(casual, slang)*
No big deal. *(slang)*
('No big deal'은 '문제 자체가 중요하지 않으므로 신경 쓸 필요가 없다.'는 의미이다.)

② S: Sorry (about that).

해설   '미안합니다.'라는 표현은 영미권에서 가장 흔히 사용된다. 길에서 앞사람을 지나칠 때에 필자의 경험으로는 미국에서는 'Excuse me.'가 흔히 사용되는 반면, 영국에서는 'Sorry.'를 흔히 사용하였다. 물론 군대에서 상관의 앞을 지나갈 때는 'By your leave, sir.' 하고 지나간다.

syn   I'm very [terribly, awfully] sorry (about that). *(formal, very polite)*

Sorry, that was my fault.

Please accept my apologies (about that). *(formal)*

Forgive me.

It's my fault, please forgive me.

참고   **감정을 나타내는 표현**

① 좋은 일 (Good News)

A: There was a car accident but I was not hurt.

B: Thank goodness! / Thank God! (천만다행이군!)

A: I passed my driving test. / I just got engaged. /
I just got a new job.

B: Congratulations! / Well done! / You did a good job!
=Good job! (축하한다! 잘했다!)
(That's)Great! / Wonderful! / Marvelous! / Fantastic!
/ Terrific! (잘됐구나!)

A: I just won a free trip to Los Angeles.

B: Incredible! / Amazing! / Unbelievable!
(믿을 수 없는 일이군!)

② 나쁜 일 (Bad News) 또는 염려

    A: I'm worried about the exam tomorrow.

    B: Try not to worry! (걱정하지 마!)

       It'll be all right! (괜찮을 겁니다!)

    A: I broke your pen.

    B: Don't worry too much! (걱정하지 마! 염려하지 마!)

    A: I lost my passport and all my money.

    B: I'm sorry! / That's too bad. / That's terrible! / What a pity! / What a shame! / How awful! / How terrible! (참 안됐군요.)

    : 이 경우 A는 혼잣말로 'Oh, my gosh'(이런)라고 표현할 수 있다. 흔히 'Oh, shit'라고도 하지만 이 표현은 좋지 않으므로 사용하지 않는 것이 좋다.

    A: He scratched his partner's favorite record.

    B: Oh no! (저런!)

    A: My bird just died.

    B: How sad! / Oh dear!

       (어찌 그런 일이! (나이 든 여자들이 주로 사용))

    A: Double-parking! It drives me nuts! [It makes me crazy!]

       (이중 주차! 정말 화나게 만들어!)

    B: Chill out. / Cool it. / Calm down. / Relex. / Take it easy.

       (진정해라.)

③ 놀라운 감정

    A: I saw a UFO last night.

    B: Really? (정말?)

③ Congratulations. *(formal)*

해설 주로 생일이나 진급 등 중요한 기념일에 사용된다. 그 외 "(일을) 잘했[됐]군요."는 다음과 같이 표현한다.

syn Good for you. *(informal)* / Well done!
Nicely done! / Congrats. *(slang*, 'congratulations'의 축약형)

참고 **축하 또는 격려와 관련된 일상적인 표현**

① 어떤 일에 성과 또는 성취를 이룬 경우 — 예를 들면, 성적 향상(good grade), 승진(promotion), 스포츠에서 공격 또는 수비를 잘한 경우, 볼링에서 Strike를 친 경우 등 — '잘했어.(잘하고 있어)'라는 의미로 사용되는 표현

Way to go! *(casual)*
(여기에서 'Way to go'는 'That's the right way it goes'의 의미로, 'go'는 'to proceed, to succeed'의 의미이다. 따라서 'Way to go'는 우리말로 '바로 그렇게 하는 거야.'라는 의미와 유사하다.)

② 일상적인 일 또는 숙제를 잘한 경우에는, '잘했다'(you've done well)는 의미로 다음과 같이 표현한다.
You did a good job! / Good job! / Good!

③ 술을 마시면서 건배(toast)를 제의할 때,
Cheers!
Bottoms up!
Here's to you [your promotion, your new job].
A toast to you [your promotion, your new job].
To you [your promotion, your new job].

('위하여'라는 의미를 지닌 'Here's to', 'A toast to', 'To' 다음에는 관련된 사람 또는 대상 등 무엇이든지 대체할 수 있다.)

Here's looking at you. *(rare)*
(위하여: 영화 'Casablanca'에 의해 널리 유행되었으나 오늘날에는 거의 사용하지 않는다.)

One shot! (*impolite,* not used in America)
('Shot'은 작은 소주잔을 말하며, 우리는 흔히 사용하지만 실제 미국에서는 사용하지 않는다.)

cf. Say when! (그만 따르기를 원하면 'when'이라고 말하세요.)
: 빈 잔에 술을 얼마나 따를지 물어볼 때 사용하는 표현으로, 받는 사람이 'When.'이라고 하면 그만 따른다.

e.g. 김 제독의 승진에 대한 축배를 제의할 경우
Congsratulations on Admiral Kim's promotion.
(김 제독의 승진을 축하합니다.)
(I propose) A toast to his promotion [him].
(제가 축배를 제의하겠습니다.)
Let's give him a toast. (축배를 듭시다.)
Please join me. (다 함께 동참해 주십시오.)
Everybody, raise your glass(es). (모두 잔을 들어 주십시오.)
(다소 강제적 표현으로 우리나라에서 많이 사용한다.)
Cheers! (위하여!)

④ 생일 또는 기념일, 신년인사
Wishing you many happy returns.
(다복하기를 바랍니다.)
Congratulations on your birthday [wedding anniversary].
(당신의 생일[결혼기념일]을 축하합니다.)

Wishing you every happiness [every joy, much joy] for 2006.
(2006년에는 만복[즐거움]이 가득하기를 기원합니다.)

⑤ 기타
시험이나 일의 성공을 바랄 때: Good luck.
편지 말미에: Best wishes.
저자인 '존(John)'이 책을 상대에게 증정할 경우
With compliments from John (존 근정)
With the compliments of the author (저자 근정)
With the author's compliments (저자 근정)

C. 소개

┌───┐
│ ① I'll (just) introduce myself. │
└───┘

해설   소개드리겠습니다.
: 'Introduce'를 사용하면 비교적 정중한 표현이다.

syn   Allow me to introduce myself. *(formal)*
Let me introduce myself.
Let me tell you a little about myself.
I'll (just) tell you a little bit about myself.

cf. Let me say a few words about myself.
('저에 대해 몇 말씀드리겠습니다.'는 일상적인 소개에서는 사용하지 않으며 주로
공식적인 담화에서 본론에 앞서 자신의 이력을 말할 필요가 있을 때 사용한다.)

주의   일상적인 경우에는 사용하지 않지만, 높은 사람을 공식적으로 소

개할 경우에는 'present'를 사용하기도 한다.

e.g. I'm going to present our president to all of you. *(very formal)*
=Let me [Allow me] to present our president to all of you.
=I am pleased [honored] to present our president (to all of you.)(우리 회장님을 여러분에게 소개해 드리겠습니다.)

I present to you, our new CEO, Mr Robert Armstrong.
(우리 사장님, 로버트 암스트롱을 여러분에게 소개해 드립니다.)

일상적인 경우에는 'present'를 사용하면 어색한 표현이 된다.
I'll introduce Mary to you. *(usual)*
*I'll present Mary to you. *(awkward)*

---

② My name is [I'm] Michael Jones. **(Just) Call me Mike.**
I'm your new teacher. I'll be teaching you English this year.

해설 　내 이름은 마이클 존스입니다. 마이크라고 불러 주세요. 나는 여러분의 새 선생님으로 올해 여러분에게 영어를 가르치게 되었습니다.

주의 　'I am called…', 또는 'Call me…'는 자신의 이름과는 다른 축약된 명칭(shortened name) 또는 별명(nickname)이 있는 경우에만 주로 사용하며, 별명 없이 이름을 그대로 쓸 경우에는 사용하지 않는다.

syn 　I'd like to be called Mike.
Everyone refers to me as Mike.
You can call me Mike.

I prefer to be called Mike.
Call me Mike.

*Call me Michael. *(not used)*
*I am called Michael Jones. *(not used)*

---

③ My name is Han Sunhi. My family name is Han, spelled H, A, N.
I'm from Seoul. And what about you? Can you introduce
yourself?

해설   나는 한순희입니다. 성은 한이고, 철자는 H, A, N입니다. 나는 서
울 출신입니다. 당신은? 자신을 소개해 주시겠습니까?

syn   I come from Seoul.
My hometown is Seoul.
I grew up in Seoul.
Seoul is where I call home. *(rare)*
Seoul is my stomping grounds. *(informal, cliché)*

주의   'Korea is my hometown.'은 잘못된 표현이다. 고향(hometown)
은 반드시 도시 또는 읍(city or town)과 같은 지명이 되어야 하며
국가가 될 수 없다.

---

④ Who is your teacher?

해설   담임[담당] 선생님은 누구지?

syn   Who's teaching this class?
Who's in charge here?

Who's in charge (of your class)? *(informal)*

cf. Who's got the con? (지휘관이 누구냐?)
(함정이나 항공기에서 지휘관이 누구인지 물어볼 경우에 사용한다. 'con'은 '지휘'라는 의미를 지닌다.)

⑤ I am a student teacher and **I'll be teaching you this week.**

해설   나는 교생입니다. 이번 주는 제가 가르치겠습니다.

syn   I'm your teacher this week.
I'll be teaching you for six days.
I'll be subbing in for the next 6 days.
I'll be filling in for your teacher this week.
I'll be your substitute while your teacher is away.

⑥ Minsu: **Kilsu, meet Sumi.** She was in my math class last
semester.
Kilsu: Hello, **Sumi. Nice meeting you.**
Sumi: Hi. **Glad to meet you, too.**

해설   위의 대화는 민수가 길수에게 수미를 소개하는 장면이다. 동료 간
이어서 일상적인(informal) 표현을 사용하고 있다.
민수: 길수야, 이쪽은 수미야. 그녀는 지난 학기 나와 같은 수학수
업에 들어왔어.
길수: 수미야. 만나서 기뻐.
수미: 나도 만나서 기뻐.

syn   Minsu: Kilsu, this is Sumi Park. / Kilsu, I want you to meet

Sumi.

Kilsu: Hi, Sumi. Glad to meet you.

Sumi: Nice meeting you, too.
(이 경우 'Same here', 'The pleasure is mine.' 'Me, too.' 등으로 응답할 수도 있으나 대체로 위와 같이 상대편의 말을 되풀이한다.)

---

⑦ Minsu: **Professor Kim, I would like to introduce my academic advisor, Mr. Park.** Professor Kim is teaching in the Korea Naval Academy.

Prof. Kim: How do you do, Mr. Park? I'm pleased to meet you.

Mr. Park: **It's a pleasure to meet you,** Professor Kim. What are you teaching?

해설   민수가 김 교수에게 자신의 학업지도교수인 박 선생님을 소개하는 장면이다. 선생님이어서 상호 정중한(formal) 표현을 사용하고 있다.

민수: 김 교수님, 학업지도교수 박 선생님을 소개합니다. 김 교수님은 해군사관학교에서 가르치고 있습니다.

김 교수: 박 선생님, 처음 뵙겠습니다. 만나서 반갑습니다.

박 선생님: 김 교수님 만나서 반갑습니다. 무엇을 가르치십니까?

syn   Minsu: Professor Kim, may I introduce my academic advisor, Mr. Park?(=Professor Kim, I would like you to meet my academic advisor, Mr. Park.)

Prof. Kim: It's nice to meet you.
(=It's a pleasure to meet you.)

Mr. Park: I'm pleased to meet you.

참고 대통령과 같이 높은 사람에게는 'I'm really honored to meet you, Mr. President.' 등으로 표현할 수도 있다.

누구나 영어로 가르칠 수 있다

◆ 교실영어의 화용적 특징

교실 현장에서 사용하는 원어민의 발화는 대부분 무표적인(unmarked) 형태를 지닌다: 즉, 질의 행위(elicitation)와 확인행위(check)는 대부분 의문문으로 표현하고, 학생에게 정보를 제공하는 행위(informative)는 주로 평서문으로 표현하며, 평가행위(evaluative)는 평서문과 문장단편(sentence fragment)으로 표현하며, 지시행위(directive)는 명령문으로 표현한다. 아래 예문에서 보는 바와 같이 우리나라 교실의 교과학습활동에서 원어민은 유표적(marked) 표현보다 무표적 표현을 선호한다고 볼 수 있다.

1 질의 행위

What's the opposite of 'borrow?'
('Borrow'의 반의어는 무엇입니까?)
Do you know 'night owl?'
('Night owl'을 압니까?)
Are you an introvert or an extrovert?
(당신은 내향성 인간입니까. 외향성 인간입니까?)

2 확인행위

Any further questions?
(또 다른 질문 있어요?)
What else?
(그 밖에 또?)
Understood?
(알았어요?)

3 정보제공행위

'Pros' means positive things and 'cons' the negative things.
('Pros'는 긍정적인 것을 'cons'는 부정적인 것을 의미합니다.)
Hold your head down: We call it just a moment of silence.
(고개를 숙인다: 우리는 그것을 묵념이라 합니다.)

'God bless you' or 'God bless' because when we sneeze our breath stops for a second.
('God bless you' 또는 'God bless'는 우리가 재채기할 때 숨이 잠시 멈추기 때문입니다.)

4 평가행위

(Wow), This is incredible. *(for good report)*
((*좋은 리포트에 대하여*) (와) 믿을 수 없구나.)
I'm impressed.
(감동했어.)
You made me feel better. *(when he hears a good answer)*
((*대답을 잘 할 때*) 기분이 좋구나.)
Excellent presentation! Let's give them a hand. *(clap! clap! clap!)*
(멋진 발표! 그들에게 박수를 보냅시다. *(짝! 짝! 짝!)*)
Thank you for giving me the right answer.
(정답을 말해서 고마워요.)

5 지시행위

Today is Friday, so please don't forget to fill out the survey before you leave the class.
(오늘이 금요일입니다. 교실에서 나가기 전에 설문지 꼭 작성하세요.)
Give it to me. Let me see.
(나에게 달라. 한번 보자.)
This is very important, so make sure you have all this written down on your notebook.
(이것은 매우 중요하다. 반드시 이것을 모두 공책에 적으시오.)

　　이 결과는 여러 학자들의 연구와 대체로 일치한다. Wesche & Ready(1985)에 의하면 원어민 영어교사들은 효과적인 의사전달을 위하여 외국인 학생들에게는 비한정적 동사보다는 시제가 있는 한정적 동사를 더 많이 사용한다. 또한 Henzl(1973)는 원어민이 외국인과 대화할 때에는 다른 시제보다 단순 현재시제 동사로 표현하는 비율이 더 높다는 것을 발견했다. 또한 Chaudron(1988)도 '교사는 초급수준의 학습자에게는 자신들의 전달내용을 어느 정도 무표적인(unmarked) 구문으로 수정하여 표현한다.'고 주장하였다. 그 이유는 문장구조와 그에 상응하는 화용적인 기능이 일치하는 무표적 구문이 초급 영어회화과정의 학생들에게 자신의 의도를 보다 명확하고 효과적으로 전달할 수 있기 때문이다.

실제로 교사가 초급회화 수준의 학생 개인 또는 집단에게 필요한 행동을 지시할 경우, 명령형이 다른 문법적인 형태보다 훨씬 더 적절하다: 예를 들면, 교사가 학생에게 과제를 부여할 때, 'Do your homework by next class.(다음 시간까지 숙제를 하세요.)'가 의문문인 'Would you mind doing your homework by next class, please?(다음 시간까지 숙제를 해 오겠습니까?)' 또는 평서문인 'I wonder if you could do your homework by next class.(다음 시간까지 숙제할 수 있을 것으로 생각해요.)'보다는 훨씬 명확하게 지시사항을 전달할 수 있는 것이다.

또한 오늘날 회화 수업에서 원어민 교사는 Sinclair & Coulthard(1975)의 주장과는 달리 교과활동의 조직과 관리를 위해 매우 다양한 표현을 사용한다. 과거 Sinclair & Coulthard (1975)는 교과 활동의 조직과 관리에 연관된 일곱 가지 행위 — 즉, 표시(marker), 확인(check), 촉구(prompt), 신호(cue), 지명(nomination), 용인(accept), 반복(loop) — 에 관련된 발화에는 극히 한정된 종류의 표현만을 사용한다고 하였다. 예를 들면, 교실수업 자료에서 신호행위를 나타내기 위해서 단지 세 가지 표현 — 즉, 'Hands up.(손드세요.)', 'Don't call out.(소리치지 마세요.)', 'Is John the only one?(존 한 사람밖에 없어요?)' — 만 사용했다고 했다. 그러나 오늘날의 원어민 수업에서는 동일한 언어행위를 위해서도 여러 가지 다양한 문장 형태를 사용한다는 것을 알 수 있다. 예를 들면, '손을 드세요'라는 신호행위도 상황에 따라 다음과 같이 다양하게 표현하였다.

6 신호행위

Raise your hands.
(손을 드세요.)
I want you to raise your hands.
(손을 들어 보세요.)
Raise your hands if you don't understand what I just said.
(내 말을 이해하지 못하면 손을 드세요.)
If you think you are right raise your hands.

(옳다고 생각하면 손을 드세요.)

즉, 오늘날에는 원어민들도 개인적 성향 또는 학습 환경에 따라 매우 다양한 교실 영어 표현을 구사한다고 볼 수 있다.

1. 현장예문 (Real-life Situation)

Attendance Check

교과 수업을 시작하기에 앞서 선생님이 출석을 부르면서 학생들에게 안부를 묻고 결석을 한 경우에는 이유를 확인하고 있다.

At the beginning of each class, most teachers take attendance. If everyone is present then the teacher can move on with his lesson. If students are missing then it is important for the teacher to ask follow-up questions in an effort to discover where the students are and why they are absent. Therefore, taking attendance means more than just ticking students names off of an attendance sheet. Teachers must be prepared to ask students about related information such as the date, where someone might be, and why they are missing. Teachers must also be able to use a voice of concern by casually addressing students as opposed to adopting a matter-of-fact type tone of voice.

Now listen to the dialogue.

T:	Ok. I'll check attendence now. [1] Are you listening?
Ss:	Yes, sir.
T:	Right. Jongmin?
Jongmin:	Yes.
T:	Jisu? … Does anyone know where Jisu is? [2] Is he absent?
Ss:	I don't know. Maybe he's sick.
T:	Yes, maybe. [3] Alright… Munki?
Munki:	Yes, I'm here.

T: Sumi?

Sumi: Here, sir.

T: Oh, Sumi, It's good to see you again. **4** Are you feeling better?

Sumi: Yes, thank you. I'm feeling better. Thank you for asking.

T: No problem. Now, next, Namjin?

Namjin: Present.

T: Minki? … Minki Kim?

Minki: Yes, sir.

T: Oh, I didn't see you there. Sunhi?… Where's Sunhi?…Does anybody know where Sunhi is?

Ss: She hasn't been here all morning. **5**

T: O.K. I'll call her at home after class. **6** I hope there's no problem with her. Is that everyone? Good. Let's get started. Open your books to page 22. (later)

T: Hello, Sunhi. You're late today. Why are you late? **7** Did you oversleep? **8**

Sunhi: Yes, I overslept. I'm sorry.

T: This is the second time you've been late for school. **9** Don't be late again.

Sunhi: Sorry. I won't be late again.

T: OK. Go to your seat and get ready for class. **10** Now, let's get back to work.

1 (출석 확인하겠습니다.) Let's see if everyone's here.
2 (지수는 어디 있니?)
 Where is Jisu? ; Where is he? ; Why isn't Jisu here?
3 (아마 그럴지 모릅니다.) Yes, he might be.
4 ((학교에) 다시 오게 되어 기쁘다.)
 It's nice to see you again ; It's good having you back.
 It's good [nice] to have you back ; Welcome back.
 You're back. Good.
5 (그녀는 오늘 아침 내내 보이지 않았다.) 문장의 시제가 현재완료이므로 'this morning'보다 'all morning'이 훨씬 적절한 표현이다. 간단히 다음과 같이 표현할 수도 있다:
 She isn't here this morning ; She isn't here.
6 '집으로 그녀에게 전화를 걸다'는 'give her a call at home'이라고도 한다. 반면 '집을 방문하다'는 'stop [drop, come] by her house [home]'가 일반적으로 사용되며, 문법책에 나오는 'call at her home.'은 지금은 거의 사용하지 않는다.
7 (왜 늦었니?) What's the reason you are late?
8 (늦잠 잤느냐?) Did you sleep [get up, wake up] late?
 cf. (어젯밤 늦게 잤느냐?) Did you go to bed late?
9 이 경우에는 과거와 연관되어 있으므로 '...you are late...'보다 'you've been late...'가 정확한 표현이다.
10 (수업 준비해라.)
 '...get ready to study' ; '...prepare the lesson' *(B.E.)*

선생님: 자, 모두 출석했는지 보겠습니다. 듣고 있습니까?
학생들: 예, 선생님.
선생님: 좋습니다. 종민?
종민: 예.
선생님: 지수?… 지수 어디 갔지? 결석했니?
학생들: 몰라요. 아마 아플 거예요.
선생님: 그럴지도 모르겠구나. 좋아… 문기?
문기: 예, 여기 왔습니다.

선생님: 수미?

수미: 예, 선생님.

선생님: 수미야, 너 왔구나. 이제 좀 낫니?

수미: 예, 고마워요. 신경 써 주셔서 고맙습니다.

선생님: 뭘. 그래, 다음, 남진.

남진: 왔습니다.

선생님: 민기? … 김민기

민기: 예.

선생님: 아, 거기 있었구나. 순희? 순희는 어디 있니? 순희 어디 있는지 아는 사람?

학생들: 오늘 아침 내내 없었어요.

선생님: 좋아. 수업 후에 집에 전화해 봐야겠다. 별일 없어야 할 텐데. 전부 다 불렀지요? 좋습니다. 시작합시다. 22페이지를 펴세요.

(조금 뒤에)

선생님: 안녕, 순희. 오늘 늦었구나. 그래, 왜 늦었니? 늦잠 잤니?

순희: 예, 늦잠 잤어요. 죄송합니다.

선생님: 이번이 두 번째 지각이야. 다음에는 늦지 마라.

순희: 죄송합니다. 다시는 늦지 않을게요

선생님: 좋아. 자리에 가서 수업 준비하거라. 자, 수업을 계속합시다.

2. 기본구문

여기에서는 학생들의 출결 및 날짜와 요일에 대한 표현을 다음과 같이 정리하였다: A. 출석 B. 날짜와 요일

A. 출석

> ① Now! I'm going to call [check] your names.

해설   출석을 확인하겠습니다.
:'출석을 확인하다'는 'call [check] your names' 또는 'check [take] attendance'라고 한다.

syn   Let's see who is here.
Let's see who's not here.
Let's see if you're all here.
Let's see if everyone's here.

Let's check (the) attendance.
I'll just check [take] attendance.
It's time to take attendance. *(informal)*

I'm going to call the roll. *(very formal)*
Please answer when I call your name(s).

— 학생들은 대부분 자신의 이름을 부르면 다음과 같이 대답한다.

ans   Present, sir [ma'am].
Yes, sir [ma'am].

Here, sir [ma'am].
("Sir / ma'am"을 붙이면 훨씬 공손한 표현이 된다.)
Here. *(informal, common)*
Yeah. *(rude)*

---

② T: Who is missing?
　S: Nobody is missing.

해설　T: 결석한 사람은?
　　　S: 아무도 없습니다.
　　　:'결석하다'는 'missing', 'away', 'asbent', 'not here'를 사용한다.

syn　T: Who is absent [away] (today)? *(formal)*
　　　Who isn't here? *(informal)*
　　　Who's not here? *(informal, casual)*
　　　Is everyone here? (S: Yes, I think so.)
　　　Is anybody away [absent]? (S: No, everybody's here.)
　　　Is anybody missing?
　　　Let's see if everyone's here.
　　　Let's see if anyone's away.

　　　Did anyone skip class today? *(informal)*
　　　Let's see who skipped class today. *(casual)*
　　　(누가 무단결석을 했는지 보자:'skip'은 '무단결석하다'는 의미
　　　가 있다.)

　　　Let's see who decided not to come today. *(casual)*

ans　순희가 결석한 경우
　　　S: I think Sunhi is missing.

Sunhi isn't here.

Sunhi's not here.

③ S: (I'm) Sorry I'm late.

T: **Don't let it happen again.**

해설　S: 늦어서 죄송합니다.

T: 다음에는 이런 일이 없도록 해라. [지각하지 마라.]

syn　T: It doesn't matter this time, but next time, try to be on time.

Try to be (here) on time next time.

Try to arrive on time please.

Try to be more punctual next time.

Try not to be late next time.

Make this the last time. (강한 불쾌감을 나타낸다.)

You ought to be on time. (강한 명령을 나타낸다.)

You really shouldn't have been so late. (유감을 표시할 때)

Try not to make a habit of this. (풍자적 표현)

(이런 일이 습관이 안 되도록 하여라.)

참고　**'Let'의 부정문 만드는 법**

'Let'을 부정문으로 만드는 방법은 두 가지가 있다. 하나는 'let' 앞에 'don't'를 붙이는 것이며, 또 하나는 'let's not'으로 표현하는 것이다. 이를 구체적으로 살펴보면 다음과 같다.

① 목적어가 'me'일 경우: 'Don't'로 시작하는 것이 일반적이며, 'let … not'은 매우 격식을 차린 표현으로 미국에서는 사용하지 않는다.

Don't let me go without my umbrella. *(normal)*

Let me not go without my umbrella. *(very formal, rare)*

위의 경우 'let'을 사용하지 않고, 대개 다음과 같이 표현한다.
Please, make sure I don't forget my umbrella.

② 목적어가 'us'일 경우:'Let's not'이 사용되며 'Don't let's'는 최근 미국에서는 사용하지 않는다.
Let's not wait any longer. *(usual)* vs Don't let's wait any longer. *(rare)*
Let's not go out tonight. *(usual)* vs Don't let's go out tonight. *(rare)*

③ 목적어가 3인칭일 경우:'Don't'로 시작하는 것이 일반적이다. 이 경우는 문두에 'let's'가 생략된 형태이며 다음과 같이 3가지로 표현될 수 있다.
Don't let them know about this. *(normal)*
Let's not let them know about this. *(rare)*
Don't let's let them know about this. *(not used)*

④ T: Why are you late? **Were you late getting up?**
   S: I'm sorry. I overslept.

해설   T: 왜 늦었니? 늦게 일어났니?
      S: 죄송합니다. 늦잠 잤습니다.

syn   T: Did you oversleep?
      Did you sleep through your alarm?
      Did you forget to set your alarm?

      Did you sleep in?

('Sleep in'(잠자리에서 오래 누워있다)은 'oversleep'(늦잠자다) 과 달리 깨어나서도 의도적으로 침대 속에서 일어나지 않는 경우에도 사용한다.)

cf. **늦은 이유를 묻는 질문에는 여러 가지가 있다.**

Did you get a late start? (늦게 출발했니?)=Did you start out late?
Did you go to bed late? (늦게 잤니?)=Did you have a late night?
Did you miss your bus? (버스를 놓쳤니?)

— 다음과 같이 여러 가지로 대답할 수 있다.

ans   S: I overslept. (늦잠 잤어요.)
       I slept in. (잠자리에서 오래 있었어요.)
       I was helping my mother.
       I missed my bus.
       I went to the dentist's.
       I went to the doctor.

교장선생님: 아취 군이 안 보이는군!
담임선생님: 허! 아취는 마지막 벨이 울리고 적어도 5분은 지나야 나타납니다.
교장선생님: 그러나 오늘은 아니야! 내가 아취 군이 여기 학교에서 밤을 보내도록 조치해
           놓았어요.
담임선생님: 여기 출석표 있어요! 눈으로 확인해 보세요!

교장선생님: 있을 수 없는 일이군! 2층에서 자고도 지각하다니!

담임선생님: 내기할까요?

---

⑤ What's the matter with Sumi (today)?

해설　　수미에게 무슨 일이 생겼니?

syn　　Is there a problem with Sumi?

Is Sumi OK?

What's the deal [problem] with Sumi?

What's wrong with Sumi (today)?

What's up with Sumi (today)?

Is Sumi sick?

참고　　위의 문장에서 'up'은 형용사로 '(일이)진행되고 있는', '발생한 (going on, happening)'의 의미를 지닌다. 'up'은 원래 전치사 또는 부사로 '위에' 또는 '위로'라는 의미를 지니고 있었지만 오늘날은 다음과 같이 여러 가지 다른 의미로도 사용되고 있다.

① '다가가다'(approach)

Mary went up to the policeman and asked him the way.

② '여기저기, 앞뒤로'(to and fro, backwards and forwards)

He walked up and down the room.

③ '(일이) 발생한, 진행되고 있는'

What's up? [What's the matter? Is anything wrong?]

④ '계획하고 [꾸미고] 있는'(occupied with)

What are those guys up to? [What are those guys planning to

do?] (최근 미국에서는 이 경우 'fellows'보다 'guys'를 주로 사용한다.)

⑤ '끝(장)난'(finished, ended)
It's all up with us. (We are finished. Our end is near.) *(B.E.)*

---

⑥ Does anyone [anybody] know where Dongsu is?

해설　동수는 어디 갔니?

syn　Who knows where Dongsu is?
Can anyone tell me where Dongsu is?
Where is Dongsu (today)?
Has anyone seen Dongsu?

Is Dongsu around? *(informal)*
('Around'는 '가까이에 있는'이라는 의미로, 교실에서는 보이지 않을 때 '동수가 학교에 왔느냐?'는 의미를 지닌다.)

― 다음과 같이 간접적인 질문을 할 수도 있다.
I can't find Dongsu.
I'm looking for Dongsu.
I need to know where Dongsu is.

cf. Oh, Dongsu, you're back. That's nice [good]. (아, 동수 왔구나. 잘됐다.)

---

⑦ Didn't Dongsu miss yesterday's class, too?

해설　동수는 어제도 결석하였지?

: '결석하다'는 주로 'be absent', 'miss'를 사용한다.

syn   Wasn't Dongsu absent yesterday, too?

Isn't this the second day Dongsu has missed?

Dongsu has been absent for 2 days, hasn't he?

Dongsu missed last class, too, didn't he?

(영국식 영어에서는 'last class' 대신 'last lesson'도 사용한다.)

Dongsu wasn't here yesterday, either.

Dongsu has missed two consecutive classes.

Dongsu missed two classes in a row.

This is twice [two days] in a row for Dongsu.

(동수가 계속하여 두 번째 [이틀째] 결석하였다.)

This is twice in as many days for Dongsu. *(rare)*

B. 날짜와 요일

① What time do you have? *(formal)*

해설   몇 시입니까?

syn   What time do you have?

What time is it (now)?

What's the time? *(informal)*

What does your watch [the clock] say?

Do you have the (right) time?

Have you got the (right) time?

Can you give me the time?
Time, please? *(casual)*

What time do you make it? *(rare, B.E.)*
What time are we looking at? *(rare, B.E.)*

주의 'What time do you make it?'은 미국식 영어에서는 잘 사용하지
않는다.
e.g. A: What time do you make it? *(rare, B.E.)*
   B: I make it ten to seven. *(rare)*

위의 표현을 미국식으로 나타내면 다음과 같다.
A: What time do you have, please? / What time is it?
B: I have ten to seven. / It's ten to seven.

참고 **시간과 관련된 표현**

① 시간에 대한 전치사는 'to, before, past, after' 등이 주로 사용
   된다.

(예) '3시 15분입니다.'
   It's (a) quarter past [after] three. *(formal)*
   It's three fifteen. *(informal)*
   *It's three (a) quarter. *(incorrect)*

(예) '5시 15분 전입니다.'
   It's (a) quarter to [before] five. *(formal)*
   It's four forty-five. *(informal)*

   (일부 미국인들은 'to' 대신 'of'를 사용하여 'It's quarter of
   five.'라고도 하지만 현재까지는 비문법적인 문장으로 처리

된다.)

② 5분 단위에서는 언제든지 'minutes'를 생략할 수 있다. 그 이외에 분을 시간보다 먼저 표현할 경우에는 'minutes'를 사용하여야 한다.

(예) '3시 7분입니다.'

It's seven minutes past [after] three. / It's three o'seven.

③ 시간을 나타내는 'o'clock'은 'hour(s) of o'clock [clock]'의 축약형이다. 따라서 시간만으로 끝나는 경우에는 시간 뒤에 'o'clock'을 사용할 수 있지만, 분이 수반되는 경우에는 'o'clock'을 사용하지 않는다.

e.g Let's meet at five (o'clock). (5시에 만나자.)
　　Let's meet at five o'clock sharp. (5시 정각에 만나자.)

　　Let's meet at five thirty. (5시 30분에 만나자.)
　　=Let's meet at half past five.

　　*Let's meet at five thirty o'clock. *(incorrect)*
　　Let's meet half past. *(rare)* (30분에 만나자.)
　　(서로 시간을 알고 있는 경우에 사용한다.)

---

② T: What day is it (today)? *(formal)*
　S: Today is Thursday, the fifth of December.

해설　T: 오늘이 무슨 요일이지?
　　　S: 오늘은 12월 5일, 목요일입니다.

T: What day is today?

What's the day today?

What day is this? *(casual)*

Could you tell me what day it is today?

S: Today is Thursday, December 5.

It is Thursday, December 5, today. *(redundant)*

⇒ It is Thursday, December 5. *(usual)*

('5'로 쓰여 있어도 'fifth'로 읽으며, 'five'로 읽어서는 안 된다. 또한 이 경우 'It's'가 오늘이므로 문장 뒤에 'today'를 붙이면 잉여문이 되므로 붙이지 않는다.)

---

③ T: What's the date today?
S: (It is) April 30th.

해설   T: 오늘은 며칠입니까?

S: 4월 30일입니다.

syn   T: What's today's date?

Does anyone know today's date?

What date is it today? *(rare)*

S: (It is) April 30th.

April the 30th

April 30. ('thirtieth'로 읽는다.)

The last day of April.

어휘   4월 말 [중순, 초순]은 'The end [middle, beginning] of April'이라고 한다.

참고   날짜(date) 또는 요일(day)을 모를 경우

What day is the 17th?

(17일은 무슨 요일입니까?)

Is the 17th a Tuesday or a Wednesday?

(17일은 화요일 또는 수요일입니까?)

Is Tuesday or Wednesday the 17th?

(화요일 또는 수요일이 17일입니까?)

What is the day before Tuesday called?

(화요일의 전날은 무슨 요일입니까?)

What's the date next Thursday?

(다음 목요일은 며칠입니까?)

=What's next Thursday's date?

=What's next Thursday? *(implied)*

What was the date last Thursday?

(지난 목요일은 며칠이었습니까?)

---

④ S1: When is the meeting?
    S2: (On) Wednesday, Oct 5th, at 7:00 P.M.

해설   S1: 언제 모임이 있지?

S2: 10월 5일, 수요일, 오후 7시.

: 날짜와 시간과 요일을 동시에 표현할 경우에는 요일, 날짜, 시간의 순서로 말한다.

syn   Wednesday, Oct 5(th), at 7. (P.M.) *(informal)*

(날짜는 '5'로 쓰더라도 'fifth'로 읽는다.)

On Wednesday, Oct 5th, at 1900 hours. *(military)*

(이때 '1900'은 군대에서는 'nineteen hundred'로 읽는다.)

On Wednesday, 5(th) Oct, at 7:00 P.M. *(B.E.)*

(영국식 영어로는 날짜가 달 앞에 온다.)

*Oct 5th, (on) Wednesday, at 7:00 P.M. *(incorrect)*
(요일이 날짜 앞에 와야 한다.)

참고   월, 일과 연도 읽는 법

① 월, 일을 나타낼 때
미국식은 흔히 월 다음에 정관사를 생략한다. 그러나 날짜는 반드시 서수로 발음하며, 기수로 발음하지 않는다.

e.g. '2월 10일'
February tenth *(A.E.)*, February the tenth *(B.E.)*, the tenth of February, *February ten *(incorrect)*

② 연도, 월, 일 전부를 나타낼 때
미국식은 월, 일, 연도의 순서로 적지만, 영국식은 일, 월, 연도의 순서로 적는다.

e.g. '2003년 9월 6일'
Sept. 6th, 2003 또는 Sept. 6, 2003
The 6th of Sept, 2003 *(more formal)*

③ 월, 일과 연도가 숫자로만 표기될 경우

e.g. 날짜가 '3/5/2005' 또는 '3/5/05'으로 표시되었을 경우
March fifth, two thousand five (미국식) (2005년 3월 5일)
The third of May, two thousand five (영국식) (2005년 5월 3일)

주의   필자의 경우 비행기 내에서 입국신고서를 숫자로만 써야 할 때 미국식과 영국식을 구별하지 못하여 낭패를 본 경험이 있다.

e.g. 2005년 7월 6일을 숫자로 표기할 경우
      미국으로 입국할 경우: 7/06/2005
      영국으로 입국할 경우: 06/7/2005

◆ 관용표현의 의의

인간언어는 일반적으로 두 가지 유형으로 구분할 수 있다. 하나는 문장생성규칙에 의해 매 순간 새롭게 생성되는 문법적인 표현이며, 나머지는 문법적인 생성절차를 거치지 않고 상시 기억 속에 저장되어 즉각적으로 이용할 수 있는 표현이다. 이 후자의 표현을 일반적으로 관용표현(formulaic sequences)이라고 한다. Kuiper(2004:52)는 이 관용표현의 의의를 다음과 같이 설명하고 있다:

We have an immense capacity to remember, and to retrieve very quickly from memory what we need. But we have relatively restricted processing capacities because our working memory is quite small. Formulaic speech enables us to harness these resources in an efficient way so long as what we wish to say does not need to be radically novel.
(인간은 매우 큰 기억용량을 가지고 있으므로, 자신이 필요한 것을 기억하고 메모리로부터 매우 빠르게 복구할 수 있다. 그렇지만 인간의 작업 메모리는 아주 작기 때문에 우리는 상대적으로 제한된 처리능력을 가지고 있다. 우리가 전혀 새로운 내용을 전달할 필요가 없을 경우, 관용표현은 우리가 이런 자원을 효율적으로 이용할 수 있게 해준다.)

따라서 일상생활에서 반복 사용하여 자연스럽게 기억에 축적된 다양한 관용표현을 활용함으로써 개인은 제한된 처리능력을 극복하고, 다양한 사회활동 혹은 일상적 상황을 효율적으로 처리할 수 있는 것이다.
Wray(2002)에 의하면 관용표현에 대한 용어는 약 60가지 — chunks(말뭉치), gestalt(게슈탈트), lexical phrases(어휘구), prefabricated routines and patterns(사전 조립된 상용표현과 양식), routine formulae(일상적 관용어), schemata(도식), stereotypes(상투어구) 등 — 로 학자마다 연구목적에 따라 별개의 용어를 사용하고 범주도 조금씩 다르지만, 여기에서는 이 모두를 편의상 '관용표현'으로 통일하기로 한다.
외국어를 이용하여 효과적으로 의사소통 행위를 수행하기 위해서는 관용표현을 숙달해야 한다. 왜냐하면 관용표현은 의사소통에서 발생하는 제반 상황에 가장 쉽게 대처할 수 있으며, 그 기능도 아주 다양하고 역동적이기 때문이다. 따라서 Wray(2002:5)도 '관용표현은 단순히 단어나 구문의 집합체가 아니라, 상황에 맞게 역동적으로 언어를 사용하는 것이다'고 주장하였다.

관용표현의 의의에 대한 학자들의 연구를 종합하면 다음과 같이 요약할 수 있다. 첫째, Yorio(1980)에 따르면 관용표현은 의사소통이 필요한 상황에서 그 사회의 언어집단이 가장 선호하는 효과적이고 적절한 표현이다. 예를 들어 다음 문장을 비교해 보자.

1 **a**. What do you want?　vs　May I help you? (Yorio 1980:434)
   b. As the aftermath of　vs　As a consequence of (Wray 2002:87)
   c. Are you chilly?　vs　Is it stuffy in here? (Schmidt 1983:153)

만약 미국의 상점에서 점원이 **1a**의 전자와 같이 방문한 손님에게 물었다면 손님은 놀라거나 불쾌하게 여길 것이다. 왜냐하면 의미는 같지만 이 상황에서 일반적으로 선호하며 사회적으로 널리 통용되는 관용표현은 **1a**의 후자이기 때문이다. 또한 **1b**도 둘 다 문법에 맞고 이해할 수 있지만, "as the aftermath of" 혹은 "as a repercussion of" 보다 "as a consequence of" 혹은 "as a result of"를 일상 언어에서는 더 선호한다. 또한 **1c**의 경우 하와이를 방문한 일본인이 실내가 후덥지근하여 문을 열고 싶어서, "Is it stuffy in here?"가 아닌 "Are you chilly?"라고 표현한 것이다. 그러나 'chilly'라는 표현은 하와이 사회에서는 일반적으로 '(돈이 없어) 쪼들리다'라는 의미로 해석되고 있다.

둘째, 관용표현은 화자와 청자의 처리노력을 절약하는 가장 간결한 표현이다. Perkins(1999)는 '일반적인 성인이 일상에서 관용표현을 선호하는 주된 이유는 처리과정의 간결성 때문인 것 같다.'고 주장하였다. 실제 우리의 생각을 표현하기 위해 이미 만들어지고 그 사회에 자연스럽게 통용되는 표현을 이용한다면, 문법규칙에 따라 새로운 문장을 생성하기 위한 두뇌의 처리 노력이 거의 필요 없는 것이다. 실생활에서 흔히 발생하는 단순한 상황에서도 처리과정이 필요하지 않는 관용표현이 훨씬 효과적이다. 다음 Schmitt & Carter(2004)의 예문을 보자:

2 **a.** Watch out!　vs　Watch the car coming behind you!
   　(조심해요!)　　　　　(당신 뒤에 오는 차를 주의하세요!)

b. Mind your back.　 vs 　Please be careful. I am walking close to you with a tray.
　(등뒤 주의하세요.)　 (조심하세요. 나는 접시를 가지고 당신 가까이에 걷고 있어요.)

위의 문장 상황에서 일반적인 경우 전자의 관용표현이 훨씬 처리가 간편하며 이해하기 쉽고, 청자의 즉각적인 반응이 필요할 때도 매우 유용하다. 위급한 상황에서 **2a**의 후자와 같이 표현하면 때로 심각한 결과를 초래할 수 있다. 실제 종업원이 음식을 들고 손님의 뒤를 지나갈 때, 일반적으로 **2b**의 전자와 같이 표현하며, 반면 후자의 표현은 일반적인 관용표현이 아니므로 훨씬 더 많은 의미해석이 요구되며 또한 상황에 대해 필요 이상의 주의를 요구하게 될 수도 있다.

셋째, 관용표현은 곤란한 상황을 효과적으로 처리하는 데 아주 유용하다. 난처한 상황에서 우리가 적절한 관용표현과 행동규칙을 모르면 상황을 더 악화시키거나, 매우 혼란스러워질 수 있다. Yorio(1980:438)의 주장처럼 어떤 상황에서 표현을 잘못하거나 관습에 맞지 않는 행동을 하면 잘못된 인상을 주거나 잘못된 결과를 초래할 수 있는 것이다. 다음 Olshtain & Cohen(1983)의 부정적인 상황이 발생한 경우에 흔히 사용되는 관용표현을 보자.

3　**a.** I'm very sorry. I really didn't mean it as a personal insult.
　　(매우 미안합니다. 실제 모욕을 주려고 한 것은 아니에요.)
　b. I'm sorry for knocking into you, but you were in the way.
　　(부딪쳐서 미안해요. 그런데, 당신이 가는 길을 막았어요.)
　c. I'm sorry. I completely forgot about it. Is it possible for me to make another appointment? Can we meet now? This won't happen again, I promise.
　　(미안해요. 깜박했어요. 다시 약속을 정할 수 있어요? 지금 만날까요? 다시는 이런 일 없을 겁니다. 약속합니다.)

위의 **3a**는 상대방이 자신의 말에 대해 예기치 않는 불쾌함을 표시했을 때 사용하는 표현이고, **3b**는 교통사고에서 상대방의 잘못을 부드럽지만 명료하게 표현하는 방법이며, **3c**는 약속을 잊은 데 대하여 통화상으로 사과를 표시하는 방법이다. 이런 관용표현이 없다면 서로 곤란한 상황을 효과적으로 처리하기가 매우 어려워지거나 악화

될 수도 있는 것이다.

넷째, 관용표현은 담화 장치(discourse device)로서의 기능을 가진다. 담화장치란 대개 담화의 의미와 구조를 연결하고, 담화의 방향을 설정하며, 담화를 조직적으로 관리하는 역할을 한다. Wray(2002)는 '담화표시장치(discourse marking device)'는 자료와 자료에 선행 또는 후행하는 상황 및 주변 자료에 대한 화자의 태도 또는 화제를 표시한다.'고 주장하였다. 다음 예문들을 보자.

4 Anyway. (여하튼)
   By the way (그런데)
   Turn back to the previous. (앞으로 돌아갑시다.)
   Now, it's time to talk about. (자, 이제 논의해 봅시다.)

위의 간단한 발화는 화자가 이전 혹은 이후의 화제에 대해 언급하거나, 진행되는 화제와의 선행 또는 후행관계를 표시하는 데 도움을 주는 매우 유용한 담화장치다. 이런 담화장치를 이용함으로써 화자는 자신의 담화 주제를 변경하거나, 또는 새로운 화제의 도입하고, 화자가 담화의 어느 지점에 도달했는지를 간단히 표시할 수 있다.

한편 담화조직장치(discourse organization device)는 담화의 정보내용을 전달하거나, 조직하거나, 요약하는 데 사용된다. 담화를 조직하기 위해 사용되는 관용표현은 일상 담화에 널리 사용되고 있다. 다음 Schmidt & Carter(2004)의 예문을 보자.

5 **a.** In other words (달리 말하면), In conclusion (결론적으로)
   b. Speaking of which (어느 쪽이냐 하면), As I was saying (내가 말한 바와 같이)
   c. On the other hand (한편), To put it another (달리 말하면)

위의 **5a**는 담화의 요약, **5b**는 이전 담화와의 연계, **5c**는 대립 또는 대등관계를 나타낸다. 이런 제반 표현이 관용표현으로 분류되는 이유는 이들이 동일한 의미를 가진 다른 문법적인 표현보다 훨씬 더 처리하기 쉽고 일반적으로 선호하는 표현이기 때문이다. 이런 차이는 Wray(2002)와 Schmidt and Carter(2004)의 아래 예문에서도 볼 수 있다.

6 **a.** I don't know well how to express it clearly.
  (나는 그것을 분명히 표현하는 방법을 모른다.)
        vs
  I don't quite know how to put it.
  (어떻게 말할지 잘 모르겠어.)
  b. It's time for a topic change.(화제를 바꿀 시점입니다.)
        vs
  By the way,
  (그런데,)

위의 예문에서 전자가 문법에 맞고 의미도 명백하고 정확하지만, 일상생활에서는 후자가 전자보다 훨씬 더 효율적이고 처리하기 쉬우며 널리 사용된다. 실제 영어가 모국어인 원어민이 자신의 견해를 표현하기가 어렵거나 화제를 바꾸고 싶을 때 후자의 관용표현을 더 선호하며 전자와 같이 새로운 문장을 생성하는 경우는 드물다.

다섯째, 의견제시, 논평, 사과, 요구, 의례적인 인사 등과 같은 다양한 사회활동에 관용표현이 널리 사용된다. Schmidt & Carter(2004)에 따르면 칭찬, 초대, 환영을 나타내는 일상적인 담화에서는 의사소통 행위 자체가 담화의 내용보다 더 중요하므로 상황에 따른 형식적인 관용표현이 널리 사용되는 것이다. 다음 Wolfson(1983)의 예문을 보자.

7 **a.** You explain things so beautifully. You've been a pillar of strength. We all look to you now.
  (너무 멋지게 설명하군요. 당신의 말은 힘이 있었어요. 우리 모두는 당신에게 기대를 겁니다.)
  b. You're being so nice about this. That's very rare around here.
  (당신은 이번에 너무 잘했습니다. 여기에서는 매우 드물어요.)

위의 두 종류의 찬사는 연사의 발표 뒤에 연설 또는 발표내용에 대해 초대자가 의례적인 찬사를 보내는 것이다. 위의 치사에는 연사의 행위에 대한 구체적인 언급이 하나도 없지만, 언어행위의 일반적인 규범에 따라 찬사로 인정되는 것이다. Wolfson(1983)은 이런 종류의 관용표현이 널리 사용되는 이유는 '이런 표현이 오해를 막고, 칭찬의 일차적인 목적인 담화자 간의 친밀감을 형성하고 유지하는 데 해로울 수 있는 개인적인 표현차를 최소화한다는 점에서 화자에게 매우 유리한 것이다(it is a great advantage to speakers in that it prevents misunderstanding and minimize the differences which might play havoc with the reason for the compliment having been given in the first place-the creation or maintenance of rapport between interlocutors.).'라고 주장하였다.

이제 Wolfson et al(1983)의 학교의 개학일에 발생한 의례적인 인사말을 살펴보자.

8 **A:** I really miss seeing you. (정말 만나고 싶었어.)

　　B: You're so busy, I don't want to bother you. (바쁘시죠. 귀찮게 해 드리고 싶지 않았어요.)

　　A: It wouldn't be a bother. I'd love to see you. (안 귀찮아. 만나고 싶었어.)

위의 대화에서, A는 교수이며, B는 학생이다. 두 대화자는 방학 동안 연락이 없다가 모처럼 만나서 사제가 사회적 유대관계를 돈독히 하기 위해 관용표현을 사용하고 있다. 이런 언어행위는 사교상의 윤활유 역할을 하며, 형식적이지만 대부분의 상황에서 개인 간의 유대를 공고히 하는 데 긍정적 역할을 하는 것이다.

요약하면 관용표현은 그 사회의 언어집단이 가장 선호하고 널리 통용되는 간략한 표현이며, 위급한 상황에 효과적으로 대처할 수 있는 완충기능을 가지며, 또한 담화 간의 구조와 내용을 연결하는 장치로도 이용되고, 각종 사회활동에서 의례적으로 사용하기에 매우 유용한 일상적인 표현이라고 볼 수 있다.

1. 현장예문 (Real-life Situation)

Classroom Discipline

날씨가 더운 오후, 수업을 시작하기 전 에어컨을 틀고 산만한 분위기를 통제하면서 수업을 진행하는 장면이다.

As teachers we know that one of the guiding principles for success in the classroom is establishing effective classroom discipline with your students. However, as language instructors we must make sure that we do not scare the students by using strong or formal disciplinary language. This unit provides you with the language needed to keep control of a class without sounding overly stern. It also introduces language that is more formal and disciplinary in case classes become difficult to control. The unit covers situations like controlling noisy students, door slamming, dark classrooms, and giving students basic instructions during a lesson.

Now listen to the dialogue.

T: Good morning, class 6. How are you today?

Ss: Fine, thanks. How are you, Mr. Kim?

T: Fine, thanks. Is it really hot in here?[1]

Ss: Yes, it is. We're boiling!

T: Well then, let's turn on the air-conditioner to get some fresh air.[2] Minsu, would you turn on the air-conditioner next to you?

Minsu: Sure.

T: That's much better, but there is some noise from the air-conditioner. Is that OK with you?**3**

Ss: Yes. Noise is better than heat.

T: OK, everyone. Quiet now please! No more talking! Minsu, stop talking now.**4** And you, Sunhi. Let's see, we're on number 5. Whose turn is it?

Mija: It's my turn.

T: Mija, sorry, just a moment! Nari and Miri, please stop that.**5** Sit down and be quiet... Thanks. Go ahead, Mija, number 5, please.

Mija: 'Minsu went to Seoul for...'

Hankil: 'To Suwon for...!'

T: Hankil, please don't interrupt while Mija is speaking. Listen and see if she is right. OK? And Sunhi, don't write while we're doing the exercises. Just pay attention!

Sunhi: I'm sorry.

T: That's OK. Hankil, I told you to stop talking. Now cut it out! I'm sorry, Mija. You can go ahead now.

주

1 (교실 안이 무척 덥구나.)
Wow! It's hot in here ; It's really hot [stuffy, humid, steamy] in here ; It's like an oven in here; It's like a sauna in here.
여기에서 'here'는 명사로 사용되었으므로 전치사 'in'이 항상 수반되어야 한다.

2 'Air-conditioner'는 'A/C'([ei si]로 발음한다)라고도 하나, 'air-con'이라고 하지는 않는다. 그 외 '선풍기를 틀다'는 'turn on the fan', '전열기를 틀다'는 'turn on the heater'라고 하며, 만약 건물 전체의 난방을 틀 경우에는 'turn on the heat'라고 한다.

3 사물이 아닌 상황을 나타낼 때는, 일반적으로 'it'이 아닌 'that'을 사용한다. 따라서 'Is it OK with you?'가 아닌 'Is that OK with you?'라고 한다.

4 (잡담 그만하세요.) Stop gabbing now.

5 (그만해.) Stop it.

:위의 대화에서 선생님은 조금씩 감정이 격해지고 있다. 처음에는 공손하게 'Quiet now please!'를 사용하고 다음에는 'Please stop that.'이라 말하며, 마지막에는 'Cut it out!'라고 단호하게 말하고 있다.

해석

선생님: 6반 안녕. 별일 없지요?

학생들: 예. 선생님은요?

선생님: 좋습니다. 좀 덥지 않나요?

학생들: 예. 매우 더워요.

선생님: 맑고 시원한 공기가 들어오도록 에어컨을 틉시다. 민수야, 에어컨을 틀어 줄래?

학생들: 예, 그렇게 할게요.

선생님: 훨씬 낫구나. 그런데 에어컨에서 소리가 난다. 괜찮니?

학생들: 예, 더위보다는 잡음이 나아요.

선생님: 좋아요. 자, 조용히 하세요. 이야기 그만 하세요. 민수야, 잡담 그만 하거라. 그리고 순희도. 자, 5번 문제지. 누구 차례지?

미자: 제 차례입니다.

선생님: 미자, 미안, 잠깐만! 나리, 미리. 그만해라. 조용히 앉아 있어. 그래, 미자 5번을 해라.

미자: '민수는 서울에 갔다.'

한길: '수원에…'

선생님: 한길아, 미자가 말할 때 방해하지 마라. 잘 듣고, 그녀의 말이 맞는지 보아라. 그리고 순희, 연습문제를 푸는 동안 필기하지 마. 잘 듣기만 해라.

순희: 죄송합니다.

선생님: 좋아. 한길아. 너 조용히 하라고 했지. 입 다물어! 미자야, 미안, 계속 하거라.

2. 기본구문

여기에서는 수업 분위기 조성에 필요한 학생들의 자세 및 교실 환경, 그리고 교실에서의 이동에 대해서 다음 순서로 정리하였다: A. 주목·태도 B. 환기·조명 C. 이동 및 정돈

A. 주목·태도

① Now then, pay attention, please.

해설　자, 주목해 주세요.
　　　: 수업 시작을 알리는 신호로 가장 흔히 사용된다.

syn　OK.
　　　Please pay (close) attention.
　　　Would you please pay attention? *(very formal)*
　　　Could I have your attention, please?
　　　Pay close attention to me.
　　　I need your undivided attention. *(formal, serious)*
　　　Please look at me.

참고　**'Now then'의 용법**
　　　'Now then'은 선생님이 수업을 시작할 때 가장 널리 사용하는 표현으로 '자, (그러면)' 또는 '조용히 해라'라는 의미이다. 이것은 군대에서 교관이 집합시켜서 처음에 'Attention'(주목)하고 말하는 것과 비슷한 의미를 지닌다. 원래 'now'는 'at this time'의 의미를 가지지만, 차츰 이야기의 서두에서 막연히 사용하는 부사어 — 우리말의 '자', '그런데'와 비슷함 — 로서의 구실을 하게 되었다.

e. g. Now, once upon a time there was a handsome prince...
Now, this prince was about to marry.

② Stop talking (now) so (that) we can start.

해설   조용히 하세요. 수업 시작하겠습니다.

syn   We won't start until everyone is quiet.
I won't begin until you all settle down.
Settle down now, so we can start.
Class will begin once everyone settles down.
Class won't begin until everyone is [has] settled down.

③ Quiet, please!

해설   조용히 하세요!

syn   Be quiet (now). / Quiet down! / Quiet (please)! *(formal)*
Be quiet, please.
Be quiet, will you [would you]?
Would you please be quiet? / May I have some quiet, please?

May I have silence, please?
Enough! (그만 됐어. *impolite*)
Stop (your) talking (now).

Calm down.
Silence! *(impolite)*
Shut up! *(rude)*

Shut your trap. *(rude)*

Put a lid on it. *(impolite)*

Can it. *(impolite)*

Zip it up! *(impolite)*

Ssshhh!

— 강한 명령 또는 불쾌감을 나타내기 위해서는 다음과 같이 말할 수 있다.

Do be quiet now. / Just be quiet now.

Don't talk.

Not another word, please.

---

④ Don't make so much noise.

해설 떠들지 마세요.

syn Please try not to make so much noise. *(polite)*

Would you please keep it down?

Not so much noise, please.

Turn it down a notch. *(casual)*

Pipe down a little bit. *(casual)*

Put a sock in it, will you? *(casual, rude)*

Can it! *(rude, among friends only)*

Chill out. / Cool it. *(casual)*

(상대방이 화가 났을 때 '진정해'라는 의미도 지닌다.)

Knock it off. / Cut it out. *(slang, impolite)*

⑤ Don't do that! Settle down.

해설   그만(하고 조용히) 하세요.
       : 학생들이 장난칠 때 주로 사용하는 표현이다.

syn   Would you please stop doing that (and settle down)?
       (very formal, polite)
       That type of behavior is not permitted (in) here. *(very formal)*

       Take it easy (now). *(informal)*
       Stop (doing) that! / Stop it!
       No, don't.

       That's enough. *(casual)*
       I've had enough.
       Enough.

       I've had it up to here. *(casual, angry)*
       ('목까지 [머리까지] 올라왔어. (더 이상 못 참아.)'라는 의미로 이
       경우에는 손짓으로 목 또는 머리를 가리키는 동작을 수반한다.)

   cf. Are you ready to take this seriously?
       (지금부터 중요한 이야기를 할 테니 잘 들으세요.)
       = Please start taking this seriously.

⑥ Please don't fool around. Calm down, please. *(usual, polite)*

해설   쓸데없이 빈둥거리며 장난치며 돌아다니지 마세요.

syn   You shouldn't be playing around.

No (more) playing around! *(casual)*
Stop playing [fooling, horsing] around. *(colloquial)*
Stop it! *(colloquial, impolite)*
Stop goofing [slacking] off
Would you mind not fooling around? *(polite)*

cf. Stop acting like a fool. *(coll.)*
Stop goofing around in the hall or you'll get detention.
(복도에서 빈둥거리는 것을 중단하지 않으면 방과 후 남을 것이다.)

⑦ Look this way, please.

해설   이쪽을 보세요.

syn   Would you please look this way? *(formal)*
Look in this direction.
Hey, over here. *(informal, between friends)*
Look over here, please. / Look at me. / Look.

주의   'Look at here'*(incorrect)* 또는 'Look here'*(threatening)*라는 표현
은 사용하지 않는 것이 좋다. 'Look at here'는 'here'가 부사이기
때문에 전치사의 목적어가 될 수 없고, 'Look here'는 문법적으로
는 옳지만 위협적인 의미를 가진다. 반면 'Look!'은 '조심해라.'라
는 의미로도 사용된다.

⑧ Turn around, please.

해설   몸을 돌리세요. [뒤를 보세요.]
:'몸을 돌리다'는 'turn' 또는 'face'를 이용하여 표현할 수 있다.

Would you please turn around?

Turn to the other side.

Please turn the other way.

Face the other way. *(casual)*

Face the rear. / Face the back.

Turn to the back of the room, please. *(very formal, very polite)*

Make an about turn. *(formal, military)*

About face! (뒤로 돌아!, *military*)

cf. '몸을 360도 한 바퀴 돌리세요.'

Turn all the way around. *(rare)*

참고   방향과 관련된 표현

① '앞을 보세요.'

Look straight ahead.

Look straight [directly] in front of you.

Look right in front of you.

Eyes to the front, please.

Face the front. *(casual, polite)*

② '왼쪽 [오른쪽]을 보세요.'

Look left [right].

Look to your left.

Would you please look to the left?

Please look to the left.

Focus your attention to the left. *(formal)*

⑨ Sit up straight.

해설   똑바로 앉으세요. [움직이지 마세요.]

syn   Stay in your seat. / Sit still. / Stand [Keep] still.
      Don't move. Nobody move.

⑩ Stand up, please.

해설   일어서세요.

syn   Would you please stand up? (*polite*)
      Would you mind standing up?

      Out of your chair, please.
      Up out of your chair, please.

⑪ S: May I sit (down)?
   T: Sure. **Please have a seat.**

해설   S: 앉아도 좋습니까?
      T: 물론입니다. 앉으세요.

syn   다음과 같은 수사적 표현을 붙일 수 있다.
      S: Do you mind if I sit down?
         Please allow me to sit down.

         If it's OK with you, I'd like to take a seat.
         If it's possible may I have a seat?

I'd like to sit if you'll allow it.

Is it OK for me to sit down?

If you don't mind, I think I'll sit. *(formal, rare)*

If it's not too much trouble, may I sit down? *(formal, rare)*

T: Sure, sit down, please.

By all means, sit down.

Sure, take the load off. *(coll.)* (편히 앉으세요.)

Certainly not. Please have a seat. ('mind'가 포함된 질문에 대한 대답)

---

⑫ Close your eyes, please.

해설   눈을 감으세요.

syn   Would you close your eyes? *(polite)*

Eyes closed.

Cover your eyes. *(casual)*

Shut your eyes.

Don't look [peek]. *(less polite)*

No looking [peeking].

---

⑬ Minsu, that's not the way to behave in class.

해설   민수야, 교실에서는 그렇게 행동해서는 안 된다.

syn   Minsu, would you please try to behave?

Minsu, behave yourself in class.

Minsu, try to control your behavior.

Minsu, please act your age. *(informal, impolite)*

Minsu, behave! *(informal, imperative)*

어휘 behave oneself: 품위 있고, 상황에 맞게 행동하다.

(act in the way that people think is correct and proper.)

참고 ## 체벌(punishment)에 관한 표현

서구에서는 학생들에 대한 구타는 금지되어 있으며 대부분의 경우 교장 또는 교감선생님에게 가서 훈계를 듣는 것이 일반적이다. 그렇지만 법적인 범위 내에서 선생님이 학생들에게 제재를 가하는 다양한 방법이 있다. 그 중 몇 가지만 열거하면 다음과 같다.

① 직접적인 제재

Face the wall. (벽을 보고 서 있어.)

Stand in the corner [in the hall]. (구석에 가서 서 있어.)

Stand outside. (밖에 서 있어.)

Get out (of the classroom). (교실에서 나가.)

Go outside. (교실에서 나가.)

Go stand in the hallway. (복도에 가서 서 있어.)

Put your head down (for 10 minutes).

(책상 위에 머리를 (10분간) 엎드리고 있어.)

Do 30 push-ups.

(엎드려뻗쳐 30회: 주로 운동부에서 많이 사용)

Go to the board and write 'I will not talk in class' 30 times.

(칠판에 가서 '나는 교실에서 떠들지 않겠습니다'를 30번

쓰라.)

— 다음과 같은 체벌은 미국에서는 불법이므로, 실제 시행하지
는 않는다.
Kneel down. (무릎 꿇어.)
You'll get a spanking (with hand).
((손으로) 엉덩이를 맞을 거야: 주로 가정에서 어린아이에게)
You'll get a paddling (with a stick). (회초리로 맞을 거야.)
Hands in the air. (손들고 있어.)
Show me your hands. (손바닥 내밀어.)

② 간접적인 제재
Stay after class [school]. / (You have) Detention after class
[after school]. (방과 후에 남을 것.)

I'm writing your name on the board, and you'll have to stay
after school [after class].
(칠판에 이름 적힌 사람은 방과 후 남으세요.)
No recess. (휴식시간에 나가지 말고 교실에서 대기할 것.)
(You can't play during free time but must stay in the classroom.)

(Go to the office and) Report to the principal. / Go to the
principal's office.
(교장선생님에게 보고할 것: 서구에서 가장 일반적으로 사용되
는 방법이다. 서구에서는 교장선생님이 주로 훈계를 담당함.)

Go to the detention room.
(훈육실에서 대기할 것: 격리되는 장소가 따로 있음.)

I think you need (a) time-out.
('너 잠깐 나갔다가 와.': 주로 어린 학생에게 사용하며, 이 경우

어린이는 교실에서 나와 잠시 훈육실이나 대기실에 들렀다 와
야 한다.)

Hawitzer 교감: 안녕, 나는 리버데일 고등학교 교감, 패튼 호위츠입니다. 내 임무에는
                 지각, 어지럽히는 학생, 다양한 말썽꾼들을 훈육하는 것이 포함되어
                 있습니다. 나의 가장 자랑스러운 업적은 우리 학교의 새로운 훈육시
                 설을 설치했다는 것입니다. 모든 훈육 대상들은 소란을 막기 위해서
                 개개인의 칸막이 좌석을 가지고 있습니다. 내가 확신컨데, 학생들은
                 스스로 새 훈육실이 크게 개선되었다는 사실에 동의할 것입니다. 계
                 속 써 내려가도록!
학생1:   저! 이번이 교도소에 처음 온 거니?
학생2:   다음에는 족쇄를 채울 거야!

⑭ Tom, please come here.

해설   탐, 여기로 와!

syn   Would you come here, Tom?
        Tom, can I see you over here please? *(formal, polite)*
        Come here, Tom.
        Tom, over here please.
        Tom, up here please. *(informal)*
        Come. *(rare, impolite)*

참고   **'Please'의 위치**
        'Please'는 대개 문두, 문미, 본동사 앞에 위치한다. 그리고 'please'
        가 동사 앞에 위치하면 정중한(formal) 표현이 된다.

        동사 앞에 위치할 경우   동사 뒤에 위치할 경우

(공손한 표현)	**(일상적인 표현)**
Tom, please come here.	Tom, come here, please.
Please, Tom, come here.	Come here, please, Tom.
Please come here, Tom.	Come here, Tom, please.

⑮ Please don't slam [bang] the door.

해설   문을 꽝 닫지 마세요. [문을 조용히 닫으세요.]

syn   Try not to slam the door.
        Don't slam the door like that!

        Close the door gently [quietly].

Gently close the door.

Please be careful closing the door.
Close the door quietly.

cf. Exit [Enter] quietly. (조용히 나가세요 [들어오세요].)

B. 환기·조명

① **Would you (please) turn on the lights?** Then we can see better.

해설　전깃불을 켤까? 그러면 더 잘 보일 거야.

syn　Would you mind turning on the lights?
We need some light in here.
We could use some light in here.
Let's get some light in here.
It's too dark in here.
It's always dark in here. Let's turn on a light or two.

활용　상황에 따라 'turn on' 대신 'turn off [up, down]' 등을 대체할 수 있다.

— '전깃불을 끕시다.'는 다음과 같이 표현할 수 있다.

ant　Would you mind turning off the lights?
Turn the lights off, please.
Turn out the lights.
Turn the lights out.
Time to turn off the lights.

Lights out! *(impolite, directive)*

> ② T: Don't you think it's too dark in here?
> S: Yes, it is a little dark.

해설   T: 좀 어둡지 않습니까?
        S: 예, 좀 어둡습니다.

어법   여기에서 'here'는 'this place'의 의미를 가진 명사로 사용되었으므
        로 전치사 'in'이 수반되어야 한다.

syn   T: Isn't it too dark in here?
        Is it light enough for you?
        Is it too dark or can you see alright?
        It's too dark in here, isn't it?

        — 어둡지 않을 경우
        S: I think the lighting is adequate [sufficient, fine], thank you.
        It's alright for me, but if you want I can turn on the light.
        It's perfectly OK for me, but feel free to turn on the light if
        you like.

        — 어두울 경우
        S: Yes, it's pretty [quite, somewhat, a little, a bit] dark.
        Yes, I'll turn on the light. / Yes, why don't we open the
        blinds?
        I think it's alright. / I don't mind (it).

③ T: Is it a bit warm in here?
S: Yes, could we turn the heat down a little?

해설   T: 조금 덥지 않니?
S: 난방을 조금 낮추면 어떻습니까?

syn   T: Are you (a bit) hot?
Don't you find it hot in here?
Is it too hot for you in here?

— 다음과 같이 대답할 수도 있다.
S: Yes, it's a little warm.
Yes, it's terribly hot in here.
Yes, it's a bit toasty in here.
Yes, we're roasting. *(casual)*
Yes, we're sweating up a storm. *(casual)*

④ T: Would you mind turning off the heater?
S: No, that would be fine.

해설   T: 전열기를 끌까요?
S: 그렇게 합시다.

syn   T: Would you mind if we turned off the heater?
Would it be OK if I turned off the heater?
If you don't mind, could we just turn off the heater?
Could you [someone] please turn off the heater?
Let's turn the heat off for a while. *(coll.)*
S: Okay.
No problem.

Right away.

Sure, I'll be glad to.

That's a good idea.

---

⑤ Minsu, please open the curtains. *(casual)*

해설   민수야, 커튼을 열어라.

syn   Minsu, could [would] you open the curtains?
       Minsu, why don't you open the curtains?

ant   '민수야, 커튼을 닫아라.'
       Minsu, close [shut, pull down] the curtains.
       Minsu, pull the curtains closed [shut].
       Minsu, draw the curtains.

어휘   'Draw the curtains'는 상황에 따라 '커튼을 닫다' 또는 '커튼을 열
       다'라는 두 가지 의미를 가진다. 따라서 의미를 분명히 하기 위해
       서는 다음과 같이 표현하기도 한다.
       Draw the curtains back. (커튼을 닫아라.)
       Draw the curtains across. (커튼을 쳐라.) *(rare)*

---

⑥ T: **It's a little stuffy in here**. Why don't you open the window
      nearest you? Let's have some fresh air.
   S: Ms. Kim, I'm sorry, but I have a cold. Could we just open
      the windows up front?
   T: Sure, no problem.

해설   T: 교실이 좀 답답하구나. 가까이에 있는 창문을 열어 맑은 공기

를 들어오게 하여라.

S: 김 선생님, 저는 감기 걸렸는데요. 앞문만 열면 안 돼요?

T: 그래, 그러자.

syn   T: Isn't it a little stuffy in here?

It's a little stuffy in this classroom, isn't it?

— 다음과 같이 대답할 수도 있다.

S: Yes, why we don't turn on the air-conditioner [the A/C]?
(에어컨을 틀지요?)

Yes, why don't we open the window? (예, 창문을 열지요?)

Yes, we need to get some air in here.

No, it's alright. (아니, 갑갑하지 않습니다.)

No, it's OK. (아니, 좋은데요.)

어휘   up front(앞쪽의)=at the front (of the classroom)

cf. Is the room uncomfortable? = Are you uncomfortable?
('Uncomfortable'은 'stuffy'보다 넓은 의미로 사용된다.)

---

⑦ **The bulb [The light] is blown (out).**

해설   전구가 나갔다.

syn   The bulb blew out. *(usual)*

The bulb [The light] has burned out.

The bulb has gone. / The bulb is dead.

The bulb is out.

C. 이동 및 정돈

> ① (Please) Move your chairs over here.

해설   너의 의자를 여기로 옮겨라.

syn   Could you move your chairs this way please?
      Would you mind moving your chairs this way please?
      Put [Place, Situate] your chairs over here.

> ② Let's make a bigger space here.

해설   여기에 공간을 만들어라.

syn   Let's open up some space here. *(usual)*
      Would you mind making a bigger space here please?
      Why don't we make a bigger space here?

> ③ Please clear a path through here. *(formal, usual)*

해설   이쪽에 길을 여세요. [통로를 만드세요.]

syn   Could you make a way [a path] through here please?
      Make way (please). *(usual)*
      (거리에서 앞을 지나갈 때)

참고   길을 비켜달라거나 지나갈 때 사용하는 표현

Excuse me (please). *(usual)*
Coming through (please).
(길 좀 비켜주세요: 자신이 직접 지나갈 때.)
Clear the way. (비켜주세요!)
(Look out.) Here I come. ((조심하세요.) 길 좀 비켜주세요.)
Out of the way. *(very impolite,* (긴급상황에서) 비켜!)
Move (aside).
(선박과 같은 좁은 공간에서 높은 사람이 지나갈 때 옆에서 소리
치는 표현. 과거에 선박에서는 이 경우 'Gangway!'(길 좀 비켜
줘!)라고 했으나 오늘날에는 거의 사용하지 않음.)

④ Please leave your boots in the hallway and hang up your coats on the hook.

해설   신발은 복도에 놓고, 코트는 옷걸이에 걸어라.

syn   Please take your boots off in the hall and hang your coat up on the hook.
Please let your boots in the corridor... *(rare, B.E.)*

어휘   'Boots' 대신 'shoes', 'sneakers', 'gym-shoes' 등으로 대체할 수 있다.

⑤ S: Do you mind if I change places [spots]? *(polite)*

해설   자리를 바꾸어도 되겠습니까?

syn   May I change places [my place]?
Would you mind changing seats?

Is it all right if I change places?

Is it OK if I change seats?

Is it OK to change seats? (*casual*)

Is it OK if we change places [spots]?

cf. 자리이동과 관련된 표현들

Can I move and sit in the shade? (그늘 쪽으로 옮겨도 괜찮습니까?)

= Is it alright if I move and sit in the shade?

Is it alright to move to the back of the room?

(교실 뒤로 이동해도 될까요?)

I'd like to change places with you if you don't mind.

(괜찮으면 너와 자리를 바꾸고 싶다.)

---

⑥ S: Where is our next class?

해설   다음 수업시간에는 어느 교실로 갈까요?

syn   Which room should we go to for the next class?

Which room should we go to next class [lesson]?

Which room should we go to next time around? (*rare, B.E*)

: 영국식 영어에서 'next time' 과 'next time around'는 모두 '다음 시간에'라는 의미로 사용된다. 그러나 미국식 영어에서 'next time around'는 약간 다르게 '다음 기회에 다시 하게 되면(when we do it again)' 또는 '다음에 다시 모이게 되면(when we get together)의 의미로 사용된다.

e.g.   We'll talk about Korean history next time around.

: 다음 시간에는 한국 역사에 대해 이야기하자. (B.E.)

다음에 (이 문제를) 다시 다룰 기회가 있으면 한국 역사에 대해 이야기하자. (A.E.)

> ⑦ S: May I (please) be excused (for a minute)? *(formal, polite)*

해설   잠시 나가도 좋습니까?

syn   (Please) excuse me for a moment [for a minute].
I need to be excused for a moment.

May I go out for a minute? *(formal, polite)*
Would you excuse me for a minute?
May I please leave the room?
Please allow me to leave for a minute.

I need to go out for a minute.
I need to leave the room for a minute.
I'll be right back.

— 위의 표현은 수업 중 학생들이 화장실에 가거나 부득이 잠깐 나갈 때 사용하는 가장 일반적인 표현이다. 그 외 아래와 같은 직접적인 표현도 사용할 수 있으나, 품위 있는 표현은 아니다.

May I go to the lavatory [restroom, bathroom, potty, ladies' [men's, boys', girls'] room] please? (어린이들이 사용)

I have to go.
I have (got) to pee! *(slang,* 어린이들이 사용*)*
Nature calls! *(slang, colloquial)*
I have to see a man about a horse. *(slang,* 남자만 사용*)*

cf. May I go and get a drink? (물 마시고 오겠습니다.)

May I leave ten minutes early? (10분 먼저 나가도 될까요?)

참고   **'Relieve'의 용법**

① May I be relieved for a moment?

(잠시 자리를 이탈해도 괜찮습니까?)

I have to relieve myself. (자리를 비워야 하겠습니다.)

(보초나 임무 수행 중에 식사를 하거나 어떤 사정으로 잠시 자리를 비울 때, 상대편에게 대신해서 자리를 지켜달라는 표현이다.)

② 'Relieve oneself [nature]'는 '화장실에 간다'는 표현으로도 사용한다. 이 경우에는 자기 자신이 아니라, 다른 사람이 당사자를 찾는 경우에 대답으로만 사용한다.

A: Where is Tom going?

B: He is relieving himself. (용변 보러 간다.)

: 대개 위의 경우 아래와 같이 대답한다.

To the bathroom. *(usual)*

He is going to the bathroom.

---

⑧ S: Please move to the side. I can't see.

해설   옆으로 옮기세요. 보이지 않습니다.

syn   Excuse me. I can't see.

You're in the way. I can't see. *(casual, rude)*

You're blocking my view. Please move.

Please move out of the way. I can't see.

⑨ S: Do you want a hand with the table?

해설   테이블을 옮기는 것을 도와 드릴까요?

syn   Do you want a hand moving the table?
       May [Can] I help you move the table?
       Can I give you a hand with that table?

◆ 교실 관용표현의 유형과 효과

교실관용표현의 유형과 효과를 차례로 살펴보기로 한다.
일상적인 관용표현에 대한 연구 성과를 외국어 습득 및 교육에 처음으로 적용한
Yorio(1980)는 교실 관용표현을 다섯 가지 유형 — 상황용 관용표현(situational
formula), 격식용 관용표현(stylistic formula), 의례용 관용표현(ceremonial
formula), 책략어(gambit), 완곡어(euphemism) — 으로 구분하였다.
첫째, 상황용 관용표현이란 특정 상황에서 모국어 화자들이 즐겨 사용하는 표현이다.
상황용 관용표현을 사용할 때에는 상대방의 성, 사회적 역할, 위계질서, 발화의 배경,
담화의 진행상황 등 여러 가지 조건뿐만 아니라 문화적 특성도 고려해야 한다. 다음
예문을 보자.

1 **a.** This hurts me more than it hurts you. (이 일로 너보다 내가 더 상처가
       크다.)
   b. You have to be there. (그만 해라.)

위의 **1a**는 부모가 자녀에게 체벌을 가할 때 사용하는 표현이며, **1b**는 상대방의 농
담이나 이야기가 계속 되풀이되거나 지나쳐서 오히려 부정적 영향을 나타낼 때 일상
적으로 사용하는 표현이다. 교실현장에서 원어민 교사들은 주로 학생들의 수업태도,
대답에 대한 평가 또는 대답을 독려하는 경우에 상황용 관용표현을 흔히 사용한다.

2 **a. 듣기에 주목을 시킬 때**
      Pay attention please. I am not saying this twice.
      (주의를 기울이세요. 두 번 말하지 않습니다.)
   b. 대답을 잘 했을 때
      You make me smile. You made my day.
      (나를 미소 짓게 하는군. 몹시 행복하다.)
   c. 질문에 반응이 없을 때
      Be brave. Take initiative. Make mistakes.
      (용기있게 해 봐. 솔선해서 해 봐. 실수도 해 봐.)

위의 **2a**는 학생들이 주의깊게 들으라고 지시할 경우, **2b**는 학생의 대답이 매우 만족스럽고 전체 학생들에게 자극을 불러일으키고 싶을 때, **2c**는 선생님의 질문에 학생이 대답하지 않거나 소극적 태도를 보일 때 흔히 사용한다.

두 번째, 격식용 관용표현은 특정 상황에서 일반적으로 사용하는 어법 또는 문체를 말한다: 예를 들면, 모르는 사람에게 처음 보내는 편지의 서두에서, 'To whom it may concern(관계자에게)' 또는 연설에서 사용하는 'Ladies and gentlemen(신사 숙녀 여러분)' 등의 표현이 이런 유형에 속한다. 영어의 격식용 관용표현은 상황용 관용표현보다 비교적 단순하고 제한적으로 사용되며, 주로 인사말 또는 감탄어법에 많이 나타난다. 실제 우리 학생들을 가르치는 원어민의 회화수업에서는 표현을 반복하거나, 학생들의 토론에 개입하거나, 과제를 부여하거나 풀이할 경우에 격식용 관용표현이 종종 사용되고 있다:

3 **a.** Sorry? Can you speak a little bit louder please?
    (다시? 조금 크게 말할 수 있어요?)
   b. Can I talk? (내가 끼어들어도 될까?)
   c. There is the possibility of losing marks [points] if you don't do these correctly. (이것을 정확히 하지 않으면 점수를 잃어요.)
   d. For your homework, I want you to do this exercise.
    (숙제로 이 연습문제를 해 오세요.)

3a는 학생의 대답이 들리지 않거나 정확하지 않을 때, **3b**는 학생들 간의 토론에 선생님이 끼어 들 때, **3c**은 과제물을 정확히 해올 것을 지시할 때, **3d**는 과제를 부여할 때 사용한 관용적인 표현이다. 이 표현들의 문장구조는 전부 의문문 또는 평서문이지만 내용은 요구 또는 지시사항을 공손하게 표현한 간접화행이다.

세 번째, 의례용 관용표현은 의례적인 인사말 혹은 감정표현에 많이 사용된다. 이 경우에는 상대방과의 관계, 위계질서 등이 고려된다: 예를 들면, 불어의 'vous(귀하)'와 'tu(너)'의 구분, 우리말과 일어 등에 나타나는 다양한 경어가 여기에 포함된다. Ellis(1984)도 인사말이 주로 여기에 포함된다고 주장하였다. 실제 우리 학생들을 가르치는 원어민 선생님도 회화수업에서 다음과 같이 수업시작 전 인사말, 감정의 공감, 상담, 학생의 대답에 대한 반응에 흔히 사용한다.

4　**a.** Good morning, folks. You guys look lively today.

　　(안녕, 여러분. 오늘 활발해 보이네요.)

　b. Oh my goodness! You guys have very tight schedule.

　　(어이구! 여러분들 일과가 벅차군.)

　c. Please come in and be my guest. (어서 들어오십시오. 편하게 하세요.)

　d. Thank you for giving me the right answer. (정답을 맞추어서 감사합니다.)

위의 **4a**는 수업시작 전 아침인사, **4b**는 학생들의 생활에 대한 감정적 공감 표시, **4c**는 학생들이 상담하기 위해 방문했을 때, **4d**는 학생의 정확한 대답에 대한 감사의 표시에 사용되었다. 이런 표현은 평서문 또는 공손형 명령문 또는 문장단편으로 표현될 수 있으며, 실제 상황에 관계없이 매우 의례적인 의미를 지니고 있다.

네 번째, 책략어(gambit)는 상호활동과정에서 상대방의 행동을 유발하거나 담화를 시작 또는 조직하기 위해 사용되는 표현이다. 책략어는 담화의 구체적인 내용은 담고 있지 않지만 담화 또는 행위의 시작, 종료, 전환을 알리는 중요한 역할을 한다. Wray(2002:177)는 책략어를 다음과 같이 규정하고 있다:

Gambits are formulaic expressions whose primary role is strategic rather than propositional in nature; they serve to guide the hearer through the discourse by semantically framing propositional information, by facilitating turn exchanges and by marking discourse boundaries.

(책략어는 일차적 역할이 본질적으로 명제가 아닌 전략적 역할을 하는 관용표현이다. 그것은 의미론적으로 명제의 정보를 조직화하고, 말차례를 용이하게 하고, 담화경계를 분명히 함으로써 담화활동에서 청자를 유도하는 데 도움이 된다.)

책략어에 대한 구분은 현재까지 명확하게 정립되어 있지 않지만 대체로 다음과 같다. Yorio(1980)에 따르면 책략어는 담화용 책략어(conversational gambit)와 조직적 책략어(organizational gambit)로 구분할 수 있다. 먼저 담화용 책략어는 직접적인 담화활동을 하기 위한 전초로 사용되는 표현이다: 여기에는 "Pardon me.(실례합니다.)", "I think that(내가 생각건대)", "Speaking of...(말해보면...)",

"Surprise!(놀랍군!)" "Guess what.(추측해 보세요.)" 등 담화를 시작하거나 유발하기 위한 표현 등이 포함된다. 반면 조직적 책략어는 담화활동과정에서 담화를 새로 시작하거나 종료할 때 또는 담화내용을 조직하기 위해서 사용되는 고정된 표현이다: 예를 들면, "Let's call it a day.(수업 마치겠습니다.)", "Take five.(5분간 휴식.)" 등과 같은 수업을 종료할 때 사용하는 표현, "We'll now take questions from the floor.(참가자로부터 질문을 받겠습니다.)"와 같은 담화 차례를 넘기거나 새로 시작할 때 사용하는 표현, "First of all(우선)", "To summarize(요약하면)", "Finally(끝으로)" 등과 같이 학습과정을 표시하는 자료용 책략어(text gambit) 등이 여기에 포함된다. 그 외 Austin(1965)의 "Thank you.(감사합니다.)", "I apologize.(사과합니다.)"와 같은 발화내용 자체가 언어행위를 나타내는 관용표현과 아래의 문장 속에 있는 이탤릭체로 쓰여진 감탄사 등도 일종의 조직적인 책략어에 포함되기도 한다.

5 **a.** There were... *oh*...15 people. (approximately, 대략)
    (대략 15명입니다.)
   b. There were... *ah*...15 people. (counting, 수를 셀 때)
    (아...15명입니다.)

실제 우리 학생들을 가르치는 원어민 선생님들의 회화수업에서도 책략어는 모든 교과활동을 조직하거나 시작 또는 종료할 때 널리 사용되고 있다. 예를 들면 교과활동을 조직하기 위한 조직적 책략어에는 다음과 같은 표현도 있다:

6 **a.** Ready (for class)? (준비됐어요?)
   b. Revise for the past class. Close your books.
    (지난 시간 복습해 봅시다. 책 덮으세요.)
   c. Today we are going to talk about [will discuss] the importance of mood in the poem. (이 시간에는 시에 나타난 분위기에 대해 토의하겠습니다.)
   d. It's time to wrap up. (마칠 시간입니다.)
    You are dismissed. See you. (수업 끝. 잘 가요.)

위의 표현들은 각각 학습시작, 복습, 학습목표, 수업 종료 등에 흔히 사용하는 관용표현이다. 직접적인 교과내용이 아닌 교과의 진행과정에 대한 표현으로 의문문, 명령문, 평서문 등 다양한 문장형태를 지니며 매번 교과활동에서 사용되고 있다. 반면 담화를 유도하기 위한 담화용 책략어로 원어민 교사는 다음과 같은 표현을 흔히 사용한다.

7 **a.** Come on. Isn't it your turn? (자. 너 차례지?)

   b. Any further questions? Anything special? (또 다른 질문은? 특별히 없어요?)

   c. Be more specific. (보다 구체적으로 말하세요.)

   d. Do you know this word, "induction", in English?
   (너는 영어단어 "입문 교육"을 아니?)

위의 표현은 각각 학생들의 적극적인 교과활동, 교과내용에 대한 세부적인 질문, 학생들의 표현의 구체화, 어휘의 의미에 대한 질문 등에 사용된 표현이다. 이들 표현은 대개 의문문 또는 명령문의 형태를 지닌다.

마지막으로 표현에 신중을 기하기 위해 사용하는 완곡어도 관용표현의 한 유형으로 분류하였다. 예를 들면 사망하거나 퇴직했을 때 사용하는 표현 — "He passed on/away.(그는 돌아갔습니다.)", "Mr. Smith is no longer with this company.(스미스씨는 이 회사에 없습니다.)" — 또는 터부시되거나 공개적으로 드러내기를 꺼려하는 주제에 대한 표현 — "I'd like to wash my hands.(손을 씻고 싶습니다.)", "I'm going to be sick.(구역질나요.)", "We are comfortable.(우리는 부럽지 않아요. (부자라는 의미로 사용한다.))" — 도 완곡어에 포함된다. 이런 완곡어도 역시 문화와 깊은 연관이 있다. 교실에서 원어민이 우리 학생들에게 사용하는 다음과 같은 표현도 여기에 속한다고 볼 수 있다.

8 **a.** There is no need to rush. Please take your time.
   (서두르지 마세요. 천천히 여유를 가져요.)

   b. You should use your own imagination on the writing.
   (글쓰기에는 상상력을 사용하세요.)

   c. I'm extremely disappointed. (나는 매우 실망했어.)

d. You all did a decent job on your work. But you guys should be more enthusiastic about making presentations.

(모두 그럭저럭 했어요. 그러나 발표에 좀 성의가 있어야 됩니다.)

위의 **8a**는 질문에 대해 학생에게 응답할 여유를 줄 때, **8b**는 학생들이 제출한 리포터가 성의가 없거나 인터넷의 자료를 복사했을 때, **8c**는 학생들이 숙제를 하지 않았을 때, **8d**는 학생들의 발표가 매우 성의가 없었음을 완곡하게 표현한 것이다. 이런 표현은 모두가 부정적인 내용을 완곡하게 표현한 것이며, 개별 문화에 따라 표현 방법이 다를 수 있다.

이상과 같이 Yorio(1980)와 Ellis(1984)의 구분 방법에 따라 교실에서 사용되는 다양한 관용표현을 살펴보았다. 그러나 어떤 표현은 복합적인 성격을 지니고 있다. 예를 들어 원어민이 수업 중 사용한 아래의 관용표현을 보자:

9 **a.** Hello, ladies and gentleman. Welcome to our English class.

(안녕, 남녀 여러분. 내 수업에 온 것을 환영합니다.) **격식용+의례용**

b. I am worried that you can't follow the text.

(진도를 따라오지 못할까 걱정된다.) **상황용+완곡어**

c. You make me smile. You made my day.

(나를 미소 짓게 만들구나. 너는 나를 즐겁게 만든다.) **상황용+의례용+완곡어**

d. *It's a great job,* but you should concentrate more on the vocabulary.

(잘했지만, 어휘에 좀 집중해야겠다.) **상황용＋완곡어**

9a는 수업 첫 시간에 사용하는 의례용 관용표현이지만, 동시에 학생들에 대한 호칭은 영미문화에 따른 격식용 관용표현으로 볼 수 있다. **9b**는 학생이 책을 가져오지 않았을 때 사용한 상황적 관용표현이지만, 표현 방법으로는 오히려 매우 우회적인 완곡어라고 볼 수 있다. **9c**는 학생의 태도가 적극적이고 대답이 정확했을 경우에 사용하는 상황적 관용표현이며, 또한 감탄의 의미를 가진 의례적인 관용표현인 동시, 정확한 대답임을 강조하기 위해 사용한 완곡어법이라고 볼 수 있는 것이다. **9d**는 학생이 제출한 과제에 대한 평가에 사용되는 관용표현이면서, 어휘 사용이 틀렸다는 것을 간접적으로 표현한 완곡어인 것이다. 여기에서 전반부에 완화된 표현(mitigation)을 사용한 것은 추후의 학습활동 및 학생과의 유대를 고려하기 위한 것으로 볼 수 있다.

다음으로 영미 원어민이 우리 교실에서 사용하는 교실영어를 중심으로 교실관용표현의 효과를 살펴보자.

원어민 교사들은 교실현장에서 다양한 교과 관용표현을 사용하여 학습효과를 높이고, 학습자와 유대감을 형성하며, 학습자의 부담도 완화한다. 관용표현은 원어민과 학습자의 문화적 차이 또는 학습자의 빈약한 회화 능력을 보완하는 데도 도움이 된다. 왜냐하면 초급영어를 수강하는 대부분의 학생들은 원어민 수업에서 적극적으로 상호활동을 하는 것을 주저하고 자신감이 결여되어 있으므로 강제성이 완화된 관용표현이 학습자를 격려하고 학습활동을 원활히 진행되는 데 도움이 되기 때문이다. 원어민 교사가 빈번하게 사용하는 관용표현이 가진 효과는 대체적으로 네 가지 ― 자연스러움(naturalness), 경제성(economy), 완화(mitigation), 유대감 형성(establishing rapport) ― 로 구분할 수 있다. 이제 관용표현이 가진 이 네 가지 효과에 대해서 좀 더 구체적으로 살펴보자.

첫째, 원어민 교사가 교실활동에서 사용하는 영어가 자연스럽고 부드럽게 들리는 근본적인 이유는 그들이 모든 학습활동에 적합한 다양한 교실 관용표현을 적절히 구사하기 때문이다. 이 점은 Schmidt & Carter(2004)의 '유연하게 말하는 사람은 극히 제한된 시간 안에 많은 정보를 전달하기 위해서 많은 관용표현을 사용한다(smooth talkers use formulaic language a great deal in order to convey large amount of information under severe time constraints).' 는 주장에 부합한다. 다음 원어민 선생님의 표현을 살펴보자.

10 Come on, I'm waiting.   vs   Why don't you answer quickly?
(자, 기다리고 있어요.)   (빨리 답하세요.)
We don't say that.   vs   That is incorrect.
(그런 말 안 해요.)   (그건 틀렸어요.)
Be more specific.   vs   You explanation is not understandable.
(자세히 말하세요.)   (너의 설명을 이해하지 못하겠어.)

비록 문법과 의미 전달 면에서 후자가 더 정확할지 모르지만, 교육적으로는 학습자의 활동을 위축하고 교과활동에도 부적절한 표현이다. 실제 후자와 같은 공격적이고 노골적인 표현은 학생들의 의사소통 활동에도 도움이 되지 못하고, 미래의 언어활동에도 나쁜 영향을 미칠 수 있는 것이다.

두 번째로, 원어민은 교과활동에서 매우 간단한 관용표현을 효과적으로 사용한다. 간단하고 쉬운 관용표현을 이용하여 원어민은 처리시간을 줄임과 동시에, 진행되는 담화활동에 대한 평가나 또 다른 교과활동에 집중할 수 있다(Wray 2002). 예를 들면, 학습자의 이해를 확인하거나 행동을 통제하기 위해서 다음과 같은 한 단어로 된 관용표현을 흔히 사용한다.

11 See? Alright? Quite. Shoot. Absolutely. Excellent. Pardon? Tired? Behave! Sorry!
    (알겠어요? 됐습니까? 거의 맞아요. (시작) 해 봐요. 맞아요. 아주 좋아요. 다시 말해요. 피곤해요? 점잖게 행동해! 미안!)

또한 관용표현에 사고나 논평을 덧붙여 적절히 활용한다. 아래의 원어민의 교실영어에서 보는 바와 같이 'Raise your hand.(손을 드세요.)'라는 교실 관용표현에 덧붙여 다양한 부가적 활동을 하고 있다.

12 Raise your hand *if you don't understand what I just said*. **확인, 질의**
    (설명한 내용을 이해하지 못하면 손을 드세요.)
    If you know the answer, raise your hand. **이해**
    (답을 알면 손을 드세요.)
    If you think you are right raise your hand. **발표**
    (옳다고 생각하면 손을 드세요.)
    Don't call out. Raise your hand. **통제**
    (소리치지 마세요. 손을 드세요.)

또한 일상적으로 이용되는 사전 조립된 구문(prefabricated pattern) 형태의 관용표현은 학생들의 발화에 대한 수사적 또는 문법적 수정에도 종종 이용된다:

13 *Don't say* "Why not" *but* "May I ask you why?" or "Sorry?"
    ("왜요"라고 말하지 말고 "왜 그렇습니까?" 또는 "한 번 더 말해 주세요."라고 하세요.)
    We don't say "played canoeing". We went canoeing.

(우리는 "카누를 타고 놀았다"라고 하지 않습니다. 카누를 탔다.)

세 번째, 원어민들은 회화 수업에서 다양한 관용적인 완화장치(mitigation device)를 사용한다. 먼저 완화에 대한 규정을 간단히 살펴보자.

Blum-Kulka(1983:43) defines mitigation as "the intentional softening or easing of the force of the message - a modulation of the basic message intended by the speaker." and says that the linguistic means available for mitigating an act or for aggravating it can be language specific.

(블룸 쿨카(1983:43)는 완화를 "화자가 의도한 기본적인 전달내용의 조정, 즉 전달 내용의 힘을 의도적으로 약화 또는 이완"이라고 규정하고, 행위를 완화하거나 악화 시키는 데 이용되는 언어적 수단은 개별언어마다 다르다고 말했다.)

Ellis(1984)도 외국인 어린이들에 대한 연구에서 원어민 교사들도 학습자의 언어 능력에 맞게 다양하게 문장 내부에 대한 내적 수정(internal modification) 또는 별도의 표현을 부가하는 외적 수정(external modification)을 이용한 완화 장치 (mitigation device)를 교실영어에서 사용한다는 사실을 발견하였다. 원어민 교사 들은 교과활동 및 교실관리를 위해 다음과 같은 완화된 형태(mitigated form)를 종종 사용한다.

14 내적 수정

Would you speak more clearly?
(보다 분명히 말해 주겠어요?)
I want you to take your notebooks out.
(여러분 공책을 꺼내주세요.)
Who would like to answer this question?
(이 문제에 답해 볼 사람 있어요?)
You guys *need to know* about this grammar perfectly.
(이 문법을 완벽히 알 필요가 있어요.)

15 외적 수정

Please don't say the word.
(미안하지만 그 단어 사용하지 마세요.)
Parden me. I didn't mean to hit you like that.
(실례합니다. 나는 당신에게 상처를 줄 의도가 아니었습니다.)
You are speaking too soft. Please speak up.
(너무 조용히 말해요. 크게 말해요.)
Don't be afraid of making mistakes. *I am here to correct you.*
(실수하는 것을 두려워 마세요. 내가 고쳐주기 위해 여기에 있어요.)
In English, please! I can't understand you *if you talk in Korean.*
(영어로 말해요! 당신이 한국어로 말하면 나는 이해 못해요.)
You all did a decent job on your homework. But you should be more enthusiastic about making presentations.
(여러분 모두 숙제를 열심히 했어요. 그러나 발표에 좀 더 열성적이어야 합니다.)

위의 예에서 보는 바와 같이 원어민 교사들은 문장 내부의 구조를 수정하는 내적 수정 또는 별도의 어휘나 구문을 첨가하는 외적 수정 등 다양한 수정 방법을 이용하여 학습자의 부담을 완화하는 것이다. 구체적으로 살펴보면 문장 내부의 수정을 위해 양태를 나타내는 조동사를 이용하거나, 의문문을 이용한 간접적인 요청을 하였다. 반면 문장 외부의 수정을 위해 'please', 근거를 나타내는 별도의 문장(grounder), 또는 'if'절과 종속절을 이용하였다. 이런 다양한 관용표현은 학습자의 스트레스를 줄이고 상호 불편한 상황을 극복하는 데 효율적이다.
끝으로, 원어민들은 학생과의 유대를 형성 또는 유지하기 위해 간단한 관용표현을 매우 빈번히 사용한다. 원어민들은 수업 시작 전 친밀한 분위기를 형성하고 원활하게 수업을 진행하기 위해 종종 간단한 인사말 또는 잡담을 한다(Wray 2002, Wolfson 1983). 또한 학습자의 태도에 대한 적극적인 피드백에도 관용표현을 사용한다. 이런 표현들은 교실환경을 교사주도가 아닌 학습자 중심의 분위기로 이끌어 가는 데 매우 도움이 된다.

16 What did you do over the weekend?
(주말에 뭐했니?)

Thank you for being well-mannered.
(학습 태도가 좋아서 고마워요.)

이상과 같은 다양한 교실 관용표현을 적절히 활용함으로써 원어민 교사들도 학습자
와 협력적 분위기를 형성하여 교육 목적을 효과적으로 달성하기 위해서 노력하였다.

1. 현장예문 (Real-life Situation)

Discussing Personal Hygiene

학생들의 개인위생 및 건강관리에 대한 구체적인 대답을 유도하는 상황이다.

At the beginning of class, during a break, or at the end of class teachers may want to lighten up a bit and socialize with the students. By showing concern for students personal hygiene, and demonstrating an interest in facets of students lives beyond the classroom a teacher can strengthen and solidify his rapport with the students. This unit reviews language used to ask students about their general health and well-being, as well as other personal information such as weekend plans, summer vacation plans and hobbies.

Now listen to the dialogue.

T: Now, let's think about personal hygiene.[1] Okay? When you get up in the morning, what should you do to take care of your body?[2]

Ss: Exercise.[3]

T: You said you should exercise. Okay, what else?

S1: Keep yourself clean.

T: Keep yourself clean. What else?

S2: (In a low voice) Brush your teeth.[4]

T: Speak up.[5] I can't hear you.

S2: Get a proper amount of rest.[6]

누구나 영어로 가르칠 수 있다

T: Get a proper amount of rest, brush your teeth. Anything else?

S3: Have [Eat] a good breakfast. [7]

T: I can't hear you. (She cups her ear.)

S3: Have a good breakfast.

T: Okay. Anything else? Yes? (Points to S4.)

S4: When you get up in the morning, wash your face.

T: Okay. Anything else? Those are all things that are related to personal hygiene. [8] Now, let's look it up in the dictionary. [9]

주

1 'Think about' 대신 'talk about'라고 할 수도 있다.

2 (건강을 돌보기 위해 무엇을 해야 합니까?) We should do something to help us take care of our body. What should we do?

3 'Hygiene'(위생)에는 'exercise'가 포함되지 않으므로 잘못된 대답이다. 반면에 개인건강(personal health)에 대해 말할 때는 'exercise, swimming, jogging' 등이 포함된다.

4 '이빨을 닦다.'를 흔히 우리가 사용하는 'clean (up) one's teeth'로 표현하면 잘못된 표현이다. 반면 'clean'(청소하다)과 'clear'(제거하다)는 다음과 같이 사용될 수 있다.

　e.g. He went to the dentist to have his teeth cleaned, and cleared [scraped, removed] tartar. (그는 치과에 이를 손질하러 가서 치석을 제거했다.)

　또한 우리가 흔히 '스케일링 하겠다.'는 의미로 사용하는 'I'll scale my teeth.'는 잘못된 표현이며, 이 경우에는 다음과 같이 표현해야 한다 ;

　I'm having my teeth scaled. (나는 이빨을 스케일링 하겠다.)

5 (더 크게 말하세요.) Speak louder.

6 (충분히 휴식을 취하세요.) Get enough rest.

7 'Have [Eat] a good breakfast'는 '아침을 차려 먹는다'는 의미이고, 'Get a good breakfast'는 '아침 식사를 사 먹다(buy a good breakfast)'라는 의미로 흔히 사용되므로 구별해야 한다.

8 (개인 건강에 관계된…)'... that are centered around personal hygiene.'

9 (사전에서 그 의미를 찾아봅시다.)

　Let us know what it is saying in the dictionary.

　Let's look up the dictionary meaning.

선생님: 자, 개인위생에 대해 생각해 봅시다. 알겠지요? 아침에 일어나면 건강을 위해 무엇을 해야 합니까?

학생들: 운동.

선생님: 운동이라고 했어요. 좋아요. 그 밖에는?

학생1: 세수를 해야 합니다.

선생님: 세수한다. 그 밖에는?

학생2: (낮은 목소리로) 이를 닦아야 합니다.

선생님: 크게 말하세요. 들리지 않습니다.

학생2: 적당한 휴식을 취합니다.

선생님: 적당한 휴식을 취하고, 이를 닦아라. 그 밖에는?

학생3: 아침을 잘 먹어야 합니다.

선생님: 잘 들리지 않습니다. (자신의 귀를 컵 모양으로 만든다.)

학생3: 아침을 잘 먹습니다.

선생님: 좋아요. 그 밖에 다른 것은? 그래 말해 볼래? (네 번째 학생을 가리킨다.)

학생4: 아침에 일어나면 얼굴을 씻습니다.

선생님: 좋아요. 그 밖에는? 그런 것들이 모두 개인위생에 관계된 것들입니다. 자, 이제 사전에서 그것의 의미를 찾아봅시다.

2. 기본구문

여기에서는 수업 분위기 조성을 위해 선생님과 학생 간에 이루어지는 일상 대화와 관련된 사항을 다음과 같이 정리하였다: A. 외모·건강 B. 취미·여가활동·상담

A. 외모·건강

---

① I hope you're feeling better today, Minsu.

해설 민수야, 오늘은 좀 나았으면 좋겠다.

syn I hope you're feeling well today, Minsu.
I hope you have recovered, Minsu.

I hope you have recouperated [have been recouped]. *(rare)*

I hope you have come around. *(B.E., casual)*
: 미국영어에서는 'come around'가 '결국에는 생각을 바꾸어 동의하다(to change one's opinion and finally agree with someone)'의 의미로 주로 사용된다.

e.g. Mary came around when Tom told her the whole story.
(탐이 그녀에게 모든 사실을 말해주자 메어리가 입장을 바꾸게 되었다.)

누구나 영어로 가르칠 수 있다

② T: Sunhi looks tired today, doesn't she?
S: Yes. I don't think she's feeling well.

해설   T: 순희가 오늘 피곤해 보이는구나.
       S: 예, 그녀는 몸이 안 좋아요.

syn   T: Sunhi doesn't look very [too] good.
        Sunhi looks a bit pale today.
        Sunhi looks a bit knackered today. *(rare, B.E.)*
        Sunhi looks as sick as a dog.
        [=Sunhi looks very sick.]
        I think she's not feeling well.
       S: Maybe she's ill.
        I think she's under the weather.

주의   서양 문화권에서는 개인의 몸 상태에 대해 — 'look good' 또는 'look tired' 등 — 언급하는 것을 싫어하므로 가능하면 당사자에게 는 사용하지 않아야 한다.

cf. **'제가 몸이 안 좋습니다'라고 할 때는 다음과 같이 표현한다.**
I'm afraid I'm not feeling very well today. *(very formal, polite)*
I'm feeling a bit under the weather.
I'm really sick today.
I think I've come down with something.
I'm feeling a bit knackered [tired, exhausted] today.
I'm as sick as a dog [very sick].

③ T: **God Bless you,** Sunhi! It sounds as though you're catching a cold.

Sunhi: Thank you.

해설　상대편이 재채기(sneeze)를 했을 때 말하며, 간단히 'Bless you'라고도 한다. 대답은 간단히 'Thank you'라고 한다.

④ T: Is that a new shirt (**you have on**)? It's nice.

S: Sure is. Glad you like it.

해설　T: 네 윗도리 새 옷이니? 좋구나.

　　　S: 맞아요. 마음에 든다니 기뻐요.

syn　T: Is that shirt you've got on new?

　　　Is that a new shirt you've got on?

　　　Is that a new shirt you are wearing?

　　　Is that a new shirt you are sporting? *(rare)*

　　　— 다음과 같은 대답도 가능하다.

　　　S: Yes, it is new. Thanks.

　　　Yes, it was a birthday present. Thanks.

B. 취미·여가활동·상담

① Come and [to] see me after class [the lesson]. I'll deal with it then.

방과 후 나에게 오너라. 그때 그 문제를 처리하자.

syn   Would you come see me after class? I'll deal with it then.
        Come see me later on. I'll help you then.
        If you see me later, I can help you.
        See me later.

     cf. Please stay (behind) after class and I'll see you. I can help you with
        that later. (방과 후 남아서 나를 만나라. 그때 그 문제를 도와주겠다.)

---

② What is your major?

해설   전공이 무엇이니?

syn   What do you major in?
        What subject do you specialize in? *(rare)*
        ('특별히 어떤 분야가 전공이냐?'는 의미로, 주로 대학원 이상에서
        '특정 분야'의 전공을 물을 때 'specialize in'을 사용한다.)

     e. g. I major in English. [I am an English major.]
         I am major in English. *(incorrect)*
         I specialized in English semantics.

---

③ T: **What did you do after school yesterday, Minsu?**
Minsu: I went to the concert.
T: Could you tell us more about that?

해설   T: 어제 방과 후 무엇을 하였니?
        Minsu: 연주회에 갔습니다.

T: 좀 자세히 이야기해 줄래?

syn T: Did you do anything special after school yesterday, Minsu?

Tell me what you did yesterday after school, Minsu.

cf. '여가시간에는 무엇을 합니까?'

What do you do in your spare time?

= How do you spend your free time?

④ T: Do you have any plans for the summer?
S: I'm planning to visit my grandparents in Seoul.

해설 T: 여름에 무엇을 할 거니?
S: 서울에 계시는 조부모님을 방문할 계획입니다.

syn T: Are you planning anything for the summer?

What are your summer plans?

What are your plans for the summer?

Do you have anything interesting planned for the summer?

Are you going anywhere this summer?

What are you going to do this summer?

What's on the go for your summer vacation? *(B.E.)*

What are you doing this summer?

How about your summer? *(not clear)*

(처음부터 사용하면 의미가 막연하다.)

S: I'm going to visit my grandparents in Seoul.

I'm visiting my grandparents in Seoul.

'How about'의 용법

화제를 처음 도입(opening question)할 때는 'how about'를 잘 사용하지 않는다. 예를 들어 친구를 만나서 여름방학에 대한 대화를 나눌 경우를 가정해 보자. 이 때 '여름방학에 어떻게 할 예정이냐?'라고 할 경우 위의 표현뿐만 아니라 다음과 같이 다양하게 표현할 수 있다.

What do you plan (to do) for[in, during] (the) summer vacation?
What is your plan for (the) summer vacation?
What will you do this summer?

그러나 위의 표현 대신 'How about your summer vacation?'이라 물으면 내용이 불분명하다. 만일 위와 같이 질문하면 상대방은 다음과 같이 되물을 수 있는 것이다.
What do you want to know about my vacation?
(나의 방학에 대해 무엇을 알고 싶으냐?)

반면에 이전에 여름방학에 대한 토의를 했으나 어디로 떠날지 결론이 나지 않고 다음에 다시 만났을 때, 다시 한 번 확인(follow-up question)할 경우에는 다음과 같이 질문할 수 있다.

e.g. A: How about your summer vacation?
     Have you decided where to go?
   B: Yes, I'll go to Jeju-do.

---

⑤ T: What are your hobbies?
  S: My hobbies are watching movies, swimming and playing soccer.

해설   T: 취미는 무엇이니?

S: 영화, 수영, 축구입니다.

T: Have you got any hobbies? / Do you have any hobbies?
What are you interested in?
What types of things interest you?
What are your interests?
What do you like to do? / What do you like doing?

S: I like to watch movies, swim and play soccer.
I watch movies, swim and play soccer

참고 개개인이 한 가지 이상의 취미가 있으므로 표현은 "What are your hobbies?"가 "What is your hobby?"보다 자연스럽다.

---

⑥ How was your weekend?

해설 주말에 무엇을 하였니?

syn Did you do anything special over the weekend?
What was your weekend like?
What did you do on the weekend?
What did you do this weekend?
Did you [everyone] enjoy the weekend?
Did you [everyone] have a nice [good] weekend?

---

⑦ S1: **What do you do on weekdays?**
S2: I go to school.
S1: Then, **what do you do on the weekend?**
S2: I **usually go hiking on Sundays.**

S1: 주중 [평일]에는 무엇을 하니?

S2: 학교에 간다.

S1: 그럼, 주말에는 무엇을 하니?

S2: 하이킹 [등산] 간다.

syn S1: What do you do during the week? *(usual)*

What do you do weekdays? *(coll.)*

*What do you do on (the) weekday? *(incorrect)*

주의1 'I often go hiking in the mountains on Sundays.'는 잉여문이 된
다. 'hiking'은 'walking up the mountains'의 의미를 가지고 있기
때문이다.

'평일'이란 의미로는 'during the week' 또는 '(on) weekdays'가 있
고, 'on (the) weekday'는 틀린 표현이다.

S1: What do you do on weekends?

What do you do every weekend?

*What do you do on weekend? *(incorrect)*

주의2 '주말'이라는 의미로는 'on the weekend'가 일반적이고, 'on
weekends', 'during the weekend'라고도 하나 'on weekend'는 틀
린 표현이다.

cf. He goes bike-riding on Sundays. (그는 일요일에 자전거를 탄다.)

참고 레저(leisure)에 관한 다음 표현들도 우리나라 사람들이 흔히 잘
못 사용하는 대표적인 문장이다. 다음은 미국인 영어선생님과의
토의 내용이다.

① 'Hiking'과 'climb'의 차이는?
일반적으로 장비 없이 산에 올라갈 경우에 미국인은 'hiking'이
라고 하며, 특별히 등산장비를 갖추고 험한 산을 탈 경우에만

'climb'이라고 한다.

e.g. He goes hiking (in the mountains) on Sunday mornings.
(그는 일요일 아침에는 산행을 [하이킹을] 즐긴다.)

반면, "그는 이번 여름 (장비를 갖추고) 설악산을 등반할 예정
이다."는 다음과 같이 여러 가지로 표현된다.

He plans to climb Mt. Jiri this summer. *(usual)*
(Mt.는 'mount'로 읽는다.)
He plans to climb Jiri Mtn. [Jiri Mountain] (OK)
(Mtn.은 'mountain'으로 읽는다.)
He plans to climb Jirisan. *(awkward)*
He plans to climb Mt. Jirisan. *(awkward, redundant)*
:'지리산'은 'Mt. Jiri' 또는 'Mount Jiri'('Mt.'는 [maunt]라고
발음해야 한다.)가 올바른 표현이며, 'Jiri Mtn'도 가능하며,
'Jirisan'은 외국인이 'san'의 우리말 의미를 알 경우에만 가능하
다. 마찬가지로 일본의 후지산은 'Mt. Huji', 에베레스트산은
'Mt. Everest'라고 한다.

② 'Go shopping [fishing, bowling, hiking]'의 의미는?
:이 경우 'go'는 특별한 의미 없이 관용구로 사용되며, 단순히
쇼핑하다(shop), 낚시하다(fish), 볼링하다(bowl), 하이킹하다
(hike)로 해석되어야 한다. 그렇지 않고 '쇼핑 [낚시, 볼링, 하
이킹]하러 가다'로 해석할 경우 이들 뒤에 전치사 'to'를 붙이는
오류를 범하게 된다. 다음 예문을 보면 분명히 알 수 있다.

e.g. She went shopping at [*to] the department store.
(=She shopped at the department store.)
(그녀는 백화점에서 쇼핑을 했다.)

He went fishing in [*to] the sea [in / on the lake].

(=He fished in the sea.)
(그는 바다에서[호수에서] 낚시를 했다.)

She went bowling at [*to] the bowling alley.
(=She bowled at the bowling alley.)
(그녀는 볼링장에서 볼링을 했다.)

반면 '쇼핑[고기잡이, 볼링]하러 갔다'는 다음과 같이 표현된다
She went to the department store to go shopping.
(그녀는 백화점에 쇼핑하러 갔다.)
He went to the sea to go fishing.
(그는 낚시하러 바다에 갔다.)
She went to the bowling alley to go bowling.
(그녀는 볼링하러 볼링장에 갔다.)

한편 'go hiking'(하이킹하다)의 경우는 보다 흥미롭다. 다음 예문을 보자.
*He goes hiking to the suburbs on the weekend.
(incorrect)
*He goes hiking to the mountains on the weekend.
(incorrect)
He goes hiking in the mountains [hills] on the weekend.
(redundant, OK)
He hikes in the mountain on the weekend.
(redundant, OK)
He goes hiking on the weekend.
(correct)

위의 첫 번째 문장의 'go hiking'은 '하이킹하다[산행하다]'이 므로 'to'를 쓸 수 없다. 둘째 'suburbs'는 '교외'가 아니라 '변 두리 거주지역'(a residential district on the outskirts of a city)이므로 산행을 할 수 없다. 따라서 수업에서도 'suburbs'를 우리말로 '교외'가 아니라 '변두리 주택가'라고 해석한다면 이런 오류를 피할 수 있을 것이다. 셋째 'hiking'(산행하다)에는 'in the mountains [hills]'의 의미가 포함되어 있으므로 일반적인 산행의 경우에는 중복되는 의미가 있는 표현이 되므로 쓸 필요가 없다. 실제 사전의 우리말 해석으로 인한 오류도 연구해 볼 필요가 있다.

◆ 공손 행위

의사소통의 목적을 효과적으로 달성하기 위해서는 상대방의 감정과 정서에 부합하고 체면을 지켜주는 언어행위가 필요하다. 상대방의 체면을 지켜주기 위해서는 상호 간의 사회적 직위와 친소관계 그리고 문화적 차이 등을 고려하여 상황에 맞게 적절한 표현을 사용해야 한다(Yule, 2010). 공손행위에 대한 선구적인 이론을 정립한 Brown & Levinson(1987)은 공손행위를 네 가지 — 노골적 명시적 (bald on record), 적극적 공손(positive politeness), 소극적 공손(negative politeness), 간접적 비명시적(off-record indirect) — 행위로 분류하였다. 먼저 노골적 명시적 행위는 발화의 효율성을 우선으로 하며, 문법상으로는 대체로 명령문으로 표현된다. 둘째, 적극적 공손행위는 상호 간의 친밀감과 유대감에 중점을 두며 주로 'Let's' 로 시작한다. 셋째, 소극적 공손행위는 청자의 체면을 중시하는 언어행위다. 마지막으로, 간접적 비명시적 표현은 상대방의 체면을 유지하기 위해 의미 전달의 효율성을 희생하더라도 최대한 간접적으로 표현하는 행위다.

원어민과 학생들과의 교수활동에서는 대개 최초 시발행위(starter), 사교행위(sociate), 훈육행위(discipline)에서 공손행위가 두드러지게 드러나고 있다.

먼저 단원을 시작하는 시발행위에는 노골적 명시적 표현이 다수를 차지하며, 주로 간결한 명령문으로 구성되어 있다. 이는 학습활동을 시작하기 위한 교사의 태도를 분명히 하여 학생들이 수업 준비 또는 활동을 신속하게 하기 위한 전략이다.

> Listen first, then repeat, alright?
> (먼저 듣고, 다음에 따라하세요. 알겠죠?)
> Read (question) number nine please. (9번 읽으세요.)
> Now, it's time to talk about what you did during the weekend.
> (자, 지난 주말 여러분이 한 일을 이야기할 시간입니다.)
> Begin with 10 minutes discussion. You should give a discussion in 10 minutes. (10분 토론으로 시작합니다. 10분 후에 토의 결과를 말하세요.)
> Today we have our debate contest. Are you guys all prepared for it?
> (오늘은 토론시합을 합니다. 모두 준비되었어요?)
> Now, we'll begin with Mr. Kim. And we'll go around.
> (자, 김군부터 시작합니다. 그리고 차례로 할 겁니다.)

We are going to talk about the importance of mood in the poem.
(시에서 분위기의 중요성에 대해 이야기할 것입니다.)

다음으로 상호협력활동을 강조하는 적극적 공손은 교과활동 중에 많이 사용되며 대체로 아래와 같이 'Let's'로 시작하는 경우가 일반적이다.

Let's have a look at the flash cards.
(플래시 카드를 봅시다.)
Let's talk over your homework.
(숙제에 대해 이야기 합시다.)
Let's practice conditional clauses with 'if' clauses.
('if' 조건절을 연습합시다.)
Let's start dialogue two.
(대화 2번을 시작합시다.)

즉 원어민의 학습활동은 단원의 도입부에서는 대체로 교사 중심으로 시작하지만, 교과활동과정에서는 학생들과의 상호협력관계를 위하여 적극적 공손형을 흔히 사용한다. 한편 학생에 대한 관심, 약속, 격려, 낙관 등을 나타내는 사교적 행위를 위한 경우에도 적극적 공손형을 가장 빈번하게 사용하지만, 아래 예문과 같이 학생에 대한 염려, 동정, 공감 등을 포함하는 소극적 공손형도 종종 사용한다.

You look guys lovely today.
(너희들 오늘 착하게 보이는구나.)
Hey, tell me what's eating you.
(야, 걱정거리 있으면 말해.)
What's your favorite food?
(무슨 음식 좋아하니?)
I see that you have a very tough schedule, but don't be stressed.
(일과가 매우 힘들지만, 스트레스 받지 마세요.)

위의 모든 발화는 학생들의 신변과 일상생활과 관계가 있으며, 교과와 직접 관계가 없다. 이런 사실은 원어민 교사들이 본격적인 학습활동에 앞서 학생과의 교감을 형성하기 위해서 노력한다는 것을 보여주고 있다.

마지막으로 훈육 행위의 경우에는 대부분 노골적 명시적 표현으로, 사교적 행위와는 매우 다른 전략을 사용하고 있다.

What's the attitude?
(태도가 뭐니?)
Concentrate!
(집중해!)
Be more polite.
(좀 공손해.)
Behave!
(품위있게 행동해!)
Don't make phone call unless it's your parents or in case of an emergency.
(부모님이나 긴급한 경우가 아니면 전화걸지 마세요.)

위의 모든 발화는 의문문 또는 명령문의 형태지만 부정적 의미를 함축하고 있다. 발화를 상호적인 발화와 비상호적인 발화로 나눌 때(Cook 1989), 위의 발화는 교사와 학습자의 상호활동이 아닌 일방적 전달을 위한 비상호적인 발화임을 알 수 있다.

또한 아래와 같이 훈육에 사용되는 간접적 비명시적인 표현도 실제 내용상으로는 강한 불만과 비난을 함축하고 있는 점은 주목할 만하다.

How many times did I say (not to use the red pen)?
((붉은 펜을 사용하지 말라고) 몇 번이나 말했니!)
I'm not judging you.
(너를 판단하는 것은 아니야.)
What are we doing? (when a student doesn't listen to him)
((학생이 듣지 않을 때) 뭘 하고 있어?)

위의 표현은 구조상으로는 모두 의문문 또는 평서문이지만, 의미상으로는 학습자의 행위 및 태도를 비난하는 반어적, 부정적 표현이다.

사교와 훈육을 위한 발화행위는 교과활동을 위한 목적이 아니며, 질문(elicitation), 대답(reply), 평가(evaluative)와 같은 주요 교과 행위에도 포함되지 않는다. 그렇지만 이런 언어행위가 상당 부분을 차지한다는 것은 오늘날 우리의 교실환경 또는 학습자의 태도가 때로 통제하기 어려우며 원어민의 교과활동에 상당한 부담을 주고 있다고 볼 수 있다.

Unit 5 교보재 및 시청각 장비

1. 현장예문 (Real-life Situation)

Teaching with Tapes

비행기에서 일어난 사건에 대한 듣기연습을 위해 플러그를 꽂고, 테이프를 수업할 위치로 옮긴 뒤에 음질을 조절하는 과정에서 이루어지는 선생님과 학생 간의 대화이다.

Regardless of the type of English course you are teaching, there are bound to be occasions when instructors use teachers aids to facilitate the lesson. This unit presents you with the English language that is required when such teachers resources are being used. The unit covers common classroom situations like asking students to help you set up over-head projectors and audio-visual machines, instructing students to follow along with a recording, and asking students their opinions on the sound or visual quality of the teaching material.

Now listen to the dialogue.

T: You are going to hear a story about something that happened on a plane.[1] After you listen write the answer for each question. Now, I'm going to play the tape. *(Later)* OK, I have to fast-forward the tape. Hold on a minute.[2] *(Later)* OK, this is it. Now, listen up. Ready?

Ss: Yes, we're ready.

T: Good. Here we go.[3] Is it loud enough?

Ss: No, could you turn it up?

T: How's that? Is that better?

Ss:	Good... *(Students can't understand the tape recording.)*
T:	Before you listen again, read the questions below. (Later) OK, I'm going to play it one more time. Listen carefully.
Ss:	It's too fast. I can barely hear.[4]
T:	Do your best.[5] Ready?
Ss:	Ready.
T:	Here goes... Did you get that?
Ss:	One more time, please.
T:	OK, listen once more. I just have to rewind the tape... Now listen carefully... How much did you catch?[6] Can anybody answer the first question? Where did the plane take off?
Ss:	In Seoul.
T:	Right! It seems you got most of it.[7]

주 ─────────────────────────

1 (…에 대한 이야기를 듣겠습니다.) You're going to listen to a story...

2 (잠깐만 기다려.) Wait just a minute ; Wait a second.

오늘날 미국영어에서는 'Hold on for a minute [moment]'보다 전치사가 생략된 'Hold on a minute [moment]'가 일반적으로 널리 사용된다.

3 (자, 시작합니다.) Let's begin ; Here goes.

한편 'Here goes'는 야구 또는 골프시합 등에서 내 차례가 되어 '해 보자!'(I'll try)라는 의미의 혼잣말로 사용될 수도 있다.

4 (거의 들리지 않습니다.) I can hardly hear ; It's not coming through very well.

5 (최선을 다하세요.)

Do the best you can ; Give it your best ; Give it a shot; You can do it ; Try your best

6 (얼마나 이해했습니까?)

How much did [could] you get [understand]? ;

Did you catch it all? ; Did you get most of it? ; Did you get it all?

7 (여러분은 대부분을 이해하는 것 같다.)

It seems you got the majority of it.

It seems you understood it. / It sounds like you got most of it.

I'm fairly [pretty] certain [sure] you got the gist of it.

해석 ────────────────────────────────────

선생님: 이제 비행기에서 일어난 사건에 대한 이야기를 듣겠습니다. 들은 뒤에 각각의 질문에 대한 답을 쓰세요. 자, 테이프를 틀겠습니다. (잠시 후) 좋아요, 테이프를 앞으로 감아야 되겠습니다. 잠깐 기다리세요. (잠시 후) 좋아요, 됐습니다. 자, 잘 들으세요. 준비되었습니까?

학생들: 예, 준비되었습니다.

선생님: 좋아요. 자 시작하겠습니다. 음의 높이가 충분합니까?

학생들: 아니요, 음을 좀 높여 주세요.

선생님: 이제 어때요? 훨씬 낫습니까?

학생들: 좋아요.

(학생들이 테이프 내용을 이해하지 못한다.)

선생님: 다시 듣기 전에 아래에 있는 문제를 보세요. 좋아요, 다시 틀겠습니다. 잘 들으세요.

학생들: 너무 빨라요. 잘 들리지 않습니다.

선생님: 최선을 다하세요. 준비되었습니까?

학생들: 준비되었습니다.

선생님: 자, 틉니다. 이해했습니까?

학생들: 한 번만 더 틀어 주세요.

선생님: 좋습니다. 한 번 더 들으세요. 테이프를 되감아야 합니다. 자, 잘 들으세요. … 얼마나 이해했습니까? 첫 번째 문제의 답은 무엇입니까? 비행기는 어디에서 이륙했지요?

학생들: 서울에서요.

선생님: 좋습니다. 내용을 대부분 다 이해한 것 같군요.

2. 기본구문

여기에서는 수업에 사용되는 유인물, 보조자료 및 시청각 자료의 활용과 연관된 표현을 다음과 같이 정리하였다: A. 교재 및 자료준비 B. 장비 및 주의사항 C. 음질·화질

A. 교재 및 자료준비

① This is for you, (Sunhi).

해설   선생님이 학생들에게 유인물이나 시험지를 배부할 경우, '자, 여기에 있어.'라는 의미로 사용된다.

syn   Here's one for you, (Sunhi).
    Here you are [go], (Sunhi).
    There you are [go]. *(casual)*
    Take this. *(casual)*
    This is yours. *(casual)*
    Here. *(casual)*

참고   위의 표현들은 상황에 따라 다양한 의미로 사용될 수 있으므로 유의해야 한다.

    ① '이건 너의 것이야.': 선물이나 물품을 개인별로 나누어 줄 때 사용한다.
    This is for you.
    Here is something for you.

    ② '바로 그것이야. 맞았어.': 어떤 질문이나 문제에 대한 해답을

상대편이 마침내 알아내었을 때,

There you go. ('Go'에 강세를 둔다.) (=You are right.)

There we [you] are.

    e.g. S: I think it is Peace Street.

          T: There you are, you see! I knew you'd say that.

③ '거기에 있었구나!': 마침내 사람을 찾았을 때 사용한다.

There you are! ('There'에 강세를 둔다.)

④ '자, 시작하겠습니다.'(Now, we'll start.): 수업뿐만 아니라, 경연대회를 처음 시작할 때에도 사회자가 흔히 사용한다.

Here we go. [Here goes.] / Here it comes (now). / Let's go.

⑤ '자, 이제 도착했습니다.' (Now, we've arrived.)

Here we are.

② S: May [Could] I have another copy?

해설   유인물을 한 장 더 가져도 될까요?

syn   Have you got an extra sheet?

       Do you have an extra sheet?

       Do you have any extras?

       Are there additional copies?

참고   위의 경우 미국식 영어에서는 'may'를, 영국식 영어에서는 'could'를 선호함.

    cf. I'm sorry I haven't got a pen, could someone lend me one?

      (펜이 없는데, 누가 빌려 줄래?)

③ T: Did you leave your book at home [behind]?
Minsu: **Yes, I did.**
T: **Don't forget to bring it next time.** Sunhi, please **share with Minsu today.**

해설 T: 책을 집에 놓고 왔니?
    Minsu: 예.
    T: 다음에는 잊지 말고 가져오너라. 순희야, 민수와 함께 보아라.

syn Minsu: I'm afraid so.
     I'm afraid I did.
     Yes. Sorry, I (simply) forgot it.

  — '다음에는 가져오너라.'라고 할 경우 다음과 같이 표현할 수 있다.
  T: Oh well, you can bring it next time.
   Forget about it, just don't forget it next time.

   Make sure you bring it next time.
   Be sure to remember it next time.

   Don't anybody forget it next time. *(demanding)*
   ('다음에는 잊어서는 안 됩니다.')

  — '함께 보다'라는 의미로는 주로 'share, look on with, pair up with'가 사용된다.
  T: Would [Could] you share with Minsu today?
   You will have to share with Minsu.
   You and Minsu share.
   Just share with Minsu (this time).
   Why don't you share with Minsu?

Would it be all right if Minsu shares your book?

Look on with Minsu. *(casual)*
May Minsu look on with you?

Join in with Minsu.
Why don't you pair up with Minsu?
Sit with Minsu. *(implied)*

④ S: I'm afraid I left my homework at home.

해설　숙제를 가지고 오지 않았습니다.

syn　I'm sorry I forgot to bring my homework.
（영국식 영어에서는 이 경우 현재완료 'have forgot'를 사용함.)

cf. 숙제를 안 한 경우 다음과 같이 변명할 수도 있다.
I'm terribly sorry I haven't done my homework.
May I do my homework tonight? I didn't have time yesterday.

⑤ T: Has anyone found a workbook?
　 S: I haven't found it.

해설　T: 학습장 본 사람 없습니까?
　　　S: 못 보았습니다.

syn　T: Who has found a workbook?
　　　My notebook has disappeared.
　　　I've misplaced my notebook.

I'm looking for a notebook.

S: I haven't.
Not me. *(casual)*
Sorry, I can't help you.
No, but if I find it I'll hold on to it for you.
(hold on to=keep)
No, but if I find it I'll let you know.

⑥ T: Whose pen is this?
   S: Mine.

해설   T: 이 펜 누구 것이니?
       S: 제 것입니다.

syn   T: Has anyone lost this pen? *(polite)*
       Who lost this pen?
       Who does this pen belong to?
       Would someone like to claim this pen?
       Is anyone the owner of this pen? *(rare)*
       Will the owner of this pen please stand up?
       Whose is this pen? *(rare)*
       Whose is this? *(OK, implied)*

    — 다음과 같이 여러 가지로 답할 수 있다.
    S: It's his [hers, mine]. / I'm sorry, I don't know. / I think it's John's.

참고   **의문대명사의 문법적 성질**
        의문대명사는 비한정대명사(indefinite pronoun) — 'somebody',

'anybody', 'nobody' 등 ─ 와 마찬가지로 문법적으로는 반드시 단수로 취급되지만, 의미상으로는 단수 또는 복수 둘 다로 해석될 수 있다.

e.g. Q: Who is going to visit our school?
　　 A: Many school inspectors.
　　 Q: Did you see anyone in the library?
　　 A: Yes, several people.
　　 Q: What's on the menu today?
　　 A: Lots of things.

그러나 다음 문장을 보자.
Who are your guests? (손님들은 누구냐?)

위의 문장에서는 'your guests'가 주어이므로 복수형 'are'를 쓴 것이다.

---

⑦ Please bring [fetch, get] the comparison chart.

해설　비교급에 대한 차트를 가지고 오너라.

syn　Please get the 'comparisons' wall chart.
　　 Could someone go and bring the wall chart(s) of the 'comparisons'?
　　 Bring the comparison. *(implied)*

cf. Bring the English dictionary from the teacher's room.
　　 (the teacher's room (교무실) = the staff room)

⑧ We need the sticky tape to stick [hang] this picture up (with).

해설   이 그림을 붙일 접착테이프가 필요하다.

syn   We'll use the tape to stick this picture up.
The tape is required to stick this picture up [to stick up this picture].

We need the tape. It's to stick this picture to the wall.
Without the tape we can't put this picture up.

활용   경우에 따라 'the sticky tape' 대신 'the drawing pins', 'the scissors' 등으로 대체한다.

cf. We need the scissors to cut these pictures out [to cut out these pictures]. (이 그림들을 자를 가위가 필요하다.)
= We need the scissors. They are for cutting these pictures out.
We need the scissors. They are used to cut these pictures out.
The scissors are required for cutting these pictures.
Without the scissors we can't cut out these pictures.

⑨ Could you put it up here? Is that straight?

해설   여기에 걸어라. 똑바로 걸렸니?

syn   Would you put [place] it here?
Put it on the wall here, please.
Hang it. (사진틀일 경우)

ans   It is crooked. (기울어져 [굽어] 있다.)

=It doesn't look right. / It's off-center.

cf. **cf. 설치상태에 대한 표현**

Is that high enough? (높이가 맞습니까?)

Can you all see it? (모두 잘 보입니까?)

어휘 벽 위에 설치하는 경우에 흔히 사용되는 표현들은 다음과 같다: 'hang it up'(걸어라), 'place [put, position] it'(설치해라), 'nail [tack, pin] it, stick it up'(고정시켜라)

---

⑩ **Put your books away now.**

해설 (책상에서) 책을 치우시오.

syn I don't want to see any books on your desk. Books away!*(slang, rare)*

cf. 책 또는 가방의 처리에 대한 표현들

Put your schoolbag away. (가방을 치우세요.)

(schoolbag(책가방) = knapsack, bag, satchel, backpack, briefcase.)

Put your bag on the floor [under your seat.]

(가방을 바닥에 [좌석 아래에] 놓으세요.)

Put your bag in your desk. (가방을 책상 안에 두세요.)

Put [Place] your books face down. (책을 뒤집어 놓으세요.)

[= Turn your books over.]

B. 장비 및 주의사항

① How does it [this machine] work? *(usual)*

해설   이 장비 작동방법을 아니?
: '작동하다'는 의미로는 'operate' 또는 'work'를 많이 사용한다.

syn   How do you operate it?
How is it operated?
Do you know how to make it work?
Do you know how it works?

How does it [this thing] work?
How do you work [run] this machine?
How do you work this thing?
Can anybody work this machine?
Does anyone know how this (machine) works?

How do we get this thing going? *(coll.)*
How shall I do it? *(implied)*

② This (tape) recorder isn't working.

해설   이 녹음기가 작동되지 않는다.

syn   There's a problem with this recorder.
Something's up with this recorder.
I'm having trouble working this recorder.
I'm having trouble getting this recorder to work.

There seems to be something wrong with this recorder.
This recorder doesn't seem to be working.

Can anyone help me?
Do you know how it works?
How do you operate it?
How does it work?
Do you know how to make it work?

---

③ It won't work. **I'll just see if it is on.**
Oh, it's OK now! **There we are.** We can begin now.

해설   이것이 작동하지 않는구나. (이 장비가) 켜져 있는지 보겠다. 아, 이제 되었다. 자, 시작하자.
: '살펴보다'라는 의미로는 'check', 'look', 'see'가 주로 사용된다.

syn   I'll check to see if it's turned on.
I'll check it out.
Let me run a check on it.

Let me take a look at it.
Let's have a closer look.

Let's see what the problem is.
Let's see if we can [can't] locate the problem.

— There we [you] are. = There it is: 여기에서는 '자, 이제 되었습니다.'라는 준비완료의 의미로 사용된다.

syn   There we go.

Got it!

This might do it.

I think we have it.

---

④ Is it (turned) on [off]? Turn it on [off].

해설   켜 [꺼져] 있니? 켜라[꺼라].

syn   Is it on [off]? Switch it on [off].

    cf. Could someone turn the recorder off?
    (녹음기 스위치를 끄세요.)

---

⑤ Would you plug the tape recorder in, please?

해설   녹음기의 플러그를 꼽아라.

syn   Plug it in.

Would you please plug the recorder in over there?

Plug it into the socket over there.

You can put it in over there.

Put the plug in. *(rare)*

Put this plug in the socket over there. *(rare)*

ant   Please pull out the plug.

Unplug it.

Could someone unplug it, please?

Pull the plug out of the wall.

Could someone take the plug out, please?

활용   'The tape recorder' 대신 'cassette player', 'videoplayer', 'TV monitor', 'O. H. P. (overhead projector)' 등으로 대체할 수 있다.

⑥ Is your headset working?

해설   헤드폰이 작동되니?

syn   How's your headset? *(casual)*
Is your headset OK?
Are you having trouble with your headset?
Is there a problem with your headset?

어휘   headset=headphone with a small microphone

⑦ Check to see if your microphone is turned [switched] on.

해설   마이크가 켜져 있는지 보아라.

syn   Make sure the [your] microphone is on.
Don't forget to test your mike.
Be sure to check your microphone and see that [if] it's working.

어휘   'Microphone' 대신 축약형 'mike'도 종종 사용된다.

⑧ Could you move to another booth? Number 17 is free.

해설　다른 자리로 옮겨라. 17번 자리가 비었다.

syn　Why don't you try a different booth? Number 17 is available.
　　　Could you move to an empty booth? Number 17 is free.
　　　Please find yourself another booth.

cf. Number 11 is out of order. Try number 17.
　　Number 11 is down. Try #17.
　　That booth isn't working. Try another.

⑨ Please be careful not to drop that.

해설　떨어뜨리지 않도록 조심하여라.

syn　Be careful with that. Don't drop it.
　　　Watch what you're doing with that.
　　　Handle it with care. *(formal)*

cf. Mind [Be careful, Careful, Watch] you don't bang your head on the
　　door. (문 위에 머리가 부딪치지 않도록 유의하여라.)
　　Mind [Be careful of/with, Careful of/with, Watch] the tape recorder. (녹
　　음기를 주의하여라.)
　　Be careful you don't trip over the lead, Min-su. (민수야 줄에 걸리지 않도
　　록 조심하여라. (the lead (줄, 선) = the tape-recorder lead))

A: 어이쿠! 아래쪽 조심해!
B: 뭘 조심하라고? 보이지가 않는 걸!

---

⑩ Watch your step.

해설   발밑을 주의하라.

syn   Careful where you step. *(casual)*
       (Be) Careful when you walk there.
       (Be) Careful not to trip over the cord.
       Watch out [Look out] for the electrical cords.

어법   'Be'가 생략되면 보다 구어적인 표현이 된다.

---

⑪ Please don't touch the controls.

해설   주조종기에 손을 대지 마세요.

syn   Hands off! *(coll.)*
       Take your hands off the control.

Keep your fingers away from the controls.
Leave the controls alone.

Don't mess (around) with the controls. *(informal)*
No messing with the controls.
Stop fiddling with [around] the controls.

어휘　　mess around(- 을 가지고 장난치다.)=fiddle with, play with

---

⑫ **Please hang up your headsets [headphones] before you leave.**

해설　　떠나기 전에 헤드폰을 걸어 놓으세요.

syn　　Put your headsets back (where they belong) before you leave.
Hang your headsets on the hooks before you leave. *(informal, polite)*
Return your headsets to their right(ful) place. *(formal)*

cf. Don't leave your headset on the desk.
(헤드폰을 책상 위에 두지 마세요.)
= Don't leave your headset lying [*laying] around.
(헤드폰을 아무 곳에나 놓아두지 마세요.: 오늘날 많은 미국인들이 'lying'과 'laying'를 구별하지 않고 사용하고 있다.)

C. 음질·화질

> ① Is the sound clear enough?

해설   소리가 잘 들립니까?

syn   Is it clear enough?
Is it loud enough?
Is the volume all right?
Can you hear all right?
Can you all hear?

cf. 다음과 같은 표현도 유사한 의미를 지닌다.
Do I need to adjust the volume? (음을 조정할까요?)
Do I need to turn it up [down] a few notches?
(음을 조금 높일[낮출]까요?)

참고   다음 표현은 마이크 없이 자신의 말소리가 뒤에까지 잘 들리는지 확인하는 경우에도 사용된다.
Can you hear in the back? (뒤에서도 들립니까?)
Can you hear back there?
Everybody can hear me? (모두 내 말이 들립니까?)

> ② Oh, it's too loud. I'll adjust the volume.

해설   소리가 너무 크구나. 볼륨을 조정하겠다.

syn   I'd better turn down the volume.

I'll turn it down.
I'll turn it down a few notches.
I'll lower the volume.

---

③ I am going to mute it.

해설   (화면만 남기고) 소리를 끄겠습니다.

syn   I'll mute it, if you like.
I think I'll put it on mute.
I'm going to press the mute botton.
I'll mute the sound. *(rare)*
I'm going to hit mute.
I'm going to turn off the sound.

어휘   to mute=to make something silent

---

④ T: Is the picture bright enough?
   S: No, it's too dark. No, could you brighten it?

해설   T: 화면이 충분히 밝니?
       S: 아니요. 너무 어둡습니다. [아니요, 밝힐 수 있습니까?]

    cf. 다음과 같이 물을 수도 있다.
      T: Is the picture too dark? (밝니?)
        Is the picture clear enough? (깨끗하니?)
        Is the picture too dull? (너무 흐리니?)
      — 학생들은 다음과 같이 대답할 수도 있다.
      S: Yes, it is. / It could be.

                                     누구나 영어로 가르칠 수 있다

It could be brighter.

It's a bit dim.

It's a little dark.

⑤ Please adjust the tracking.

해설 화면조정을 하시오.

syn The tracking seems a bit off. Please correct it.

There's something wrong with the tracking.

The tracking isn't quite right. Let's adjust it.

⑥ Would you (please) pause the tape [the video]?

해설 테이프[비디오]를 정지시켜 주십시오.

syn Please pause it.

Put it on pause, please.

Pause it.

어휘 pause=the function which stops the tape momentarily without taking off the play function.

TELEVISION

◆ 공식영어formal English와 일상영어informal English의 차이
(based on Meloni, Thompson & Beley (1982))

1 화자와 청자(speaker and listener)와의 관계에 의해 그 선택이 좌우된다.
Use formal ways of speaking with boss, teacher, professor, supervisor, advisor, or stranger.
(상관, 선생님, 교수, 감독관, 조언자, 또는 낯선 사람과 이야기할 때는 공식영어를 쓴다.)

Use informal ways of speaking with friends, classmates, co-workers, or family members.
(친구, 급우, 동료, 가족 간에는 일상영어를 쓴다.)

2 두 가지 표현은 문장구조(sentence structure)와 의미에서 차이가 있다.
Formal expressions are generally longer and use more fixed phrases ; they are often more tentative and indirect.
(공식영어는 상대적으로 길고, 표현이 고정되어 있다 ; 종종 (의미가) 확정적이지 않고 간접적이다.)

Informal expressions are usually shorter, more direct, and use fewer fixed phrases ; there is usually a much wider choice of appropriate expressions.
(일상영어는 보다 짧고, 직접적이며, 고정된 표현을 사용하지 않는다 ; 대개 다양한 표현을 선택할 수 있다.)

이 두 가지 유형이 '인사와 소개'의 경우에 어떤 차이가 나타나는지 예문을 통해 살펴보자. 먼저 공식적인(formal) 표현을 적고, 다음에 일상적인(Informal) 표현을 적었다. 다음은 학교에서 이창수가 그의 여자 친구 박수미에게 김민수를 소개하고, 헤어지는 현장에서의 대화이다.

Park Sumi: **Good morning, Mr. Lee.** *(formal)*

(이름이 아닌 성을 사용한다.)

Park Sumi: Hi, Changsu. *(informal)*

Lee Changsu: **Good morning, Ms. Park. How are you today?**

(상황에 맞는 적절한 인사말과 함께 상대방의 안부를 묻는다.)

Lee Changsu: Hi, Sumi. How are you doing? *(informal)*

Park Sumi: **I'm fine, thank you. How about you?**

(축약형을 사용하지 않는다.)

Park Sumi: Good [Very well]. And you? *(informal)*

Lee Changsu: **I'm fine, thank you. Ms. Lee, I'd like to introduce you to Minsu Kim. He and I are in the same class (this year).**

(소개에 이름 전부를 말하고, 관계를 구체적으로 설명한다.)

Lee Changsu: Good. Sumi, this is Minsu. He is my classmate.

Park Sumi: **It is nice [a pleasure] to meet you, Mr. Kim. I'm Sumi Park.**

(단축형을 사용하지 않는다.)

Park Sumi: Nice meeting you, Minsu.

Kim Minsu: **It is nice meeting you, too, Ms. Park.**

(단축형을 사용하지 않는다.)

Kim Minsu: Nice meeting you, too, Sumi.

Lee Changsu: **What are your plans today, Ms. Park?**

(명사형을 사용한다.)

Lee Changsu: (Looking at Ms. Park) What are you doing today?

Park Sumi: **I have homework, so I should go to the library after** class...

Excuse me, but I have to go now, Ms. Park. Class begins at 10. See you later.

(양해를 구하고, 작별의 분명한 이유를 제시한 뒤 작별인사를 한다.)

(주의: 이 경우 우리말식으로 '그런데 가야겠어'라는 의미로 'Excuse me...' 대신 'By the way I have to go now.'라고 하면 틀린다. 왜냐하면 'By the way.'는 다른 이야기를 계속 이어 갈 경우에만 사용하며, 이야기를 중단할 경우에는 사용하지 않는다.)

Park Sumi: Not much. [Nothing special]... I've got to go (now). See you.

Lee Changsu: **Certainly. [Of course]. See you.**
Lee Changsu: Okay!

Park Sumi: (Looking at Mr. Kim) **Mr. Kim, it was nice to meet you.**
Park Sumi: (Looking at Mr. Kim) Minsu, nice seeing you.

Kim Minsu: **It was nice to meet you too, Ms. Park.**

(주의: 위의 표현 대신, 우리말식으로 '내가 기쁜 걸요.'라는 의미로 'My pleasure, Mr. Park.'이라고 표현하면 어색하다. 왜냐하면 미국영어에서는 'My pleasure.'는 상대방이 도움을 준 경우에만 사용하고, 이 경우에는 구체적인 도움을 준 것이 아니기 때문이다. 그러나 'It was a pleasure to meet you, Ms Park.'이라고 표현할 수는 있다.)

Kim Minsu: Same here. [You, too ; Nice seeing you, too, Sumi.]

Park Sumi: (Looking at Mr. Kim) **I hope to see you again.**
Park Sumi: (Looking at Mr. Kim) See you again.

| Kim Minsu: | **I hope so.** |
| Kim Minsu: | See you. |

| Park Sumi: | **Have a good day, Mr. Kim. Good bye.** |
| Park Sumi: | Bye. |

| Kim Minsu: | **Have a nice day, Ms. Park. Good bye.** |
| Kim Minsu: | Bye. |

◆ **높임형**Polite forms**의 판별기준**(adapted from J. S. Peccei (1999))

1 문장형태에 의한 구별

As an utterance becomes more polite, it becomes more indirect.
(언어표현이 공손할수록, 보다 간접적인 형태를 가진다.)

예를 들어 '식탁을 차려라.'라는 명령문은 다음과 같이 표현할 수 있다.

a. Set the table. (imperative: 명령문)

b. Can you set the table? (interrogative: 의문문)

c. Would you mind setting the table? ('mind'를 쓰면 더 공손해진다.)

d. Could I possibly ask you to set the table? (interrogative and request: 의문문과 청유)

위의 명령문도 a, b, c, d의 순서로 간접적인 표현 형태를 가지며, 동시에 점점 공손한 문장으로 변하고 있다.

한편 'Please'를 이용한 경우에는 일반적으로 훨씬 공손한 표현으로 처리된다. 예를 들어 교무실(staff room)이 시끄러울 경우 '좀 조용히 해 주세요.'는 다음과 같이 표현할 수 있다.

a. Be (more) quiet. [Be less noisy.] *(impolite)*

b. Could you be (more) quiet? *(less polite)*

c. Be (more) quiet please. *(a little polite)*

d. Please be (more) quiet. *(polite)*

e. Could you be (more) quiet please? *(more polite)*

즉, 미국인들은 의문문보다 'please'를 사용하는 것을 더 공손하게 생각하며, 또한 문두에 'please'를 사용하는 것을 문미에 'please'를 사용하는 것보다 공손하게 생각하는 경향이 있다.

2 문장의 의미에 따른 구별

Saying something good about the other person is much more polite than saying something bad.
(상대방에 대해 좋게 말하는 것이 나쁘게 말하는 것보다 공손하다.)

예를 들어 다음 두 사람의 대화를 보자.

Linda: Well, I've done it.[주] I've dyed my hair blonde.
  (그래, 나 했어. 내 머리를 금발로 염색했어.)
Tom: (a) You look awful. (보기 싫어)
  (b) You look amazing. (놀라운데.)
  (c) You look beautiful. (멋진데.)

Linda가 머리를 염색한 것이 Tom이 보기에 좋을 수도 있고, 그렇지 않을 수도 있다. 이 경우 Tom은 위와 같이 여러 가지로 반응할 수 있다. (a)는 상대방을 불편하게 하며, (b)의 '놀랍다'는 표현은 의미가 모호하고(amazing for its awfulness or its beauty?), (c)는 사실의 진위에 관계없이 상대방을 편하게 한다. 따라서 표현상으로는 (a), (b), (c) 순으로 점점 공손해지는 것이다.

(주) 'I've done it.'은 주로 과감히 무언가를 실천하였거나, 또는 어려운 것을 해냈을 때, '나 해 보았어.' 또는 '나 해냈어.'라는 의미로 사용된다.

Anyone Can Teach In English

Part 2 수업일반

Practicing for the Lesson

1. 현장예문 (Real-life Situation)

'Ghost Story' Review

앞 시간에 학습한 유령이야기(ghost story)에 대한 복습을 위해 선생님이 그 내용에 대해 질문을 하고 학생들이 대답을 하는 상황이다.

In this unit we present the language that teachers typically use in reading classes. Depending upon the particular approach of the teacher, a reading class may place more emphasis on teacher direction and participation in the lesson. The language presented in this unit includes how teachers can begin a class with a review of what was read in the previous class. Also, the unit looks at how to give students instructions in terms of page numbers, eliciting student opinions, and giving instructions for reading aloud in the classroom.

Now listen to the dialogue.

T:	Do you remember the story from the last class? (Students nod.) Where did it take place?
S1:	Korea.
S2:	America. *(pause)*
T:	Yes. The story took place first in Korea, then in America, and then back in Korea again. Let's write that on the board. (*Teacher writes: This story starts out in Korea.*)
T:	Who was involved in the story?[1]
S1:	A man.
S2:	A woman, his friend.

T:	Yes, there was a man and a woman who were friends. Were they just friends?
S1:	*Marry. [They were married.]
T:	OK. They wanted to get married. Did they get married?
S4:	*No money. [No.]
T:	No, they didn't get married ; they couldn't get married because they had no money.
	So? Do you remember what happened? *(pause)* Do you remember the story?
S2:	*America.
T:	Right. The man decides to go to America. Why? *(pause)* So that he can make his fortune and come back and marry his fianc.

(* : 비문법적인 표현)

1 (이야기에는 누가 등장하고 있습니까?)

Who were the main characters? ; Who were the key figures in the story? ; Who were the people in the story?

선생님: 지난 시간에 배운 이야기를 기억합니까? (학생들 고개를 끄덕인다.)
어디서 일어난 사건입니까?

학생1: 한국.

학생2: 미국. (잠시 멈춤)

선생님: 예, 그 이야기는 처음 한국에서 일어난 뒤, 그 다음에는 미국에서, 다음에는 다시 한국에서 일어났습니다. 이를 칠판에 쓰겠습니다.
(선생님이 '이 이야기는 한국에서 시작한다.'고 쓴다.)

선생님: 이야기에는 누가 관련되어 있습니까?

학생1: 한 남자.

학생2: 한 여자, 그 남자의 여자 친구.

선생님: 예, 친구 사이인 남자와 여자가 있었습니다. 그들은 단순히 친구였습니까?

학생1: 결혼합니다.

선생님: 맞아요, 그들은 결혼하기를 바랐습니다. 그들은 결혼했습니까?

학생4: 돈이 없습니다.

선생님: 그들은 결혼하지 않았습니다. 그들은 돈이 없어 결혼하지 못했습니다.
그래서? 무슨 일이 일어났는지 기억합니까? (잠시 멈춤) 이야기를 기억합니까?

학생2: 미국.

선생님: 맞습니다. 그 남자는 미국에 가기를 결정합니다. 왜? (잠시 멈춤) 돈을 벌어와, 그의 약혼녀와 결혼하기 위해서.

2. 기본구문

여기에서는 학과 수업의 도입단계에서 수업준비를 지시하고, 전 시간에 학습한 내용을 복습한 뒤에, 금일 수업을 준비하는 과정과 관련된 사항을 다음과 같이 정리하였다: A. 수업 시작, 교과 진행 및 지체 B. 예습과 복습 C. 페이지 찾기

A. 수업 시작, 교과 진행 및 지체

> ① Are you [we] all ready?

해설   준비되었습니까?
: '준비된'이라는 표현은 'ready' 또는 'set'이 흔히 사용된다.

syn   All set? *(casual)*
Are you all set?
Is everybody ready to start [to begin]?
I hope you are all ready for class.
Is everybody ready to start class?

참고   **동음어구의 의미 차이**
동음어 - all ready / already, all right / alright, all together / altogether, any way / anyway, everyday / every day, every one / everyone - 의 의미 차이를 간단히 살펴보자.

   ① all ready (all prepared: 모두 준비가 된)와 already (before the given time: 이미)
      e.g. The children were all ready for the picnic. (모두 준비된)
            (=All of the children were prepared for the picnic.)

They had already gone when we arrived. (이미)
(=They had gone before we arrived.)

② all right (in good condition, satisfactory, acceptable: 상태가 좋은, 만족한)을 미국영어에서는 속어로 간단히 'alright'으로 쓰기도 한다.

　e.g.　All she's worried about is whether he is all right. (몸이 좋은)

③ all together (united with each other: 모두 함께)와
altogether (completely, totally, entirely: 아주, different from other people or things: 전혀 다른)

　e.g.　The children were all together in one room. (모두 함께)
　　　　His tour may have to be cancelled altogether. (완전히)
　　　　He was an altogether different type. (전혀)

④ any way (by any method: 어떤 방식이든)와
anyway [anyhow] (true or relevant in spite of other things: 어 쨌든)

　e.g.　Organize these any way you like. (어떤 방식이든 간에)
　　　　I wasn't qualified to apply for the job but I got it anyway. (어쨌든)
　　　　(미국영어에서는 'anyhow'보다 'anyway'가 널리 쓰임)

⑤ everyday (형용사)와 every day (빈도의 부사)

　e.g.　Going to work is just part of everyday life.
　　　　(형용사로 'life'를 수식하므로 'every day'를 사용할 수 없음)
　　　　I run five miles every day. (Not *everyday)
　　　　('매일'이라는 의미를 가진 부사구이므로 'everyday'를 쓸 수 없음)

⑥ 부정대명사, everyone(all the people: 모든 사람들)과

명사구 every one(all of them: 그들 각각 모두)

e. g. Everyone wants success. (Not *Every one)

(모든 사람은 성공하기를 바란다.)

Every one of their children did well in school. (*Not everyone)

(어린이들 각자는 학교에서 잘하였다.)

(미국영어에서는 'in school'이 'at school'보다 널리 쓰임)

---

② Let's start (our) class now.

해설 수업을 시작하겠습니다.

:'시작하다'라는 의미로는 'begin', 'start', 'get (down) to work'가 주로 사용된다.

syn Let's begin (today's class). / Let's get started (to work).

It's time to start class. / It's time for class to start.

Ok, let's get to work. /

Now we can get down to (some) work. *(informal)*

Let's get down to business. / Let's get on with our work.

All set. *(casual)* / Let's get this show on the road.

Are you ready to roll? /

Let's get the ball rolling. *(informal, A.E.)*

I think we can start our class now. *(rare)*

Let's get cracking. (=Let's hurry.) *(slang)*

참고 오늘날 미국 영어는 단순화를 지향하고 있다. 따라서 과거와 달리 상세하게 나타낼 목적으로 불필요하게 덧붙이는 표현은 잘 사용하지 않는다.

① 시작합시다.

I can get started. *(usual)* vs I can get started to work. *(redundant)*

② 금액이 '합계 얼마입니까?'는 간단히 'How much is it?', 또는 'How much?' 라고 하며, 'owe'를 사용할 경우에는 다음과 같이 표현한다.

How much do I owe you? *(usual)* vs How much do I owe you in all? *(redundant)*

③ 내일 전화 걸게.

I'll call you tomorrow. *(usual)* vs I'll call you up tomorrow. *(redundant)*

미국인은 종종 문제나 상황을 복잡하게 처리하려고 애쓸 때 - 예를 들면 스위치를 안 켜서 전기가 꺼졌는데, 형광등을 분해하고 있을 때 - 친밀한 사이에서 흔히 'KISS'(Keep it simple, stupid.) (바보, 간단히 처리해.)라고 말한다.

---

③ T: Where did we stop last time?
S: Last time we got to line 23 on page 32.

해설　　T: 지난 시간 어디까지 했습니까?
S: 지난번에 32페이지 23째 줄까지 했습니다.

syn　　T: Where did we leave off last time?
How far did we get last time?
How far have we gotten?
Where were we? *(casual)*
What were we talking about last time?
Where did we stop working last time? *(rare, B.E.)*
Where are you up to? *(casual, rare)*
How far into it are you? *(especially for longer readings)*

(장문의 읽기에서 어느 부분인지 모를 때)

④ Let's see. Last time we talked about cars made in Korea.
   (usual)

해설   자, 지난 시간에 우리는 국산차에 대해 이야기했습니다.

syn   Last time we talked about Korean (manufactured) cars.
       Last time we talked about cars of Korean make. *(rare)*
       Let me refresh your memory. Last time we talked about cars of
       Korean make.

어휘   'Make', 'mark', 'brand', 'trademark', 'label'의 차이
       'Make(제작, 제조, …제)'는 제품의 크기, 모양, 기계장치 등을 총
       칭하는 표현으로 전자 및 기계제품에 흔히 사용한다.
       e.g. Sonata III is a car of Korean make.

       반면 'mark(상표)', 'brand', 'trademark'는 서로 동의어로 사용될
       수 있으며, 어떤 회사가 자사의 제품을 다른 회사의 제품과 구별
       하기 위하여 사용하는 부호(symbol)를 말한다. 원래 'brand'는 가
       축(소)이나 위스키 병에 불을 태워(burning) 표시한 표시(brand)
       를 말하며, 소유권(ownership) 또는 품질(quality) - 예를 들면 'a
       brand of cigarettes' - 을 나타내기 위해 사용되었다.
       e.g. Hanaro is a brand of cigarettes. (하나로는 담배의 상표다.)

       그리고 'label (꼬리표, 레테르, 딱지표)'은 어떤 물건에 부착된 종
       이 또는 플라스틱 자체를 의미한다.
       e.g. He peered at the label on the bottle. (병에 붙은 표를 보았
             다.)

⑤ This is the way we'll do it.

해설   (수업은) 다음과 같이 진행하겠습니다.

syn   This is the way to do it.
This is how we shall do it.
This is how we shall proceed. *(very formal)*
This is how it should [ought to] be done.
This is how to get it done.

You ought to do it this way.
You should do it this way.

Let me show you how to do it.
Let me explain what I want you to do.

Please do it like this.
Would you do it this way [like this]?

I would like you to do it in the following way.

Before you begin, let me explain [tell you] how I want you to do it.
Before you begin, let me explain what I want you to do.

cf. '지난 시간에 했던 것과 같은 방식으로 하세요.'
Try to do it the way we did it last time [last class].
Do it the same way as last time [last class].

⑥ First of all, we're going to practice new vocabulary.

해설 먼저, 새로 나온 어휘를 연습하겠습니다.

syn Let's practice new words first.
Let's begin by going over the new vocabulary.
First, let's go over the new vocabulary.
Let me introduce some new words.
Let's take [have] a look at the new vocab.

어휘 'Vocabulary'를 구어에서는 'vocab.'라고 말하기도 한다. 'First of all', 'the first thing we'll do', 'to begin with'는 'first'보다 격식적인 표현이다.

new vocabulary=new words, new vocabulary words
화용적으로는 단어가 별도의 목록으로 된 경우에는 'new vocabulary words', 문장 속에 나타나는 경우는 'new vocabulary'가 적합하나 대개 구별하지 않는다.

참고 **'First'와 'at first'의 차이**
'First (or firstly)', 'first of all', 'to start (off) with', 'to begin with (먼저, 우선)'는 단순히 행동의 순서를 나타내는 반면에, at first [in the beginning] (처음에는)는 추후 상반되거나 대비되는 행동을 수반한다.
e.g. First we shall sing, and then we shall work.
(먼저 노래를 부른 다음에 수업을 시작하겠다.)

At first he was kind to me, but then he became cruel.
(처음에는 그는 나에게 친절했으나, 나중에는 잔인해졌다.)

(주의:'first'의 반의어는 'last', 'lastly', 'to finish with'(끝으로)이며,

'at last'(마침내)와는 구별되어야 한다.)

---

⑦ After that we're going to do some reading.

해설   그 다음에는 읽기를 하겠습니다.

syn   Then we'll do some reading after that.
We'll follow up by doing some reading.
Thereafter, we'll do some reading. *(very formal, rare)*
The next thing we'll do is some reading.
After that, we'll read.

어휘   then=after that, following that, to follow up, once we've finished that

---

⑧ Later (on) I want you to practice conversation.

해설   그 다음에는 회화를 연습하겠습니다.

syn   Later (on) I want you to have some conversation practice.
Later (on) I want you to practice having conversations.
Later (on) I'd like you to practice conversation.

---

⑨ By the end of the lesson you'll be able to talk about [discuss] your likes and dislikes.

해설   수업을 마치면, 여러분은 자신의 기호를 표현할 수 있을 것입니다.

syn   When you've finished this lesson, you'll have learned how to
       say what you like and dislike.
       Upon completion of this lesson, you'll be able to say what you
       like and dislike.
       By the time we're finished, …

    cf. By the end of the lesson, you'll be able to use the present perfect
        tense of the verb to determine what has happened.
        (수업을 마치면, 여러분은 일어난 일을 확인하기 위해 현재완료시제를 사용할
        수 있을 겁니다.)

⑩ If we finish this in time, we'll learn something new.

해설   이것을 시간 내에 끝내면, 다른 것을 배울 것입니다.

syn   Time permitting [If we have time], we'll learn something new.
       If time permits [If time allows it], we'll learn something new.
       If we have time after we finish, we'll learn something new.
       If there's time when we finish, we'll begin something new.
       When we finish this, if time permits [if time allows], we'll go
       onto something new.

어휘   if time permits=if time allows, if we have time

참고   영어에서는 문두, 문미, 문장 가운데의 순서로 강조된다. 따라서
       아래와 같이 표현하면, 'when'이 이끄는 시간의 부사절이 'if조건
       절보다 강조된다.
       When we've finished this, if there's time, we'll learn something
       new.

⑪ We'll take a break at the end of the lesson.

해설   수업이 끝나면 쉬는 시간입니다.

syn   At the end of the lesson let's take a (short) break. *(usual)*
… we'll take a break for a moment or two. *(formal)*
… we'll break for a couple of minutes.
… we'll recess for a few seconds.
At the end of the lesson, we're going to have a break for a few moments. *(awkward)*
(원칙적으로 부사구 뒤에는 쉼표(,)를 사용하지 않으며, 위의 경우에는 'be going to have'보다는 'will take'가 간단하고 자연스럽다.)

cf. At the end of the lesson we'll pause for a few moments. (not clear) ('잠시 동안 멈춘다.'는 말은 '잠시 동안 쉰다.'는 의미와는 다소 차이가 있다. 이 경우 의미가 분명하지 않을 수 있다.)

참고   실제 수업현장에서 사용되는 수업 단계별 표현들은 대체로 다음과 같다.

기능(Functions)	표시어(Signals)
Introductions (도입)	I'm going to talk about… / My topic is… / My subject is …Our topic today is…
Sequencing (나열)	First… / Next… / Then… / After that… (The / My next point is… / Finally…
Changing topic (화제전환)	Now let's look at… / Now let's turn to… / Moving on…
Giving examples (예시)	For example… / As you can see from (the picture)… / The graph (picture / chart) shows…
Conclusion (요약, 결론)	In conclusion… / To sum up… / Let me sum up by saying… / Finally…

   누구나 영어로 가르칠 수 있다

⑫ I'm sorry about the delay.

해설 (수업이) 지연되어 미안합니다.
: '지체하다'라는 의미로는 'wait', 'delay'를 주로 사용한다.

syn Sorry for making you wait.
Sorry to keep you waiting.
Sorry you had to wait.
Sorry about the wait.

Sorry for being late (with this).
Sorry for my tardiness.

My apologies for the delay.
I apologize for the delay. *(very formal)*

⑬ Let's get back to work.

해설 (잠시 중단한 후) 수업을 계속합시다.

syn Let's get back to what we were doing.
Let's start again.

We'll go on with our work.
Let's go back to where we were.
Let's get on with [start] our work.
Alright, let's get started.
Right. Back to work.
Let's resume working.
Let's resume what we were up to. *(rare)*

— 다음과 같이 부사절로 시작할 수도 있다.

To continue what we were doing, …

To pick up where we left off, … *(slang)*

---

⑭ **Now where was I?** *(informal, usual)*

해설   좀 전에 어디까지 하였습니까? : 수업을 잠시 중단한 뒤 다시 시작할 때 사용하는 표현이다.

syn   What were we talking about before I was interrupted?

What was I saying before I was interrupted?

Where were we before I was interrupted?

---

⑮ **Let's go on to the next exercise [exercise 3].**

해설   다음 연습문제 [연습문제 3번]로 넘어갑시다.

: '넘어가다'는 'go on to, go ahead to, move on to, proceed to' 등으로 표현한다.

syn   Let's take a look at the next exercise.

Let's move on to the next exercise.

Let's proceed to the next exercise. *(formal)*

Now we'll go ahead to the next exercise.

Go to the next exercise. *(informal)*

어휘   go on to=move on to, begin

cf. 문제풀이와 관련된 표현들

Which question are you on? (몇 번 문제를 풀고 있니?)

Let me explain what I want you to do next. (다음에 해야 할 것을 설명하겠습니다.)

---

⑯ When you have done that, continue with number 5.

해설   그 문제를 푼 다음에 5번 문제를 계속하세요.

syn   After you complete that, you may continue with number 5.
       Once you've finished [completed] that, …
       When you get through with this exercise, move on to number 5.
       (rare)
       Then go to number 5. *(informal)*

B. 예습과 복습

---

① Let's go over it again (quickly).

해설   잠시 복습하겠습니다.

syn   We're going to review it once more.
       Let's summarize. *(casual)*
       Summarize it for me.
       Sum it up for me.
       Let's review quickly.

       Let's go over it (one more time).

In a nutshell, we... *(slang)* (요약하면, …)

어휘   again=one more time

cf. Who can summarize for me? (요약해 볼 사람?)

---

② Who can tell me what we learned last time?

해설   지난 시간에 무엇을 배웠는지 압니까?
       :상황에 따라 'learned' 대신 'practiced', 'discussed', 'talked about',
       'studied', 'went over', 'look at', 'read', 'go over' 등을 사용한다.

syn   Can anyone remember what we covered [studied] last time?
       Who can recall what we learned last class?
       Let's review what we learned last time [class].

---

③ We looked at [dealt with] these forms last week.

해설   지난 시간에 이런 유형을 학습했습니다.

syn   We went over [worked on] these forms last week.
       We did these forms last week.
       We tackled these last week. *(casual)*
       We reviewed these last week.

참고   **'Can not'과 'cannot'의 차이**
       원래 중세(Middle Ages) 영어에서는 같은 자음이 중복되면 단어
       위에 사선(bar: -)을 긋고 연결하여 표시하였다. 따라서 'cannot'
       은 'cañot'으로 표기하였다. 그 후 표기법이 변화하여 오늘날 사선

(bar)표기법이 사라진 뒤에도 영어에서는 'can not' 또는 'cannot'을 둘 다 허용하게 되었다. 그러나 'may not' 등에서는 동일 자음 중복이 없으므로 'maynot'으로 붙여서 표기하면 안 된다. 향후 컴퓨터 시대에는 'can not'을 다른 단어들과 마찬가지로 편의를 위해 띄어 쓸지 모른다.

④ Have you all read this chapter?

해설   이 장을 읽어왔습니까?

syn   Did [Has] everyone read this chapter?
       Have you gotten through this chapter?

       Have you all prepared this chapter? *(not clear)*
       (위의 우리말식 표현은 이 장을 읽었는지, 단어를 외웠는지, 문제를 풀었는지 물음의 의미가 명확하지 않으므로 미국인들은 적절한 질문이 아니라고 본다.)

C. 페이지 찾기

① T: Where did we stop last time?
   S: I think [believe] we were on page 16.

해설   T: 지난 시간 어디까지 했습니까?
       S: 16페이지까지 했습니다.

syn   T: Where were we last time? *(casual)*
       What were we talking about last time? *(formal)*

What were we doing (in our) last class?

How far did we get last time?

Where did we leave off last time?

Where did we stop working last time?

   S: We stopped on page 16.

If memory serves (me correctly), we were on page 16.
(formal, coll.)

I believe we left off on page 16.

If I remember correctly, we were on page 16.

('Correctly' 대신 영국식 영어에서는 'rightly'가 사용될 수 있다.)

cf. 보다 구체적으로 다음과 같이 답할 수도 있다.

Last time we got to line 23 on page 16.

= We're on page 16, line 23.

(지난 시간 16페이지 23째 줄까지 했습니다.)

---

② T: Do you know **where we are?**
  S: It's (somewhere) near the bottom (of the page).

해설   T: 어디인지 알겠습니까?

S: 아래쪽 가까이에 있습니다.

:'어느 페이지'라고 할 경우에는 'where we are', 'the right page' 등
의 표현을 사용한다.

syn   T: Have you all found the right page?

Is everyone on the right page?

Are you all on the right page?

Is there anyone who doesn't know where we are?

Are you all looking at the right page?

Is there anyone who still hasn't found the right place?

Have you all found the place? *(B.E.)*

S: It's somewhere near the bottom.

It's close to the bottom of the page.

(다음과 같이 답할 수도 있다.)

It's somewhere near [around] the middle of the book.

It's in the bottom right-hand [top left-hand] corner.

It's right around the middle of the page.

어휘 near=toward, bottom=end, bottom ↔ top

활용 'near the bottom of' 대신 'at the bottom [top] of', 'in the (very) middle of', 'on the right [left]' 등으로 대체할 수 있다.

---

③ S: What [Which] page are you on?

해설 몇 페이지입니까? (지금 몇 페이지를 하고 있습니까?)

: 학생이 진도를 모를 때도 선생님에게 위와 같이 질문할 수 있다.

syn Where are you?

Where are you up to?

What [Which] page is it on? *(formal)*

Which page is it? *(informal)*

Where are we?

Where is it?

How far have you gotten?

How far did you get?

cf. **진도와 관련된 질문**

Which number [What number] are you on? (몇 번을 하고 있습니까?)

What [Which] page should we read? (몇 페이지를 읽을까요?)

What [Which] page should we do? (몇 페이지를 할까요?)

참고   'Which page'는 기사(article)나 짧은 논문의 경우에 주로 사용하고, 'what page'는 책, 잡지에 주로 사용한다.

---

④ It's ten lines from the top [bottom].

해설   위에서 [밑에서] 10째 줄에 있습니다.

syn   Go down ten lines.
From the top [bottom] it's ten lines down [up].
It's the tenth line from the top [bottom].

어휘   읽기자료에는 'line'이 주로 사용되고, 도표, 통계 등에서는 'row'가 많이 사용된다.

cf. **교재의 위치를 정정할 때 사용하는 표현**

Not the next line, but the one after that.
(다음 줄이 아니라, 그 다음 줄입니다.)
Not the previous line, but the one after that. (앞줄이 아닌 그 다음 줄)
Go five lines farther down [up]. (다섯 줄 더 아래 [더 위])

주의   정도의 의미를 가진 'further'와 구별할 것.
The government's economic policies have further depressed
living standards.

⑤ Let's look at page 36.

해설   36페이지를 보세요.
:'(페이지를) 펴다'는 'turn to', 'open to'를 주로 사용한다.

syn   Everyone turn to page 36. *(informal, casual)*
Open your books to page 36.
Take out your books and open them to page 36.
(미국영어에서는 'open' 뒤에 'to' 대신 'at'을 사용하지 않는다.)
Let's take a look at page 36.

어법   'Page+숫자'의 경우 페이지 앞에는 정관사 'the'를 붙이지 않는다.

주의   'Open'은 반드시 목적어로 사물을 필요로 하므로, '36페이지를 펴시오'를 '*open to [at] page 36' 또는 페이지를 목적어로 '*open page 36'로 표현해서는 안 된다.

    cf. 책의 페이지와 관련된 표현들
    It is on page 36.
    Turn to [Move to] page 36.
    Take out your books and open them to page 36 [lesson 7].

⑥ Look at the exercise on page 56.

해설   56페이지의 연습문제를 보세요.

syn   You'll find the exercise on page 56.
Take [Have] a look at the exercise on page 56.
The exercise is on page 56.
Look at exercise 3 on page 56. (연습문제 3번일 경우)

참고   페이지 읽는 법

① 1페이지부터 99페이지까지: 일반적인 단위(full number)로 읽을 것.

    e.g. page 36: page thirty six

             page three six *(incorrect)*

② 100페이지 이상은 단위로 읽거나, 한 자리씩 따로 읽어도 된다.

    e.g. page 136: page one hundred and thirty six.

                     page one-three-six.

        page 107: page one hundred and seven.

                     page one-o [ou]-seven.

---

⑦ Look at the second word in line 7.

해설   7째 줄 두 번째 단어를 보세요.

syn   Line 7, (the) second word. *(casual)*

        (The) Seventh line, (the) second word.

    cf. 책의 페이지를 지시할 경우에 사용되는 표현

        Look at the last line of [in] the third paragraph.

        Look at the second to the last line in paragraph two.

        Look at the colored box beneath [underneath].

        Look at the paragraph beginning with [starting with] 'He said...'

        Look at the second [third, fourth] to (the) last word in line 7.

⑧ Turn to the next page.

해설   다음 페이지로 넘기세요.

syn   Let's go [move on] to the next page.
       Let's turn the page.
       Next page, please.
       Turn the page. *(casual)*
       I want you to turn [go] to the next page.

   cf. '앞 페이지를 보세요.'
       Let's go back to the previous page.
       Go [Turn] back to the previous page.
       Look back at the previous page.

◆ 현대영어의 3단계 단순화 과정

(adapted from Question Box in ELT Journal by Simeon Potter (1976))

오늘날 영어는 시대 상황에 따라 단순화 과정을 겪고 있다. 그 과정은 대체로 문장 [절] ⇒ (전치사를 포함한)구 ⇒ (소유격을 포함한)단어 ⇒ 단어 [또는 복합명사]의 3단계 순서로 진행된다고 볼 수 있다. 구체적으로 예문을 통해 살펴보기로 하자.

e.g. **Workers [Those who work] should participate** (in the running of their factory.) ((공장의 경영에) 노동자들도 참여해야 한다.)

: 여기에서 '노동자들이 참여하다'는 '주어+동사'로 표현되어 있다.

① 1단계: 위의 고딕체 부분으로 된 절은 다음과 같이 전치사를 포함한 명사구로 변한다.

The participation of workers (is essential.)

② 2단계: 이 명사구는 소유격의 수식을 받는 명사로 전환된다.

Worker's participation (is essential.)

③ 3단계: 간단히 복합명사 (명사+명사)로 표현된다.

Worker participation (is essential.)

일상적인 회회문의 경우에도 이와 유사한 현상이 나타나고 있다. 다음 예문을 보자

e.g. **Would you please look (to the) left?** (왼쪽을 보시겠습니까?)

① 1단계: 주어와 의문조동사가 생략되어 명령문으로 나타난다.

Please look (to the) left. (왼쪽을 보세요.)

② 2단계: 동사가 생략되어 부사구로 표현된다.

To the left. (왼쪽으로.)

③ 3단계: 전치사가 생략되어 부사로 변화되었다.

Left. (왼쪽.)

특히 전치사구를 포함한 명사구에서 전치사가 탈락되고 복합명사로 변하는 현상은 오늘날 광범위하게 나타난다.

e.g. the training of teachers (교사들의 연수)
    ⇒ teacher training (교사 연수)
    the shooting of tigers (호랑이의 사냥)
    ⇒ tiger shoot (호랑이 사냥)
    members of the family (가족의 구성원)
    ⇒ family members (가족 구성원)
    members of the staff (참모의 구성원들)
    ⇒ staff members (참모진)
    wall chart of the 'comparisons' (비교급에 대한 차트)
    ⇒ the 'comparisons' wall chart
    a wrestler with broad shoulder (넓은 어깨를 가진 레슬러)
    ⇒ a broad-shouldered wrestler (어깨 넓은 레슬러)
    a boy with bare legs (맨발을 한 소년)
    ⇒ a bare-legged boy (맨발 소년)

또한 명사가 수식어로 그대로 사용되는 경우도 많다. 예를 들면 '교육제도'는 영어로 'educational system' 또는 'education system' 둘 다로 표기될 수 있다. 그리고 오늘날 명사를 수식어로 사용하는 추세에 비추어 장차 후자가 널리 사용될 것으로 보인다.

이와 같이 절이 단어로 표기되고, 단어의 경우도 복합어의 경우 형용사 대신 명사 자체가 형용사로서 직접 수식을 하는 구조로 변화하고 있는 원인은 대체로 다음 세가지로 볼 수 있다.
첫째, 언어 단순화 현상 때문이다.
둘째, 통사적 전치화 경향(syntactic switch to front position) 때문이다: 언어 사용에서 현대인은 전치사구에 의한 후위수식보다 전위수식을 할 수 있는 명사부가어(premodifying noun adjunct)를 선호하기 때문이다.
셋째, 일상적인 표현(inforaml expression)에 대한 선호 현상 때문이다.

실제 최근 영국의 한 장관은 스페인의 '발렌샤 대학의 철학 교수진'에 대한 표현을 다음과 같이 하였다.

① Valentia University's Philosophy Faculty

　위의 말은 원래 다음과 같이 표현해야 하는 것이다.

② The Faculty of Philosophy in the University of Valentia

위의 공식적인 표현인 ②에는 전치사가 3개 포함되어 있으나, ①의 일상적인 표현에는 소유격 하나로 대체되어 있다. 장관이 ①과 같이 표현한 것은 언어단순화 현상이외의 또 다른 수사학적인(rhetoric) 이유 때문으로 보인다. 즉, 장관은 의도적으로②와 같은 공적 또는 공식적인(official or formal) 표현을 회피하고, ①과 같이 일상적인 표현을 사용함으로써 우의 있고, 상냥하게 보이기 위해 노력한 것이다.

1. 현장예문 (Real-life Situation)

Word Games With Cards

(adapted from Richard Young(1983))

초급영어에서는 학생들이 간단한 구문을 쉽게 활용할 수 있도록 다양한 게임을 한다. 여기에서는 홍콩의 영국영사관에서 9~10세 사이의 홍콩초등학교 학생들을 대상으로 다년 간 시행해온 카드의 짝을 맞추는 게임을 살펴보기로 한다.

먼저 학생들을 4~5명 단위의 소그룹으로 나눈다. 선생님은 각각 20~25개의 단어가 적힌 카드와 그 단어에 대한 그림카드를 만든다. 각 그룹의 학생 개개인에게 4장씩의 카드를 나누어 준다. 그룹의 한 학생이 자기가 가진 문자카드와 같은 그림카드를 찾기 위해 그룹의 다른 사람에게 카드를 요청한다. 요청 결과 같은 카드를 가지고 있으면 받아서 자기 카드와 짝을 지어 내려 놓고, 카드가 없으면 다음 사람에게 요청권이 넘어간다. 최종적으로 카드를 먼저 전부 내려놓은 사람이 이기는 게임이다.

간단한 몇 가지 구문을 활용하여 말하기 연습을 할 수 있는 효과적인 방법이다. 또한 이런 종류의 게임은 아이들의 주의가 게임에 집중되므로, 배운 언어를 활용하는 언어습득체계(language acquisition system)의 향상에 도움이 된다.

아래는 'Will you give me', 'Here you are', 'Sorry, I don't have one'의 구문과 학습한 단어를 활용하는 게임에 대한 예문이다.

This unit reviews the language needed to give instructions when playing games. Teachers will need to do such things as instruct students how to play, correct student errors during the game, and give orders to students during the game itself if necessary. Aside from word games, this unit also covers how to guide students through course textbook exercises.

For instance, it presents language on giving exercise instructions, eliciting student responses, answering student questions, and moving from one exercise to the next.

Now listen to the dialogue.

Word Games with Cards [Word games using Cards]

T: OK. Today, we'll play word games with cards. You're going to be divided into groups. 4 members, in each group.[1] Now, get into a group with your neighbors.[2]

Jim: I can't find a team. All the teams are full.

T: Then. Why don't you join in with Mary's team?[3]

Jim: It's full.

T: That's OK. Then Mary's group will have 5 members. All members should be seated facing each other, so arrange your desks... By the way, where is Tom?

Ss: He dropped out last week.[4]

T: Oh, that's too bad... Ready? Now I'll give you some cards. Each member will get 4 letter cards and 4 picture cards. Don't show your cards to the others. Next, make a pair with your cards by asking the others the matching card. And when you make a pair, put the matching pair on your desk. When you ask for a card you should use the following expressions:

Will you give me...? Here you are. Sorry, I don't have one.[5]

When one of you has made all your pairs and has laid them down on the table, the game ends. OK? Begin...

May: Will you give me a bag, please?

John: *(He hands the bag picture to May)* Here you are.

May: Thank you. *(She lays her pair down on the table.)*

John: Will you give me a watch, please?

Bonnie: Sorry, I don't have one. Will you give me a shoe, please?

Sandra: Sorry, I don't have one. Will you give me a watch, please?

May: Sorry, I don't have one. Will you give me a watch, please?

John: *(He hands watch picture to May)* Here you are.

May: Thank you.

John: *(To Sandre)* Will you give me a radio, please? (pause) Will you give me a radio, please?

Sandra: *(She hands the radio picture to John)* Here you are.

John: Thank you. *(He lays his pair down on the table.)*

Bonnie: Will you give me a car, please?

Sandra: Sorry, I don't have one. *(pause)* Will you give me a camera, please?

May: Sorry, I don't have one. Will you give me a shoe, please?

Sandra: *(She hands the shoe picture to May)* Here you are.

May: Thank you.

   (She lays her last pair on the desk and shows her empty hands to the other players to show she is the winner.)

T: When you have finished, collect the cards and pass them to the front...

1 (각 그룹은 4명입니다) Each group consists of members. / 4 members, each group
2 (옆 사람과 그룹을 만드세요) Make a group with your neighbors.
3 'Join in with'(가입하다)는 간단히 'join', 'get into', 'go into'로도 표현한다.
4 'Drop out'(학교를 자퇴하다) = 'drop out of school', 'leave school', 'guit school'

  e.g. He dropped out (of school). (그는 자퇴했다.)
        He is a drop-out.
        'Fail out' ((성적 부진으로) 퇴학당했다) = 'fail out [flunk out] of school'

  e.g. He failed out [flunked out] (of school).
        He is a failure. (이 문장도 같은 의미지만 '실패자'라는 극히 부정적인 의미가
        있으므로 잘 사용하지 않는다.)

  반면 불량 행동으로 학교에서 쫓겨난 경우에는

  e.g. He was expelled out of school.
        He was kicked out (of school).

5 'Here you are.'(여기에 있습니다.)는 'Here', 'Here it is.', 'Here you go.' 'I haven't
  got one.' 등으로 다양하게 표현할 수 있다.

  <활용> 위의 대화를 중급과정에 활용할 경우에는 좀 더 복잡하게, 카드를 받아야 할 타
       당한 이유를 제시한 다음에 받아올 수 있게 할 수 있다.

  Sandra: Will you give me a pig, please? (돼지 한 마리 줄래?)
  May: Why? (왜?)
  Sandrs: We want to put it in our farmyard together with our hen. (농장
           에 닭하고 같이 놓아두려고.)
  May: Sorry, we don't have one. (미안, 없어.)
           (or) Here you are. (여기에 있어.)

선생님: 이번 시간에는 카드를 이용한 단어게임을 하겠습니다. 그룹으로 나누겠습니다.
        각 그룹은 4명으로 구성되겠습니다. 자, 옆 사람과 그룹을 만드세요.
짐: 저는 팀이 없습니다. 모든 팀이 짜여졌어요.
선생님: 메어리의 팀에 들어가거라.
짐: 짜여졌는데요.

선생님: 좋아. 메어리 팀은 5명이다. 모든 사람은 서로 마주 보고 앉도록 책상을 정리하세요. 그런데 톰은 어디에 있습니까?

학생들: 지난주 자퇴했습니다.

선생님: 안됐군…. 준비되었습니까? 자, 카드를 주겠습니다. 각각 4장의 문자카드와 그림카드를 가지세요. 카드를 다른 사람에게 보여주지 마세요. 그리고 상대방에게 짝이 되는 카드를 요청하여 여러분의 카드와 한 짝을 만드세요. 그리고 짝을 지었을 때에는 그 두 장을 책상 위에 놓으세요. 상대에게 카드를 요구할 때에는 다음 표현을 사용해야 합니다:
Will you give me…? Here you are. Sorry, I haven't got one.
여러분 중 한 사람이 모든 짝을 맞추고 책상 위에 내려놓으면 게임은 끝납니다. 자, 시작하세요….

메이: 가방 주시겠습니까?

존: (메이에게 가방 그림을 준다) 여기 있습니다.

메이: 고맙습니다. (메이는 자신의 카드 짝을 탁자 위에 둔다.)

존: 시계 주시겠습니까?

보니: 미안합니다. 없습니다. 신발 주시겠습니까?

산드라: 미안합니다. 없습니다. 시계 주시겠습니까?

메이: 미안합니다. 없습니다. 시계 주시겠습니까?

존: (메이에게 시계 그림을 준다.) 여기 있습니다.

메이: 고맙습니다.

존: (산드라에게) 라디오 주시겠습니까? (잠시 멈춤) 라디오 주시겠습니까?

산드라: (존에게 라디오 그림을 준다.) 여기 있습니다.

존: 고맙습니다. (존은 그의 패를 책상 위에 둔다.)

보니: 차를 주시겠습니까?

산드라: 미안합니다. 없습니다. (잠시 멈춤) 카메라 주시겠습니까?

메이: 미안합니다. 없습니다. 신발 주시겠습니까?

산드라: (신발 그림을 메이에게 준다.) 여기 있습니다.

메이: 고맙습니다. (그녀는 자신의 짝을 책상 위에 놓고, 자신의 빈손을 다른 상대에게 보여주며 자신이 이겼음을 알린다.)

선생님: 끝났을 때에는 카드를 모아 앞으로 넘기세요.

2. 기본구문

여기에서는 수업 중에 선생님이 학생에게 질문 또는 문제풀이를 지시하거나, 판서를 지시 또는 지우기 위해 사용하는 표현들을 다음과 같이 정리하였다: A. 질문 및 문제풀이 B. 지시와 지명 C. 판서

A. 질문 및 문제풀이

① The purpose of this exercise is (for you) to practice the future tense.

해설   이 연습문제를 통하여 미래시제를 연습하겠습니다.

syn   The idea [objective] of this exercise is to practice the future tense. *(usual)*
The idea behind this exercise is to practice the future tense.
This exercise teaches you the future tense.
This exercise takes you through the future tense.
This exercise helps you (to) understand the future tense.
With this exercise we will practice the future tense. *(rare)*

What this exercise does is (to) make you practice the future tense. *(formal)*

What we're trying to do with this exercise is (to) make you practice the future tense. *(redundant)*
What this exercise is trying to do is (to) make you practice the future tense. *(redundant)*
(위와 같이 우리말의 표현방식으로 'does' 대신 'is trying to do'를 사용하면 중복되는 의미를 가진 표현이 된다.)

cf. The idea of [behind] this exercise is (for you) to practice the conditional.
(이 연습문제의 목적은 조건법을 연습하는 것이다.)

= This exercise is to practice using the conditional.

This exercise was designed for you to practice the conditional.

This exercise teaches you the conditional.

This exercise helps you (to) understand the conditional.

With [In] this exercise we will practice...

The purpose [point, focus] of this exercise is to practice...

② Any questions?

해설   질문 있습니까?

syn   Does anyone have any questions?

Are there any questions?

Is anyone having trouble [difficulty]?

Let me know if you run into a problem.

Does anyone need any help?

Who needs help? *(casual)*

I'll help you if you get stuck. *(slang, common)*

Who can't manage on his [her] own? *(rare)*

어휘   get stuck=unable to continue doing it because it is too difficult
(어려워서 해결할 수 없는)

cf. Any other questions? (또 다른 질문 있습니까?)

syn   Do you have any other [further] questions?

Is there anything more you want to ask?

Is there anything else you want to ask?

③ Is anyone having trouble [difficulty] (with this)?

해설   (이것에 대해) 모르는 사람이 있습니까?

syn   Let me know if you run into a problem. *(formal)*

Does anyone need any help? *(informal)*

Who needs help? *(casual)*

Is anyone having a hard [tough, difficult] time with this?

Who can't manage on his [her] own? *(rare)*

I'll help you if you get stuck. *(slang)*

> **cf.** If you run into a problem, raise your hand.
> (문제가 생기면 손을 드세요.)

이 망할 내 옷장은
항상 필요한 순간에 안 열린단 말이야!

④ Answer these questions.

해설   다음 질문에 답하시오.

syn   Answer the following questions.

Complete these questions.

What are the answers to these questions?

Write appropriate answers to the following questions.
What answers do you have [have you got] for these questions?

---

⑤ Try exercise 3.

해설   연습문제 3번을 하세요.

syn   I want you to do exercise 3.
Let's get into [engage in, tackle, work on] exercise 3.
Let's go on [move on, proceed] to exercise number 3.
Let's focus our attention on exercise 3.
I want you to try to do exercise 3 on your own.

cf. **연습문제 풀이와 관련된 지시문**
Let's try [go on to, move on to] the next exercise.
(다음 연습문제로 넘어갑시다.)
Sun-hi, (you) try number 5. (순희야, 5번을 해 보아라.)
Do part [some] of the exercise. (연습문제를 풀어보세요.)
Do the whole [entire, all the] exercise. (연습문제를 전부 풀으세요.)
Do the exercise in pencil. (연습문제를 연필로 하세요.)
We'll do the exercise orally. (연습문제를 구두로 풀겠습니다.)
Look at the exercise under [by, above] the picture on page 16.
(16페이지의 그림 아래에 [옆에, 위에] 있는 연습문제를 보세요.)

---

⑥ You don't have to do number 5.

해설   5번 문제는 할 필요가 없습니다.

syn   There's no need for you to do number 5.

Don't worry about number 5.

Don't pay attention to number 5.

Don't bother doing #5.

Don't bother with number 5.

Just omit number 5.

Ignore [cross out] number 5.

We are not going to do number 5.

cf. If you get stuck, skip the question.
(어려우면, (다음 문제로) 넘어가세요.)

---

⑦ Choose the correct alternative.

해설   대체할 수 있는 단어를 선택하세요.

syn   Choose the correct alternate word.
       What is the alternative choice?

참고   **문제풀이에 대한 지시문**
       1) 객관식
       Choose the word or phrase which best completes each sentence.
       (각 문장을 완성하기에 가장 적절한 단어나 구를 고르세요.)
       Choose [underline, circle, find, cross out] the verb that best
       fits each sentence.
       (각 문장에 가장 적절한 동사를 택하세요. [밑줄 치세요, 동그
       라미를 치세요, 찾으세요, 줄을 그으세요.])

       You have to find the right word for each blank [gap].
       (빈 칸에 적절한 단어를 찾으세요 ; 'blank'가 'gap'보다 널리 사
       용된다.)

Match the questions with the right [correct] answers.
(문제에 대한 올바른 답을 짝 지우세요.)
Mark the right alternative.
(대체할 수 있는 단어를 표시하세요.)
Match the questions to the right answers.
(문제에 대한 올바른 답을 짝 지우세요.)
Put one word from the list below in each gap [blank].
(각각의 괄호에 아래에 열거된 단어 중 하나를 적으세요.)

Cross out the incorrect word. (틀린 단어를 삭제하세요.)

Write T [or ∨] if the following sentence is correct. If it is incorrect put an F [or ×].
(문장이 맞으면 T [또는 ∨]를, 틀리면 F [또는 ×]를 쓰세요.)

2) 단답식
Fill in the missing words. (빈 칸을 채우세요.)
Fill in the blanks. Use only one word in each space.
(괄호를 채우세요. 각각의 괄호에 한 단어만 사용하세요.)

3) 주관식 (문장 전환 및 수정)
Rewrite this sentence in correct English.
(다음 문장을 올바른 영어로 다시 쓰세요.)
Start [Make use of] a given word or words in the bracket at the end of each sentence ; change the form but keep the meaning.
(각 문장의 끝의 괄호 속에 있는 단어(들)를 이용하세요. 형태는 바꾸되 의미는 바꾸지 마세요.)

e.g. He liked the theater but hated the play. (Although…)
⇒ Although he liked the theatre, he hated the play.

⑧ [You must] Construct sentences using the words given [given words].

해설   주어진 단어를 이용하여 문장을 만드세요.

어휘   이 경우 'construct' 대신 'write', 'make', 'build', 'put together'로 대체할 수 있다.

> **cf. 문장[구, 절]의 조합에 대한 표현**
> [You have to] Arrange the sentences into a good paragraph.
> (문장을 배열하여 하나의 글로 만드세요.)
> Combine each pair of sentences, using 'in case.'
> ('In case'를 사용하여 각 쌍의 문장을 결합하세요.)

⑨ You should write [put] your name at the top.

해설   맨 위에 이름을 적으세요.

> **cf. 이름과 관련된 지시문**
> Hand in the [your] papers as you leave and make sure your names are on them.
> (나가면서 시험지를 제출하고, 이름이 위에 적혔는지 확인하세요.)
> Don't forget to put your names on the sheets.
> (시험지에 이름을 적는 것을 잊지 마세요.)

⑩ Let's look at this chapter [topic] in more detail.

해설   이 장[주제]을 좀 더 자세히 살펴봅시다.
    : '보다 자세히'는 'more closely', 'in more detail', 'in greater

depth' 등으로 표현한다.

syn　We'll look at this chapter in more detail [in greater depth].

　　Let's look at this chapter more closely.
　　Let's look more closely at this chapter.
　　('more closely' 대신 'closer'를 사용할 수 없다.)

　　Let's look more closely at this chapter.
　　Let's take a deeper look at this chapter.
　　Let's delve more deeply into this chapter. *(rare)*

cf. We have (quite) a lot of work to do on this topic [chapter].
　　(이 주제[장]를 하는 데는 많은 노력이 필요하다.)
　　= We need to focus more energy on this topic [chapter].
　　　We're going to pay greater attention to this topic [chapter].

---

⑪ Let's look at some of the difficult points.

해설　몇 가지 어려운 점을 살펴보겠습니다.
　　　:'살펴보다'라는 의미로는 'point out', 'take a look at', 'identify' 등
　　　이 사용된다.

syn　I'd like to point out some difficulties.
　　Let's take a look at some of the problem areas.
　　Let's identify some of the trouble areas.

⑫ I'll give you ten minutes to finish (this) (off).

해설   10분 안에 끝내시오.
: '10분 만에 풀다'는 'have [take, spend] 10 minutes'로 주로 표현한다.

syn   You have 10 minutes to get through this.
You have 10 minutes to polish this off.
You only have 10 minutes. *(casual, implied)*

You can take up to 10 minutes to finish this.
I'm afraid you can only spend 10 minutes on this.
Don't spend more than 10 minutes on (doing) this.

You can spend ten minutes on this.
You'll have to stop in ten minutes. *(rare)*

cf. 10분의 한계를 보다 명확히 할 때는 다음과 같이 표현할 수도 있다.
You have 10 minutes tops to finish this.
(이 문제를 푸는 데 최대 10분까지 주겠습니다.)
= You have a maximum of 10 minutes to complete this.
   You have a 10 minute time limit for this exercise.

⑬ Finished? *(casual)*

해설   (문제풀이를) 모두 끝마쳤습니까?
: 문제풀이나 시험 시간의 종료를 알릴 때 흔히 사용하는 표현이다.

syn   Done?
Are you done (yet)?

All through?

Through?

Have you all finished?

Is everyone finished?

Have you done everything?

(Have you) Done them all?

(주로 'Have you'를 생략하고 사용한다.)

cf. Who hasn't [isn't] finished? (끝마치지 못한 사람 있습니까?)

= Is there anybody who hasn't finished?

Is there anybody who isn't finished?

Anybody [Anyone] not finished?

Anybody [Anyone] who (still) hasn't finished? *(B.E.)*

Is anyone done [finished] yet? (벌써 끝마친 사람 있습니까?)

어법 'Finished'는 완료시제 (have+과거분사)에서는 동사로, 'be'동사 뒤에서는 형용사로 사용된다.

---

⑭ **The last thing we'll do is listen to a radio program.** *(formal)*

해설 마지막으로 라디오 프로그램을 듣겠습니다.

syn In our final piece of work today we will listen to a radio program.

Finally we will conclude today's class by listening to a radio program.

Last but not least, we have a radio program to listen to.

cf. **수업 종료 직전의 학습활동에 대해 흔히 사용되는 표현**

For the last few minutes finish the dialogue you're practicing and then we'll stop.

(마지막 몇 분간 여러분이 연습하는 대화를 끝내고, 마치겠습니다.)

Finish the question you're (working) on at the moment, and do the rest at home.

(여러분이 하고 있는 문제를 마치고, 집에 가도록 하겠습니다.)

Please complete the question [task] you're on now and then we'll stop.

(여러분이 하고 있는 문제를 마친 다음, 그만하겠습니다.)

Go through this section again on your own at home.

(집에 가서 개별적으로 이 장을 다시 복습하세요.)

---

⑮ S: Excuse me, sir. **May [could] I ask you a question?**
　T: Sure. What would you like to know?

해설　S: 질문을 해도 좋습니까? (개인적으로 질문할 때 흔히 사용된다.)
　　　　T: 그래 무슨 문제인데?

syn　S: Do you have time to answer a few questions?
　　　　I have some questions (to ask you).
　　　　Sir, I hope I'm not bothering you. I just have a few questions. *(polite)*
　　　　May I interrupt [trouble] you for a moment?
　　　　I'd like to pick your brain if you don't mind. *(casual)*

cf. 질문을 할 때는 다음과 같은 표현도 흔히 사용한다.

Excuse me, Mr Kim. May I ask [say, add] something?

(김 선생님, 할 말이 있는 데요.)

Can you explain what you said about...?

(…에 대한 말을 설명해 주시겠습니까?)

Can you explain the sentence beginning...?
(…로 시작되는 문장을 설명해 주시겠습니까?)

참고 **개인적으로 연구실을 방문하여 질문하는 경우에 일반적으로 사용하는 표현**

① 방문할 때 사용하는 표현
Excuse me, sir. Are you busy? May [Could] I ask you a question?

② 질문을 마친 뒤에 하는 표현
I understand. / I see. / I've got it. (알았습니다.)
Thank you very much for your help. / Thank you for everything. / Thanks.

---

⑯ S: What's the answer to number 7?

해설 7번 문제의 답은 무엇입니까?

syn Could you read the answer to number 7 aloud [out loud]?
What do you have for number 7?

어휘 number 7=question number 7, question 7

cf. What's Mrs. Kim doing in picture 2?
(두 번째 그림에서 김 여사는 무엇을 하고 있습니까?)

⑰ S: Will these do? *(casual)*

해설   이러면 되겠습니까? [맞습니까?]
: 선생님이 지시한 문제를 풀이한 뒤에 맞는지 확인할 때 흔히 사용한다.

syn   Are these alright? *(informal)*
Will these suffice?

어휘   'Alright' 대신 'right', 'correct', 'acceptable', 'fine', 'doable'을 쓸 수 있다.

⑱ S: Why was what I wrote wrong?

해설   내가 쓴 것이 왜 틀렸습니까?
: 틀린 이유를 물을 때 흔히 사용하는 표현이다.

syn   Why did you mark this wrong? *(informal)*
What's wrong with this? *(casual)*
Where did I go wrong?
How did I mess up? *(slang)*

cf. Why did you put a line under this word? *(informal)*
(이 단어 아래에 왜 밑줄을 그었습니까?)

⑲ Is there **an error** in sentence 5?

해설   5번 문장에 틀린 곳이 있습니까?

syn   Isn't there a mistake [a problem] in sentence 5? *(informal)*

Is there anything to correct in sentence 5?

Are there any mistakes in sentence 5?

Can you check sentence 5 for me?

Is sentence 5 OK?

cf. 오류에 대한 지적

Shouldn't the verb be in the past tense?

(동사가 과거형이어야 하지 않습니까?)

I think you've made a mistake on the blackboard.

(칠판에 쓰인 것이 틀립니다.)

I'm afraid you made several mistakes in this exercise. You'd better do it again.

(연습문제가 여러 곳 틀립니다. 다시 해 오세요.)

---

⑳ **What's the difference between A and B? *(formal)***

해설   A와 B의 차이는 무엇입니까?

syn   How do A and B differ?

How are A and B different?

cf. Is A the same as B? (A와 B가 같습니까?)

㉑ **S: Would [Could] you explain it again, please?**

해설   다시 한 번 설명해 주시겠습니까?

주의   'Explain'은 타동사이므로 목적어 'it'을 생략하지 말 것.

cf. 설명을 되풀이하기를 요구할 때 사용하는 표현

When you said... did you mean that we should...? *(very formal, very polite)*

(…한 말씀은 우리가 …해야 한다는 뜻입니까?)

Can you explain what you said about....?

(…에 대해 하신 말씀을 설명해 주시겠습니까?)

Would you mind explaining the sentence beginning....?

(…로 시작되는 문장을 설명해 주시겠습니까?)

㉒ **S: What shall we do when we've finished?**

해설　마친 다음에는 무엇을 할까요?

syn　What's next?

What's up next?

What are we going to do next?

What do we (have to) do next? *(casual)*

Where do we go from here?

㉓ **S: I didn't write that down. Would [Could] you say it again?**

해설　받아 적지 못했습니다. 다시 한 번 말씀해 주시겠습니까?

어휘　write down(적다, 받아쓰다)=get down, note, take down, jot down

cf. 받아쓰기와 관련된 표현

Could you repeat the instructions, please? (지시문을 반복해 주십시오.)

Could you repeat the last bit? (마지막 부분을 되풀이해 주시겠습니까?)

Would [Could] you write it up on the blackboard, please?

(칠판에 적어 주시겠습니까?)

B. 지시와 지명

① This is difficult [a difficult problem].
Who'd like to try (it)?

해설   이것은 어려운 문제입니까? (설명 또는 풀이)해 볼 사람?
: 위의 표현은 문제뿐만 아니라 여러 가지 상황에서 널리 사용되는 표현이다.

syn   Who wants to volunteer?
Who'd like to volunteer?
Who'd like to answer (it)?
Who'd like to try to answer (it)?
Who'd like to answer this question?

Who'd like to give it a shot? *(usual, informal)*
(여기에서 'shot'은 'attempt'의 의미를 가지며, 도전을 자극하는 의미로 널리 사용된다.)

② **Raise your hand if you know the answer.**
If nobody voluteezrs [is willing], then I'll have to choose somebody.

해설   답을 아는 사람은 손을 드세요. 아무도 말하지 않으면 지명하겠습니다.
: 교실에서 '손을 올리다 [들다].'는 'raise'를 주로 사용한다.

Would you raise your hand before you answer?

Let's see some hands if you know the answer.

Hands in the air if you know the answer.

Those of you who know the answer, raise your hand [put your hand up].

Raise your hand first.

Up with your hand. *(casual)*

Hands up *(before you answer)*.

ant   Put your hands down. *(casual)*

Hands down.

Lower your hands.

어법   강도가 '손들어'라고 할 경우에는 '(Put your) Hands up.'이라고 표현하며, 경관들이 고속도로에서 '손들어'라고 할 경우에도 간단히 'Hands up.'이라고 한다.

— '손을 드세요'는 'Raise your hand'로 단수 'hand'를, '손을 내리세요'는 'Put your hands down'으로 복수 'hands'를 주로 사용한다.

cf. I don't see any volunteers. (지원자가 없습니까?)

Now this time, don't raise your hand. I'll point [I'll pick someone].

(자 이번에는 손을 들지 마세요. 제가 지명하겠습니다.)

I see [keep seeing] the same hands all the time.

(항상 같은 사람들만 손을 듭니다.)

③ Please don't talk while I'm writing (on the blackboard).

해설   (칠판에) 쓰는 동안 말하지 마세요.

syn   There'll be no talking while I write. *(formal)*

Please be quiet while I'm writing.

Would you please be quiet when I'm writing. *(polite)*

No talking while I write.

You'd better not talk while I'm writing. *(impolite, warning)*

Keep quiet while I write. *(impolite, warning)*

---

④ Don't write while I'm talking, please.

해설   설명하는 동안 필기하지 마세요.

syn   You must not write while I'm speaking.

While I'm talking please lay down your pencils. *(formal)*

Please put your pencils down when I'm speaking.

No writing while I'm talking.

It's better if you don't write while I'm talking.

cf. Don't write it down until I tell you to.

(지시가 있을 때까지 필기하지 마세요.)

= Don't write until I tell you to.

I'll tell you when to write.

You may [can] start writing when I give the signal.

Don't start until I say so. *(implied)*

---

⑤ Sunhi, to the front, please. *(informal)*

해설   순희야, 앞으로 나오너라.

syn   Sunhi, would you come up to the front?

Sunhi, come up [come out] to the front of the class.

Sunhi, come up and join me at the front of the class.

> **cf. 교실 앞으로 나오라고 할 때 사용하는 표현**
>
> Come up and write it on the board. (나와서 그것을 칠판에 쓰세요.)
>
> Sun-hi, come up front [here] and face the class.
>
> (앞으로 나와서 학생들을 보세요.)

⑥ Go back to your seat(s) please.

해설   자리로 돌아가세요.

syn   Back to your place(s). *(casual)*

Take your seats (please).

Return to your seats.

Please be seated, once again.

> **cf. 'Back'과 연관된 표현**
>
> Go and sit at the back of the class. (교실 뒷좌석에 앉아라.)
>
> Go out and we will call you back in.
>
> (교실 밖으로 나가라. 다시 부를 것이다.)

⑦ Everybody should be working alone [on his own].

해설   각자 혼자서 풀어야 합니다.

: 동료와 상의하는 것을 금지할 때 사용한다.

syn   Everybody work alone [on his own, by himself].

Please work by yourself on this one.

누구나 영어로 가르칠 수 있다

Everybody work individually on this one.

Do your own work please.

Please work on your own.

---

⑧ Are there any mistakes in the sentences on the board?

해설　칠판 위에 적힌 문장에서 틀린 데가 있습니까?
　　　:'틀린 곳을 알다'는 'see [notice, find, identify] errors [problems, mistakes, anything wrong]' 등으로 표현한다.

syn　Do you notice anything wrong with what's witten on the board?
　　　Can you see anything wrong with the sentences on the board?
　　　Are there any problems with the sentences on the board?
　　　Do you see any mistakes in the sentences on the board?
　　　Can anyone find any mistakes in the sentences on the board?
　　　Can you identify any errors in the sentences on the board?
　　　Are the sentences on the board correct?
　　　Do these sentences look OK? *(informal)*

cf. Read the sentences on the blackboard out loud.
　　(칠판에 적힌 문장을 큰 소리로 읽으세요.)

C. 판서

---

① Everyone look at the board, please.

해설　칠판을 보세요.

syn   Focus on (what is written on) the board.
Would you all please look at the board?
Turn your attention to the notes on the board.
Take a look at the board.
Let's look at the sentences [words] on the board.
Pay attention to what I've written on the board.

---

② Please write this down.

해설   이것을 적으세요.

syn   I would like you to write this down.
Take this down.
Please take notes.
Jot this down. *(casual)*

---

③ T: Can you all see? Sit (somewhere) where you can see.
  S: Move to one side so that we can all see what you've written.

해설   T: 모두 보입니까? 잘 보이는 곳에 앉으세요.
       S: 필기한 것을 볼 수 있도록 옆으로 비켜주세요.

syn   T: Can everyone see this [the board]?
Does everyone have a view of the board? *(rare)*
Does everyone have an unobstructed view? *(formal, rare)*

S: Please move out of the way so that everyone can see what you've written.
Now move away so everyone can see. *(informal)*

Move so we can see. *(casual)*

Step aside so that the class can see what you've written.

Get out of the way, so everyone can see. *(very impolite)*

---

④ T: Would you (please) erase the blackboard?
   S: Yes, I will.

해설   T: 칠판을 지워라.
       S: 예.
       : '(칠판을) 지우다'는 'erase'를 주로 사용하며, 간혹 'clean (off)'
       또는 'clear (off)'라고도 한다.

syn   T: Erase everything, please.
          Erase the board, will you?
          Erase it all, please.

          Can you please clear (off) the board? *(rare)*
          Please clean (off) the blackboard. *(rare, B.E.)*
          Clean everything off, please. Thanks. *(B.E.)*

어휘   '칠판을 지우다'라는 의미로, 미국식 영어에서는 일반적으로
        'erase'를 많이 사용하지만 영국식 영어에서는 'clean (off)', 'rub
        off', 'wipe off'를 쓰기도 한다. 'clean off'(깨끗이 청소하다)와
        'clear off'(깨끗이 치우다)는 구별해서 사용되기도 한다.

---

⑤ T: Would you erase the top left-hand corner?
   S: Yes, of course.

해설   T: 왼편 위쪽을 지워 주세요.

S: 예.

syn   Would you erase the words in the top left-hand corner?
Please erase the words on the top left.
Just get rid of the words in the top-left corner.

어휘   the top left-hand corner(왼편 위쪽)=the words on the left at the
top the bottom
right-hand corner(오른편 아래쪽)=the words on the right at the
bottom.
the bottom [upper] half of the board (아래쪽 [위쪽] 반)

cf. 칠판 지우기와 연관된 표현

Just erase the left, if you would.
(왼쪽을 지워 주세요.)
I'd really appreciate it if you would erase the list of vocabulary words.
(어휘부분을 지워 주세요.)
Erase everything except the top right-hand corner.

(오른쪽 위쪽을 제외하고 모두 지우세요.)
= Erase everything excluding the top-right corner.

---

⑥ T: Would you mind clearing some space on the board?
S: Certainly, Mr Kim. This part [space] here?
T: Just erase this half. Not that half. Thank you.

해설   T: 칠판을 좀 지워 주겠어요?
S: 예, 김 선생님. 이쪽을 지울까요?
T: 아니 이쪽. 그쪽 말고. 고마워.

syn   S: Do you mean here? *(casual)*
Here?
Here, do you mean? *(rare)*
This part [bit, section, area, portion, section] right here?
T: Leave that half [part]. Thanks. *(casual)*
Don't touch that half of the board.

---

⑦ Would you mind getting some chalk from the office?

해설   사무실에서 분필을 가져오세요.
: '분필을 가져오다'는 'get [fetch, bring, grab] some chalk'로 표현
한다.

syn   Please go to the office and get some chalk.
Please fetch me some chalk from the office for me. *(rare)*
Please go to the office for some chalk.
Go and bring some chalk from the office. *(casual)*
Could you grab some chalk from the office for me? *(normal)*

분필(chalk)과 관련된 표현들

Please go next door and ask for some chalk.

(옆 교실에 가서 분필 좀 가져오너라.)

= (Go and) See if there's any chalk next door.

Would you go get some chalk from the supply closet?

(비품창고에서 분필 좀 가져오너라.)

= Would you go see if you can get some chalk from the supply closet?

Does anyone know where the colored chalk is kept?

(색분필이 있는 곳을 아는 사람?)

= Has anybody seen the colored chalk?

Who knows where the colored chalk is?

◆ 질문의 기능과 수정 방법

질문의 기능과 효과를 살펴보고, 다음으로 질문의 수정 방법에 대해 살펴보기로 한다. 어떤 발화가 의문문의 형태를 가지고 청자로부터 반응 또는 언어적 행위를 기대할 경우 대개 '질문(question)'이라고 규정한다. 질문은 IRF/E(Initiation-Response- Follow-up / Evaluation)로 구성된 3단계 전형적인 교과활동에서 최초 발의의 역할을 하며, 교사의 질문은 대상언어의 생성과 학습내용에 대한 학생의 정확하고 의미있는 응답을 용이하게 한다(Chaudron 1983).
Banbrook & Skehan(1989), Richard & Lockhart(1996), Banbrook & Skehan(1989), Steve(2006) 등의 연구를 종합하면, EFL/ESL 수업에서 질문이 지닌 기능과 효과는 다음과 같이 정리할 수 있다:

1 **교사의 질문은 학습자가 담화에 직접적으로 참여하게 한다.**
   e.g. Minhi, what was your first impression on the opera?
   (민희야, 그 오페라에 대한 너의 첫인상이 어땠니?)

2 **교사의 질문은 학습자의 흥미를 자극하고 유지한다.**
   e.g. Who can tell me why we make homepages and how they are used?
   (우리가 왜 홈페이지를 만들고 그것이 어떻게 사용되는지 말해 볼 사람?)

3 **교사의 질문은 학습자가 학습내용을 생각하고 집중하도록 돕는다.**
   e.g. Many of us still do not fully understand the differences among various cultures. Who will start out by explaining why we have to be careful towards other people from different parts of the world?
   (우리 중 다수는 아직도 다양한 문화 간의 차이를 충분히 이해하지 못한다. 다른 지역에서 온 타인에 대해 왜 우리가 주의해야 되는지 설명을 시작해 볼 사람?)

4 **질문을 통하여 교사는 학습자의 표현을 명확히 하고 수정할 기회를 준다.**
   e.g. S: What mean 'irrigate?' ('관개하다'가 무슨 뜻입니까?)

T: Say it once again. (한번 더 말해 보세요.)

S: What mean 'irrigate?' ('관개하다'가 무슨 뜻입니까?)

T: No. What does 'irrigate' mean? Or What's the meaning of the word, 'irrigate?'

(아니. 'What does 'irrigate' mean?' 또는 'What's the meaning of the word, 'irrigate?')

5 질문을 통하여 교사는 학습자에게 요구되는 특정 문장구조나 어휘를 이끌어 낼 수 있다.

e.g. T: Minsu, make a sentence with 'if.'

Minsu: If you are unmarried, you'll save much money.

T: If you remain single, you'll save a lot of money.

6 질문을 통하여 교사는 학습자의 이해 정도를 확인할 수 있다.

e.g. T: 'Bully' is someone who threatens. What does it mean to threaten? ('부랑아'는 위협하는 사람이다. '위협하다'는 무슨 뜻입니까?)

Ss: Too aggressive. (지나치게 공격적인.)

7 질문은 학습자가 교과 또는 담화활동에 참여하도록 자극한다.

e.g. T: Kilsu, what did you do last weekend? (길수, 지난주 무엇을 하였니?)

S: I went yachting. (요트 탔어요.)

T: Who else went yachting? (그 밖에 요트 탄 사람?)

8 질문을 통해 학습자의 대답의 오류를 수정할 수 있다.

e.g. T: What did you do, Sumi? (수미야, 너는 뭘 했니?)

Sumi: I play canoeing. (카누 타고 놀아요.)

T: We don't say 'play canoeing.' We went canoeing. Repeat. We went canoeing.

('카누 타고 놀다'라고 하지 않습니다. '우리는 카누를 탔다.' 따라하세요. 우리는 카누를 탔다.)

요약하면, 질문의 용도는 매우 다양하며 학습자가 교과활동에 참여하고, 학습자의 발화를 수정할 기회를 제공하며, 학습하는 언어를 훨씬 쉽고 실용적으로 사용할 수 있게 해주는 역할을 한다.

다음으로 질문의 수정 방법을 살펴보기로 한다.
교육 목표를 달성하기 위해서 교사는 교과 활동 중에 질문을 수시로 수정해야 한다. 이 경우 질문을 적절히 수정하기 위해서는 교사는 질문의 수정 방법을 알고, 다음으로 어떤 종류의 수정 방법이 적절한 지를 결정해야 한다. 여기에서는 질문의 수정 이론에서 가장 널리 알려진 세 가지 유형의 수정 방법을 검토해 본다.(Chaudron 1988, Richard & Lockhart 1996, Ellis 2008).
첫째, 단서(clue)를 제공하여 질문에 대한 응답의 범위를 축소(narrowing)함으로써 학습자가 쉽게 응답하게 하는 전략이다. 교사는 자신의 질문의 의도를 분명히 하기 위해 먼저 질문에 대한 단서를 제공하여 학습자의 응답을 용이하게 한다. 다음 예문을 보자.

> T: Who knows deskex?... If you want to move this desk, call it deskex. Then what would I say if I want to move this chart?
> ('책상실습'을 아는 사람?... 여러분이 이 책상을 움직이고 싶으면 '책상실습'이라고 합니다. 그러면 이 차트를 움직이고 싶으면 무엇이라고 하지요?)
> S: Chartex. (차트실습.)

위의 대화에서 교사는 필요한 단어를 가르치기 위해, 먼저 'deskex'에 대한 예를 들었다. 그런 다음 교사는 이를 통해 학습해야 할 단어에 대한 질문을 하였다. 이 결과 주어진 단서를 이용해서 학습자는 어려움 없이 질문에 대한 답을 할 수 있었다.
둘째, 질문을 반복하거나 환언(rephrasing)하는 것이다. 교사들은 학습자의 응답을 용이하게 하기 위해서 자신들의 최초의 질문을 선택형 질문(alternative question) 또는 택일형 질문('or-choice' question)으로 환언할 수 있다.

> T: What would you like to drink? ...(pause) Would you like coffee, tea or beer?
> (무엇을 마시고 싶니? ...(멈춤) 커피, 차, 또는 맥주를 마시고 싶니?)

Long(1981)은 원어민 간의 담화보다 원어민과 외국인과의 담화에서 택일형 질문이 두 배 정도 많이 발생하는 것을 발견하였다. White & Lightbown(1984)도 교사는 질문을 반복하거나 환언함으로써 질문을 지속할 수 있다는 점을 지적하였다. 한편 Ellis(2008)는 외국어학습에서 학습자가 초급수준일 때는 교사들은 흔히 같은 질문을 반복한다고 주장하였다. 또한 환언된 질문은 학습자의 참여와 주제에 대한 응답을 용이하게 하는 효과가 있다.

> T: *Do you know what this is?* (이것이 무엇인지 아니?)
> Ss: No, sir. (모릅니다, 선생님.)
> T: *What does it look like?* (무엇과 닮았니?)
> Ss: It looks like a P3C. (P3C기와 비슷합니다.)
> T: Are you sure? Look again. (정말. 다시 한 번 봐.)

위의 담화에서, 교사의 첫 번째 질문에는 학습자의 유의미한 대답이나 참여를 이끌어 낼 수 없었다. 그러나 질문을 환언함으로써 주제에 대한 학습자의 응답을 유발하고, 이를 통해 교사는 학습자의 지식수준을 알아내고, 주제에 연관된 토의를 자연스럽게 이끌어 갈 수 있었다.

셋째, 교사는 학습자의 응답을 얻기 위해서 질문을 단순화(simplification)할 수 있다. Richard & Lockhart(1996)는 언어를 사용하여 질문을 단순화하는 네 가지 방법을 예를 들어 설명하였다:

1) 어휘를 단순화하는 것이다: 예를 들면, 어려운 어휘를 일상적인 어휘로 대체한다:"What do you think this picture depicts?(이 그림이 무엇을 묘사한다고 생각하니?)" 대신 "What do you think this picture shows?(이 그림은 무엇을 보여준다고 생각하니?)"로 단순화하는 것이다. 그러나 단순화하기 위해서 학습자가 익숙하지 않은 관용이나 복잡한 표현을 사용해서는 안 된다: 이를테면 "Do you understand the word?(그 단어를 이해하니?)" 대신 "Are you comfortable with the word?(그 단어에 익숙하니?)"와 같은 관용구나 복잡한 표현을 사용하지 않아야 한다. 왜냐하면 외국인에게는 'are comfortable with(익숙하다)'가 'understand(이해하다)'보다 오히려 명료하지 않은 것이다.

2) 문장구조를 단순화하는 것이다. 교사들은 흔히 문장의 문법적인 구조를 단순화한다. 교사는 교실 밖에서보다 교실 안에서는 종속절을 훨씬 적게 사용하며, 복잡한 시

제를 피하는 경향이 있다.

3) 최초의 질문을 구체화함으로써 단순화시킬 수 있다. Chaudron(1988)도 원어민 교사는 외국어 학습자가 쉽게 이해하고 대답할 수 있도록 처음부터 질문을 수정하거나, 또는 학습자의 반응에 따라서 자신의 질문을 수정한다고 주장하였다. 다음 대화를 보자.

> T: What will change in the future, Myungghi? (명기야, 미래는 무엇이 변할까?)
>
> Myungghi: Lifestyle will be changed. (생활양식이 변할 것입니다.)
>
> T: Lifestyle? And? Keep going, Myungghi. (생활양식? 그리고? 계속 말해봐, 명기.)
>
> Myungghi: (no answer) …. (대답없음.)
>
> T: What will happen to you in 50 years? (50년 후에 너에게 무슨 일이 일어날까?)
>
> Myungghi: My hair will be white. (머리가 희게 될 것입니다.)

위의 담화에서 교사는 자신의 두 번째 질문에 대한 담화가 연결되지 못하자, 명기 개인에 대한 질문으로 수정했으며, 그 결과 명기는 자신의 생각을 보다 쉽게 표현할 수 있었다.

4) 다음으로 예를 들어 단순화시키는 경우를 보자.

> T: When speaking in English, there are certain ways to show politeness?
>
> (영어로 말할 때는 공손을 표시하는 어떤 방법이 있지요?)
>
> S: Could you say that specifically?
>
> (자세히 말해 줄 수 있습니까?)
>
> T: Okay. Instead of saying "Give me the salt", you could ask "Would you pass me the salt?" to be polite. *Let's think about expressions that show politeness.*
>
> (그래. "소금 주세요"라고 하지 않고, 공손히 "소금 건네 주시겠습니까?"라고 묻습니다. 공손을 표시하는 표현에 대해 생각해 봅시다.)

S: How about saying "I really appreciate you're doing this for me?"
("나를 위해 이 일을 해 주신 것을 진심으로 감사드립니다"는 어떻습니까?)

T: Yes, it's more of a polite answer. Can you think of anything else?
(그래, 그것이 보다 공손한 대답이다. 그 밖에 다른 예는?)

위의 대화에서 교사는 자신의 첫 번째 질문 내용에 대해 구체적인 예를 들어 설명한 뒤에, 첫 번째 질문보다 단순하고 보다 구체적인 수정된 질문을 학생에게 하였다.

요약하면, 질문을 수정하기 위해서는 내용을 축소 또는 쉽게 하기 위한 단서를 제공하거나, 질문을 환언 또는 반복하거나, 어휘·문법·담화내용을 단순화 또는 구체화하는 세 가지 방법을 사용할 수 있는 것이다.

1. 현장예문 (Real-life Situation)

Question and Answer With Mr. Best's Ladder

(adapted from A.W. Hornsey(1971))

간단한 문장을 이용하여 필요한 어휘 및 구문을 학습할 수 있다. 이 경우 선생님은 먼저 필요한 문장을 학생들이 충분히 익히게 한 다음에, 다양한 질문을 통해 활용하도록 해야 한다. 다음 예문을 통해 구체적으로 살펴보자. Best 씨가 밤늦게 친구들과 어울려 놀다가 집에 와보니 문이 잠겨 있다. 다행히 창고에 사다리가 있어 이것을 이용하여 창문을 통해 집안에 들어가려고 한다. 이 경우 'Best 씨는 창고에서 사다리를 가져 왔다.'는 다음과 같이 표현할 수 있다.

Many teachers dedicate some time to listen and repeat drill sessions in order to ensure that their students have a grasp of English pronunciation and have a chance to listen to the voice of a native speaker. This unit focuses on how to take students through listen and repeat exercises, particularly how to set them up and initiate the exercises. Also, it looks at setting up role play activities. More specifically, it provides language on setting up small groups, assigning roles to students, and pairing students up with each other.

Now listen to the dialogue.

Mr Best got a ladder from the shed.

이제 위의 구문을 이용하여 여러 가지 필요한 문형 — 'to get something

from somewhere', 'to get something', 'preposition' 등 — 의 활용 및 표현 방법을 익히게 할 수 있다.

T: What did Mr. Best get [take] from the shed?

S1: A ladder.

T: What was it Mr. Best got from the shed? (asked to another pupil.)

S2: A ladder.

(Two forms of the same question but the form of the second allows the teacher to let his pupils hear the form 'got.')

T: Where was the ladder? In the shed or next to it?

S3: In it.

T: Where did Mr. Best get the ladder from?

S4: The shed.

T: Where did he get the ladder?

S5: From the shed.

(If the class is slow, then alternatives could have been used more extensively: Did he get the ladder from the shed or from the bedroom? or the preposition could have been furthur stressed by asking where Mr. Best went to get the ladder.)

T: Who got a ladder from the shed?

S6: Mr. Best.

(This last question gives 'got' again and also allows the students to say 'Best' and the teacher to ensure that it is pronounced correctly. The ground is now prepared and the teacher can proceed to more demanding questions, requiring full-sentence answers.)

T: What did Mr. Best do?

S6: He got a ladder from the shed.

T: What happened?

S7: Mr. Best got a ladder from the shed.

경우에 따라 'ladder' 대신 'spade', 'potato-peeler', 'tin-opener', 'lighter' 등이 포함된 단문을 이용하여 다양한 질문과 연습을 할 수도 있다.

해석

선생님: 베스트 씨는 창고에서 무엇을 가져왔습니까?
학생1: 사다리.
선생님: (또 다른 학생에게 질문한다) 베스트 씨가 창고에서 가져온 것은 무엇입니까?
학생2: 사다리.
(같은 질문을 두 가지 형태로 하였는데, 두 번째 형태는 선생님이 학생들이 과거형 'got'을 듣도록 해 준다.)
선생님: 사다리는 어디에 있습니까? 창고 안에 또는 옆에?
학생3: 창고 안에.
선생님: 베스트 씨는 어디에서 사다리를 가져왔습니까?
학생4: 창고.
선생님: 그는 사다리를 어디서 구했습니까?
학생: 창고에서?
(학생들의 반응이 느리면, 다음과 같이 다른 형태의 질문도 널리 사용된다: 그는 사다리를 창고에서 또는 침실에서 가져왔습니까? 또는 베스트 씨가 사다리를 가지러 어디에 갔는가를 물음으로써 전치사에 강세를 둘 수도 있다.)
선생님: 누가 창고에서 사다리를 가져왔습니까?
학생6: 베스트 씨.
(마지막 질문에는 'got'을 다시 사용하고, 학생들이 Best라고 말함으로써 올바르게 발음되고 있는 것을 확인할 수 있다. 이제 충분히 준비가 되었으므로 보다 어려운 질문, 즉 문장으로 답을 해야 하는 단계로 넘어갈 수 있다.)
선생님: 베스트 씨는 무엇을 했습니까?
학생6: 그는 창고에서 사다리를 가져왔습니다.
선생님: 무슨 일이 일어났습니까?
학생7: 베스트 씨가 창고에서 사다리를 가져왔습니다.

2. 기본구문

여기에서는 수업 중에 선생님이 학습한 내용을 반복 연습하거나 활용하기 위해 사용하는 표현들을 다음과 같이 정리하였다: A. 반복 학습과 역할분담 B. 개별 및 단체연습

A. 반복 학습과 역할분담

---

① Again, (please.)

해설　　다시 한 번 되풀이하시오.

syn　　Repeat, (please).
　　　　Would you repeat that, please?
　　　　Would you mind repeating what you said?
　　　　Once more [Once again], please.
　　　　One more time please.
　　　　Would [Could] you say that again?
　　　　Would [Can] you say it again?
　　　　Say it again [once more]. *(casual)*
　　　　Try it one more time.
　　　　Would you mind repeating what you said?

---

② Yes, well done. **Let's all repeat it together.**

해설　　예, 잘했습니다. 이제 다 같이 반복해 봅시다.

syn　　All together now. / In unison.

Let's all say that together.

Everyone! *(informal, implied)*

cf. Again, but faster / quickly [more clearly] this time.

(다시, 이번에는 더 빨리 [더 분명하게])

I'll read first and then you (all) will read [repeat] after me.

(내가 먼저 말하면, 따라하세요.)

---

③ Repeat after me, please.

해설　내 말을 따라하세요.

syn　Say (it) after me.

Listen and repeat (after me).

I want all of you to repeat this sentence.

Now, everybody. Would you listen carefully and repeat after me?

활용　'All of you' 대신 'you all', 'everybody', 'the whole class' 등으로 대체할 수 있다.

cf. 선생님과 학생이 다 함께 읽을 경우

Say it with me. (나와 같이 읽자.)

---

④ Let's do it again. Ready?

해설　다시 한 번 해봅시다. 준비되었습니까?

syn   One more time. Ready?
       Let's try it again. Are you ready?
       Let's give it another shot. *(casual)*
       Let's give it another go. *(casual)*
       Why don't we give it another try?

⑤ Now everybody, listen and repeat aloud.

해설   모두 [전부] 다 함께, 듣고 크게 따라하세요.

syn   The whole class, please. Listen and repeat (it) out loud.
       All together, now. Listen and say it loudly.
       I want you all to join in. Would you listen carefully and repeat out loud?
       Let's all say it together. Listen and repeat aloud.
       Everyone! *(casual, implied)*

⑥ Once again, but more loudly. *(casual)*

해설   다시 한 번, 좀 더 크게 말하세요.

syn   Say it a little [a bit] louder.
       Say it so that everyone can hear you.
       Say it so that we can all hear.
       Say it so you won't have to repeat yourself.
       I can't hear you. Say it again, but this time louder.
       I can't hear you! *(impolite)*

다음과 같이 간단히 표현할 수도 있다.

누구나 영어로 가르칠 수 있다

Louder, please.
Speak up.

주의 'Say'는 타동사이므로, 목적어 'it'를 생략하면 — 즉, '*Say loudly
(aloud).' '*Say louder.' '*Say again.' '*Say so that we all hear.' 등
— 비문법적인 문장이 된다.

어휘 음의 높이를 의미하는 'Speak up'(크게 말하다)과 지지를 의미하
는 'Speak out'(대변하다, - 를 위하여 말하다.)는 구별해야 한다.

cf. **표현 방법과 관련된 문장**

What you said sounded fine, but could you say it louder?
(너의 말이 좋은 것 같은데, 좀 더 크게 말해볼래?)
Yes, a good answer. But a bit louder please. Again?
(예, 좋은 답입니다. 좀 더 크게. 다시?)
You speak too low. You'll have to speak up.
(말이 너무 작습니다. 크게 말하세요.)
Tom spoke out strongly for [against] letting girls join the club.
(탐은 여자들이 그 클럽에 가입하는 것을 강하게 찬성[반대]하였다.

---

⑦ **Not so loud.**

해설 너무 크게 말하지 마시오.

syn Softer.
Pipe down a bit. *(slang)*
There's no need to shout. I'm not deaf. *(impolite)*
Don't shout. *(B.E.)*

⑧ Not so fast, please. I can't keep up with you.

해설   너무 빨리 말하지 마세요. 따라갈 수가 없습니다.

syn   A bit slower please so I can keep up.
       Slow down, please. I can't follow.
       You're speaking too fast. I can't follow. Not so fast, please. I can't follow. *(casual)*
       (이 경우 'fast'(속도가 빠른)가 'quickly'(행동이 민첩한)보다 적절하다.)

⑨ I'm sorry. I didn't catch what you said.

해설   무슨 뜻인지 모르겠습니다. 교과내용을 못 알아들었거나 설명한 것의 의미를 모를 때 흔히 사용된다.

syn   Sorry? What did you say?
       I missed that. What did you say?
       I beg your pardon?
       I beg your pardon. I thought you said...
       Come again. I didn't hear you. *(usual, between friends)*

       (다음 표현은 주로 설명한 것의 의미를 잘 모를 때 사용한다.)
       I didn't get all of what you said.
       I'm not entirely clear on what you said.
       I didn't understand [catch] (what you said).
       I need further clarification.

       I'm sorry I don't know. (incorrect)

누구나 영어로 가르칠 수 있다

(Li'L='Little'의 축약형임)

아빠: 징크스야, 숙제 했니?

징크스: 아직 안 했어요!!

아빠: 숙제를 하는 것은 매우 중요해! 알고 있지, 너의 세대는 자라서…. 세상을 책임 지고, 오늘날의 무질서를 바로잡아야 한다. 자, 내 말 알아듣겠니?

징크스: 예! … 아빠 세대는 숙제를 하지 않았다는 것을!

주의 I'm sorry I don't know. ((답을) 모르겠습니다.)

=I have no idea.

=I don't know the answer.

: 이 표현은 상대방의 질문에 대한' 답을 모른다.'는 의미이다.

'무슨 말인지 모르겠습니다.'라는 의미가 아니므로 유의해야 한다.

cf. 일상생활에서 상대방의 말을 알아듣지 못했을 때, '다시 한 번 말씀해 주시겠습
니까?'라는 의미로는 다음과 같은 표현도 흔히 사용된다.

Run that by me again?

Could you run that by me again?

Come again?

I'm afraid I didn't hear you.

(I'm) Sorry?

Pardon?

Excuse me?

What? *(casual)*

Huh? *(casual)*

어법 'Sorry'는 'Say it again?'[Sorry?]의 의미로 사용될 때에는 끝이 올
라가며 (rising intonation), 'I am sorry.'[Sorry.]의 의미로 사용될
경우에는 끝이 내려간다 (falling intonation).

cf. 학생들이 설명이나 지시를 이해하지 못했을 때 흔히 사용하는 표현

I don't understand what I'm supposed to do.

(무엇을 해야 할지 모르겠습니다.)

I missed the beginning of what you said.

(설명의 앞부분을 못 들었습니다.)

⑩ I can't [couldn't] hear what you are saying [said] because of
the noise.

해설   소음 때문에 말을 알아들을 수 없습니다.

syn   I can't hear you above [over] the noise.
        I'm sorry, the noise is drowning you out.
        I can't hear what you are saying for the noise. *(B.E.)*

어법   위의 예문과 같이 주절과 종속절이 연결된 행위는 일반적으로 주
        절과 종속절의 시제를 일치시킨다.
        *I can't hear what you said because of the noise. *(incorrect)*
        *I can't hear what you have said for the noise. *(incorrect)*

---

⑪ S: Slow down, please! *(casual)*

해설   천천히 말씀해 주십시오.

syn   Could you please slow down?
        Would you please speak more slowly? *(formal)*

    cf. You're speaking too fast for me. (너무 빨리 말해서 모르겠습니다.)
       = You're speaking way too fast. *(slang)*
        You're speaking too quickly.

---

⑫ Now, I am A and **you are B.** Listen to what A says [I say] and
reply using one of the cues.

해설   나는 A이고 너는 B이다. A가 하는 말을 잘 듣고, 주어진 단서 중
        의 하나를 사용하여 대답하시오.

syn   You take B's part.

You take the part of B.

⑬ Now let's act out this dialogue.

해설   이 대화를 실제로 행동으로 표현해 봅시다.

syn   Now we will act out this dialogue.
         Now let's perform this role play.

어휘   act out(실연하다)=put into action, perform

cf. 역할분담과 관련된 표현
Now, in pairs [in twos], prepare a short story about that picture.
(이제 짝을 지어, 이 그림에 대한 짧은 이야기를 준비하세요.)
Let's watch Min-su and Sun-hi acting out the conversation. The rest of you are the audience. Will the actors and actresses come out to the front?
(민수와 순희가 이 대화를 연기하는 것을 봅시다. 나머지는 관중입니다. 남녀배우들은 앞으로 나오세요.)
I want you to make up a conversation working in twos, taking parts.
(두 명씩 짝을 지워 대화를 만들고, 역할을 맡으세요.)

make up(만들어내다, 짜맞추다) = think up, invent, plan, come up with, develop, put together, construct

⑭ Now you are a bus driver. *(casual)*

해설   이제 네가 버스기사의 역할을 하여라.

            누구나 영어로 가르칠 수 있다

Imagine [pretend] (that) you are a bus driver.

Act as though you are a bus driver.

Act as if you were a bus driver.

Try to act like a bus driver. *(rare)*

cf. 상황연기(role play) 지시

So what kind of things might they say in a job interview?

(입사인터뷰에서는 어떤 말을 할까요?)

Act as an interviewer and ask members of the class if they want to work.

(기자로서 학생 개개인에게 일자리를 원하는지 물어 보세요.)

Now ask for and give opinions on the following topics.

(다음 화제에 대해 묻고, 의견을 제시하세요.)

Imagine [Pretend] (that) you're calling your friend.

(네가 친구에게 전화를 건다고 가정하자.)

---

⑮ Sun-hi, play the part of the clerk.

해설   순희야, 너는 점원 역할을 하여라.

syn   Sun-hi, play the clerk's part.

Sun-hi, you be the clerk.

(위의 문장에서 'be'는 일종의 가정법으로 사용된 것이다.)

참고   하이픈(hyphen)의 생략

복합어의 하이픈(-)을 생략하는 것은 일반적인 현상이다. 날짜를 나타내는 'to-day', 'to-morrow', 'to-night'도 과거에는 하이픈이 있었지만, 오늘날에는 간단히 'today', 'tomorrow', 'tonight'으로 표기하고 있다.

⑯ We're going to use cue cards. Each card tells you which role you must play.

해설 역할카드를 사용하겠습니다. 각 카드는 여러분이 할 역할을 나타 내고 있습니다.

syn We're going to use role play cards. On your card it says what you have to do.

B. 개별 및 단체연습

① T: Who's next? *(casual)*
   S: Is it my turn?

해설 T: 다음 차례는 누구입니까?
     S: 제 차례입니까?

syn T: Who's turn is it next?
       Who is the next one to try?
       Who hasn't had a turn?
       Who hasn't gone yet?
       Whose turn is it to answer a question?
       Who hasn't answered a question yet?
       Is there anyone who hasn't answered a question yet?
       Who else is there?
       Who's left?

     S: Am I next?

누구나 영어로 가르칠 수 있다

Am I up next?

Is it my turn?

Shall I start?

cf. Have you all had a turn? (모두 다 한 번씩 했습니까?)

  = Have you all gone?

IN A BARBERSHOP

② Your turn, (Minsu). *(casual)*

해설   (민수야,) 너의 차례다.

syn   Now, it's your turn.
You're next, Minsu.
Aren't you next?
Aren't you up next?
Now you, [Minsu.] *(casual)*
You're up next.

You're on deck.
(야구에서 다음 타순을 가리키는 표현이다.)

cf. 차례와 관련된 표현들
Next one [person, student], please. (다음 사람.)
Come on! Isn't it your turn [go]? (자! 너의 차례이지?)
Next time you can be first. (다음에는 너부터 하여라.)

Are you next? (네가 다음이냐?)
= (Is it) You next?

③ One at a time, starting here [starting with Minsu].

해설   한 번에 한 명씩, 이쪽부터[민수부터] 차례대로 하겠습니다.

syn   One at a time. Start here.
Take turns. Start from here.
In turn.
In order, One after the other. *(rare)*

Take it in turns. *(B.E.)*

cf. One (boy) at a time! The rest of you, wait your turn.
(한 번에 한 명씩, 나머지는 차례를 기다리시오.)
= You can all have a turn, but one by one.

어휘 turn(차례)=go*(B.E.)*

---

④ Wait a second, Minsu. You just answered.
Let someone else have a turn... Yes, Sunhi?

해설 잠깐, 민수. 너는 방금 답을 하였다. 그 밖에 다른 사람이 해봅시
다. … 그래, 순희야 말해 보아라.

syn Now let's have someone else try it.
Now someone other than [besides] Minsu.
Someone please give Minsu a rest.

Not you again, Minsu.
Let's not leave it all to Minsu.

어휘 wait a second=just a minute, hold on a second,
hold your horses *(slang, impolite)*

---

⑤ Let her try it by herself [on her own].

해설 그녀가 스스로 하도록 내버려 두세요.

syn She can probably manage on her own [by herself].

I'm sure she can handle it by herself.

I'm sure she can do it on her own.

I'm sure she can manage on her own.

She can probably get it done on her own.

Don't help her. *(casual, impolite, usual)*

cf. Try it on your own, Minsu. (민수야 너 혼자서 해보아라.)

= Now, on your own, Minsu.

---

⑥ Work on your own. *(casual)*

해설   각자 풀이해 보세요.

syn   Work alone (on this one).

Try to work independently.

Everybody work individually.

Work by yourselves. *(casual)*

참고   **'To oneself'와 'by oneself'의 차이**

① To oneself=silently (소리 내지 않고)

Read the passage to yourselves.

② By oneself=individually, on one's own, alone, without other's help (혼자서)

Solve the problems by yourself.

Everybody work on his own [by himself].

(이 경우 'on his own' 대신 'for his own' 또는 'for himself'로 대체할 수 없다.)

⑦ Don't disturb [bother] your neighbor.

해설   옆 사람을 방해하지 마세요.

syn   Don't interrupt your neighbor's work.

   cf. 옆 사람에 대한 제반 행위를 금지하는 표현
       There's no need to discuss it with your neighbor.
       (옆 사람과 상의하지 마세요.)
       Don't help your neighbor. (옆 사람을 거들지 마세요.)
       Don't look at [glance at] your neighbor's work.
       (옆 사람이 한 것을 보지 마세요.)
       = No peeking at your neighbor's work.

⑧ Now, you ask Sunhi.

해설   이제, 네가 순희에게 물어라.

syn   Now it's your turn to ask Sunhi.
       Ask Sunhi the (same) question.
       Now, why don't you ask Sunhi?
       You ask Sunhi, this time.

   cf. Ask the boy (sitting) in front of [behind] you.
       (여러분 앞에 있는[뒤에 있는] 남학생에게 물으세요.)
       Then you ask Sunhi, and she asks Minsu and so on around the class.
       (네가 순희에게 묻고, 순희는 민수에게 묻고, 차례로 돌아가면서 물으세요.)
       Don't keep prompting. (재촉하지 마세요.)

⑨ Good. Have you all had a turn now?

해설   모두 한 번씩 했습니까?

syn   Well done. Has everyone had a turn?

어휘   good=well done, alright

> cf. You've already taken [had] your turn. (너는 이미 한 번 하였다.)

⑩ Who hasn't been [come] to the board yet?

해설   아직 앞으로 나오지 않은 사람?

syn   Who hasn't been up to the board?
Who hasn't come up yet?
Who hasn't come to the board?
Who hasn't been to the board? *(rare)*

> cf. You've already been up here. (너는 이미 한 번 나왔다.)
> = You have been up here once already.

⑪ Work in pairs.

해설   2명씩 연습하세요.
: '짝을 지어라'는 'work with', 'in pairs [twos]', 'find someone' 등을 흔히 사용한다.

syn   I want you to work on this in pairs. *(formal)*

I want you in pairs please.

We'll work in pairs.

Work together with a friend.

You need to work with someone.

Work in [Get into] twos. *(casual)*

Pair up. *(casual)*

In twos, with your neighbor.

Find (yourself) a partner.

Find someone to work with.

We'll work in twos, now, so find yourself a partner.

cf. 2명씩 연습과 관련된 지시문

Alright. It's time we did some pair practice.

(자, 이제 짝을 지어 연습하겠습니다.)

Find a partner. Come on, hurry up. We haven't got all day.

(짝을 찾으세요. 서두르세요. 한가하게 꾸물거릴 때가 아닙니다.)

---

⑫ **Oh, you are by yourself, aren't you?**

해설 너는 짝이 없느냐?

syn You don't have a partner, do you?

Don't you have a partner?

You don't have anyone to work with, do you

cf. Are you all by your lonesome? *(rare)*

('너는 혼자니?'라는 의미로 주로 클럽에서 사용하며, 교실에서는 사용하지 않는다.)

⑬ Why don't you join us?

해설   우리와 함께 합시다. [우리 팀에 들어오너라.]

syn   Why don't you join in?
Please join us.
Feel free to join in anytime.
Don't hesitate to join in.
Why don't you take part?
Would you like to partake? *(formal, rare)*

Why aren't you joining us?
Why aren't you participating?
(위의 두 표현은 '함께 하자'는 의미도 있지만 '함께 어울리지 않는 이유가 무엇이냐'는 의미도 있다.)

cf. What about turning around and joining [working with] them?
(뒤로 돌아서, 그들과 함께 하여라.)
= Why don't you turn around and join in with them?

어법   join=work with

⑭ Turn around and face your neighbor.

해설   뒤로 돌아서 상대를 마주 보세요.

syn   Turn and look at your partner.
Face your partner.
Look your partner in the eye.
Make eye contact with your partner.

어휘   미국식 영어에서는 주로 'round' 대신 'around'를 사용함.

      cf. Look at the person in front of [next to, behind] you.
         (여러분의 앞 [옆, 뒤] 사람을 보세요.)

---

⑮ Now then, I want you to do this exercise orally in pairs.

해설   자 그러면, 이 연습문제를 짝을 지어 말로 연습하세요.

syn   Now we'll work in pairs and practise this exercise orally.
        Practice this exercise with your partner.

---

⑯ **In pairs I'd like you to practice this dialogue.**
   When you've finished, trade roles [parts].

해설   짝을 지어 이 대화를 연습하세요. 끝마치면 역할을 바꾸세요.

syn   With your partner practis this dialogue.

어휘   'Trade roles [parts].'는 다음과 같이 여러 가지로 표현할 수 있다.
        Change parts.
        Swap.
        Switch [Trade, Change] places.
        Switch [Trade] roles.
        Then, we'll switch.
        Trade, so that you take the other part. *(usual, redundant)*

      cf. Now 'A', you ask the questions, and 'B', you answer the questions.
         Then, we'll trade [switch] roles.

(자, 너는 A로서 묻고, 너는 B로서 질문에 대답한다. 그런 다음에 역할을 바꾸어
연습하겠습니다.)

> ⑰ You move up and **form groups of three [four, five].**

해설   각자 이동하여 3명[4명, 5명]씩 짝을 지으세요.

syn   Form [Make] a group of 3 [4, 5]. *(casual)*
Work in threes [fours, fives]. *(casual)*
Work in groups of three [four, five].

I'd like you to set up groups of three [four, five].
Set yourselves up in groups of three [four, five].
We're going to work in groups of three [four, five], please.
I'll divide the class into groups of three [four, five].
I want you to form groups. Three [Four, Five] students in each
group.

어휘   'form'(구성하다) 대신 'get into', 'make', 'break up into', 'split up
into'로 대체할 수 있다.

주의   2명은 'pair'를, 3명 이상은 'group'을 사용한다.
Work in [get into] groups of two. *(awkward)*
⇒Work in [get into] pairs. *(usual)*

참고   3명 이상의 경우 그들을 1조라고 한다면 한 단어로 '수사+some'
의 형태를 취한다. 따라서 '3명 1조'라고 할 경우 'three'가 아닌
'threesome'으로 표현할 수 있다. 그러나 오늘날 'threesome'은 미
국에서는 의미가 변질되어 성적인 개념으로도 흔히 사용된다. 따
라서 'a group of four' 또는 'a group of five' 대신 'a foursome', 'a

누구나 영어로 가르칠 수 있다

fivesome'은 가능하나, 'threesome'은 사용을 피하는 것이 좋다.

e.g. T: Will you divide into groups of three and prepare the dialogues using the idioms from today's lesson?
(3명씩 그룹을 지어 오늘 배운 관용어를 이용하여 대화를 만드세요.)

　　　S: Do you want us to write the dialogues first?
(대화를 먼저 적을까요?)

　　　T: Yes, I want you to write the entire text on a sheet of paper and hand it in at the end of class.
(그래요, 대화 전부를 종이에 적어서, 뒤로 넘기세요.)

---

⑱ Get together in groups and discuss your ideas.

해설　그룹을 지어서 여러분의 생각을 토의하세요.

syn　Get together. Discuss your ideas in groups. *(informal)*
Work in groups and discuss your ideas.
Form groups and discuss your ideas.

---

⑲ Now, I'm going to divide the class in half.

해설　교실을 반으로 나누겠습니다.

syn　Now you'll work in 2 teams. *(informal)*
Now, we're going to split [seperate] the class into 2 teams.
I'm going to divide the class [you] down the middle.
Now, I'm going to divide you into 2 teams.
I want you to work in 2 teams.
I'm going to split [break] the class up into 2 teams.

Now, I'm going to divide you in half.

⑳ Now all the boys.

해설   남학생만 전부 하세요.

syn   Boys first.
Just the boys.
Boys only. *(casual)*
Let's begin [start] with the boys.
The boys will [may, can] begin.
The boys will lead off.

   cf. This row will repeat. (이 줄만 따라하세요.)

㉑ I want this half of the class to answer this question.

해설   이쪽 반이 질문에 대답하시오.

syn   I'd like this half of the class to answer this question.
Let's use this part of the class to answer this question.
Let's use the first [second] half of class to answer the question.

문법   'Answer'는 타동사로 쓰이므로 뒤에 'to'를 붙일 수 없다.

활용   상황에 따라 'this half of the class' 대신 'this row'(이 줄), 'these two rows'(이 두 줄), 'the back row on their own'(뒷줄만), 'just the front row'(앞줄만) 등의 표현으로 대체한다.

㉒ Now we'll **do** some groupwork, and this is how I want you to do it. You **will work** in pairs with one person asking the questions and the other answering. After that, you **will change places** [change up].

해설　자, 그룹활동을 하겠습니다. 이런 방식으로 하겠습니다. 짝을 지어서 한 사람이 묻고, 다른 사람이 답하겠습니다. 그런 다음에 역할을 바꾸겠습니다: change[switch] places [roles, parts]=change up. 이 경우 'change up' 대신 'change over'는 미국영어에서 사용하지 않는다.

어법　**시제의 일치**: 동일 시점에서는 동일 시제를 사용하고, 조동사도 가능한 같은 종류의 조동사를 사용하는 것이 오늘날의 미국식 영어에 가깝다. 위의 예문은 미국식 영어로 전부 미래시제를 사용하고 있다. 아래의 영국식 영어에서는 상황에 따라 미래, 현재, 조동사가 혼용되고 있음을 알 수 있다.

Now we'll do some groupwork, and this is how I want you to do it. You work in pairs with one person asking the questions and the other answering. After that, you can change places. *(B.E.)*

cf. 팀을 나눌 때 사용하는 지시문

These two rows will [can] be team 1 and these two rows team 2.
(이 두 줄은 1번 팀, 이 두 줄은 2번 팀입니다.)

Now we can have a competition with teams. For this, we're going to have teams, going from front to back.
(이제 팀으로 나누어 시합하겠습니다. 시합을 위해 앞뒤로 팀을 나누겠습니다.)

㉓ You're 1, you're 2 and so on. Count off, down the line. Now, we have 5 teams. 1 2 3 4 5. Each team! Please will you count off? Remember your numbers. We'll keep score. Hands up, all number ones! Ready?

해설 너는 1번, 너는 2번으로, 뒤로 번호를 매겨라. 자, 이제 5팀이다. 1, 2, 3, 4, 5. 각 팀은 번호를 불러보세요. 자기 팀 번호를 기억하세요. 팀별 점수를 내겠습니다. 1번 팀, 모두 손들어 보세요. 준비되었습니까?

어휘 'Count off(번호를 붙이다)'는 간혹 'number off'라고도 한다.

어법 'Score' 앞에 관사를 붙이지 말 것.

cf. 팀별 활동에 대한 지시문

Those of you on the left, you are Jim. You take Jim's part.
(왼쪽 줄에 있는 사람은, 짐입니다. 여러분은 짐의 역할을 합니다.)
Students on this side, you ask the questions. Students on that side you give the answers.
(이 줄의 학생들은 질문을 합니다. 저 줄의 학생들은 답을 합니다.)
In your groups you're going to write a short paragraph about 'Korean people'.
(그룹별로 '한국인'에 대한 짧은 글을 쓰겠습니다.)

누구나 영어로 가르칠 수 있다

◆ 의문문의 구성과 대답 방법

1 Wh - 의문문을 이용한 질문

Wh - 의문문은 의문의 종류에 따라 다양하게 질문을 구성할 수 있다. 예를 들어 다음 문장을 보자.

John opened the door.

위와 같은 대답이 나올 수 있는 질문의 유형은 크게 세 가지로 나눌 수 있다.

(1) 대상 - 'John' 또는 'the door' - 에 초점을 둘 경우
   Who opened the door? 또는 What did John open?
(2) 행위에 초점을 둘 경우
   What did John do?
(3) 사건 자체에 대해 질문할 경우
   What happened?

2 의문문에 대한 대답

1) 'Yes - No'question에 대한 대답
   (1) 'Yes'로 답할 경우 대개 다음 네 가지가 일반적이다.

     e.g. Question : Is Sunhi American?
           Answer   : ① Yes.
                       ② Yes, she is. ('Is' 이하가 생략된 경우 '*Yes, she's.'
                          로 축약하지는 않는다.)
                       ③ Yes, she's American.
                       ④ Yes, Sunhi's American.

   (2) 'No'로 답할 경우에는 훨씬 다양한 표현 방법이 있다.

e.g. Question : Is Sunhi American?
　　Answer 　: ① No.
　　　　　　　② No, she isn't.
　　　　　　　③ No, she's not.
　　　　　　　④ No, she isn't American.
　　　　　　　⑤ No, she's not American.
　　　　　　　⑥ No, Korean.
　　　　　　　⑦ No, she's Korean.
　　　　　　　⑧ No, she isn't American ; she's Korean.
　　　　　　　⑨ No, she's Korean, not American.

(3) 잘 모르거나 질문에 대해 반박할 경우

e.g. Question : Is Sunhi American?
　　Answer 　: ① Perhaps.
　　　　　　　② Well.
　　　　　　　③ I don't know.
　　　　　　　④ Maybe.
　　　　　　　⑤ I can't remember.
　　　　　　　⑥ You must be joking.
　　　　　　　⑦ What do you think she is.?

2) 의문사가 있는 의문문에 대한 대답
  의문사에 대응하는 답을 할 수도 있고, 전혀 별개의 문장으로 답할 수도 있다.
  예를 들어 다음 문장을 보자.

e.g. Where is Mr Kim going?

위의 문장은 다음 두 가지 방법으로 답할 수 있다.
(1) 일반적인 대답
  He is going to London. / To London. / London.

(2) 부정적인 대답

　　He didn't tell me. / How should I know? / Don't you mean
　　Mrs...?

한편 형태상으로도 여러 가지가 있다. 즉, 같은 의미라도 다양한 문형으로 답을
할 수 있는 것이다. 대개 세 가지 형태 - 즉, Wh - 의문사에 대응되는 주어(또는
목적어), 주어+대동사, 또는 문장 전체의 반복 - 로 대답할 수 있다.

e.g.　Question : Who arrived late?
　　　Answer　 : The girls. / The girls did. / The girls arrived late.
　　　　　　　　*The girls arrived. *(incorrect)*
　　　　　　　　*The girls did arrive late. *(incorrect)*
　　　Question : Who wanted the book?
　　　Answer　 : Me. / I did. / I wanted it.
　　　　　　　　*I wanted. *(incorrect)*
　　　　　　　　*I did want. *(incorrect)*
　　　Question : Where are you going?
　　　Answer　 : I'm going to school.
　　　　　　　　To school.
　　　　　　　　School.
　　　　　　　　*Go(ing) to school. *(incorrect)*
(외국인 영어선생님들에 따르면, 우리 학생은 위와 같이 우리말식으로 주어
만 생략하고 답을 하는 경우가 많으므로 유의해야 한다.)

1. 현장예문 (Real-life Situation)

Assigning Reading Homework

수업 후에 선생님이 과제물에 대한 세부적인 지시와 결과처리에 대해 설명하는 상황이다.

It is at the end of each class that teachers spend time introducing students homework. This unit presents the language needed for introducing homework assignments to students. More specifically, the unit looks at such things as giving homework instructions, presenting teachers expectations, assigning homework due dates, and handing out homework to the students. The unit also looks at how to review finished homework in class, comment on the quality of students homework, and elicit homework answers from students.

Now listen to the dialogue.

T: Tonight, I'd like you to do some homework.[1] I'd like you to do some reading. Look at the questions on.pages 62 and 63 of your books.[2] Read the exercises through to make sure you know what you have to do.

Ss: Will you collect the homework?

T: I didn't finish speaking yet. Listen until I'm finished. Now for Section 1 just write a very short answer. For Section 2 write the word for the feeling next to the text and bring your answers to class. We'll go over them together. However, for Section 3 write me a paragraph for each situation.

Ss: Should we sumbit our writing for section 3?

T: Of course. For section 3 write your homework on a piece of paper and hand it in on Friday.[3] Please think carefully before you write. It is related to your class participation points. If you do well, you will get a good grade.

S1: After you look over our homework, will you return it to us?

T: Sure, after I look over your homework and correct the errors with some comments, I will return it to you.[4] I hope you'll do your best. Have a nice day.

Ss: *(In a low voice)*[5] Nice day with a lot of homework! Is she making a fool of us?[5]

T: No more talking. Straighten up your desks. Put your books away. And close the windows before you go home.

1 (숙제를 내겠습니다.)
   I'd like to give you some homework ; I'm going to give you a bit of homework.
2 페이지를 2개 이상 말할 때에는 단수형 'page'가 아닌 복수형 'pages'를 쓴다.
3 (숙제를 종이에 적어서 금요일에 제출하세요.)
   Could you prepare your homework on a piece of paper and get it in to me on
   Friday?
   Please write your homework on a piece of paper and submit it to me on Friday.
   Could you do the homework on a piece of paper and get it in to me on Friday?
4 ...after I check your homework and check the mistakes with some comments, I'll
   give it back to you.
5 (낮은 목소리로) In a soft voice
6 (지금 농담하는 건가?) Is she kidding [joking, serious]?

해석

선생님: 오늘 밤, 숙제를 해 오세요. 읽기를 하세요. 교과서 62쪽과 63쪽의 문제를 보세요. 연습문제를 끝까지 읽고 무엇을 할 것인지 확인하세요.

학생들: 숙제를 제출합니까?

선생님: 내 말 아직 안 끝났습니다. 내 말을 끝까지 들으세요. 1장은 간단히 답만 쓰세요. 2장은 교과서에서 느낌에 대한 단어를 적어 오세요. 다 함께 풀어 보겠습니다. 그러나 3장은 각 상황에 대해 짧은 글을 써 내세요.

학생들: 3장을 쓴 것은 제출해야 됩니까?

선생님: 물론입니다. 3장은 숙제를 종이에 써서 금요일날 제출하세요. 쓰기 전에 잘 생각하세요. 평소 점수에 반영하겠습니다. 잘하면 좋은 성적을 받을 겁니다.

학생들: 숙제를 검사한 뒤에 돌려줍니까?

선생님: 그렇지요. 숙제를 검토한 뒤에, 틀린 부분을 고치고 평가를 쓴 뒤에 돌려줄 겁니다. 열심히 하기를 바랍니다. 즐거운 하루 되세요.

학생들: (낮은 목소리로) 숙제는 많이 내주고 즐거운 하루 되라고. 우리를 놀리나.

선생님: 잡담하지 마세요. 책상을 정리하세요. 책 챙기세요. 집에 가기 전에 창문을 닫으세요.

2. 기본구문

여기에서는 수업 중에 사용되는 각종 유인물 및 과제물의 배포, 회수, 평가에 사용하는 표현들을 다음과 같이 정리하였다: A. 과제부여 B. 과제물의 배포와 회수 C. 과제평가

A. 과제부여

---

① Now, I'd like you to do some homework.

해설   숙제를 내겠습니다.

syn   I'd like to give you some homework.
        I'm going to give you a bit of homework.

---

② Finish this exercise at home.

해설   이 연습문제를 집에서 해오세요.

syn   I want [would like, expect] you to finish this exercise at home.
        I want this exercise (to be) finished at home.

        I prefer you finish this exercise at home. *(A.E.)*
        (미국영어에서 이 경우 'finish' 대신 'finishing'은 사용하지 않는다.)

        You should do this exercise for homework.
        For homework, I want you to finish this exercise.
        I would like this exercise (to be) done (in your notebooks) at home.

You are supposed to do this exercise for homework. *(rare)*

아취: 어쩌지? 그 리포트 오늘까지 제출해야 되는데!

사브리나: 아취야, 너 노트 가지고 있니?

아취: 그래, 그렇지만 타이프 칠 시간이 없어!

사브리나: 나에게 줘! 나는 수업이 없어! 내가 해 줄게!

아취: 와! 맹세코 너는 생명의 은인이야! 5교시 전까지 해 주면 오늘밤 시내에 너랑 놀러 갈께!

사브리나: 와! 끝난 걸로 생각해!

(Consider it done=consider it finished. Don't worry about it. I'll do it for you.)

누구나 영어로 가르칠 수 있다

③ S: When is our homework due?
T: You must have this finished by this time next week.

해설 S: 숙제를 언제까지 해야 합니까?
T: 다음 주 이 시간까지 끝마쳐야 됩니다.

syn S: When do we have to do our homework?
When is the due date for our homework?
When do we have to hand in [submit, pass in, give you] our homework?
T: You must finish this a week [one week] from today.
Please finish this one week from today.
Have this finished one week from today.

어휘 today week (일주일 후 이날까지)=a week from today, this day next week
yesterday week (어제부터 일주일 후까지)=a week from yesterday
tomorrow week (내일부터 일주일 후까지)=a week from tomorrow
: 실제 전자의 'today week', 'yesterday week', 'tomorrow week'는 오늘날 미국영어에서는 거의 사용하지 않고 후자의 표현을 주로 사용한다.

주의 가까운 미래의 표현 방법
일반적으로 며칠 후 라고 할 경우에는 '주와 요일'을 이용하여 표현한다. 예를 들면 오늘이 수요일일 경우, '8일 후'는 다음과 같이 표현한다.
Next week, Thursday. *(usual)*   Thursday, next week. *(usual)*
A week from tomorrow. (OK)
Eight days hence. *(rare)*
One week counting from tomorrow. *(rare)*
*Tomorrow in seven[eight] days. *(incorrect)*

cf. Our vacation begins a week from tomorrow.

(우리의 방학은 내일부터 일주일 후에 시작됩니다.)

I have a paper due on Monday.

(나는 월요일까지 해야 하는 숙제가 있습니다.)

When (are) the grades due?(언제까지 성적을 제출합니까?)

They're due on March 15th. (= The due date is (on) March 15th.)

(3월 15일까지 제출해야 합니다.)

---

④ S: I'm (all) done. What's next?
  T: Finish the rest for homework tonight.

해설 S: 다했습니다. 다음은 무엇을 할까요?

  T: 나머지는 오늘 집에 가서 끝마치세요.

syn S: I'm through. What's next?

  I've done this. What should I do next?

  I've finished (this). What shall I do now?

  T: The rest [The remainder] of this exercise is your homework
   (for) tonight.

   Your homework (for) tonight is to do the rest of this exercise.

   Do the rest of this exercise for your homework tonight.

   The rest of this exercise is for homework tonight.

   Complete the rest of this exercise (for homework) tonight.

  cf. 숙제할 부분의 확인과 관련된 표현들

  I'm not sure what we have to do. (무엇을 해야 할지 모르겠습니다.)

  Which exercise must we do? (연습문제의 어느 부분을 해야 합니까?)

해설   23페이지 연습문제 10번을 숙제로 해오세요.

syn   Homework is exercise 10 on page 23. *(casual)*
       Tonight's homework will be exercise 10 on page 23.
       Exercise 10 on page 23 will be tonight's homework.
       Do exercise 10 on page 23 for homework.

cf. 숙제와 관련된 표현

For homework, I want you to do exercises 2 through 7.
= For homework, I want you to do exercises 2 to 7, including 7. *(rare)*

At home, I want you to go over what we've just learned.
= At home, review [read over, study] what we've just learned.

Complete up to page 35. (35페이지까지 해오세요.)
('Up to' 대신 'as far as', 'down to', 'through to', 'all the way to'를 대용할
수는 있으나, 'until'은 사용할 수 없다.)

Finish the rest for homework for the next class.
(나머지는 다음 수업시간 숙제로 해오십시오.)

⑥ Before the next class I want you to read pages 36 to 39 and
   answer the questions.

해설   다음 시간까지 36페이지부터 39페이지까지 읽고 문제를 풀어 오
       세요.

syn   For next time I want you to read pages 36 to 39 and answer the questions.

Please read pages 36 to 39 and answer the questions for next class.

You're responsible for reading pages 36 to 39 and answering the questions before our next class.

---

⑦ Write this out neatly at home.

해설   이것을 집에서 깨끗하게 써 오세요.

syn   Rewrite this more legibly at home.
Rewrite this neatly at home.
Do this again neatly at home.
This needs to be written out more neatly [neater]. Do it at home.

> **cf. 필기숙제와 관련된 표현**
>
> Write it in your notebook and turn it in [give it in] next class.
> (그것을 공책에 써서, 다음 시간에 제출하세요.)
> Write it in your notebook [on paper] and I'll go over it tomorrow morning.
> (그것을 공책에 써 오면, 내일 아침에 검사하겠습니다.)

어법   '적(어오)다', '필기하다'는 'write [take, get, put, copy]+목적어 +down' 또는 'write+목적어+down [out, up]'으로 표현할 수 있지 만, 대개 'write down[out]'을 많이 사용한다. 그리고 '간단히 적어 두다'라는 의미로는 'jot down'을 쓰기도 한다.
   e. g. Write the new words down in your exercise books.
       (연습장에 새로 나온 단어를 쓰세요.)
       Write your answer (down [out, up]) on the blackboard.
       (칠판에 답을 적으세요.)

⑧ Please write your homework on a piece of paper and hand it
in on Friday.

해설　숙제를 종이에 써서 금요일에 제출하세요.

syn　Please write your homework on a piece of paper and submit it
to me on Friday.
Could you do [prepare] the homework on a piece of paper and
give it to me on Friday?

⑨ Don't forget your homework next time.

해설　다음 수업 시간에 숙제를 꼭 가져오세요.
: '명심하다'는 'don't forget', 'make sure', 'remember' 등으로 표현
한다.

syn　Don't forget to bring your homework next time.
Make sure you bring your homework next time.
Bring it along next time.

[Be sure to] Remember your homework next time.
Remember to complete the homework assignment.
Remember (to bring, to do) your homework.

⑩ S: Should we finish this at home?

해설　S: 이것을 집에서 끝마쳐야 합니까?

syn　Are we supposed to finish this at home?

Do you want us to finish this at home?

Should we take this home to finish?

Should we do this at home?

cf. Shall we do the exercises in our workbooks?
(학습장에 연습문제를 해야 합니까?)

⑪ S: I'm sorry I didn't get my homework done.
Could I hand in my homework tomorrow?

해설　숙제를 해오지 못했습니다. 숙제를 내일 제출해도 됩니까?

syn　I couldn't be able to finish my homework. Can I give[hand, pass] it to you tomorrow?

…Is it OK if I hand it in a day late?

…Is it OK if it's a day late?

…Can I submit it tomorrow?

cf. Is it alright if I do my homework tonight? I didn't have time yesterday.
(숙제를 오늘 밤에 해도 됩니까? 어제는 시간이 없었습니다.)

B. 과제물의 배포와 회수

① Pass these papers [sheets] back.

해설　이 유인물을 뒤로 전달하여라.

syn   Pass these papers to the back (of each row).

Please pass these papers to the end of the row.

Will you pass these papers to the end of the row?

ant   Pass these papers (up) to the front (of each row).

Will you pass these papers up to the front?

---

② I have some papers to hand out today. Will you please hand these out, Sumi? Thanks.

해설   오늘 몇 가지 유인물을 나누어 주겠습니다. 수미야, 이 유인물을 나누어 주어라.

어휘   hand out(나누어 주다)=give out, pass out [around], distribute

hand in (제출하다)=turn in, submit

> **cf. 유인물의 배포와 관련된 표현**
>
> The teacher handed out the examination papers.
> (선생님이 시험지를 배포하였다.)
> I should hand in my homework by tomorrow.
> (내일까지 숙제를 제출해야 한다.)
> Pass these papers around [along].(이 유인물을 차례로 돌리세요.)
> Could you hand [pass] out these papers? (이 유인물을 나누어 주겠습니까?)

---

③ Take one and pass them on. They are for you to keep.

해설   한 장씩 가지고 넘기세요. 유인물은 개인이 보관하세요.

:'pass them on'에서 'on'을 생략할 수 없다.

syn   You may keep them.

        They are (all) yours to take home.

        You may have them to keep. *(awkward : redundant)*

> cf. I want them back at the end of the lesson. Don't write on them.
>
> (수업 후에 회수하겠습니다. 유인물에 적지 마세요.)

---

④ Could you give these flash cards out please? One (for) each.

해설   이 학습용 카드를 나누어 주어라. 한 사람에 한 장씩.

syn   Would you hand [pass] out these flash cards? One (for) each.

        Please distribute these flash cards. One card (for) each student.

        : 'each'를 강조할 경우에는 'every one of us'로 대체될 수 있으며, 보다 강조할 때에는 'each and every one of us'로 표현할 수도 있다.

어법   위의 문장에서는 전치사 'for'가 생략 될 수 있다. 이와 유사한 전치사 생략현상은 'of'의 경우에도 흔히 나타난다.

e.g.   Are you going to have all of us [us all] tested?

        (우리 모두를 시험하겠습니까?)

        All of us [We all] have to go there together.

        (우리 모두 거기에 함께 가야 합니다.)

---

⑤ One book between two people.

해설   2명당 1권씩

syn   Share the books between two people.

There's one book for every two people.

Two people share one book.

Pairs share one book.

> **cf.** One book to every three students. (3명에 한 권씩)
>
> = One book per 3 students.
>
> Three students to each book.
>
> A threesome to each book. *(rare)*
>
> A threesome per book. *(rare)*

---

⑥ **Does everyone have a copy of the article [the exercise]?**

해설   모두 그 기사[연습문제]의 복사물을 가지고 있습니까?

syn   Do you all have a copy of the article? *(usual)*

Have you all got a copy of the article? *(usual, B.E.)*

('Have you got…'은 영국식 영어이다.)

Is there anybody who doesn't have [hasn't got] a copy?

Who doesn't have a copy of the article [text]?

Is there anyone who doesn't have a copy of the article?

Has everyone got a copy of the article? *(B.E.)*

Is there anyone without a copy of the article?

Do you all have one? (*implied*: 무엇인지 이미 알고 있을 때 사용)

(모두 한 장씩 가지고 있습니까?)

⑦ I'm afraid I don't have [I haven't got] enough copies to go around.

해설   나누어 줄 유인물이 모자랍니다.

syn   I'm afraid there aren't enough copies for everybody.
I'm afraid we're running low on copies.
I'm afraid I ran out of copies.

> **cf.** There are only enough (copies) for twenty students.
> (20명에게 줄 유인물밖에 없습니다.

⑧ Please pick up a sheet as you leave.

해설   나갈 때 한 장씩 가져가세요.

syn   Pick up a sheet on your way out.
Remember to take a sheet as you leave.

⑨ I will collect [gather, take in] your work now.

해설   여러분이 한 것을 모으겠습니다.

syn   Please hand in [turn in] your work (to me).
I want to collect [gather, take in] your work now. *(rare)*
I'd like you to hand me your work.

> **cf.** Would the first person in each row collect the books, please?
> (각 줄의 첫 번째 사람이 책을 모으세요.)

누구나 영어로 가르칠 수 있다

⑩ You can have your homework back but first I'll go over a few points.

해설   숙제를 돌려주기 전에 몇 가지 사항을 검토하겠습니다.

syn   I will give your work back but I'll go over some mistakes first.
       I'll return your homework after we go over a few common errors [mistakes].

C. 과제평가

① Good (job)! *(casual)*

해설   '잘했습니다.' 과제를 잘하였거나 또는 교과수업을 마칠 때 사용하는 표현이다.

syn   Great [Excellent] job!
       Good work!
       You've all done a good job!
       You've all done quite well.
       Well done.
       This is a job well done.
       You did a very good job on that.
       You can't do much better than that.
       You seem to have a good understanding of the material. *(formal, polite)*
       You made a very good job of that. *(B.E.)*
       That was a job well done. *(rare)*

해설   좀 더 열심히 노력하여라.

syn   A bit more effort is required [needed].
(Give it) A bit more effort.
Put some [a bit of] life into it.
Give 100%.
Give it your all.

Pull your socks up! *(B.E.)*
Come on, wake your ideas up. *(rare)*

참고   **숙제 또는 리포트에 대한 평가에 사용되는 표현**
① 명사구:
Excellent work, Good stuff, Good job, Great improvement,
Too many careless slips.
② 형용사구:
Excellent, Magnificent, Marvelous, Terrific, Great, Very well
done, Good, Satisfactory, Adequate, Interesting, Much better,
Careless, Disappointing, Not up to your usual standard.
('뛰어나다'라는 의미로 사용되는 'excellent', 'terrific',
'magnificent', 'marvelous'의 의미차는 거의 없으며, 강약의 정
도는 억양에 의해 좌우된다.)
③ 동사구:
Keep it up. (꾸준히 계속하여라) Shows some improvement. (좀 나아졌다.) Could do better. (좀 더 잘해라.) Needs
to show more effort. (좀 더 노력을 요함), See me about this
(이것에 대해 나와 상의할 것.)

③ (I know) You can do better than that.

해설   '좀 더 잘하여라.' 숙제나 일이 기대에 미흡할 때 사용하는 표현이다.

syn   There's room for improvement there.
I hope you do better next time.
You need to brush up on this.
(Come on,) Can't you do any better than that? *(rude)*
You have the potential to produce much better work.

    cf. Most of you did better than last time, but you could still do better.
(대부분 지난번보다는 잘했지만, 좀 더 잘할 수 있습니다.)
: 영국식 영어에서는 과거형 'did' 대신 완료형 'have done'을 흔히 사용함.

④ It [Your homework] was rather disappointing.

해설   숙제가 다소 실망스럽구나.

syn   I wasn't very satisfied with (the way you did) that. *(formal)*
It was poorly done.
It didn't meet my expectations.
It wasn't up to par. *(slang)*
It was awful [terrible, rotten]. *(casual, rude)*

⑤ You've done the wrong exercise, haven't you?

해설   지정해 준 연습문제를 하지 않았구나.

syn   You completed the wrong exercise.

Did you do the wrong exercise?

It looks like you did the wrong one.

cf. 숙제가 잘못된 경우에 사용하는 표현

You're doing it the wrong way, aren't you? (그것을 하는 방식이 잘못되었다.)

= It looks like you're doing it wrong.

= You're going about this the wrong way.

Look. This is how you're supposed to do it.

(너는 그것을 이런 방식으로 해야 한다.)

= Let me show you how to do it.

---

⑥ Let's go over the exercise together.

해설   연습문제를 다 같이 검토해 봅시다.

syn   Let's go through this exercise.
Let's take a look at this exercise together.

어휘   go over(검토하다)=take a look at, undertake, work on, look at

---

⑦ Check your answers on page 176.

해설   176페이지의 답을 확인해 보세요.

syn   The right [correct] answers are on page 176.
Look on [Refer to] page 176 for the answers.
Check page 176 for the answers.
The answer key is on page 176.

누구나 영어로 가르칠 수 있다

Let's check the answers. (답을 확인해 봅시다.)

Change [Trade] papers with your neighbor. (답안지를 옆 사람과 바꾸세요.)

What was the answer to number 7? (7번 답은 무엇입니까?)

Could you read the answer to number 7 aloud [out loud]?

(7번 답을 큰 소리로 읽어보겠습니까?)

Shouldn't the verb be in the past tense? (동사는 과거형이어야 합니까?)

I think you've made a mistake on the blackboard.

(칠판에 쓴 것 중 틀린 곳이 있습니다.)

---

⑧ Can someone volunteer to answer number 3 for the class?

해설 누가 3번 문제에 대한 답을 말해 보겠습니까?

syn Somebody read their answer for number 3.

Can someone read aloud what they put for number 3?

(usual, incorrect) ('someone'은 대명사 'he / she'를 사용하나, 비문법적이지만 흔히 'they'도 사용한다.)

Could anybody read out what they put for number 3? *(rare)*

cf. Can you read the instructions for this exercise?

(이 연습문제의 지시문을 읽어라.)

---

⑨ What was your grade [points, score]?

해설 너는 몇 점 받았니?

: 미국에서는 성적을 주로 등급으로 나누므로 'grade'를 사용하며, 우리나라에서 점수로 표시할 경우에는 'points' 또는 'score'라고 한다. 또한 스포츠에서는 주로 'score'를 많이 사용한다.

How did you do on your test? *(usual)*

What did you get (on the exam)?

What grade did you get?

How many points did you get? (성적을 점수로 표시할 경우)

e.g. A: How was your test?

(시험이 어떠했니?: 시험의 난이도를 묻는 의미로 주로 사용된다.)

B: It was easy. I got an A. (쉬웠어. A 받았어.)

cf. 점수 및 채점과 관련된 표현

How many did you get right [wrong]? (몇 개 맞았니[틀렸니]?)

Count up your points. One point for every right answer.

(점수를 계산하세요. 한 문제당 1점입니다.)

I didn't count it as a mistake if you put 'bring'.

('Bring'을 써도 맞는 것으로 처리했습니다.)

You made several mistakes in this exercise. You'd better do it again.

(너는 이 연습문제에서 여러 개 틀렸다. 다시 하여라.)

⑩ I was a little [a bit] disappointed with your result.

해설 너의 시험결과에 약간 실망하였다.

syn I wasn't happy with your results.

You can do better.

I'm not very pleased with your results.

I wasn't impressed with your score.

cf. 등급의 구분과 관련된 표현

I've given you grades A-D.[I've given you marks out of 100.]

A [90 and over] is excellent [very good].
B [80 and over] is good [above average].
C [70 and over] is average.
D [60 to 69] is below average.
Below that is fail [failing].

⑪ S: Are these right [correct]?

해설　　이것은 맞습니까?

syn　　Are these alright? *(informal)*
　　　　Will these do? *(casual)*

cf. 답의 진위에 대한 표현들
Circle [Ring] the correct answer. (옳은 답에 동그라미 치세요.)
Cross the appropriate answer. (옳은 답에 옆줄을 그으세요.)

⑫ S: Is there an error in sentence 5?

해설　　5번 문장에 틀린 것이 있습니까?

syn　　Isn't there a mistake in sentence 5?
　　　　Is there anything to correct in sentence 5?
　　　　Are there any mistakes in sentence 5?

⑬ S: I failed physics [my physics class, the physics exam].

해설　　나는 물리를 과락하였다.

: 위의 세 가지 표현은 비슷하지만 의미가 다를 수 있다. 'Fail physcis [my physics class]'는 '물리학 수업 전체가 과락이지만, 'fail the physics exam'은 '물리학 시험만 잘 못쳤고 그 외 교과 과정에 관계된 출석, 리포트, 등에 관해서는 문제가 없으므로, 과락이 되지 않을 수도 있는 것이다.

syn   I flunked the physics exam [physics, my physics class].
       I didn't pass physics (exam).

   cf. I messed up on physics (exam). *(informal)* (나는 물리시험을 망쳤다.)
       = I screwed up on physics (exam). *(slang, impolite)*

⑭ T: **Come here for a moment, would you, Minsu.** I'd like a word with you about your homework. Why didn't you do your homework?
   S: I'm sorry I couldn't because I have [had] the flu.

해설   T: 민수야, 여기에 잠깐 오너라. 숙제에 대해 이야기하고 싶다. 왜 숙제를 안 해 왔니?
       S: 감기 때문에 하지 못했습니다.

syn   T: Minsu, over here for a second.

어휘   for a moment=for a second, for a minute, for a bit
       'The flu' 대신 'a cold', 'a temperature' 등으로 대체할 수 있다.

참고   **접속사 'since', 'because', 'as', 'for'의 구분**
       위의 4가지 접속사의 용법에 대한 구별은 매우 어렵지만 신정보 (new information)와 구정보(old [given] information)를 이용하면 비교적 간단히 구분할 수 있다. 일반적으로 'because'는 뒤에

누구나 영어로 가르칠 수 있다

신정보와 구정보 어느 쪽이나 수반할 수 있지만, 'since'와 'as'는 단지 구정보만을 수반할 수 있다. 다음 예문을 보자.

e.g. Since[As] you're here *(given)*, you might as well stay for lunch.

Since[As] it is located in the tropics *(given)*, Indonesia has a hot climate.

위의 예문에서는 'since' 다음에 구정보가 있으므로 어법에 맞다. 그러나 다음 예문을 보자.

A: Why are you here?

B: *I came, since [as] Sunhi called me. *(new)*

위의 문장에서 'since' 다음의 내용은 신정보이기 때문에 'since'가 아닌 'because'를 사용해야 문법적인 문장이 된다. 반면에 'for'는 뒤에 신정보만을 수반하기 때문에 일반적으로 문장 뒤에 위치하며, 문법에서도 부사절이 아니라 주절을 이끄는 대등접속사(coordinating conjunction)로 처리한다. 물론 이 경우에도 'because'는 언제든지 사용할 수 있다.

e.g. John set off early, for he had a long way to go. *(new)*

Since he had a long way to go *(old)*, John set off early.

◆ 외국인이 회화에서 범하기 쉬운 8가지 문법적 오류와 수정 방법

1 외국인이 회화에서 범하기 쉬운 8가지 문법적 오류
(adapted from R. R. Jordan(1990))

다음은 영어를 배우는 모든 외국인이 대화에서 흔히 범하는 일반적인 문법상의 오류에 대한 것이다. 여기에서 어떤 종류의 오류가 가장 많이 발생하는지 관찰하면 학생들의 영어회화 능력을 향상시키는 데 많은 도움이 될 것이다. 그러나 학생들이 자신들 간의 토론과정에서 이런 오류를 범하더라도, (학생 자신이 토론 중에 직접 구체적으로 묻는 경우를 제외하고) 학생들 간의 대화에 방해가 되지 않도록 절대 수정해서는 안 된다. 다만 토론이 끝나고 나서 다음 시간에 문법에 대한 학습에서 다루거나, 또는 담화를 녹화해서 추후에 별도로 분석해 볼 수는 있다.

① Omission of subject: 명령문 외에는 주어를 생략할 수 없다.
　　e.g. (It) is very important.
　　　　Why don't (you) stay a little longer?
　　cf. 앞의 의문사의 용법에서 언급한 바와 같이 우리 학생들도 대화에서 주어를 생략하는 경우가 많다고 한다.

② Omission of auxiliary: 의문문에서 조동사는 생략할 수 없다.
　　e.g. Where (do) you come from?

③ Omission of article: 보통명사의 관사는 생략할 수 없다.
　　e.g. It is (an) important target...

④ Omission of final '(e)s': 3인칭 단수 어미 's'는 생략할 수 없다.
　　e.g. She believe(s) that Tom go(es)...

⑤ Incorrect preposition: 전치사를 정확히 사용해야 한다.
　　e.g. The new method dispense *of [with] much labor.
　　　　Because *at [in] developing countries...

⑥ Irregular past participle not known: 과거분사형을 조작해서 사용해서는 안 된다.
  e.g. I've *gived [given] up smoking.
        It was *choosed [chosen] by me.

⑦ Singular / plural confusion: 단수와 복수를 혼동해서는 안 된다.
  e.g. Korea *have [has] succeeded.
        There *is [are] a lot of points here.

⑧ Vocabulary confusion: 어휘를 잘못 선택해서는 안 된다.
  e.g. So when I *tell [say] high rate of unemployment...
        Then your productivity *raise [rises / will rise / will be raised].
        My *choose [choice] is number 1.

이외에도 외국인 영어 선생님들에 따르면 우리 학생들은 다음 두 가지도 많이 틀린다고 한다.

⑨ 어순의 배열
  일반적으로 부사는 문장 뒤가 우선이며, 문장 앞도 가능하나 그 외의 경우는 틀리다.
  e.g. He studies English very hard everyday. (usual)
        Everyday he studies English very hard. (OK)
        He studies English everyday very hard. (OK but with emphasis on 'everyday')
        *He everyday studies English very hard. (incorrect)
        *He studies everyday English very hard. (incorrect)

반면, 빈도부사의 경우는 동사 앞 또는 문장 앞에 오는 것이 원칙이며, 회화에서 강세를 줄 경우 목적어 뒤에 오는 것까지는 허용되나 그 외의 경우는 잘못된 표현이다.
  e.g. I sometimes watch TV before bed on Saturday. (usual)

Sometimes I watch TV before bed on Saturday. *(OK)*
I watch TV sometimes before bed on Saturday. *(often colloquial)*
*I watch TV before bed sometimes on Saturday. *(incorrect)*
*I watch TV before bed on Saturday sometimes. *(incorrect)*

⑩ 의문의 의미를 가진 의문문의 마지막 부분을 내려서 읽는 것 (falling intonation)도 아주 일반적으로 행해지고 있는 잘못이다.
　　e.g.　Does she study hard? ↗ *(correct)*
　　　　　Does she study hard? ↘ *(incorrect)*

2　학생들의 오류에 대한 9가지 수정 방법
(adapted from Ann Malamah-Thomas(1987))
학생들의 잘못된 답에 대한 수정 방법은 다음 9가지가 보편적이며 수업의 효율성을 높이고, 교실 분위기에 맞게 적절히 선택해서 사용해야 한다.

① Teacher gives correct answer. (선생님이 올바른 답을 가르쳐준다.)

② Teacher asks other S - 'Is that right?' 'What's wrong?'
　(선생님이 다른 학생에게 옳은지 또는 무엇이 틀렸는지 묻는다.)

③ Teacher says 'No / wrong.'
　(선생님이 '아니다 / 틀렸다'라고만 말한다.)

④ Teacher says 'Again / repeat.'
　선생님이 학생에게 'again' 또는 'repeat'라고 하여 대답을 되풀이하게 한다.)

⑤ Teacher mentions terms.
　e.g.　tense, third, pronoun.
　(선생님이 틀린 부분의 문법용어 - 이를 테면 시제, 3인칭, 대명사 - 를 언급한다.)

⑥ Teacher repeats the question with change of stress.
(선생님이 어조를 바꾸어 질문을 반복한다.)

⑦ Teacher repeats student's answer up to point of error.
(선생님이 학생의 답을 틀린 부분까지 되풀이한다.)

⑧ Teacher makes physical gesture to indicate error.
(선생님이 몸짓으로 틀렸음을 표시한다.)

⑨ Teacher does not correct. (고쳐주지 않는다.)
일반적으로 교실현장에서 문장을 가르칠 때에는 선생님이 문장을 문법적으로 설명하고, 문법적 설명이 끝난 후 단체 또는 개별연습을 한다. 이때 선생님이 먼저 지명하면, 학생은 대답하고, 선생님이 그 대답을 확인(feedback) 또는 수정하는 방식으로 진행되며, 이 경우 위의 여러 가지 수정 방법이 동시에 적용된다. 예를 들어 선생님이 'Flight 308 goes to Paris.'에 대한 설명을 끝내고 학생들이 연습하는 과정을 보자.

T: *(Finishing the explanation)* Flight 308 goes to Seoul. Flight 308 goes to Seoul... Everybody. *(T makes gesture)*
SS: Flight 308 goes Seoul.
T: No. Flight 308 goes to Seoul. Again. *(gesture)*
          (여기에서, 수정방식 1번이 적용된다.)
SS: Flight 308 goes to Seoul.
T: Good... now Sunhi.
Sunhi: Flight 308 goes to Seoul.
T: Good... Myra.
Myra: Flight 308 goes to Seoul.
T: Yeah... *(T points to Kilsu.)*
Kilsu: Flight 308 go to Seoul.
T: Flight 308 go?

(수정방식 7번이 적용된다.)
Kilsu: Oh, Flight 308 goes to Seoul.
T: Good.

그 외 위의 수정방식 5번과 같이 직접적으로 문법적인 부분을 지적하여 수정하는
방식은 Part 3, Unit 1의 현장예문 'Be Going To'에 잘 나타나고 있다.

1. 현장예문 (Real-life Situation)

Ending Class and Giving Information
About Final Examination.

수업 종료 후, 학생들에게 다음 주 월요일까지 숙제를 제출하고 어휘시험
에 대비하라는 선생님의 지시이다.

As all classes must come to an end each day, it is important that the
teacher be able to wrap up his class in an efficient manner. In this unit
we provide language related to the various things a teacher might need
to do when concluding a class. Most importantly, the teacher needs to
indicate to the students a shift from the main part of the lesson to the
conclusion of the class. Other aspects considered in this unit are how to
review what has been covered in class, how to indicate precisely when
class will conclude, how to signal that class has officially ended, and
how to demonstrate anticipation and enthusiasm for the next class.

Now listen to the dialogue.

T: There's the bell. We have to stop here.

Ss: Finally![1] I thought it would never end.[2]

T: That's all for today.[3]

S1:   It better be.[4] What a terrible class![5]

T: We'll finish this exercise next time.[6]

S1:   Oh no, not the same exercise again!

T: Wait. Don't go yet, Minsu.[7] I have something to say to you.

Minsu: I wasn't going anywhere.[8] OK, I'm sorry.

T: For your homework prepare chapter six until line 16 by next Monday. [9]

Minsu: I missed that. [10] What chapter are we supposed to prepare?

S1: Six, down to line 16, by next Monday.

T: You'd better review your vocabulary because there will be a test on it.

Sujin: Oh no, not a vocabulary test!

T: Well, I'll see you on Monday.

S1: I won't be here. I have to go to the dentist on Monday.

T: All right, have a nice weekend everybody.

S2: What sort of weekend is that when you have to review for a vocabulary test?

T: OK. Go on. You're dismissed. [11]

S2: All right. Good-bye.

T: And please be quiet. [12] Other classes are still working.

S1: Okay. We'll try.

T: OK. Straighten up those desks. Right, you can go. Good bye everyone.

Ss: Good bye.

T: Have a good weekend.

1 (드디어 끝이구나.) 지겨운 일이 끝날 때 흔히 사용하며, 'At last'라고도 한다.

2 '… it would last forever'

3 (오늘은 그만 하겠습니다.)
  'That's all for today.' 또는 'That's it for today'가 가장 일반적으로 사용되며, 그 외
  'That will do for today.', 'That's good [enough] for today.' 등이 사용된다.

4 ((끝나서) 잘됐다.) 'It certainly will' 또는 'I hope so.'라고 표현하기도 한다.

5 (지겨운 수업이었어.) 'What an awful class.'이라고 하기도 한다. 영국식 영어로는
  'class' 대신 'lesson'을 사용하여, 'What a terrible lesson.'이라고도 한다.

6 (다음 시간에는 이 연습문제를 끝마치겠습니다.) 또는 '다음 시간에 이어서 계속하겠
  습니다.'로 표현할 수도 있다.
  We'll pick up where we left off next time.
  We'll go on with [continue with] this exercise next time.

7 (잠깐, 민수, 서둘러 나가지 마라.) Wait, Min-su. Don't go rushing off, Min-su.

8 무례한 표현이므로 민수가 사과한다.

9 영국식 영어로는 다음과 같이 표현하기도 한다.
  …prepare chapter six down to line 16 for next Monday.

10 (못 들었는데요.) Can you say that again? I didn't hear you.

11 (해산.) You're free to leave. You can go home now.

12 (조용히 하세요, 떠들지 마세요.)
  Keep the noise down ; Quiet down a bit ; Not so much noise.

해석 ────────────────────

선생님: 벨이 울렸습니다. 그만 해야 되겠습니다.

학생들: 결국! 언제 끝날까 싶었네.

선생님: 오늘은 그만 하겠습니다.

학생1: 그만 해야지요! 지긋지긋한 수업이었어!

선생님: 다음 시간에 이 연습문제를 계속하겠습니다.

학생1: 아니, 같은 문제를 다시 하다니!

선생님: 민수, 아직 나가지 마라. 할 말이 있어.

민수: 아무데도 안 가요. 좋아요, 미안합니다.

선생님: 숙제로 다음 월요일까지 6장 16째 줄까지 해오세요.

민수: 못 들었는데요. 몇 장을 해오라고요?

학생1: 6장, 16째 줄까지, 다음 월요일까지.

선생님: 어휘시험이 있으니 어휘도 복습해오세요.

수진: 아니, 게다가 어휘시험은 안 돼!

선생님: 자, 여러분 모두 월요일에 다시 만나겠습니다.

학생1: 나는 못 볼 겁니다. 월요일날 치과에 가야 합니다.

선생님: 좋아, 모두 즐거운 주말이 되도록…

학생2: 어휘시험 때문에 복습을 해야 하는데 무슨 주말을 보내!

선생님: 자, 해산.

학생2: 좋아요, 안녕히 계세요.

선생님: 그리고 조용히 하세요. 다른 반은 아직 수업하고 있어요.

학생1: 예, 그럴게요.

선생님: 좋아요. 책상을 정리 하세요. 자! 가도 좋아요. 잘 가요 여러분.

학생들: 안녕히 가세요.

선생님: 즐거운 주말 보내세요.

누구나 영어로 가르칠 수 있다

2. 기본구문

여기에서는 수업내용을 요약하고, 수업 종료를 한 뒤, 교실 정리정돈을 시키기 위해 사용하는 표현들을 다음과 같이 정리하였다: A. 요점정리 및 마무리 B. 수업 종료 C. 교실 정리 정돈

A. 요점정리와 마무리

---
① Let's review (what we've learned).

해설　(배운 것을) 요약하겠습니다.

syn　Let me sum up then.
　　Let me summarize what we know.
　　Let me summarize then.

　　Let's go over it one more time.
　　Let's look back at what we studied.

　　cf. Let's recap quickly. (간단히 요약해 봅시다.)
　　　　= Let's sum it all up quickly.
　　　　= Let's go over this again quickly.

---
② Please summarize the passage [what' we've learned].

해설　이 글을 요약하세요. [학습한 내용을 요약해 보세요.]

syn　Can you sum up the passage?

Give me a brief summary of the passage.

Who can summarize?

Could someone sum up what has been said so far?

Can you give me the main ideas of the passage in a nutshell? *(rare)*

---

③ Let's review the passage.

해설   이 글을 복습해 보겠습니다.

syn   Let's ask some questions about [on] this passage. *(formal)*
       Let's see [check] if you get the gist of the passage.

       Let's see if you understand this passage.
       Let's see if you've understood this passage. *(B.E.)*

어법   완료시제는 영국식 영어에서 사용하며, 미국식 영어에서는 현재
       시제를 사용한다.

---

④ You will have to finish in two minutes.

해설   2분 만에 끝마치세요. [2분 남았습니다.]

syn   You have 2 minutes to go.
       I'll (have to) stop you in two minutes.
       I'll give you 2 minutes to finish.
       You have 2 minutes (to finish).
       There are 2 minutes remaining [left].
       Please finish up what you're doing in 2 minutes.

누구나 영어로 가르칠 수 있다

① We still have a couple of minutes left. (아직 2분 정도 남았습니다.)

= There are another two minutes yet.

② We seem to have finished 2 minutes early.

(2분 일찍 끝마친 것 같다.)

= We have two minutes left.

= It seems we have two minutes to spare.

③ We have an extra two minutes. (추가로 2분 더 할 수 있다.)

어휘   'Extra'는 추가로 2분 더(additional minutes)라는 의미를 가지며, 2분 남았다(2 minutes remaining)라는 의미는 아니다. 'to spare' 는 이 경우 2분 일찍 끝마쳤다는 의미이다.

⑤ It might be a good idea to leave this exercise until next time.

해설   이 연습문제는 다음 시간으로 미루는 것이 좋겠습니다.

syn   We'll continue (with) this exercise next class.

We'll continue working on this exercise next time.

Let's finish this exercise (up) next time.

We'll finish this exercise in the next class.

We've run out of time, but we'll go on with this exercise next time.

B. 수업 종료

① Stop now.

해설   그만 하세요.
: 문제풀이, 학습활동을 중단시킬 때 사용한다.

syn   Put your pens down, please.
All right, you can stop now.
Your time is up now, I'm afraid.
I think we'll stop (doing this) now.
Everyone stop what you are doing.

> **cf. 종료[중지]와 관련된 지시문**
> I've already asked you to stop once. I won't tell you again.
> (그만 하라고 한 번 말했습니다. 두 번 이야기하지 않겠습니다.)
> There's the buzzer [bell], so you must stop working now.
> (벨이 울렸습니다. 이제 끝마치세요.)
> Time is almost up. Please finish quickly.
> (시간이 다 되었습니다. 즉시 끝마치세요.)
> Stop (doing) that. No more of that.
> (그만 해요. 더 이상 그런 짓은 하지 마세요.)

② It's time we stopped now.

해설   그만 하겠습니다.
: 수업 또는 하던 일을 끝마칠 때 사용한다. 'It's time' 다음 절에서는 가정법 과거를 사용한다.

syn (OK,) That's enough (for now).
Enough of that.

Let's stop here. / We'll stop here. / Let's stop there for now.
It's (almost) time to stop. / We'll have to stop now.
I'm afraid it's time to stop [finish] now.
I see it's almost time. / We'll have to stop here.
I think we'll stop now.

Time is running out. We have to call it a day.
This class is coming to a close. Time to wrap it up.

We'll leave off here.

That will do, thank you.
That's fine.

Let's pause here (for a moment).
Let's stop here for a while. *(awkward, redundant)*
I make it almost time. We'll have to stop here. *(rare, B.E.)*

---

③ All right. That's all for today, thank you.

해설 오늘 수업을 마치겠습니다.
: 그날 수업을 종료할 때 사용하는 표현이다.

syn That's it (for today).
That will be it for today.
That will be all.

That will do for today.
That should do it for today.
That's enough for today.

Let's finish [end] today's class.
It's time to call it a day.
Let's call it a day.
Time to close up shop. *(idiom)*

Class is over.
Class is adjourned. *(very formal)*
Class dismissed. (*formal*: 군대에서 흔히 사용)

cf. Enough of that. *(casual)*: 주로 부정적 의미로 사용되며 '그만하면 됐어.(그만
해!)'라는 의미의 명령어이다.

e.g. Hey! Enough of that!

---

④ **Close your books.**

해설   책을 덮으세요.

syn   All books closed, please.
Books closed! *(casual)*
Shut your books. *(casual, impolite)*
We are finished with our book for today.

---

⑤ **OK. Let's take a break.**

해설   쉬는 시간이 되었습니다.

syn   It's time for us to take [have] a break now.
       Now, it's time we took a break.
       Let's break for a few minutes.
       We'll take a short break.
       Let's take a short recess.
       Take 5[10]. (5[10]분간 쉬자) *(A.E.)*
       OK. Let's take a rest. *(rare)*

주의   미국영어에서 '10분간 쉬다'는 'take a break for 10 minutes', take
       10', 'rest for 10 minutes' 등으로 표현한다. 우리가 흔히 사용하는
       'take [have] a rest for 10 minutes.'는 오늘날 거의 사용하지 않는
       다.

---

⑥ **It isn't time to stop [finish] yet.**

해설   수업이 아직 끝나지 않았습니다.

syn   Class is not finished yet.
       We're not done yet.
       We're not finished yet.
       We're not through yet.

       There's still some [plenty of] time left.
       Time isn't up yet. *(casual)*
       The buzzer [bell] hasn't gone off yet.

    cf. This lesson isn't supposed to [due to] finish until five past.
       (이 수업은 정각 5분에 끝마치게 되어 있습니다.)

:'past' 다음에는 시간이 생략되어 있다.

There's [There are] still 5 minutes remaining. (아직 5분이 남았습니다.)

---

⑦ **There's no point (in) starting anything else now.**

해설   지금 다른 것을 시작할 의의가 없습니다.

syn   There's no reason to start something new.
There's not [There isn't] any point (in) starting anything else at this time. *(emphatic)*

---

⑧ **See you again on Tuesday.**

해설   화요일에 보겠습니다.

syn   Good bye, everyone, see you all on Tuesday!
I'll see you (all) again on Tuesday.
See you Tuesday! *(casual)*
Catch you on Tuesday.
Until Tuesday.
Catch you all again on Tuesday. *(rare, informal)*

cf. **수업 종료 후 인사말**
Well, I hope you all enjoy yourselves. (자, 모두 즐겁게 지내세요.)
I hope you all work hard tonight. (오늘 밤 열심히 공부하세요.)

---

⑨ **All of you, go outside now!** *(casual)*

                누구나 영어로 가르칠 수 있다

해설   모두 다 교실에서 나가세요.

syn   I'd like all of you to leave.
       Would [Will] you please leave?
       Please leave.
       All of you, get out! *(casual, rude)*
       Get out of here now. *(slang, rude)*
       Get out of my sight. *(slang, angry)*

C. 교실 정리 정돈

① Pack up your books.

해설   책을 정리하세요.

syn   Pack your books up.
       Wrap it up.
       Put away your things.

cf. Close your books and put them away. (책을 덮고 치우세요.)

② T: Would you (all) clean up your desks please?
   S: Yes, alright.

해설   T: 책상을 정돈하세요.
       S: 예, 알았습니다.

syn   T: Please get your desks in order.
Would you mind tidying your desks please?
Would you straighten up your desks please?

S: Yes, OK. / Alright. / Yeah, sure.

cf. 정리 정돈에 대한 표현
Would you put all your desks straight please? (책상을 똑바로 놓으세요.)
Before you (all) leave, would you see that you've not forgotten anything?
(가기 전에 잊어버린 물건이 없는지 살펴보세요.)

Before you (all) leave, will you make sure the desks are straight?
(가기 전에 책상이 정돈되었는지 확인하세요.)
: make sure(확인하다) = see that, check that, ensure that, see to it that,
be sure to

---

③ Put your chairs back in their places before you leave.

해설   나가기 전에 의자를 제자리에 넣어주세요.

syn   Put your chairs back where they were before you leave.
Push your chairs back where they belong before you leave.
(오늘날 미국영어에서는 'where' 앞에 'to'를 붙이지 않는다.)
Return your chairs to their usual [normal] position [place].

cf. Will you put everything back in its right place please?
(모든 것을 제자리에 도로 놓아두겠습니까?)

---

④ Throw that in the garbage, please.

해설   그것을 쓰레기통에 버려라.

syn   Please throw it away.
       Would you put that in the garbage [the wastebasket]?
       Would you put that (trash) in the trash can [the wastebasket]?
       Throw away [Throw out] the garbage. *(casual)*
       Would you put that rubbish in the dustbin, please? *(B.E.)*

       Please toss this in the trash.
       Would you mind getting rid of this garbage?

       Toss it. / Trash it. / Can it. / Get rid of it. *(colloquial)*

참고   **'쓰레기통'의 종류**
       garbage can: 가장 널리 사용되며 부엌이나 집밖에 있는 음식물
       을 포함한 쓰레기를 버리는 곳도 여기에 포함된다.
       wastebasket (or waste paper basket): 사무실이나 교실에서 휴지
       를 버리는 곳.
       trash can: 휴지 및 잡다한 쓰레기를 버리는 곳으로 거리의 쓰레기
       통도 여기에 해당된다.
       dustbin: 영국식 영어로, 'garbage can'과 비슷한 의미를 지닌다.

cf.   'What (s)he said is stupid or useless.'(그 말은 쓰레기야.)라는 표현은 다음
       과 같이 여러 가지로 표현할 수 있다. 그러나 이 표현들은 무례하므로 되도록 사
       용하지 말아야 한다.
       That's (complete) garbage. *(rude)*
       That's bullshit. *(rude, angry)*
       That's a crock of bull.
       That's a load of crap.
       That's a waste of time.
       That's useless.

◆ 수행평가 또는 인성에 대해 사용하는 표현

(adapted from Douglas Drewry (1984))

학생들의 수행평가(performance apprasal), 인성(personal traits) 또는 취업에 대한 추천서를 간혹 영문으로 작성해야 할 경우가 있다. 이 경우 미국에서 흔히 개인에 대한 평가를 쓸 경우 사용하는 아래의 표현들을 참고하면 많은 도움이 될 것이다. 개인의 인성(personal traits)은 간단히 단어로 평가할 수도 있고, 구체적으로 서술 할 수도 있다. 여기에서는 먼저 단순한 어휘에 의한 평가와 서술적 평가로 구분하여 몇 가지 예를 열거해 본다.

1 단순 평가

어휘 또는 어구를 이용하여 간단히 몇 자 이내에 평가하는 방법이다. 먼저 긍정적 또는 적극적 특성 (positive or active attributes)을 적고, 다음으로 그와 상반되는 부정적 또는 소극적 특성(negative or passive attributes)을 적는다.

① active, energetic, quick & fiery, athletic
(활동적, 의욕적, 민첩하고 급한, 건장한)
vs
inactive, passive, slow & sure, steady and studious
(소극적, 수동적, 느리고 확인하는, 꾸준하고 학구적인)

② bold, aggressive, firm, just forceful positive type
(담대하고, 공격적인, 태도가 분명하고, 매우 추진력 있는 적극적인 유형)
vs
timid, cautious, weak, negative type
(소심하고, 조심스럽고, 약하고, 소극적인 유형)

③ conceited, vain, proud and argumentative
(자부심이 강하고, 허영심이 있고, 자존심이 강하고 논쟁적인)
vs
unassuming, taciturn, unresponsive

(나서지 않으며, 과묵하고, 둔감한)

④ optimistic, talkative, nervous (낙천적이고, 수다스러우며, 조급한)

                  vs

  pessimistic, quiet, calm (비관적이고, 조용하고, 차분한)

⑤ radical, original, resourceful, ingenious, experimental
  (급진적이고, 독창적이며, 재주가 있고, 영리하고, 실험적인)

                  vs

  conservative, orthodox, conventional, painstaking, lacks
  imagina-tion
  (보수적이고, 정통적이며, 관습을 따르고, 노력하는, 상상력이 부족하다)

⑥ abrupt, hot-tempered, outspoken
  (허둥대고, 성격이 급하며, 꾸밈없는)

                  vs

  courteous, tactful, considerate
  (공손하고, 재치 있고, 사려 깊은)

⑦ grasp essentials, not especially interested in petty details,
  observant
  (이해력이 빠르며, 세세한 일에 개의치 않으며, 관찰력이 예리한)

                  vs

  slow to grasp essentials, falls back on details
  (이해력이 느리며, 사소한 점에 좌우됨)

⑧ mentally alert, reasonable, a good thinker, well balanced,
  mentally coordinated, well informed, thinks ahead, quick
  perceptions
  (정신적으로 기민하고, 합리적이며, 사고가 현명하고, 균형을 유지하며, 정신
  이 조화롭고, 상식이 풍부하고, 예측력이 있으며, 지각이 빠름)

vs

mentally dull, not an orderly thinker, jumps to conclusions, lacks mental coordination, learns slowly

(정신적으로 둔감하며, 논리가 정연하지 못하며, 성급하게 판단하고, 정신적인 조화가 부족하고, 학습이 느림)

⑨ works well under pressure, inspires respect of others

(긴장을 참고 업무에 충실하며, 타인의 존경을 이끌어냄)

vs

may burn or crack under pressure, does not inspire confidence

(긴장하면 참지 못하고, 신뢰성을 주지 못함)

⑩ pleasing personality, good sense of humor

(인간성이 쾌활하고, 유머감각이 뛰어남)

vs

colorless personality, lack of humor, serious type

(개성이 없으며, 유머감각이 부족하고, 신중한 성격)

⑪ willing to assume responsibility, self-reliant

(책임감이 강하며, 자신감이 있는)

vs

avoids or is unwilling to assume responsibility

(책임을 회피하거나 싫어함)

⑫ Well liked by juniors [subordinates], contemporaries, and seniors

(하급생[부하], 동기, 상급자가 아주 좋아함)

vs

does not inspire confidence (신뢰성이 결여됨)

2 서술적 평가

보다 구체적으로 평가할 경우에는 다음과 같이 서술적으로 기술할 수도 있다.

① Highly cooperative, always willing to help, invariably a leader in conference or group discussions.
(매우 협동적이고 항상 도움을 베풀며, 회의나 토의를 주재함.)

② Fully capable of meeting new situations head-on and applying himself/herself in a highly resourceful manner.
(새로운 상황에 정면으로 대처할 수 있는 능력이 있으며, 아주 능숙하게 적응함.)

③ Analytical, decision-making ability, and adaptability to changing situations make him competent in any situation.
(분석적이고 결단성이 있으며, 상황변화에 적응력이 있어 어떤 환경에서도 유능함.)

④ Exhibits initiative and resourcefulness in solving problems. Does not rely on outside advice or guidance.
(문제해결에 주도적이며 풍부한 지식을 보임. 외부의 충고나 조언에 의지하지 않음.)

⑤ Devoted to duty and willing to perform above what is expected.
(임무에 충실하고, 솔선하여 기대 이상을 수행함.)

⑥ Has [possesses] stamina to tackle most difficult assignments, and the judgement and ability to obtain[produce] quality results.
(어려운 문제에 도전하는 열정이 있으며, 좋은 결과를 가져오는 판단력과 능력이 있음.)

⑦ Ability to create and maintain confidence, respect, and

professionalism in any organization.
(어떤 조직에서도 신뢰와 존경과 전문성을 발휘하고 유지하는 능력)

⑧ Knowledge of profession and job is impressive and desire to use experience in assisting others is commendable.
(직업에 대한 지식이 인상적이며, 경험을 이용하여 남을 도우려는 의지가 칭찬받을 만하다.)

⑨ Team player, places high [great] emphasis on cooperation and team work.
(단체활동가, 협력과 단체활동을 중요시함.)

⑩ Facilitates communication and understanding between people with different points of view.
(의견이 다른 사람들 간의 의사소통과 이해를 원활하게 함.)

⑪ A student of human nature, displays social poise and tact (and: courteous, respectful, gracious, pleasant, frank, open-minded, even-tempered)
(인간성이 좋은 학생, 사회성과 재치를 보임 (그리고 공손하고, 예의바르고, 품위 있고, 쾌활하고, 솔직하고, 개방적이고, 침착함.)

⑫ Constantly learning, reads professional books and completes correspondence courses during off-duty and spare time.
(학구적이고, 전공서적을 읽으며, 일과 외 또는 여가 시간 동안 통신교육과정을 마침.)

1. 현장예문 (Real-life Situation)

Examination Preparation

다음은 두 친구 간의 대화로, 한 친구가 다가올 수학시험에 대비하지 않고 농구경기를 보러 가려고 하자 다른 친구가 공부할 것을 충고하는 장면이다.

The final classes in most schools and universities are often followed by final exams. In this section we introduce language that is typically used during this period of the school year. In particular, the unit addresses language related to what will be included on exams, motivating the students to study and do well on exams, taking questions from students concerning exam content, and bidding farewell to the students as it may be a teacher's last class with them.

Now listen to the dialogue.

Lee: When is our math test?[1]

Kim: This Thursday, 2nd period. It should take 2 hours. [2]

Lee: Have you studied for the math test already?[3]

Kim: I sure have. I spent all weekend studying.

Lee: Well, I haven't opened my book yet.

Kim: Are you kidding? You'd better start studying. You know you can't pass Professor Kim's tests without studying. He is very tough. [4]

Lee: But I'm going to the basketball game tonight.

Kim: I'm telling you, [5] the test will be tough.

Lee: I guess it's too late to start studying anyway.

Kim: If I were you, I'd really work hard tonight.

Lee: I really don't want to miss that game but... [6]

Kim: Listen! Go to the game and you'll be sorry. [7]

Lee: You're right. Let's get a bite to eat. [8] And then I'll go to the library.

Kim: OK. Let's go!

Lee: By the way did you take notes of everything you learned in class? [9]

Kim: Of course I did.

Lee: Then, let me get a copy. [10] I missed his class twice because I was sick. [11]

Kim: OK. No problem.

주

1 (수학시험 언제 치느냐?)

  When is our math quiz?

  When are we going to take the math test [quiz]?

  : 일반적인 시험은 'test' 또는 'quiz'라고 하며, 'examination'은 중간고사(mid-term exam), 기말고사(final exam), 종합시험(comp(rehensive) exam) 등 중요시험에 사용한다.

2 (이번 목요일 2교시. 2시간이야.)

  It is on this coming Thursday at the 2nd period for two hours.

3 (수학시험 공부해 놓았니?) Have you prepared...?

4 (그는 학점이 짜다.) He is very strict. He is a very hard[tough] grader.

  학점을 잘 주면 'He is an easy grader.'(그는 학점을 잘 준다.)

  : 영국식 영어에서는 'grader' 대신 'marker'도 사용한다.

5 (시험이 어려울 것임에 틀림없어.) Trust me, the test will be tough.

  부모와 같이 윗사람이 경고할 때는, 'I'm warning you, ...'라고 한다.

6 (그 시합을 놓치기 싫지만…) I sure hate to miss that game but...

7 (시합에 가면 후회할 걸.) If you go to the game, you will be sorry.

8 (간단하게 먹자.) Let's grab a bite [something] to eat.

    Let's get something small to eat. / Let's get a snack.

    Let's go eat. / Let's eat something together.

9 (전부 적어 두었니?) Did you write down everything...?

    cf. 필기의 경우에는 'take a note of'를 사용하나, 간단히 잊지 않기 위해 한두 가지
       사항을 적어둘 때는 'make a note' (메모해 두다.)라고 한다.

    e.g. I have a meeting on Friday. I should make a note of it. (금요일 모임이 있다.
       적어놓아야겠다.)

10 (복사 좀 하자.) Let me make a copy of them.

11 미국영어에서는 'twice' 대신 'two times'도 흔히 사용한다.

해석

이군: 수학시험 언제지?

김군: 이번 목요일 2교시. 2시간이야.

이군: 내일 있는 수학시험 공부해 두었니?

김군: 그럼. 주말 내내 공부했어.

이군: 그래, 나는 아직 책도 안 펴보았는데.

김군: 정말? 공부하는 게 좋을 걸. 너 김 교수 시험공부 안 하고 통과할 수 없다는 것을 알잖아. 그는 학점이 짜다.

이군: 그런데 오늘 밤 야구 구경 갈 건데.

김군: 단언하건데, 시험이 어려울 걸.

이군: 공부 시작하기에는 이미 너무 늦은 것 같은데.

김군: 내가 너라면, 오늘 밤 열심히 하겠다.

이군: 게임을 놓치고 싶지 않지만….

김군: 자! 게임에 가, 그러면 후회할 걸.

이군: 맞아. 간단히 먹고, 도서관에 가겠어.

김군: 그래, 가자.

이군: 그런데 너 수업시간에 배운 것 전부 필기해 두었니?

김군: 물론이지.

이군: 그래, 복사 좀 하자. 나는 아파서 두 번 빼먹었어.

김군: 좋아. 그러렴.

2. 기본구문

이 단원에서는 수업을 마친 뒤 다음 시간의 학습계획을 공고하고, 시험시간과 관련된 사항을 전달하기 위해 사용하는 표현들을 정리하였다: A. 차시예고 및 공고 B. 시험일자 및 시간

A. 차시예고 및 공고

> ① I'll test you on these lessons sometime next week.

해설   다음 주 이 과에 대한 시험을 치겠습니다.

syn   There will be a test on these lessons sometime next week.
       I will give you a test on these lessons...
       A test will be given on these lessons...
       You ought to prepare for a test on these lessons...
       Be ready for a test...
       You can expect a test on these lessons...
       You will be tested on these lessons...

> ② On Friday, which period is English?

해설   금요일 몇 째 시간에 영어 수업이 있습니까?

syn   Which period do we have English on Friday?
       When is English class on Friday?
       When do we have English class on Friday?
       Which period is English scheduled for on Friday?

Which period is English slotted for on Friday? *(rare)*
(미국영어에서는 'in' 대신 'for'를 사용한다.)

cf. Fourth period has been cancelled next Monday, so there won't be an
English lesson.
(다음 월요일 4교시가 없어져서, 영어 수업이 없습니다.)

③ There's been a room change for next week.

해설   다음 주에 교실이 바뀝니다.

syn   There's been a change of rooms for next week.
We'll change rooms for next week only.
We'll be relocating to another room next week.

④ Don't forget there's a club meeting tomorrow.

해설   내일 클럽활동이 있는 것을 잊지 마세요.

syn   Keep in mind (that) there's a club meeting tomorrow.
Please remember there's a club meeting tomorrow.
Will you please remember there's a club meeting tomorrow?
(redundant)
(위의 문장에서는 'will you'와 'please' 그리고 의문문 모두가 명령
의 내용에 대한 공손의 의미로, 중복되는 의미를 가진 문장이 된
다.)

⑤ Stay where you are for a moment.

해설   잠시 그 자리에서 대기하세요.

syn   Just a moment please.
Just) hold on a minute.
Sit [Hang] tight for a minute. *(casual)*
Hold it right there for a moment. *(impolite)*
Don't move. *(impolite)*
Wait a sec [a second]. *(slang)*
Hang on a moment. *(slang)*
Hang tight for a moment. *(slang)*

Hold your horses. *(slang, rare, rude)*
('잠깐 (끼어들지 말고) 기다려.'라는 의미이다. 주로 'Hold on a minute'라고 한다.)

⑥ I have something to tell you before you go. Would you listen, please?

해설   집에 가기 전에 알릴 것이 있습니다. 잘 들으세요.

syn   I have some announcements to make before you go.
I have a few things [a few words] to say before you leave.

⑦ Be quiet as you leave. Other classes are still working.

해설   나갈 때 조용히 하세요. 다른 반은 수업 중입니다.

syn   No noise as you leave. Other classes are still working.
Please leave quietly.
Try not to make any noise as you leave.

> ⑧ Please remember to bring money for the extracurricular activities next class.

해설   다음 시간에 과외 활동비를 가져오세요.

syn   Please remember to bring the money for extracurricular activities next class. *(B.E.)*

> ⑨ Wash your hands before lunch.

해설   점심식사 전에 손을 씻으세요.

syn   Wash your hands before eating your lunch.
Wash your hands before your lunch. *(awkward)*

> ⑩ This is my last class with you.

해설   오늘이 여러분과의 마지막 수업입니다.

syn   This is our last meeting [class] together. *(casual)*
This is our final meeting [class] together.
This is our farewell meeting.

B. 시험일자 및 시간

> ① S: When is our exam [test]?

해설   시험은 언제 칩니까?

syn   When are we going to take [have] our exam?
      When are we having our test?
      When are we going to have our test? *(formal)*
      When will we be tested?

> ② By yourselves! You've got 40 minutes to do [write] this. Start now.

해설   혼자서 할 것! 시간은 40분 주겠습니다. 지금 시작하세요.

syn   You have forty minutes to do this.

어휘   By yourselves!=Alone!, No talking!

cf. **시험 시간 및 시작에 대한 표현**
[You must] Finish this by ten to eleven.
(11시 10분 전까지 끝내야 합니다.)
Books closed! Don't make any stupid mistakes. Start now. *(rude)*
(책을 덮으세요. 어리석게 실수하지 마세요. 지금 시작하세요.)

③ Time's up. Stop working now.

해설   시간이 끝났습니다. 그만 하세요.
            : 시험 시간이 종료되었을 때 사용하는 표현이다.

syn   (Your) Time is up.
            I'm sorry, but (your) time is up. (Put your) pens down.
            I'm afraid I'll have to stop you now.
            Would you stop writing, please?
            Stop writing.
            Pens down. *(casual)*
            That's all the time you have. *(rare)*

④ Have you (all) handed in your tests?

해설   시험지를 모두 제출하였습니까?

syn   Is there anyone who hasn't turned in their test?
            Is anyone still writing?

     cf. **답안지 회수와 관련된 지시문**
         Pass your essay to the front when you've finished.
         (끝나면 여러분의 글을 앞으로 전달하세요.)
         Leave your tests [sheets, papers] on your[the] desk as you leave.
         (나갈 때 시험지를 책상 위에 놓아두세요.)

◆ 상황별 작별인사의 유형과 표현 방법

일반적으로 대화를 끝내고 헤어질 때에는 간단히 작별인사를 할 수도 있지만 가벼운 이유 또는 변명을 하는 것이 보다 품위 있는 태도이다. 여기서는 먼저 흔히 사용하는 작별인사를 구분하고, 다음으로 상황에 따른 몇 가지 작별을 위해 사용하는 자연스런 표현을 살펴보기로 한다.

1 **대화를 마치고 작별인사를 할 경우에 사용되는 표현에는 다음의 세 가지 유형이 있다.**

① 일반적으로 가장 널리 사용되며 간단히 '잘 지내'라는 의미를 가진 의례적인 표현
See you (later). (Good) Bye. Have a nice day. So long.
: 위의 표현은 서로 주고받아도 상관없다. 미국에서 'So long'은 앞의 세 가지 표현만큼 흔히 사용되지는 않는다.

② 주로 친한 사이에 사용되며, '(신경 쓰지 말고) 편안히 지내라.'라는 의미를 가진 표현.
Take care [of yourself]. Take it easy. Don't work too hard.
: 대답으로는 간단히 'OK [Alright]'라고 할 수도 있고, 위의 1)의 표현으로 답할 수도 있다.
e.g. Kilsu: Take care [of yourself], Sumi.(수미야, 편히 지내라.)
        Sumi: OK. [Alright.] You too, Kilsu.(길수야, 너도.)

③ 부모 또는 윗사람이 아랫사람에게, '몸조심해라. [말썽피우지 마라.]'라는 의미로 사용하는 표현.
Be careful. Stay out of trouble. Don't get into trouble.
: 이 경우에는 대체로 아랫사람은 'OK. Alright.'이라고 답한다.
e.g. Mother: Be careful, Kilsu. (길수야, 항상 조심하여라.)
        Kilsu: Alright [OK], mom. (알았어요, 어머니.)

2 상황에 따라 일반적으로 널리 사용하는 작별을 위한 가벼운 변명

① (At school)

A: **Now I have to go** to English class. It starts at 10. The teacher gets upset if we are late. See you later.

(이제, 영어수업에 가야겠다. 10시에 시작이야. 늦으면 선생님이 싫어하셔.)

B: Ok. See you.

② (At school or In the office)

A: **I'd love to continue this conversation, but I really need to go now.** I have to get back to class [work].

(이야기를 계속하고 싶지만 가야겠어. 수업하러[일하러] 가야 돼.)

B: Well, let's get together soon. (그래, 곧 다시 만나자.)

A: OK. Give me a call later. See you. (좋아. 나중에 전화해. 안녕.)

B: See you later. (안녕)

③ (In the street)

A: **I'm sorry but I have to go.** It was nice talking to you.

(가야겠어. 즐거운 대화였어.)

B: Same to you. [You too.] (나도.)

Have a nice day. (즐겁게 지내.)

*Same to me [Me too.] *(incorrect)*

*My pleasure. *(awkward)*

<주의> 위의 경우 'Same to you [You too.]'는 '(It was nice talking) to you.'의 준말이므로 'Same to me. / Me too'라고 답하면 틀리다. 또한 'My pleasure.'라고 할 수도 없다. 이 표현은 미국인들은 도움을 준 경우에만 (only if I do something for him) 일반적으로 사용한다.

④ (At the party)

A: **You'll have to excuse me.** I need to go. It was a pleasure talking with you. (실례하겠습니다. 가야겠어요. 즐거운 대화였습니다.)

B: You too. [Same to you.] (나도요.)

*Me too. [Same to me.] *(incorrect)*

<주의> 위의 경우와 같이 'You too'는 '[It was a pleasure talking to] you, too.'의 축약이므로, 'Me, too.'라고 하면 잘못된 표현이다.)

⑤ (In the hospital)

A: **It's time to go**. *(usual)* [Now I must be going. *(formal)*] I hope you'll get well soon. So long. (가야겠어요. 곧 회복되길 바랍니다. 잘 있어요.)

B: So long.

⑥ (Over the phone)

A: **Thanks a lot for calling**. I hope we'll get together soon. Bye. (전화 줘서 고마워. 곧 다시 만나길 바래. 안녕.)

B: I hope so. Bye.

⑦ (Over the phone at home)

A: OK. **(Now) I should hang up.** My mother is calling me. I should do some errands [I should go and run some errands]. I'll call you later. See you. (전화 끊어야겠어. 엄마가 나를 부르고 있어. 심부름해야 돼. 나중에 전화할게. 안녕.)

B: Bye. Have a nice day.

A: You too. Bye.

⑧ (When invited at home)

Guest: **It's late**. I enjoyed having dinner with you. (늦었습니다. 저녁 맛있게 먹었습니다.)

Host: My pleasure. Why don't you stay a little longer? (뭘요. 좀 더 놀다 가지요?)

Guest: No, I must hurry. See you.
(아니요, 서둘러야 되겠습니다. 안녕히 계세요.)
Host:　See you.

Part 3 분야별 학습

Practicing Each Part

1. 현장 예문 (Real-life Situation)

Using 'Be Going To'
(adapted from Nancy Salama(1973))

다음은 처음 나온 단어 혹은 구를 학습한 뒤 그것을 응용하는 방법에 대한 현장 예문이다. 선생님이 미래의 예정(future intended tense)을 나타내는 'be going to' 구문에 대한 설명을 마친 뒤에, 학생들의 연습과 그 과정에서 발생하는 학생들의 오류를 선생님이 수정하는 상황이다.

Although the title of this unit is Using be going to, the focus is placed primarily on the language needed when questioning or being questioned by students on how to say something in English. It is a common occurrence in classes taught by Korean teachers for students and teachers to use their mother tongue in the classroom. This unit provides language for teachers to instruct, encourage and motivate the students to speak in English and to identify the correct English phrases for Korean words. It also addresses such classroom occurrences as how to praise students for improvement or correct answers, how to generate more questions from the students, how to elicit more information from the students, and how to motivate students to continue doing their best in the classroom.

Now listen to the dialogue.

T: Sunhi, are you going (to go) to the movies Thursday night?[1]
Sunhi: No, I'm not.
T: Why aren't you going (to go) to the movies?[2]
Sunhi: (Because) I'm going to visit my friend.

T: Fine. Now, who would like to have their conversation first? All right, Minsu and Sujin.

(They come to the front and laugh a little from nervousness and ask the teacher who should start first. The teacher says 'Whoever can start, start!' After a second of silence, Minsu starts and the conversation begins.)

Minsu: *Are you going to make your homeworks tonight?

Sujin: Yes, I am.

Minsu: *Where are you going to make it?

Sujin: *I'm going to make my homeworks in the library from eight to ten o'clock.

T: That was good, because you used the future intended tense correctly. However, remember that we say that we 'do our homework'. We don't say 'make' with 'homework' and the word 'homework' never has an 's' at the end. Everyone repeat after me: I'm going to do my homework.

(repeated in chorus by the class)

T: I'm not going to do my homework tonight.

(repeated in chorus by the class)

T: Would you repeat your conversation now quickly and correctly while the rest listen again?

(They do so.)

T: All right. Now Minsu and Sujin will repeat their conversation and you will (all) repeat each question and (each) answer.

Minsu: Are you going to do your homework tonight?

Ss: *(Looking at Sujin)* Are you going to do your homework tonight?

Sujin: Yes, I am.

Ss: Yes, I am. *(Then the class looks at Minsu and listens for the next question.)*

Minsu: Where are you going to do it?

Ss: *(Looking at Sujin)* Where are you going to do it?

Sujin: I'm going to do my homework in the library.

T: That was very good. Thank you. Who is next?[3] All right. Dongsu and Nami.

(The class listens carefully because it is interesting to find out what they will say and because they must repeat it soon.)

Dongsu: Nami, are you going to the dance on Saturday night?

Nami: No, I'm not.

Dongsu: Why aren't you going?

Nami: I don't have any money.

Dongsu: Oh, that's too bad. Is your sister going (to go) to the dance?

Nami: I don't know. Are you going to ask her to (go with you)?

Dongsu: I can't. *I don't have no money either.

(During the dialogue the teacher said nothing. She watched the students and noted errors mentally only.)

T: Fine. You used what you learned in class yesterday, so that was very good.[4] There was one small problem when Dongsu said, 'Are you going to the dance?' This is correct but it is a special use of the present continuous tense with the near future. Remember we used that form last week. Repeat after me: Are you going to school tomorrow? *(Class repeats.)*

T: We can say it another way using the future intended tense.[5] Repeat.

Are you going to go to school tomorrow? *(Class repeats.)*

T: Are you going to go to the dance on Saturday night?

(Class repeats.)

T: Why aren't you going to go? *(Class repeats.)*

T: Another small problem was the statement:'I don't have no money.'

It should be 'I don't have any money.'

(If the rule for the use of 'any' has not been taught yet, it should not be mentioned now.)

T: Repeat. I don't have any money. *(Class repeats.)*

T: I don't have any time to do my homework. *(Class repeats.)*

T: Dongsu and Nami, please repeat while the rest listen. *(They do so.)* All right. Now let's do the conversation again. (You all) listen and repeat.

Dongsu: Are you going to the dance on Saturday night?

(Class repeats, looking at Nami.)

Nami: No, I'm not.

(Class repeats and then turns to Dongsu.)

Dongsu: Why aren't you going?

(Class repeats looking at Nami.)

Nami: I don't have any money.

(Class repeats and then turns to Dongsu.)

Dongsu: Oh, that's too bad. Is your sister going to go to the dance?

(Class repeats looking at Nami.)

Nami: I don't know. Are you going to ask her to go with you?

(Class repeats, looking at Dongsu.)

Dongsu: I can't. I don't have any money either.

(Class repeats.)

(* : 비문법적인 표현)

1 (목요일 밤에 영화 보러 갈 거니?)

Are you going to the movies [a movie] on Thursday night?

Are you going to see a movie on Thursday night?

Are you planning to go to a movie on Thursday night? ; 'go to the movies'와 'go to a movie' 둘 다 맞지만, 전자가 보다 일반적으로 사용된다.

2 (왜 영화 보러 안 가니?) Why not?

3 (다음은 누구 차례지?) Who's up next?

4 (네가 어제 [지난 시간에] 배운 것을 적용한 것은 매우 잘한 것이다.)

It's great that you applied what we learned last class.

5 (그것을 미래예정시제를 사용하여 달리 표현할 수 있다.)

Thaere's another way of saying it using the future intended tense.

Let's try using the future intended tense.

Why don't we try saying it using the future intended tense?

해석 ─────────────────

선생님: 순희야, 목요일 밤에 극장에 갈 예정이니?

순희: 아니요, 안 갑니다.

선생님: 왜 안 가니?

순희: 친구를 방문할 예정입니다.

선생님: 좋아요, 대화를 나누고 싶은 사람 없습니까? 좋아요, 민수와 수진.

(그들은 교실 앞으로 나와서 긴장한듯 약간 웃으면서 선생님에게 누가 먼저 시작할 것인지를 묻는다. 선생님이 "누구든지 시작할 수 있으면 해라."라고 말한다. 잠시 후 한명이 시작하며 대화가 시작되었다.)

민수: 너 오늘 밤 숙제를 만들거니?

수진: 그래, 할 거야.

민수: 어디서 만들거니?

수진: 8시부터 10시까지 도서관에서 숙제를 만들 예정이야.

선생님: 좋아요, 미래예정시제를 잘 사용했습니다. 명심할 것은 우리는 '숙제를 한다.'라고 말합니다. 그리고 숙제를 '만든다'는 말로 표현하지 않으며, 그리고 숙제 뒤에는 's'가 붙지 않습니다. 모두 나를 따라하세요: 나는 숙제를 할 예정입니다.

(학급 전원이 합창으로 되풀이 한다.)

선생님: 나는 오늘 밤 숙제를 하지 않을 작정입니다.
(학급 전원이 합창으로 되풀이 한다.)

선생님: 이제 너희들은 대화를 빠르고 정확하게 다시 한 번 반복하고, 나머지는 다시 듣도록 합시다.
(학생들은 대화를 되풀이한다.)

선생님: 좋습니다. 이제, 민수와 수진이는 대화를 되풀이하고, 나머지는 모두 질문과 답을 따라합니다.

민수: 오늘 밤 숙제를 할 예정이니?

전학생: (수진이를 보면서) 오늘 밤 숙제를 할 예정이니?

수진: 예, 그럴 예정입니다.

전학생: 예, 그럴 예정입니다.
(그 다음 전 학생이 민수를 보고 다음 질문을 듣는다.)

민수: 어디서 숙제를 할 예정이니?

전학생: (수진이를 보면서) 어디서 숙제를 할 예정이니?

수진: 도서관에서 숙제를 할 예정입니다.

선생님: 좋아요. 다음은 누가 할 겁니까? 좋아. 동수와 나미.
(학생들은 그들이 무슨 말을 할지 궁금해 하며, 그들도 곧 그 대화를 따라해야 하기 때문에 주의 깊게 듣는다.)

동수: 나미야, 토요일 밤에 무도회에 갈 거니?

나미: 아니, 안 갈 거야.

동수: 왜 안 가는데?

나미: 돈이 없어.

동수: 저런. 너의 여동생은 무도회에 갈 거니?

나미: 몰라. 그녀에게 너와 함께 가자고 요청할 거니?

동수: 안 돼. 나도 돈이 없어.
(대화 동안 선생님은 아무 말도 하지 않았다. 그녀는 학생들을 지켜보고 마음속으로만 잘못된 부분을 기록해 두었다.)

선생님: 좋아요. 어제 수업시간에 배운 것을 사용해서 매우 좋았습니다. 동수가 '춤추러 갈 거니?'하고 물을 때 약간 문제되는 부분이 있었습니다. 이 말은 맞지만, 그것은 가까운 미래를 나타내기 위한 현재진행시제의 특별용법입니다. 지난주에 이 형태를 이용한 것을 기억하지요. 나를 따라하세요: 내일 학교에 갈 예정이니?
(학급 학생들이 따라한다.)

선생님: 미래의 의도를 나타내는 시제를 사용하여 달리 표현할 수도 있습니다. 따라하세요. 내일 학교에 가려고 계획하고 있니? (학급이 따라한다.)

선생님: 토요일 밤에 무도회에 가려고 계획하고 있니? (학급이 따라한다.)

선생님: 너는 왜 갈 계획이 없니? (학급이 따라한다.)

선생님: 그 다음 말도 약간의 문제가 있습니다:'I don't have no money.'라는 문장은 'I don't have any money.'로 되어야 합니다.
(만약 'any'의 용법에 따른 규칙을 아직 가르치지 않았다면 언급하지 않아야 합니다.)

선생님: 따라하세요:'I don't have any money.' (학급이 따라한다.)

선생님: 'I don't have any time to do my homework.' (학급이 따라한다.)

선생님: 동수와 나미는 다시 반복하고, 나머지는 듣도록. (나머지는 듣는다) 좋아요. 대화를 다시 합시다. 여러분 모두 듣고 따라하세요.

동수: 토요일 밤 무도회에 갈 예정이니? (학생들은 따라하고, 나미를 본다.)

나미: 아니, 안 가. (학생들은 따라하고, 동수를 본다.)

동수: 왜 안 가니? (학생들은 따라하고, 나미를 본다.)

나미: 돈이 없어.(학생들은 따라하고, 동수를 본다.)

동수: 저런. 너의 여동생은 무도회에 갈 거니? (학생들은 따라하고, 나미를 본다.)

나미: 몰라. 그녀에게 너와 함께 가자고 요청할 거니?
(학생들은 따라하고, 동수를 본다.)

동수: 안 돼. 나도 돈이 없어. (학생들이 따라한다.)

2. 기본구문

여기에서는 실제 수업에서 영어로 말하기 또는 표현 방법과 연관된 제반 활동을 다음과 같이 정리하였다: A. 표현 방법 및 평가 B. 질문과 토론 C. 상황 묘사

A. 표현 방법 및 평가

---
① In English, please.

해설   영어로 말하세요.

syn   Say it in English, please.
Use English.
Try using English.
Use the English that you know.
Use your best English.
This is supposed to be an English lesson, so let's speak English.

---
② It's almost the same in English.

해설   영어도 비슷합니다.
: 말의 의미나 구조가 서로 유사할 경우에 사용하는 표현이다.

syn   The English word (for it) is almost the same.
The English word (for this) is very similar.

③ Can you say it another way?

해설   다른 방식으로 표현해 보세요.

syn   Is there another way to say the same thing?
       Can you say the same thing in another way?
       How else can you say the same thing?
       In what other way can you say the same thing?
       What would be another way of saying it?

       Could you rephrase it please?

       Is there another way of saying the same thing?
       Can you say the same thing, using different words?
       Give me a phrase that means approximately [more or less] the
       same thing.

       Try to put it into other words.
       Can it be put another way?
       What else could you say? *(casual)*
       How else could you say it? *(casual, common)*

   cf. Is there a better [a shorter] way of saying the same thing [this]?
       (좀 더 좋은 [간단한] 표현 방법이 있습니까?)
       = Can you come up with a better way to say it?
       What's a better way to say it?
       What's a better way of saying it?
       Can anyone improve on that?

       Could you phrase it differently?
       Could you phrase it slightly differently? *(awkward)*

(이 경우 영어에서는 표현의 의미가 분명하지 않으므로 'slightly [a little]'와 'differently'를 함께 사용하지 않는다. 따라서 우리말식으로 'slightly [a little] differently'(약간 다른 방법으로)라고 표현하면 어색해진다.)

- 아취가 말한다 -
음식이 아주 좋습니다만 배가 부르군요! 더 이상 한 입도 못 먹겠습니다.

(그러나 아취의 속마음은 다음과 같다.)
우! 이 음식 되게 맛없구나!

- 베티가 말한다 -
멋있는데요. 좀 덜 화려한 것은 없습니까?
(그러나 베티의 속마음은 다음과 같다.)
아름답지만, 돈이 없어요! 좀 싼 것 없습니까?

- 워더비 씨가 말한다 -
얘들아 즉시 수업하러 들어가거라!
(그러나 워더비 씨의 속마음은 다음과 같다.)
복도에서 꾸물거리지 마라, 안 그러면 훈육실로 데리고 가겠다!

---

④ Almost right. Try it again.

해설   (비슷하나) 정답은 아닙니다. 다시 한 번 말해보세요.
       : 대답이 정확하지 않을 경우에 사용한다.

syn   Almost right. Give it another try. [Have another try.]
       Not exactly. Keep trying. [Keep working on it.]
       Not quite right…
       Not quite…
       Good try, but not quite right…
       I'm afraid that's not quite right… *(very formal)*

       You're getting close [warm]. Give it another [one more] shot.
       (casual)
       You're close…
       That's very close…

       Close but no cigar.
       (과거 미국에서 축제(carnival) 또는 행사에서 주어진 문제를 맞

히거나 또는 병을 쓰러뜨리는 놀이 등에서 이기면 보상으로 '담배'를 상으로 주었던 데서 유래한다.)

You're almost there.
That's almost it.
You've almost got it.

Keep at it. You're getting close.

cf. There was a small mistake in what you said. (네가 한 말은 약간 틀렸다.)

---

⑤ No, that's wrong. *(casual)*

해설 틀렸습니다. [아닙니다.]

syn You can't say that, I'm afraid.
     You are not there yet.

---

⑥ **In a way, perhaps.** Under what circumstances might [would] you do that?

해설 그럴 수도 있지.
     : 대답이 정확하지는 않으나 상황에 따라 맞을 수도 있을 때 사용하는 표현이다.

syn It might be, I suppose.
     Perhaps. / Possibly. / It may be possible.
     It depends. / It depends on how you look at it.
     Sort of, yes.

Could be. / It could be, I guess.

Yes or no. ('맞을 수도 있고, 틀릴 수도 있다.')

---

⑦ That's right.

해설 맞습니다. [정답입니다.]

syn That's correct.
There's nothing wrong with your answer.
You didn't make a single mistake.
What you said was perfectly right.
I couldn't have given a better answer myself.
You hit the nail right on the head.
Bingo.
Bullseye! *(rare)*
(골프클럽 등의 상품에 간혹 적혀 있음.)

---

⑧ That's much [a lot] better.

해설 훨씬 나아졌습니다.
: 앞의 대답이나 표현보다 정답에 더 가까울 때 사용하는 표현이
다. '나아지다'는 'improve' 또는 'get better'로 표현한다.

syn That's more like it. *(casual)*
You have made a lot of progress.
You've improved a lot [a little].
You're improving.
That's an improvement.

You're getting better (at it) all the time.
You've improved to no end. *(awkward, rare)*
Keep up the good work. *(informal)*
(To keep up=to go on, not to stop, to continue)

⑨ Try to manage without your book.

해설   책을 보지 않고 해 보세요.
: 문장을 반복하거나, 따라서 연습할 때 흔히 사용하는 표현이다.

syn   Try it without your book.
Now close your book and try it.

⑩ Take it easy. I'll help you if you get stuck.

해설   여유 있게 행동하여라. [편안하게 생각하여라.] 막히면 도와줄게.
: 학생이 대답을 서두르거나 당황할 때 사용하는 표현이다.

syn   What's your hurry? There's plenty of time.
What's the big hurry [rush]? There's plenty of time.
There is no need to hurry [rush].
There's no hurry [no rush]. We have plenty of time.
Relex. We have plenty of time.

참고   **'Take it easy'의 두 가지 의미**
'Take it easy'는 위의 예문과 같이 'to go or act slowly and carefully(천천히 조심스럽게 행동하다)'라는 의미와 'to avoid hard work or worry, have an easy time(신경 쓰지 않고 살다, 편안하게 살다)'이라는 두 가지 의미로 사용된다.

① Take it easy. The roads are muddy. (=Drive slowly and carefully.) (천천히 (운전)해라. 길이 질퍽하다.)
② Judy likes to take it easy. (=Judy doesn't like to work hard.) (존은 모든 것을 가볍게 생각하기를 좋아한다.)

---

⑪ You'll need to practice these words. *(informal)*

해설 이 단어를 (발음)연습해 보아야 한다.

syn You need some more practice with these words. *(formal)*
You need to become better acquainted with these words.
You need to familiarize yourself with these words.
You'll have to spend more time practicing these words.
(very formal)
You should focus on these words.

---

⑫ That's an interesting suggestion.

해설 재미있는 생각입니다.
: 문제 해결에 대한 답이 독창적이거나 특이할 때 사용하는 표현
이다.

syn That's a very good point. I never thought of that.
That's one way of looking at it.
That's some interesting feedback. *(rare)*
That's a novel way of looking [to look] at it.

⑬ 'How are you?' is a bit too formal. You should use 'Hi!' if you are talking to friends.

해설   'How are you?'는 다소 격식적인 표현이다. 친구에게는 'Hi!'라고 말해야 한다.

cf. 'Hi!' is rather colloquial. You should use 'How are you?' if you're writing a formal letter (to a person you don't know'.)
('Hi!'는 다소 구어적인 표현이다. 공식적인 편지를 (당신이 모르는 사람에게) 쓰는 경우에는 'How are you?'라고 써야 한다.)

B. 질문과 토론

① Any questions? *(casual)*

해설   질문 있습니까?

syn   Alright. Does anyone have any questions?
Is there anything else you want to ask?
Is there anything more you want to ask?
Do you have any other questions?

cf. Got it? (이해하겠습니까?)
I got it. (알았습니다.)

해설   왜 그렇게 생각하니?

syn   Can you support what you say?

Do you have any supporting information?

Do you have any proof?

What proof do you have for saying that?

Do you have any proof [support, evidence] to back up what you say?

What reasons do you have for saying that?

Is there any evidence to support what you say?

cf. 이유를 물을 때 흔히 사용하는 표현

Why do you suppose the girl is doing that?

(그 소녀는 왜 그것을 합니까?)

∴'suppose'는 'think'보다 격식 있는 표현이다.

What could have happened earlier? Why do you think that?

(앞에 어떤 일이 있었습니까? 왜 그렇게 생각합니까?)

What might happen in a few minutes? Why do you think that?

(몇 분 뒤 무슨 일이 일어나겠습니까? 왜 그렇게 생각합니까?)

Look at these pictures of clothes. Which do you like best? Why?

(이 그림 속의 옷을 보세요. 어느 옷이 가장 좋습니까? 그리고 그 이유는?)

③ Do you really think so? *(casual)*

해설   너는 분명히 그렇게 생각하니?

syn   Are you absolutely certain?

Is that your honest opinion?

Is that what you honestly think?

Do you actually believe this?

Are you 100% sure about that?

Would you bet your life on it?

Are you convinced of that? *(rare)*

④ I'm not sure what you mean.

해설   당신 말의 의미[의도]를 모르겠습니다.

syn   Be more specific.

Be a little more precise. *(rare)*

What exactly do you mean?

Where are you going with this?

Get to the point. *(rude)*

Could you explain what you mean?

What exactly are you trying to say?

I'm not sure what you are getting at?

I'm not sure what you are driving at? *(slang)*

Could you go into more detail?

Could you expand on that a little?

DIRECTIONS

누구나 영어로 가르칠 수 있다

⑤ Who agrees with Jim?

해설   짐의 말에 동의합니까? [짐의 말에 동의하는 사람은?]

syn   Who agrees with what Jim said?
        Does anybody share Jim's opinion [views]?
        Do any of you feel the way Jim does?
        Does anyone echo Jim's opinion?

⑥ Do you have [Have you got] anything to add to what Jim said?

해설   짐이 한 말에 보충할 것이 있습니까?

syn   Does anybody have anything to say about what Jim said?
        Would anyone care to elaborate on what Jim said?
        Does anybody else have a response to what Jim said?
        Does anybody else want to respond to what Jim said?

    cf. Does anybody else have a response to what Jim said?
       (그 밖에 또 짐의 말에 덧붙일 사람 있습니까?)
       : 문장 속에 'else'를 덧붙이면 이미 누군가가 Jim의 말에 대해 이미 의견을 덧붙였다는 의미를 포함하게 된다.

⑦ Which (ones) would you buy for yourself? Arrange them in order of preference.

해설   당신이라면 어느 것을 사겠습니까? 선호하는 순서대로 나열하시오.

cf. 우선순위 및 선택과 관련된 토론에서 흔히 사용되는 표현

Which of these would you take with you camping? Persuade another pair that your choice is best.

(캠핑을 갈 때 이것들 중 어느 것을 가지고 가겠습니까? 당신의 동료에게 당신의 선택이 최선이다라는 것을 설득해 보세요.)

(여기에서 'camping'은 'when you camp'의 의미이다.)

Which kind of tools would you use at work? Discuss your choice with your neighbor.

(작업에서 어떤 종류의 도구를 사용하겠습니까? 옆 사람과 선택한 것을 상의해 보세요.)

C. 상황 묘사

---

① **If you were in that situation, how would you continue the conversation?**

해설   여러분이 그런 상황에 처해 있다면, 어떻게 담화를 계속하겠습니까?

syn   Under those circumstances, how would [should] you proceed in the conversation?

In that context, how would you respond?

cf. 대화를 연속하기 위한 표현

You could expand [carry on] the conversation with a personal opinion.

(개인적인 의견으로 담화를 계속해 나갈 수 있습니다.)

You could ask for further information.

(보다 자세한 정보를 요청할 수 있습니다.)

You could accept the offer or say 'No' and explain why.

(그 제의를 받아들이거나 또는 '아니오'라고 말하고, 그 이유를 설명하세요.)

---

② For example, if a stranger needs information quickly, what should he ask [say]?

해설 예를 들어 낯선 사람이 정보를 빨리 원한다면, 그는 어떻게 물어야 합니까?

syn If a stranger requires immediate feedback how should he inquire?
Suppose a stranger needs information, what should he ask?
Supposing a stranger needs information, what could he ask?
(*awkward ;* complex)

어휘 for example=for instance, let's take an example, I'll give you an example

---

③ Does anyone know what you say in English when you give directions to a place?

해설 장소에 대한 안내를 할 때 영어로 표현하는 방법을 아는 사람 있습니까?

syn Does anyone know how to give directions in English?
Who knows how to give directions (to a place) in English?

(redundant)

Who knows how to say this in English when you give directions to a place? *(awkward)* (한 문장에 의문사가 세 개 이상 사용되면 의미가 명료하지 못하다.)

cf. So, how would you say that in English?
(그래, 그 말을 영어로 어떻게 표현합니까?)

④ If it were an informal situation you could say that. However if it were a formal setting then what would you say?

해설 일상적인 상황에서는 그렇게 말할 수 있습니다. 그러나 격식을 차려야 할 경우라면 어떻게 표현하겠습니까?

syn If it were someone you knew well you could say that. If it were a stranger then what would you say?
With your peers you could say that. But, what if it were someone more important?

⑤ Explain what happened in your own words.

해설 일어난 사건을 우리말로 설명하시오.

syn Tell me in your own words what happened. *(informal)*
Use your own words to describe what happened. *(formal, polite)*
Explain the meaning of this situation[accident, painting, paragraph], using your own words. *(very formal)*
I wonder if you could say what happened in your own words.

(very formal, very polite)

cf. '화재'를 주제로 한 여러 가지 지시문

Someone asks Ali how (he thinks) the fire started.

(누군가가 알리에게 화재가 어떻게 발생했는지 묻는다.)

Mr. Lee, ask Sumi what the students did when they saw the smoke.

(이군, 수미에게 화재가 난 것을 본 학생들이 무엇을 했는지 물어 보아라.)

Ask your neighbor who telephoned the fire department.

(옆 사람에게 누가 소방서에 전화 걸었는지 물어 보아라.)

: fire department(소방서) = fire brigade, fire company

Ask your partner how long it took to put the fire out.

(동료에게 불을 끄는 데 얼마나 걸렸는지 물어 보세요.)

Ask each other how much damage it caused.

(서로서로 그 화재가 얼마나 피해를 입혔는지 물어 보세요.)

---

⑥ Look at the names of the people in the picture.
They want to buy one of these things. *(informal)*

해설 그림 속에 있는 사람들을 보세요. 그들은 다음 중 하나를 사려고 합니다.

syn They want to purchase one of these items.
They want to pick up one of these items.
They want to take home one of these items. *(colloquial)*

---

⑦ Look at the people's names [photos] on the board.
They want to do one of these things.

해설 칠판에 있는 사람들의 이름[사진]을 보세요. 그들은 다음 중 하나를 하려고 합니다.

syn   Read the people's names on the board.
Take note of the people's name on the board.
*Look at the people on the board. *(incorrect)*
: 칠판 위에 사람들이 있는 것이 아니라 사람들의 이름이나 사진
이 있는 것이므로 'the people'을 직접목적어로 사용할 수는 없다.

---

⑧ Can you make a sentence about each person in the picture?

해설   그림 속의 각 개인에 대한 문장을 하나씩 쓰시오.

syn   Write a sentence about each person in the picture.
I want you to make a sentence about each person in the picture.

cf. 그림과 관련된 지시문
Now, in twos, look at the picture and make up a short dialogue like this.
(자, 짝을 지어서, 그림을 보고 이런 식으로 짧은 대화를 만드세요.)
Listen and tell me which picture [sentence, table] this refers to.
(잘 듣고, 이 말은 어느 그림[문장, 표]을 가리키는지 말하세요.)

◆ 발화에 대한 평가

학습자의 발화에 대한 평가행위는 학습자에게 수행 정도를 알려 주고, 동기유발을 하며, 협조적인 학습 분위기를 조성하기 때문에 교수활동에서 매우 중요한 역할을 한다 (Richard & Lockhart 1996). 학습자의 대답 또는 발화 내용에 대한 평가는 세 가지 유형 — 긍정적, 부정적, 중간적 — 으로 구분할 수 있다. 중간적 평가는 학생의 대답에 대해 전제조건을 부가하여 수용 또는 부정하거나, 수용 또는 부정에 대한 표시 없이 대답을 그대로 인정하는 행위를 말한다(Bowers 1980).

먼저 학습자의 발화를 긍정적으로 평가할 경우에는 원어민은 관용적인 문장단편을 빈번하게 사용한다. 특히, 긍정적 평가를 위해서는 'good' 또는 'good'을 포함한 다음과 같은 표현을 매우 빈번하게 사용한다.

Good job [work, effort, stuff, answer, attempt, try, writing, English].
Cool.
Fantastic.
There you go. [You're right.] (잘했습니다.)
That's good. (좋습니다.)
Oh, good stuff! (좋았습니다.)
Keep up the good work! (계속 잘하세요.)
You speak good English. (영어 잘하네요.)
OK, you deserve it. (좋아요, 칭찬 받을 만해요.)
Hold it there; what you just said was really good.
(잠깐, 방금 한 말이 아주 좋아요.)
This is very good writing. You are improving rapidly.
(잘 썼어요. 빠르게 향상되네요.)
Good, good. I am very satisfied with all of your efforts.
(잘했어요. 여러분의 노력에 매우 만족해요.)
Wow, you surely did a superb job. Let's give him/her a round of applause.
(넌 정말 잘 했구나. 그에게 박수를 보냅시다.)

위의 평가행위는 대부분 교실에서 흔히 사용하는 관용표현(formulaic expression)이다.

반면 중간적 평가는 학생의 대답을 논평없이 그대로 인정하는 행위를 말한다.

It's Okay. (좋아요.)
You got it! (맞아요!)
Okay, I understand. (그래, 알았어요.)
All right, next one. (좋아요. 다음 사람.)
Try to make it simple. (간단히 말하도록 하세요.)
This is a very common mistake for students. (이것은 학생들이 흔히 범하는 오류입니다.)
Difficult to pronounce it, isn't it? (발음하기 어렵지요?)
Watch out for simple mistakes. (간단한 실수에 유의하세요.)
Read it with emotions. (감정을 넣어 읽으세요.)

끝으로 부정적 평가행위는 대부분 아래와 같이 평서문의 형태를 지니고 있다.

You should use your own imagination. (상상력을 이용하세요.)
Some people are confused. We'll go over it again.
(몇몇 학생은 잘 모르군요. 다시 한번 살펴보겠습니다.)
A little bit but it's still confusing. (조금 비슷하지만, 여전히 모호하다.)
That does not make sense, does it? (그 말은 이치에 맞지 않는다.)
This doesn't look like your own work. Did you copy and paste?
(이것은 너가 쓴 것이 아닌 것 같다. 복사해서 붙였니?)
You've learned English for seven years. And you're still afraid of speaking English. That's crazy, silly, ridiculous.
(여러분은 영어를 7년 동안 배웠다. 그래도 영어를 말하기를 두려워한다. 그건 정말 이상하고 어리석고 터무니없다.)
You all did a decent job on your work. But you guys should be more enthusiastic about making presentations. (여러분 모두 과제를 그럭저럭 잘 했어요. 그러나 좀 더 열정적으로 발표하세요.)

부정적 평가에서는 'mistake', 'confuse', 'worried', 'disappointed' 등의 단어를 포함한 문장을 흔히 사용한다. 흔히 문장 단편으로 표현되는 긍정적 평가와 달리, 원어민은 부정적 평가를 할 경우에는 먼저 합리적 근거를 제시하거나 또는 평가에 대한 이유를 밝히는 평서문을 사용하여 논리적인 근거를 분명히 함으로써 부정적인 영향을 최소화하려고 노력한다고 볼 수 있다.

1. 현장예문 (Real-life Situation)

Reserving a Room from a Receptionist
(adapted from E. Raman(1987))

테이프를 이용한 듣기 연습에는, 먼저 녹음된 자료를 선생님이 들려주고 학생이 주어진 문제를 직접 풀거나, 또는 테이프를 듣기 전에 선생님이 먼저 몇 가지 질문을 제시한 뒤 테이프를 듣고 문제를 푸는 방식이 있다. 여기서는 테이프를 듣고 학생이 답을 적은 뒤에 풀이하는 방식을 보자.

다음은 손님이 호텔에 전화를 걸어서 안내대의 접수계원(receptionist)에게 예약을 하는 과정에서 발생하는 대화이다.

At some point all language teachers employ some form of listening comprehension into their lesson plan. This unit provides the language needed to get through the different stages involved in teaching such a class. Teachers should be prepared to introduce the listening activity, describe the type of technology that will be used to facilitate the activity, check for student comprehension, and conclude the listening activity. If necessary he should also solve problems with the audio equipment.

Now listen to the dialogue.

1. 듣는 내용

- Telephone rings -
(Note: R stands for Receptionist, G for Guest.)

R: Good morning. Orient Hotel. May [Can] I help you? [How can I help you?]

G: Good morning. I'd like to reserve a room for next week.

R: Yes, sir. Which days next week?

G: Monday thru [to] Friday, please.

R: Do you want a single or a double room?

G: A single with an attached bath.

R: All our rooms have attached bathrooms, Sir. Do you want full board?

G: No. Just bed and breakfast, please.

R: So - that's a single room, bed and breakfast, for four nights. Can I have your name and address, please?

G: Yes. It's Mr. K.D. Kim, 14 Prince Street, Colombo.

R: Thank you, Mr. Kim. Can you confirm the booking before Monday?

G: Yes. I'll confirm it. Can you tell me how much the room will be?

R: 90 dollars a night, bed and breakfast, sir.

G: Thank you. Goodbye.

R: Goodbye, sir.

2. 위의 내용에 대한 진위형 문제

- True / False Questions -

a. Mr. Kim wants to stay at the Orient Hotel.

b. Mr. Kim wants a double room.

c. There are no rooms with baths available.

d. Mr. Kim wants to have lunch and dinner at the hotel.

e. Full board at the Orient Hotel costs 190 dollars.

3. 문제풀이

위의 문제를 풀이하기 위해, 선생님은 다음과 같이 학생들과 자료의 내용을 토의함으로써 학생들의 이해와 표현능력을 향상시킬 수 있다.

T: I want you to just say where the conversation is taking place: Where is it, OK? Check if you can hear.[1]

(plays the beginning of the taperecorded conversation. Telephone rings ; Voice says: Good morning, Orient Hotel. Can I help you?)

T: So, that's it. Where is the conversation taking place? *(pause)* What did you hear on the tape just now?[2] *(pause)* Anyone want to answer?[3] What did you hear?

S: Hotel.

T: Hotel. Did you get the name of the hotel?

S: Orient Hotel.

T: Orient Hotel. Right. *(pause)* Do we know anything else about the conversation?[4] *(pause)* Is it two people in the hotel?

S: No.

T: No? Why not? *(pause)* Are there two people in the hotel talking? *(pause)*. Where is the conversation taking place? It's in a hotel, but we know something more, don't we? What kind of conversation is it? *(pause)* Listen again. *(Teacher replays only the sound of the telephone ringing)* So what kind of conversation?

S: Telephone. *(very faint)*

T: A telephone conversation. Right. So, it's a conversation in a hotel. What do you think it's about? It's a telephone conversation in a hotel. What do you think the conversation is about? (pause) No

누구나 영어로 가르칠 수 있다

ideas? *(points to a student)* What do you think it's about?[5] *(pause)* What do you think the conversation is about?

S: I think it's a receptionist. *(very faint)*

T: It's a receptionist in a hotel. Fine. O.K. So one person is the receptionist and who is the other person? *(pause)* What do you think?

S: *(incomprehensible)*

T: One of the...?

S: Passenger.

T: You don't call it a passenger?

S: Maybe a lodger. *(very faint)*

T: What do you call somebody who stays in a hotel?

S: Lodger.

T: Not a lodger, no. Hotel-? *(pause)* Somebody who stays in a hotel. Yes? What do we call that person? Hotel...? Know this word? *(writes 'g' on the board)*

S: *(very faint)* Guest.

T: Guest. Right. ...

1 (들리는지 확인해 보세요.) Check if you can understand.
2 ((테이프에서) 무엇을 들었습니까?) What did you hear?
3 (답해 볼 사람?) Does anyone want to answer?
4 (그 밖에 대화 내용에서 알 수 있는 것은?)
   What else do you know about the conversation?
5 (무엇에 대한 이야기입니까?) What are they talking about?

해석 _____

선생님: 대화가 어디에서 일어나고 있는지 말해 보세요: 어디죠? 듣고 확인하세요.
(녹음된 대화의 시작 부분을 들려준다: 전화가 울리고 목소리가 나온다: 안녕하세요, 오리엔털 호텔입니다. 무엇을 도와드릴까요?)

선생님: 자, 이겁니다. 대화는 어디에서 일어나고 있습니까? (잠시 멈춤) 지금 테이프에서 무엇을 들었습니까? (잠시 멈춤) 누가 답해 볼 사람? 무엇을 들었습니까?

학생: 호텔.

선생님: 호텔. 호텔의 이름을 들었습니까?

학생: 오리엔털 호텔.

선생님: 오리엔털 호텔. 맞습니다. 그리고 (잠시 멈춤) 대화에서 그 밖에 어떤 것을 알았습니까? (잠시 멈춤) 호텔 안에 두 사람이 있습니까?

학생: 아니오.

선생님: 아니라. 아니? 왜 아니지? (잠시 멈춤) 호텔 안에서 두 사람이 이야기하고 있지 않습니까? (잠시 멈춤) 대화는 어디에서 진행되고 있습니까? 호텔이지만, 그 밖에 다른 것은 없습니까? 이것은 어떤 종류의 대화입니까? (잠시 멈춤) 다시 들으세요. 어떤 종류의 대화인지. (선생님은 전화가 울리는 소리를 재생한다.) 자, 어떤 종류의 대화지요?

학생: 전화. (매우 약한 목소리로)

선생님: 전화 대화. 맞습니다. 그래요 호텔에서의 대화입니다. 무엇에 대한 대화입니까? 이것은 호텔에서의 전화 대화입니다. 그 대화는 무엇에 관한 것입니까? (잠시 멈춤) 모릅니까? (한 학생을 지명한다) 무엇에 대한 대화입니까? 그 대화는 무엇에 대한 것이라고 생각합니까?

학생: 안내요원이라고 생각합니다. (매우 약한 목소리로)

선생님: 호텔 안내요원입니다. 좋아요. 한 사람은 안내요원입니다. 그리고 다른 사람은

누구입니까? (잠시 멈춤) 어떻게 생각합니까?

학생: (이해하지 못함)

선생님: … 중의 한 사람?

학생: 승객.

선생님: 승객이라고 부르지 않지요?

학생: 아마, 하숙하는 사람. (매우 약한 목소리로)

선생님: 호텔에 투숙하는 사람을 무엇이라고 합니까?

학생: 하숙하는 사람.

선생님: 하숙하는 사람이 아닙니다. 호텔? (잠시 멈춤) 호텔에 머무는 사람. 그래요? 그 사람을 무엇이라고 하지요? 호텔…? 이 단어를 알아요? (칠판에 'g'를 쓴다.)

학생: (매우 약한 목소리로) 손님.

선생님: 손님. 맞습니다.

2. 기본구문

여기에서는 시청각 자료를 통하여 학습자료를 듣고 문제를 풀이하는 과정에 대해 다음과 같이 정리하였다: A. 듣기준비와 방법 B. 듣기연습 및 문제

A. 듣기준비와 방법

① Now, listen (to the tape).

해설   자, (테이프를) 들으세요.

syn   Let's listen. *(informal)*
Now, let's listen to the tape [the recording].
Now pay attention to the tape.
Focus your attention on the tape.
See if you can catch what's being said. *(coll.)*

Listen to the tape recording. *(usual, redundant)*
('the tape' 또는 'the recording'만으로도 충분히 의미가 전달되지만 분명히 나타내기 위해서 둘 다 사용하기도 한다.)

Listen carefully.
Listen up.
Listen up carefully. *(awkward)*
('up'에 'carefully'의 의미가 이미 포함되어 있다.)

어휘   '녹음기'와 '(녹음)테이프'는 구별하여 사용해야 한다.
녹음기: cassette player, player

녹음테이프: cassette tape, cassette, tape

② Let's listen to the conversation [dialogue].

해설 담화[대화]를 들으세요.

syn Now listen to the conversation on the tape.
Let's begin by listening to the conversation.
We're going to listen to the conversation.
Everybody listen up. I'm going to play the conversation on the tape.
First (of all), listen to the conversation.

③ First, let's listen to the dialogue [conversation].

해설 먼저, 다음 대화[담화]를 들으세요.

syn To start with listen to the dialogue [conversation] on the tape.
To begin with, you can listen to the dialogue [conversation] on the tape.
Let's start off by listening to the dialogue.
Let's get started.

You can hear the dialogue [sentences] on the tape. *(rare)*
: 수업 중에 '(자료를)듣다'는 의미로는 'hear'가 아닌 'listen to'를 사용한다.

어휘 first=to begin with, the first time , firstly

'Hear'와 'listen to'의 차이

일반적으로 'hear'와 'listen to'의 차이를 주의(attention)를 기울이는가 그렇지 않은가로 구분하지만 이것은 잘못된 기준이다. 다음 예문을 보자.

> e.g. I once heard [*listened to] Brendel play all the Beethoven concertos.

위의 경우는 베토벤의 협주곡 전부를 귀를 기울여 들은 것이다. 이 경우에는 'listen to'보다 'hear'가 더 적절하다. 따라서 그 규칙은 다음과 같이 수정되어야 한다. 즉, 다음 두 가지 경우에는 원칙적으로 'hear'를 사용한다는 것이다.

① 주의를 기울이지 않는데, 소리가 들려올(come to one's ears) 경우
> e.g. Did you hear that noise?

② 그 순간에 진행되는 활동(ongoing stimulus)이 아니라, 전체적인 행위(complete event)를 나타낼 경우.
> e.g. Have you heard his latest album?

cf. When he phoned I was listening to the radio.(동작의 진행)
(= He phoned while I was listening to the radio.)
(그가 전화를 걸었을 때, 나는 라디오를 듣고 있었다.)

---

④ Books shut, then. Ready to listen? Ann speaks first.

해설 책을 덮으세요. 자 준비 되었습니까? 앤이 먼저 말합니다.

syn Let's close our books and listen. Ann will speak first. *(formal)*

Close your books. Ready to listen? Ann will begin[start, lead-off].

Close your books. Ready to listen? It's Ann who speaks first. *(rare)*

cf. 듣기 연습에 연관된 표현들

OK, I want you to practice a short dialogue.

(짧은 대화를 연습하겠습니다.)

Well, now, We're going to listen to a short dialogue today.

(자, 이제, 짧은 대화를 듣겠습니다.)

I want you to listen again and this time, repeat Ann's part, all together.

(자, 다시 듣겠습니다. 이번에는 앤의 말을 다 함께 반복하세요.)

Alright then, work in pairs and I'll come round and listen.

(자, 짝을 지어 연습하세요. 나는 둘러보겠습니다.)

---

⑤ Ready? I'll turn it on.

해설 준비되었습니까? 틀겠습니다.

syn OK? Let's start.
All set? Then, let's begin.
Everybody ready? Let's start.
If you're ready I'll start the tape.
If you're ready let's get started.
Ready (to start)? We're gonna' start now. *(casual)*

어휘 'Turn the volume down [up]' (음을 내리다(높이다), 'adjust the tone'(음을 조정하다), 'adjust the focus'(촛점을 맞추다) 등도 흔히 사용되는 표현이다.

Listen carefully to the instructions. (지시사항을 잘 들으세요.)

Listen again and this time, when I stop, complete the sentence.
(다시 듣고, 이번에는, 내가 중지하면, 문장을 완성하세요.)

So, are you ready to listen and answer these questions? I'll start the tape.
(그래, 듣고 질문에 답할 준비가 되었습니까? 테이프를 틀겠습니다.)

---

⑥ Here goes.

해설 '자! 시작합니다.'라는 의미이다. 즉 어떤 언어적 설명을 실제 행동으로 시범을 보일 때 사용하는 관용어이다. 이때 'go'는 'to behave in a certain way ; gesture, act, or make sounds as specified or shown' (언어적 설명을 실제로 몸짓, 행위, 소리 등을 통하여 시범을 보인다.)의 의미를 지닌다. 간단히 'O.K.'라고 말하고 수업을 시작하는 선생님이 많다.

syn O.K.
Here we go.
Here it goes. *(rare)*

cf. 구별해야 할 표현
Off we go then. (= Let's leave.) (자, 갑시다.): 떠날 때 사용.
Here it comes. (자, 간다.): 주로 물건을 (던져서) 건네줄 때 사용된다.
Here it comes now. (= Now we'll start): 연극이나 공연의 시작을 알릴 때.

참고 **'Here we go'의 용례**
다음은 미국 방송인 'Oprah Winfrey Show'에서 청소년 문제에 대해 이야기를 시작할 때에 나왔던 대사이다.
The secret emotional life of boys is next. Here we go...
American boys are living what many of them have described as

"a double life" from the outside...
(다음으로 청소년들의 겉으로 드러나지 않는 정서생활에 대해 말씀드리겠습니다. 자, 시작하겠습니다. ⋯미국 소년들은 겉으로 흔히 말하는 이중생활을 하고 있습니다. ⋯)

---

⑦ It's not in properly.

해설   테이프를 잘못 [반대 방향으로] 넣었습니다.
: '잘못 넣었다'는 'wrong', 'on the wrong side', 'in the wrong way' 등으로 표현한다.

syn   I seem to have put it in on the wrong side.
It's in wrong. *(informal)*
It's in the wrong way.

I seem to have put it in upside down.
It needs to be re-inserted.

---

⑧ This is the wrong tape.

해설   다른 테이프를 가져온 것 같습니다.

syn   I seem to have brought the wrong tape.
This isn't the right tape.
This isn't the tape I need.

⑨ I'll play it twice.

해설 두 번 듣겠습니다.

syn I'm going to repeat it.
I'll play it two times.
You'll hear it [the tape] twice.

cf. 반복과 관련된 표현들
① '다시 한 번 더 듣겠습니다.'
Let's listen again.
Let's have a second listen. *(rare)*
Let's go over it again.

② '한 번만 듣겠습니다.'
I'm not going to repeat it.
I'll only play it once.
This is the first and last time I'll play it.
I'm playing it one time only.

③ '테이프를 되감고 다시 들어 보십시오. [재생하시오.]'
Rewind your tapes and listen again.
Replay the tape.
Rewind and play the tape again.
Play back the tape.
Go back to the beginning[start] and play the tape again.

④ '필요하면 여러 번 들려주겠습니다.'
I'll play it as many times as necessary.
I'll play it over and over.
I'll play it repeatedly if you want.

누구나 영어로 가르칠 수 있다

I'll play it continuously if necessary.
If you want, I can play it again.

---

⑩ Review the tape as many times as you like.

해설　　필요하면 여러 번 들어도 좋습니다.

syn　　Play it (over again) as often as you need to.
Repeat the tape as often as you like.
Replay it as many times as you need.
Feel free to stop the tape as many times as you want.
Keep listening until you get it.
Keep listening until you feel comfortable.

---

⑪ There are two people talking, A and B. A asks a question and B answers. Listen.

해설　　두 사람, A와 B가 대화를 하고 있습니다. A는 묻고, B는 답을 합니다. 잘 들으세요.

syn　　A poses a question and B responds.
A says something and B answers. *(rare)*

---

⑫ Look at the questions while I find the place.

해설　　내가 학습할 부분을 찾는 동안 문제를 보세요.

syn　　Look over the questions while I find the place.

cf. Please review [go over] the questions while I fast-forward the tape. (내가 테이프를 앞으로 감는 동안 문제를 검토해 보세요.)

어휘 fast-forward (앞으로 감다)=advance, wind, move along
reverse (되감다.)=rewind
play back (다시 틀다)=play again

B. 듣기연습 및 문제

① Listen and repeat (out loud).

해설 듣고 (크게) 따라하세요.

syn Repeat after the tape.
Listen (to the tape) and say it (out loud).
All together, after the tape. *(rare)*

*Say after the tape. *(incorrect)*

cf. Repeat along with the tape. (테이프를 따라 반복하세요.)
= Let's speak along with the tape.
*Say along with the tape. *(incorrect)*

Read along with the tape.
(테이프를 따라 읽으세요 ; 읽기자료가 있을 경우)

참고 'Repeat after the tape'는 테이프를 들은 뒤에 되풀이하는 것이고, 'repeat along with the tape'는 테이프와 동시에 말하는 것이다.

② Let's listen to it once more [once again].

해설 한 번 더 들읍시다.

syn Now we'll listen to it again.

cf. 반복 듣기 연습과 연관된 표현들

Listen (again) and say it after me [repeat after me].
(듣고, 내 말을 반복하세요.)
Just listen. Don't say anything. (듣기만 하세요. 아무 말도 하지 마세요.)
I want you to listen again, and this time, repeat Ann's part all together.
(다시 듣고, 이번에는 앤의 말을 모두 반복하세요.)
Alright then, work in pairs and I'll come round and listen.
(좋아요. 짝을 지어 연습하세요. 나는 돌아다니면서 듣겠습니다.)
Now, before we practice in pairs, shall we repeat it once more all together?
(짝을 지어 연습하기 전에, 다시 한 번 모두 반복해 보겠습니다.)

③ Did you catch that? I'll go back and play it again.

해설 이해하였습니까? 처음부터 다시 들려주겠습니다.

syn Were you able to understand that? We'll go back and listen again.
Could you understand? Let's play it again.
Did you get it? Listen again.
Has it sunk in now? Should we play it again? *(slang)*
Do we need to repeat that? OK, let's play it again.

④ Wait. Was that correct? Listen again.

해설   잠깐, 그것이 [그 말이] 맞습니까? 다시 들으세요.

syn   Just a minute, was that right? …
       Careful! Are you sure about that? …
       I'm not sure that was correct. Check your answers.

어휘   wait=just a minute, hold it, hold on, wait a minute, let's stop
       there

⑤ As you listen, fill in the missing words.

해설   들으면서, 빈 단어를 채워 넣으세요.

syn   While you are listening [While listening], fill in the blanks.

cf. 듣기와 문제풀이
       Listen again and this time, when I stop, complete the sentence.
       (다시 들으세요. 그리고 이번에 내가 멈추면, 문장을 채우세요.)

⑥ Before listening (again), read through the questions.

해설   (다시) 듣기 전에, 문제를 읽어 보세요.

syn   Before listening (again), familiarize yourself with the questions.
       Before listening (again), go over the questions.
       Before listening (again), take a good look at the questions.

read through=read over, go over

⑦ Before we go on, let me ask you some questions.

해설   계속하기 전에, 몇 가지 질문을 하겠습니다.

syn   Before we go on, I'll ask you some questions.
       Before we move on, I'd like to check your understanding
       [comprehension].
       (이 경우에는 'understanding'이 'comprehension'보다 흔히 사용된다.)
       Before we move (further) ahead, …
       Before we move forward, …
       Before moving on, …
       Before we go [proceed] any further, …

   cf. 듣기 문제의 풀이방법에 대한 지문
       Now we'll take the test. Let me explain what I want you to do. First you
       must listen to the tape. You'll hear it only once. After that you must
       answer the questions by checking the right choices.
       (자, 시험을 치겠습니다. 방법을 설명하겠습니다. 먼저, 테이프를 듣습니다. 한
       번만 들려주겠습니다. 들은 다음, 질문에 대해 바른 답을 표시하세요.)

어휘   checking=marking, ticking

◆ 미국영어와 영국영어의 차이점(어휘와 구문)

다음 차이점은 반드시 절대적인 것이 아니며, 미국의 각 지역 그리고 개인 간에 차이가 있다는 점을 유의해야 한다.

A. 어휘

미국영어와 영국영어는 다소 차이가 있는데, 그 중에 특히 6가지 분야 ― 사업과 재정(Business and Finance), 의복(Clothes), 교육(Educa-tion), 식사와 음료수(Food and Drink), 가구와 숙박(Household and Accommodation), 여행(Travel) ― 에서 뚜렷한 차이가 있다. 여기에서는 이 중 가장 널리 사용되는 몇 가지 사항만 정리하였다. 각각의 표현에 대한 간단한 논평은 미국인들과의 대화를 통해서 종합한 내용이다. 실재 미국인들도 개인차가 크므로, 이런 구별이 절대적이라고 단정하기는 어렵지만, 대체적으로 구별해서 사용하면 예기치 않은 실수를 방지하는 데 도움이 될 것이다.

1 사업과 재정(Business and Finance)

	American English	British English
(식당의) 계산서	check	bill
	: 미국영어에서도 둘 다 혼용이 되지만 식당의 계산서는 'check', 각종 공과금은 'bill'을 많이 사용한다.	
당좌예금	checking account	current account
저축예금	savings account	deposit account
외무부	the State Department	the Foreign Office
(전화를)걸다	call someone up	phone someone
수신인 지불로 걸다	call collect	reverse charges

: 이때 'collect'는 부사로서 '수신인 지불로'라는 의미를 지니며, '수신인 지불 전화'는 'collect call'이다. 물론 미국에서도 교환수에게 'reverse charges'라고 하면, 충분히 이해된다고 한다.

주식	stocks	shares
	: 미국영어에서 'stocks'는 일반적인 주식을 의미하고, 'share'는 '주'를 의미한다.	
(상점)점원	sales clerk	shop assistant
채권	bonds	stocks
변호사	lawyer, attorney	solicitor

2 의복(Clothes)

	American English	British English
바지멜빵	suspender	braces
양말대님	garters	suspenders
턱시도	tuxedo	dinner jacket
실내복	bathrobe, robe	dressing gown
(여자용)핸드백	pocketbook, purse	handbag
	: 미국에서는 여자들의 휴대용 작은 가방(주로 돈, 화장품을 넣음)을 'purse', 다소 큰 휴대용 가방을 'pocketbook'이라고 하며, 'handbag'이라는 말은 거의 사용되지 않는다.	
작은 돈지갑	change purse	purse
잠옷	pajamas	pyjamas
팬티스타킹	nylons, pantyhose	tights
바지	pants, slacks	trousers
	: 미국에서는 'slacks'라는 말은 주로 양복바지가 아닌, 일반적인 바지를 일컫는다.	

속옷	underwear, underpants, panty, briefs, boxers	underpants panties,
	: 일반적으로 미국에서 속옷은 'underwear'라고 한다. 반면 좀 더 세부적으로는 여자들의 속옷을 'panty', 남자들의 속옷을 'briefs' 또는 'boxers'라고 한다. 또한 여자들의 속에 입는 모든 것 – 브래지어(brassiere), 소매 없는 속옷(camisole) 포함 – 을 통칭하여 'lingerie'(란제리)라고 한다.	
상의속옷	undershirt	vest
	: 미국에서는 상의 겉옷 바로 아래 입는 소매 없는 옷을 'undershirt'라고 한다.	
조끼	vest	waistcoat

3 교육(Education)

	American English	**British English**
학년	grade	class, form
초등학교	grade school[elementary school]	primary school
중등학교	high school	secondary school
공립학교	public school	state school
(2년제)초급대학. 실업전문대학	junior college, community college	technical college
	: 미국에서는 전문기술을 배우는 2년제 대학을 'technical college'라고 한다.	
대학원생	graduate	postgraduate
	: 미국에서는 학부과정을 'undergraduate courses', 대학원 석사과정을 'graduate courses', 박사과정을 'postgraduate courses'라고 한다.	
(대학, 중등) 교원, 교수단	faculty	staff
강사	instructor	lecturer

: 미국에서는 전임강사를 'instructor', 시간강사를 '(part-time) lecturer'라고 한다. 또한 강의를 전담하는 사람도 'lecturer'라 한다. 태권도와 같은 운동 또는 훈련을 시키는 사람을 'instructor'라고도 한다.

조교수	assistant professor	senior lecturer
부교수	associate professor	reader
(정)교수	senior / full professor	professor
이력서	resume, C.V.	curriculum vitae, C.V.
	: 미국에서는 이력서를 주로 'resume'이라고 한다.	
리포트	paper, report, essay	essay
숙제	asssignment, homework	homework
	: 미국영어에서도 'assignment'와 'homework'는 둘 다 널리 사용된다.	
논문	thesis	long essay, paper
	: 미국영어에서 석사학위 논문은 'thesis', 박사학위 논문은 'dissertation'이라고 한다.	

4 식품과 음료(Food and Drink)

	American English	British English
감자튀김	French fries	chips
	: 미국영어에서 'Frech fries'와 '(potato)chips'는 다른 종류의 간식이다.	
물을 타지 않은	straight, straight up	neat
얼음(덩어리)을 넣은	on the rocks	with ice
	: 미국에서는 'on the rocks'뿐만 아니라 'with ice'도 널리 사용된다.	
청량음료	soda, pop	soft drink
	: 미국영어에서는 주로 'soda'라 하고, 'pop'은 가끔 사용된다.	
술	liquor	spirits

사탕	candy	sweets
하이볼(위스키에 소다수를 섞은 술)	highball	whiskey cocktail

5 가구와 숙박 (household and accomodation)

	American English	**British English**
알루미늄	aluminum	aluminum
(창문)가리개	shade	blind
	: 미국에서도 'shade'뿐 아니라 'blind'도 널리 사용된다.	
커튼	drapes, drapery	curtains
	: 미국영어에서 'drapery'는 긴 커튼을, 'curtains'는 짧은 커튼을 말한다. 찬장 closet cupboard	
찬장	closet	cupboard
	: 미국에서는 부엌 싱크대 위에 있는 문이 달린 찬장이나, 책장(bookcase)이라도 문이 달려 있으면, 쇠로 되었건 나무로 되었건 모두 'cabinet'이라고 한다. 반면 돈 넣는 금고는 'safe'라고 한다.	
고무젖꼭지	pacifier	dummy
쓰레기통	garbage / trash can	dustbin
부동산 중개업자	realtor, real estate agent	estate agent
아파트(건물)	apartment building	block of flats
아파트(세 들어 사는)	apartment	flat
아파트(분양받은)	condominium / condo	flat
1층	first floor	ground floor
2층	second floor	first floor
임대	ease / rent	let
엘리베이터	elevator	lift

수도꼭지	faucet / tap	tap
설거지하다	do the dishes	wash up
세수하다	wash up	wash
	: 미국에서 'wash up'은 '설거지하다'라는 의미가 아닌 'wash one's face(세수하다)'라는 의미로 사용된다.	

6 여행(Travel)

	American English	**British English**
예약하다	make a reservation	book
	: 미국에서는 '예약하다'라는 의미로 'book'도 흔히 사용된다.	
주차장	parking lot	car park
휴대품 보관소	coatroom, checkroom	cloakroom
	: 미국에서는 'coatroom'이 일반적으로 사용된다.	
우회로	detour	diversion
(전차, 버스, 열차의) 차장	conductor	guard
	: 오늘날 미국에서 'conductor'는 '차장'이라는 의미로 거의 사용되지 않으며, 주로 '(기차, 지하철 등) 전동차를 운전하는 사람'을 지칭한다.	
(도로의) 교차점	intersection, junction	junction
고속도로	freeway, highway, express way	motorway
	: 영국과 미국에서 집 근처 찻길은 'driveway'라고 한다.	
번호판	license plate	numberplate
인도	sidewalk	pavement, footpath
휘발유, 가솔린	gasoline, gas	petrol
화장실	bathroom, restroom, washroom	public convinience, toilet
	: 미국에서는 일반적으로 'bathroom'이 널리 사용된다.	

철도	railroad	railway
(호텔의) 접수계원	receptionist, desk clerk	receptionist
왕복표	round-trip ticket	return ticket
편도표	one-way ticket	single ticket
	: 미국에서 'single ticket'은 '일인용 표'라는 의미를 가진다.	
지하도	underpass	subway
시간표, 예정표	schedule	timetable
지하철	subway	tube, underground

B. 문법과 구문

미국영어(American English: A.E.)와 영국영어(British English: B.E.)는 발음, 철자, 어휘, 문법에서 다소간의 차이를 보인다. 영문법의 기준은 현재까지는 영국영어로 하고 있다. 여기에서는 일상적으로 널리 사용되는 문장을 중심으로 차이점을 몇 가지 기술해 보겠다. 물론 문법적인 사항에 대한 관점은 개인에 따라 다소 차이가 있으므로 반드시 절대적이라고 할 수는 없다.

1 **형용사와 부사:** 수식어로 미국영어는 부사의 위치에 형용사형을 널리 사용한다.
   e.g. He drives really fast. *(B.E.)* vs *He drives real fast. *(A.E., incorrect)*
       We had a really good time. vs *We had a real good time. *(incorrect)*
       : 구어에서 'real'이 'really'보다 널리 사용되는 것은 분명하지만, 아직 문법적으로는 틀린 것으로 처리되므로 유의해야 한다.

2 **완료형과 과거형:** 영국영어는 완료형을, 미국영어는 과거형을 선호한다. 이것은 미국영어에서 완료형이 점점 축소되는 경향 때문으로 보인다.
   e.g. Have you finished it already / yet? *(B.E.)*
       vs Did you finish it already / yet? *(A.E.)*
       I've seen it already. *(B.E.)* vs I saw it already. *(A.E.)*

: 몇몇 미국인들은 이 두 개의 의미를 다른 것으로 생각한다.

'Did you finish it already?'는 '벌써 마쳤니?'라는 예상보다 빠르다는 의미로, 'Have you finished it yet?'은 '이제는 마쳤니?'라는 조금 늦었다는 의미로 사용하기도 한다.

3 **관사의 사용:** 영국영어에서 관사를 붙이지 않는 경우에도, 미국영어에서는 관사를 사용하는 경우가 있다.

    e.g. be at table *(B.E.)* vs be at the table *(A.E.)*
          be in hospital vs be in the hospital
          go to university vs go to a university
          in future vs in the future

4 **조동사의 용법**

  ① 일부 조동사 - 'dare', 'need' - 의 부정형: 영국영어에서는 직접 'not'을 붙이는 반면, 미국영어에서는 일반적으로 'don't'를 사용한다.

    e.g. I daren't do it.*(B.E.)* vs I don't dare do it. *(A.E.)*
          You needn't go. vs You don't have to go.

  ② 미국영어에서는 'would'도 과거의 규칙적 행위를 나타낼 수 있다.

    e.g. We went [used to go] there every day. *(B.E.)*
              vs
          We would go there everyday. *(A.E.)*

  : 미국에서는 단순한 사실을 이야기할 때는 과거형을, 이야기나 추억을 이야기할 때에는 'would'를 사용하기도 한다.

5 **명사의 단수형과 복수형:** 스포츠, 학문에서 영국영어와 미국영어는 다소 차이가 있다.

    e.g. He has decided to study maths. *(B.E.)*
              vs
          He has decided to study math. *(A.E.)*

          She is excellent at sport. *(B.E.)*

                        vs
   She is excellent at sports. *(A.E.)*
   : 미국에서는 수학은 'math'로, 스포츠는 'sports'로 주로 표기한다.

6 **전치사:** 영국영어와 미국영어는 선호하는 전치사가 다르다.

British English	American English
He hid it behind the house.	He hid it in back of the house.
I've tried talking to her.	I've tried talking with her.

(미국에서는 단순히 말을 걸 때에는 'talk to', 대화를 나눌 때는 'talk with'를 주로 사용한다.)

It's five past four. It's five after four.
(둘 다 널리 사용된다.)

Please fill in this form.	Please fill out this form.
They were in a sale.	They were on sale.

(미국영어에서 'in a sale'은 사용하지 않는다.)

Rows A up to and including D Rows A through D
(are reserved for non-smokers.)   (are reserved for non-smokers.)

7 **대명사:** 선행사 'one' 뒤에는 영국영어는 'one'을, 미국영어는 'he / she'를 선호한다.
   One should always do what one knows is right. *(B.E.)*
   One should always do what he / she knows is right. *(A.E.)*

8 **부정사:** 영국영어는 동사 뒤에 부정사를 사용하는 반면, 미국영어는 접속사 또는 생략형을 널리 사용한다.
   Come to see me tomorrow *(B.E.)*
   vs Come (and) see me tomorrow. *(A.E.)*
   You should help to clean the car
   vs You should help clean the car.

We ordered him to be followed.
vs We ordered him followed.

9 **가정법:** 영국영어에서는 'should'가 주로 사용되나, 미국영어에서는 둘 다 사용된다.
He advised me that we should be set free. *(B.E.)*
He advised me that we be set free. *(A.E.)*

1. 현장예문 (Real-life Situation)

Solving Cloze Test

(adapted from Yeghis Aslanian(1985))

독해자료에 대한 토의는 자료의 내용과 자료에 대한 학생의 이해와의 차이를 분명하게 알 수 있게 해 준다. 또한 실제 학생이 문제 이외의 내용 중 자신이 이해하지 못한 부분을 확인할 수 있게 해 주며, 논리적 표현력도 길러준다.

다음은 뉴욕에 있는 어느 대학의 학생에게 독해자료에 대한 이해력을 구두로 질문한 것이다. 학생은 미국에서 7년 이상 머물고 있는 외국인 학생이다. 이 학생은 유창한 영어를 구사하지만, 문장에 대한 이해력 및 논리적 설명력은 약하다.

이 자료는 독해뿐만 아니라 회화교육에도 도움이 될 것이다.

Solving cloze tests is a lesson activity that effectively engages students in reading both individually and with a partner using a more communicative and interactive approach. Therefore, it is important that the teacher use English to facilitate these activities so that the students are motivated to do so themselves. This unit focuses on questioning the students about correct or incorrect word choices, checking for reading comprehension, engaging the students in the activity, and asking the students to read aloud.

Now listen to the instructions, passage, and dialogue.

Instructions

Read this passage and choose one of these words for the blanks. After you finish reading and fill out the spaces, I will ask you to give me reasons for your choices. Then you will tell me what you have understood from the passage. You can read the passage as many times as you wish to.[1]

Bridges

Bridges are built to allow a continuous flow of highway and railway traffic across water lying in their paths. Engineers can't forget the fact that river traffic, too, is essential to our economy. The role of (1) _____ is important. To keep these vessels moving freely, bridges are built high enough, when possible, to let them pass underneath. Sometimes, however, channels must accommodate very tall ships. It may be uneconomical to build a tall enough bridge. The (2) _____ would be too high. To save money, engineers build movable bridges.

(1) a. wind   b. boats   c. weight   d. wires   e. experience
(2) a. levels   b. cost   c. standards   d. waves   e. deck

〈문제 풀이〉

(Note: the grammar of the students' responses has not been corrected.)

T:　What is the word that you have chosen for question(1)?[2]

Ss:　Boats.[3]

T:　Why did you choose that?[4]

Ss:　Because I figure it's talking about boats, you know. The path, engineers, the river…

T:　Why do you think the others are not correct?[5]

Ss:　We are not talking about the wind, etc. They are talking about bridges. We are talking about traffic, so it's got to be boats.

T:　What about question 2?

Ss:	I picked levels. They are talking about... it's talking about how to build tall enough bridges.
T:	Could you read the sentence with your choice?
Ss:	The levels will be too high. To save money, engineers... OK. The cost would be too high.
T:	What made you change your mind?[6]
Ss:	OK. I changed my mind because to save money engineers build movable bridges. So we're talking about money. So it could be cost.
T:	Why do you think levels was not the correct answer?[7]
Ss:	cause we are talking about economics, so it has to do with money.
T:	Now, tell me everything you understood from this passage.
Ss:	The passage is mainly about the bridge... the boat should not be built at too high a level because of the bridge. It would be uneconomical to build another bridge. So to economize, we shouldn't build boats too high.
T:	Is that what you get from the passage?[8]
Ss:	Yes.
T:	Is there any word you don't understand in this passage?[9]
Ss:	Movable bridge. I'm not sure about it... I haven't seen one.
T:	Let's go back to the beginning of the first passage for a moment. Can you tell me what the first sentence means?
Ss:	It's trying to say that bridges are built high for the water path and the flow like the waves would not interfere with the bridge.
T:	Where does it say that?
Ss:	It says bridges are built to allow continuous flow of highway and railway traffic across the water lying in their paths.
T:	What does the word 'uneconomical' mean?
Ss:	OK. 'Uneconomical' would be like inflation, things that are happening.

T:	If something is uneconomical, how do you think it is?
Ss:	It means no use.
T:	Why is it no use building high bridges?
Ss:	I think it's no use because they haven't had any trouble: you know, that the ships are going under the bridge. Maybe the level is OK. It's no use to build it higher.
T:	Do you have any comments?[10]
Ss:	My other problem is that I just don't like to read.[11]

A cloze test is a gap-fill exercise using a longer text with a consistent number of words between gaps (e.g. every 9th word). The word 'cloze' is often incorrectly used to describe any gap-filling task. (From Jim Scrivener(1994))
(Cloze Test(규칙적인 괄호 채우기)는 장문의 문장에서 일정한 차례대로 - 예를 들면, 매 9번째 단어 - 단어를 비워 두고 채우는 시험이다. '클로즈'라는 단어는 종종 잘못하여 단순히 괄호 채우기(gap-filling) 문제를 설명하기 위해서 사용되기도 한다.)

1 (글은 여러 번 읽어도 좋습니다.)
   Read as often as you like ;
   You can read the passage as many times as you need to.
2 (1번 문제에 대해 선택한 단어는 무엇입니까?)
   What did you choose for question (1)?
   What is your answer [choice] for question (1)?
3 (보트입니다.) I think it's boats ; Question (1) is boats.
4 (왜 그것을 선택했습니까?) Why do you think it's boats?
5 (다른 것들은 왜 맞지 않습니까?) What was wrong with the others?
6 (왜 생각을 바꾸었습니까?) What caused you to change your mind?
7 ('Levels'는 왜 정답이 아닙니까?) What was wrong with 'levels'?
8 (그 글에 대해 당신은 그렇게 이해했습니까?)
   Is that your understanding of the passage?
9 (이 글에서 모르는 단어가 있습니까?)
   Any words that you don't understand in this passage?
10 (또 할 말이 있습니까?) Do you have anything to add?
11 (나의 문제점은 독서를 싫어한다는 것입니다.)
   Another problem is that I just don't like to read.
   : 'Another'와 'my'는 함께 쓸 수 없으므로, 'Another my problem'은 잘못이다.

〈지시사항〉
다음 글을 읽고 괄호 속에 들어갈 단어를 고르세요. 읽고 괄호를 채운 다음에는, 여러분이
선택한 이유를 물을 것입니다. 그러면 여러분은 이 글에 대해 이해한 사실을 말해야 합니
다. 글은 여러 번 읽어도 좋습니다.

〈다리〉
다리는 도중에 있는 고속도로와 철로가 물을 가로질러 계속적으로 연결되도록 하기 위해
서 세워집니다. 그러나 기술자들은 강의 수로도 우리 경제에 필수적이라는 것을 알고 있
습니다. (1)의 역할은 중요합니다. 이 배들이 자유롭게 항해하기 위해서는, 가능한 한 다리
가 지나갈 수 있을 정도로 충분히 높아야 합니다. 때로, 그렇지만, 수로는 매우 큰 배를 수
용해야 합니다. 여기에 충분한 높은 다리를 짓는 것은 비경제적입니다. (2)는 너무 높습니
다. 경비를 절약하기 위해서, 기술자들은 움직일 수 있는 다리를 건축합니다.

(1) a. 바람   b. 보트   c. 무게   d. 쇠줄   e. 경험
(2) a. 높이   b. 비용   c. 표준   d. 파도   e. 갑판

〈문제 풀이〉
(주의: 학생들의 대답에 대한 문법적인 사항은 수정하지 않았다.)
선생님: (1)번 문제에 대해 선택한 단어는 무엇입니까?
학생들: 배.
선생님: 왜 그 단어를 선택했습니까?
학생: 그 글이 보트에 대해 이야기하고 있다고 생각하기 때문입니다. 길, 기술자, 강….
선생님: 왜 다른 단어는 맞지 않습니까?
학생: 이 글은 바람에 대해 이야기하지 않습니다. 다리에 대해 이야기하고 있습니다.
교통에 대해 이야기하고 있으므로, 그것은 보트가 되어야 합니다.
선생님: 2번 문제는 어떻습니까?
학생: 높이를 선택했습니다. 그들은 이야기하고 있습니다. … 그 글은 충분히 큰 다리
를 짓는 방법에 대해 이야기하고 있습니다.
선생님: 선택한 단어를 넣어서 문장을 읽어보세요.
학생: 높이가 너무 높다 경비를 절약하기 위해서, 기술자들은… 맞아. 비용이 너무 높다.
선생님: 왜 생각을 바꾸었습니까?
학생: 그래요. 경비를 절약하기 위해서 움직이는 다리를 짓기 때문에 생각을 바꾸었
습니다. 그래서 우리는 비용에 대해 이야기하고 있습니다. 그래서 그것은 비용

입니다.

선생님: 왜 높이가 올바른 답이 아니라고 생각합니까?

학생: 비경제적인 것에 대해 이야기하기 때문에, 그래서 그것은 돈과 관계되어야 합니다.

선생님: 자, 이 글에서 당신이 이해한 모든 것을 말해 보세요.

학생: 그 글은 주로 다리에 대한 것입니다. … 다리 때문에 보트는 너무 높이 건조되지 않아야 합니다. 다른 다리를 짓는 것은 비경제적입니다. 그래서 절약하기 위해서, 너무 높은 배를 건조하지 않아야 합니다.

선생님: 그것이 그 글에서 알아낸 것입니까?

학생: 예.

선생님: 이 글에서 모르는 단어가 있습니까?

학생: 'Moveable bridge'. 나는 그것에 대해 잘 모릅니다. 나는 그런 것을 본 적이 없습니다.

선생님: 잠깐 첫째 단락의 앞부분으로 돌아갑시다. 첫 번째 문장의 의미는 무엇입니까?

학생: 다리가 높이 세워지는 것은 수로 또는 파도와 같은 물의 흐름이 다리에 방해가 될 수 있기 때문입니다.

선생님: 어느 부분에 그런 말이 있지요?

학생: 글에서 다리가 세워지면 고속도로와 철도가 물을 가로질러 갈 수 있다고 합니다.

선생님: 'Uneconomical'은 무슨 뜻입니까?

학생: 좋아요. 비경제적은 인플레이션과 같습니다. 흔히 일어나는 것들.

선생님: 어떤 것이 비경제적이면, 어떻다고 생각합니까?

학생: 그것은 소용없다는 의미입니다.

선생님: 높은 다리를 건축하는 것이 왜 소용이 없습니까?

학생: 높은 다리는 아무 문제가 없기 때문에 소용이 없다고 생각합니다: 배는 다리 아래로 갑니다. 아마 높이는 좋습니다. 다리를 더 높이 세우는 것은 소용이 없습니다.

선생님: 다른 할 말은 없습니까?

학생: 또 다른 문제는 읽기가 싫어요.

누구나 영어로 가르칠 수 있다

2. 기본구문

여기에서는 일상수업에서 널리 활용되는 각종 읽기 자료의 연습, 이해와 설명, 토의 및 내용에 대한 제반 문제풀이 등에 연관된 표현을 다음과 같이 정리하였다: A. 읽기연습 B. 내용파악 C. 해석 및 토론

A. 읽기연습

① Read the passage silently.

해설　그 글을 소리 내지 말고 읽으세요.

syn　Read the passage to yourselves.

Take a few moments to read over the passage by yourselves.

cf. 읽기연습과 관련된 표현

Let's read the text aloud. (본문을 크게 읽으세요.)

Now, read the first paragraph silently and find the answer to this.

(첫째 단락을 소리 내지 말고 읽은 다음, 이 문제에 대한 답을 찾으세요.)

Now, before we practice in pairs, shall we repeat it once more all together?

(짝을 지어 연습하기 전에, 다시 한 번 다 같이 반복하겠습니다.)

② Who would like to read Jim's part? *(informal)*

해설　짐의 대사를 읽을 사람은?

syn　Who would like to read the part of Jim? *(formal)*

Who wants to take the part of Jim?

Who wants to play the role of Jim?

cf. 읽을 차례에 대한 지시문

Go on reading, Minsu. (민수야, 계속해서 읽어라.)

Read the next section, will you, Minsu? (민수야 다음 부분을 읽어라.)

Minsu, pick up where Sunhi left off.

(민수야, 순희가 중단한 부분부터 읽어라.)

(= Minsu, go on from where Sunhi left off.)

③ Let's read the conversation again. Minsu, please read the part of Mr. Best.

해설   대화를 다시 읽읍시다. 민수, 베스트 씨의 대사를 읽어라.

syn   Let's read the conversation again, with you, Minsu, reading the part of Mr. Best.

Let's go through the conversation again, and Minsu will take the part of Mr. Best.

Let's read the conversation again. Minsu, you play the role of Mr. Best this time.

Let's try it again, but this time with Minsu as Mr. Best. *(informal)*

What if you read Mr. Best's part, Min-su? *(casual, request)*

What [How] about (you) reading Mr. Best's part, Minsu? *(casual, opinion)*

누구나 영어로 가르칠 수 있다

(전자의 'what if...'는 '베스트 씨의 대사를 읽어 볼래?'라는 가벼운 요구의 뜻이 있는 반면, 후자의 'what[how] about...'는 '베스트 씨의 대사를 읽어 보는 것을 어떻게 생각하니?'라는 상대방의 의견을 묻는 의미가 강하다. 따라서 교실 현장에서 선생님의 지시문으로는 전자가 더 적합하다.)

What do you think of reading Mr. Best's part, Minsu?
(not used)
(문법적으로는 옳지만 교실 현장에서는 사용하지 않는다.)

*What about if you read Mr. Best's part, Minsu? *(incorrect)*
('About'와 'if'를 동시에 사용할 수 없다.)

---

④ Read (down) to the end of the chapter.

해설   그 장의 끝까지 읽으세요.

syn   Read as far as the end of the chapter.

cf. 읽을 부문에 대한 지시문
Read one sentence each. (각각 한 문장씩 읽어라.)
Read the first paragraph [the first ten lines].
(첫째 단락[처음 열 줄]을 읽어라.)
Start reading from line 6. (여섯째 줄부터 읽어라.)

Read what it says at the top of the page first.
(먼저 그 페이지의 위에 있는 내용을 읽어라.)

B. 내용파악

---

① We'll look at some difficult points in this passage.

해설   이 글에서 어려운 부분을 살펴보겠습니다.

syn   Let's have a look at some of the difficult points.

Let's start with a look [by looking] at the difficulties in this passage.

There are one or two difficult points we should look at.

I'd like to point out some difficult words and constructions.

I'd like to take you through some of the difficult areas in the passages.

cf. Let's look at the passage in more detail.

(이 글을 좀 더 자세히 살펴봅시다.)

= (Perhaps) We should have a detailed look at the passage.

---

② T: Are there any questions about this text?
  S: I am not familiar with this expression.

해설   T: 이 글에 대한 질문이 있습니까?
      S: 이 표현을 모르겠습니다.

syn   T: Any questions?

Do you have [Have you got] any questions about this text?

Do you understand everything (we've covered) in the text?

Is there anything else you would like to ask about?

Are there any points you're not sure of?

Would you like something [anything] explained?
Does anyone have [Has anybody got] anything to ask about this text? *(rare)*
Is everybody clear?

S: This expression is unfamiliar [foreign] to me.
I don't know [get] this expression.
I'm not aware of this expression.
I don't understand.

③ What does it say at the top of the page?

해설   그 페이지의 위쪽에는 무엇이라고 쓰여 있습니까?

syn   Tell me what it says at the top of the page.
       What does the author say at the top of the page.

   cf. 본문의 대명사 또는 어휘의 의미에 대한 질문
       In line 8 [the 8th line from the top,] what does the author mean by 'it'?
       (여덟째 줄의 'it'의 의미는 무엇입니까?)
       In the 3rd line in paragraph 2, what do you think 'which' refers to?
       (둘째 단락의 3째 줄의 'which'는 무엇을 지칭합니까?)
       In the sentence beginning 'the man', why does he use the word
       'moreover'.
       ('The man'으로 시작되는 문장에서, 그는 왜 'moreover'라고 했습니까?)
       Near the bottom, why does he repeat the words '____'?
       (아랫 부분에서, 그는 왜 그 말'_____'을 반복하고 있습니까?)
       Look at line 7 for a moment. In line 7, you see the word 'it'.
       (일곱째 줄을 잠깐 보세요. 일곱째 줄에서, 'it'이 있습니다.)
       Look at the end of the very first line. (첫째 줄 끝을 보세요.)
       A little further down, about two lines from the bottom...
       (조금 더 아래, 밑에서 둘째 줄쯤에….)

④ Look at the third line of the second paragraph. You can see
   the word 'mean'.

해설   둘째 단락의 3번째 줄에 있는, 단어 'mean'을 보세요.

syn   Second paragraph, third line, the word 'mean'. *(casual)*
       I'd like to draw your attention to the word 'mean' in line 3 of

paragraph 2.

It's worth noting [noticing] how the word 'mean' is used in line 3 of paragraph 2.

⑤ S: I am not clear about the difference.

해설 차이점을 잘 모르겠습니다.

syn The difference is still not clear [apparent] to me.

I still don't see the difference.

I still can't pick up the difference.

I still don't know what the difference is.

참고 **'Still'의 네 가지 의미**

① '지금까지 (at this time), 아직까지'라는 의미를 지닌다.

It's still raining.

I'm still hungry.

위의 의미는 부정문에 사용되는 'yet'의 의미와 대응된다.

It hasn't stopped raining yet.

I'm not satisfied yet.

② 비교급을 수식하여 '훨씬(even, much)'의 의미를 지닌다.

: 오늘날에는 이 용법은 거의 사용되지 않는다.

Tom is tall but Mary is still taller. (훨씬(even, much))

③ '그럼에도 불구하고 (in spite of that)'의 의미를 지닌다.

We told him the car was no good, but he still bought it.

(그에게 그 차가 쓸모없다고 말했지만, 그는 그것을 샀다.)

④ 형용사로서 '조용한, 움직이지 않는(quiet or not moving)'의

의미를 지닌다.

Keep still. (가만히 있어라.)

---

⑥ What's the title? What could it be about?

해설   제목은 무엇입니까? 이 글은 무엇에 대한 것입니까?

syn   What do you think it is about?
      What's it about?

주의   What do you think of this?=How about this?(이것에 대해 어떻게
      생각합니까?): 주로 사물 또는 대상에 대한 의견이나 선택의 의미
      로 쓰임.

> **cf.** 주제 및 내용파악에 대한 질문에 사용되는 표현
>
> What do you think the author will go on to say next?
> (저자는 다음에 어떤 말을 이어나갈 것이라고 생각합니까?)
> What kind of people is the author writing for, do you think?
> (저자는 어떤 종류의 사람을 위해 글을 쓰고 있습니까?)
> So what do you think the author wanted to tell his readers?
> (그래 저자는 독자에게 무엇을 말하고 싶어 한다고 생각하느냐?)

C. 해석 및 토론

---

① Explain what happened in your own words [in Korean].

해설   사건 내용을 우리말[한국어]로 설명하세요.

syn Tell me in your own words what happened.

Use your own words to describe what happened.

Explain the meaning of this sentence, using your own words.

I wonder if you could say what happened in your own words.

cf. In your own words, what does it [the sentence] mean?
(너희 나라 말로 그것[그 문장]의 의미는 무엇이냐?)

---

② Now we've read about the problems of pollution together.
Can you discuss in twos[pairs] what you would do?
Write down five things in order of importance.
I'll come around and see what you think.

해설 이제 공해문제에 대하여 다 함께 읽었습니다. 2명씩 짝을 지어 여러분이 할 것을 토의하세요. 중요도에 따라서 5가지를 적으세요. 나는 둘러보면서 여러분이 생각하는 것을 보겠습니다.

syn Discuss in pairs what you would do.
With a partner, discuss what you would do.

---

③ **Now we'll present the problems in [when] choosing a career.**
Can you discuss in groups how these might might affect you?
Write down six ways in order of importance.
I'll come around and help you.

해설 이제 직업 선택에 있어서의 문제점을 보겠습니다. 집단별로 이 문제점들이 여러분에게 어떻게 영향을 미치는지 토의해 보세요. 중요한 순서로 6가지를 적으세요. 나는 둘러보면서 도와주겠습니다.

syn Now we've got some ideas about the problems of [in, when] choosing a career. *(rare)*

어휘 present=go over, review, discuss, examine

---

④ We have pairs of advertisements which are almost the same. Ask each other questions to find out what is different about them.

해설 거의 비슷한 두 쌍의 광고가 있습니다. 그 둘의 차이점을 찾아내기 위하여 각자에게 질문을 하세요.

syn We have pairs of advertisements which are almost the same. Ask each other questions to find out how they differ.
We have a couple of ads which are similar. Discuss their differences.
We have pairs of advertisements which are almost exactly the same... *(redundant)*

어휘 almost=practically, nearly, relatively

주의 'Almost'(거의) 대신, 우리말식으로 'almost exactly'(거의 정확하게) 'almost similar'(거의 유사한)라고 표현하면 중복되는 의미를 가진 문장이 되므로 간단히 'almost' 또는 'similar'로 표현해야 한다.

누구나 영어로 가르칠 수 있다

◆ 여러 가지 숫자와 부호 읽는 법

다음 숫자와 부호들은 일반적으로 널리 사용되는 것으로 익혀둘 필요가 있다.

1 일반적인 숫자

① 3.721 : three point seven two one

② 253,491 : two hundred (and) fifty three thousand four hundred (and) ninety one

(오늘날에는 백 단위 다음에도 'and'를 생략하는 것이 일반적임)

③ 0.5% : zero point five percent / point five percent

2 분수 및 제곱

① $2\frac{1}{2}$: two and a half

② $33\frac{1}{3}$: thirty three and a third / thirty three and one third

③ A / B : A over B / A divided by B

④ 7^1 : seven to the first power

⑤ 7^2 : seven to the second power / seven squared

⑥ 7^3 : seven to the third power / seven cubed

⑦ 7^5 : seven to the fifth power

3 산수

① 4+3=7 : Four plus three is [equals] seven.

② 6-2=4 : Six minus two equals four.

③ 73+20-43=50 : Seventy-three plus twenty minus forty-three equals fifty.

④ 25÷5=5 : Twenty five divided by five equals five.

⑤ 33×3=99 : Thirty three times three equals ninety nine.
Thirty three multiplied by three equals ninety nine.

⑥ $7^3 \times 7^5 = 7^8$: Seven to the third times seven to the fifth equals seven to the eighth (power).

⑦ $2\frac{7}{8} \times 3\frac{2}{7} = 9\frac{1}{28}$: Two and seven eighths times [multiplied by] three and two sevenths is [equals] nine and one twenty eighth.

⑧ $1\frac{2}{3} \div 1\frac{1}{7} = 1\frac{11}{24}$: One and two thirds divided by one and one seventh is one and eleven twenty fourths.

⑨ $(8 \div 2) + 3 \times (2-4) = -2$: Eight divided by two plus three times two minus four is negative two.

(이 경우 숫자 사이의 괄호(parenthesis)는 통상 읽지 않는다. 답이 '+2'일 경우에는 'positive two'라고 읽는다.)

4 전화번호

① (714) 597-4019 : (seven one four) five / nine / seven-four / O / one / nine

② (800) 761-4000 : (eight hundred) seven / six / one-four thousand

5 객실

① Room 217 : room two seventeen

② Room 2450 : room twenty-four fifty

6 금전

① $1.03 : one dollar (and) three cents, one O three.

② $8.75 : eight dollars (and) seventy five cents.
eight seventy five.
eight seventy five cents. *(incorrect)*
('Dollars'를 생략할 경우에는 마지막에 'cents'도 붙이지 못함.)

③ $25.17 : twenty-five dollars (and) seventeen cents.
twenty-five seventeen.
twenty-five seventeen cents. *(incorrect)*

④ $875 : eight hundred (and) seventy five dollars.
eight seventy five.
('car sale' 또는 'rent'에서 가끔 사용함.)

⑤ $875.15 : eight hundred (and) seventy five dollars (and) fifteen ents.

(금액이 클 경우에는 단위 모두를 분명히 발음하는 것이 좋다.)

eight seventy five fifteen. (ok)

eight seventy five dollars fifteen cents. *(incorrect)*

⑥ $2,500 : two thousand five hundred dollars.

twenty five hundred dollars.

(백 달러 이하에 첨가되는 돈이 없을 경우에 주로 사용함.)

cf. 1달러 이하의 경우

기념주화 이외의 미국화폐는 1달러 미만의 동전(coin)인 센트(cent)와 1달러 이상의 지폐(bill)인 달러(dollar)로 구분되며 다음과 같다. 각각의 표시는 상점에서 물품 구매시 유용하므로 표시를 잘 살펴보도록 해야 한다.

1 cent : 'penny'라고 하며, 1￠, 또는 $ .01로 표시한다.

5 cent : 'nickel'이라고 하며, 5￠, 또는 $ .05로 표시한다.

10 cent : 'dime'이라고 하며, 10￠, 또는 $ .10로 표시한다.

25 cent : 'quarter'라고 하며, 25￠, 또는 $ .25로 표시한다.

(전화를 걸 경우거나 가판대의 신문을 구입할 경우에 필요하다.)

50 cent : 'half dollar'라고 하며, 50￠, 또는 $ .50로 표시한다.

(실제 사용되는 경우는 거의 없다.)

1 dollar : 'dollar'라고 하며, 100￠, 또는 $ 1.00으로 표시한다.

예를 들어 상점에서 물건을 산 후에 거스름돈 36센트를 줄 경우에는 다음과 같이 여러 가지로 거슬러 준다.

1 quarter, 1 dime, and a penny

3 dimes, 1 nickel, and a penny

3 dimes and six pennies

7 신용카드(credit card)의 유효기간

(만기일이 2007년 11월인 경우) Exp. Dt 11/07

Credit Card Expiration Date eleven two thousand seven

November two thousand seven

eleven 0 seven

eleven zero seven *(not used)*

8 거리 및 크기

① 0.001m(milimeter), 0.01m(centimeter), 0.1m(decimeter),
10m(dekameter), 100m(hectometer), 1000m(kilometer)

② 1 mile=1.609 kilometer.

: One mile is one point six zero nine kilometers.

③ Water freezes at 32°F, i.e., 0°C.

: thirty two degrees farenheit, that is, zero degrees centigrade.

④ The picture measured $2'6\frac{1}{2}''\times5'8\frac{1}{4}''$.

: two feet six and a half inches by five feet eight and a quarter
inches.

9 운동경기

① 축구에서 이긴 경우

We won 3:0. (football)

: three (goals) to zero / three-zero [zip, nil].

② 축구에서 3:3으로 무승부가 난 경우:

'무승부(가 나다)'를 미국영어에서는 주로 'tie'라 하고, 영국영어에서는 'draw'
라고도 함.

Brazil and England's game tied 3:3

Brazil and England's game was a 3:3 tie. [a 3-3 tie.]

:three all, three (to) three

Brazil and England drew 3:3. *(rare, B.E)*

③ 축구에서 0:0으로 비긴 경우

They tied zero. / They tied at zero.

④ 테니스에서 자신이 이기고 있는 경우

The score is 15:0 [30:0, 40:0] to me at the moment. (tennis):fifteen
love [thirty love, forty love]

cf. 테니스에서 Becker가 이기고 있는 경우

The score stands at 15:0, Becker.

10 인용부호 : 참고문헌 등의 인용부호는 하나씩 읽는 것이 원칙이다.
Please quote reference no. 8/2-771.(번호 8/2-771을 인용하세요.)
: eight slash [stroke] two dash seven seven one. *(usual)*
eight slash [stroke] two dash double-seven one. *(rare)*

11 로마자(Roman Numerals) 읽는 법
오늘날 우리가 사용하는 숫자는 아라비아 숫자이지만 로마인들은 로마자를 사용
했으며, 현재도 시계나 책의 장을 표시할 때에 종종 사용한다.
I (1) II(2) III(3) IV(4) V(5) VI(6) VII(7) VIII(8) IX(9) X(10)...XX(20) XXIX(29)
XXX(30)
XXXI(31)... L(50)...
C(100)...D(500)... M(1,000)...

위의 숫자를 읽는 데에는 다음 두 가지 규칙이 적용된다.

규칙 1) 같은 크기 또는 작은 크기의 숫자가 뒤에 오면 더한다.
     e.g. XXVIII=10+10+5+3=28
         MMV=1000+1000+5=2005

규칙 2) 작은 숫자가 앞에 오면, 뒤의 큰 숫자에서 앞의 작은 숫자를 뺀다.
     e.g. XLIX=(50-10)+(10-1)=49
         CDXLIV=(500-100)+50-10)+(5-1)=444
         MCMXCIX=1000+(1000-100)+(100-10)+(10-1)=1999

Unit 4 쓰기

1. 현장예문 (Real-life Situation)

Using Pictures from the Story, 'Cow and Frog'
(adapted from S. Sarkar(1977))

그림 또는 삽화를 이용하는 수업은 학생들의 흥미를 유발할 뿐만 아니라 학습에 매우 효과가 있으므로, 모든 단계의 교육 과정에서 널리 쓰이는 방식이다.

삽화를 바탕으로 수업을 진행하는 방법은 다음과 같다: 먼저 선생님은 학생들과 다 함께 아래의 그림에 등장하는 동물의 이름을 확인한다. 그리고 첫 번째 그림을 보며 그 배경과 등장인물 또는 동물이 무엇을 하는지 질문한다. 다음으로 선생님은 질문에 대한 학생들의 답을, 자연스럽게 대화를 통하여 올바른 용어와 문법에 맞는 표현이 되도록 구두로 수정을 해 주거나 칠판에 적는다. 그리고 그 결과를 종합하여 첫 번째 그림에 대한 이야기(story)를 적는다. 선생님이 첫 번째 그림에 대해 학생들의 대답을 이용하여 하나의 문단(paragraph)을 완성하는 것을 보고, 학생들은 이야기 전개 방식에 대한 요령을 터득하게 된다. 다음으로 두 번째 그림부터는 학생들을 그룹별로 나눠 자기들끼리 상의하거나, 때로 선생님에게 물어보면서 이야기를 전개하도록 지시한다. 그리고 각각의 장면에 대한 적절한 이야기를 전체적으로 일관성 있게 전개하여, 가장 논리적이고 적절한 어휘를 구사하였으며 내용이 풍부한 이야기를 구성한 그룹을 가장 우수한 팀으로 결정한다. 구체적으로 이솝 우화에서 황소와 개구리의 이야기를 발췌해 이용한 수업 진행 과정을 살펴보자.

먼저, 위의 첫 번째 그림에 대한 이야기를 전개하기 위한 선생님의 질문과 질문에 대한 답을 이용하여 이야기를 구성하는 과정을 살펴보자. 먼저 그림 속의 'cow'와 'frog'를 확인한 뒤 선생님은 이야기를 만들기 위해 다음과 같이 학생들에게 질문한다.

여기에서는 선생님이 상태와 사건에 대해 의문사 — Who, What, When, Where, Why, How — 를 이용하여 세부 사항을 질문하는 형식으로 진행하고 있다.

🔊 This unit gives teachers the language needed to use pictures in their lesson plans, particularly in terms of telling a story (pictures are also covered again in Unit 6). It addresses how to ask students to explain what they see in a picture, how to ask students to comment in detail on a picture, and how to elicit additional information about a picture. The unit also covers how to call on students for written answers in the classroom. This includes how to prepare them for a written response in the classroom, asking them to write something down, and questioning them on the meaning and legibility of their writing.

Now listen to the dialogue.

T: What is the cow doing?

S: It is eating grass.

T: Yes. When an animal eats grass while moving around in an open space we also call it 'grazing'.

S: The cow is grazing.

T: That's right. Where is it grazing?

S: In a field.

T: Field or meadow. Both words mean a large open space, a flat land where grass grows. What do you think the cow is feeling while it is eating? Do you think it's angry, or happy, or just peaceful and content?

S: It's peaceful because it's eating.

T: Yes, it's not bothering [troubling] anyone else, is it? It's just grazing peacefully. Now let's begin the story about the frog and the cow. Once upon a time-that's the way we begin a story which happened some time in the past - a cow was grazing peacefully in a field. What did the cow look like? Was it thin?

S: It was big and fat.

T: What color was it?

S: Brown.

T: All right. A big brown cow was grazing peacefully in a field. What time of the day was it, do you think?

S: It was in the morning.

T: And was it raining that morning?

S: No, it was very hot.

T: I wonder what day of the week it was.

누구나 영어로 가르칠 수 있다

S: It was a Saturday morning.

T: So we have-One hot Saturday morning a big brown cow was grazing peacefully in a field. What kind of grass was it eating? Was it hard and dry?

S: No, soft and sweet.

T: Good. Now, can you tell me what we call a fruit, let's say an orange, which is full of water, sweet water?

S: Juicy.

T: Yes, 'juicy'. Another word is 'succulent'. The grass was succulent or juicy.

S: So the cow was eating juicy grass.

T: Yes, juicy green grass. Now, when the cow was eating the juicy green grass, something suddenly happened. A frog came. Where did it come from?

S: From river.

T: From a river. How does a frog move?

S: It jumps.

T: Or hops [leaps]. Why did it come there?

S: To see the cow.

T: Now we have-When the cow was eating the juicy green grass a frog jumped up to see the cow.

S: Why did it want to see the cow?

T: Let's see. Because it had never seen such a big animal before?

S: No, the frog was sleeping peacefully and the cow's chewing noise disturbed it.

T: That's a very good idea! The noise of the cow's chewing disturbed it. Sometimes we use the word 'munching' instead of 'chewing'. When we chew something crisp and juicy for a long time we are munching.

Now let's see what we have: One hot Saturday morning a big brown cow was grazing peacefully in a field. It was eating juicy green grass when suddenly a frog jumped up to him. The frog had been sleeping in the grass near the river but the noise of the cow's chewing woke him up. And so on.

위와 같이 첫 번째 그림에 대한 이야기를 완성한 다음, 두 번째부터는 그룹별로 상의하여 이야기를 전개하도록 지시하고, 선생님은 필요할 경우 도움을 준다.

해석

선생님:	소는 무엇을 하고 있습니까? (사건)
학생:	풀을 먹고 있습니다.
선생님:	예. 동물이 야생에서 돌아다니면서 풀을 먹고 있을 때, 우리는 그것을 '풀을 뜯고 있다.'고 말합니다.
학생:	소가 풀을 뜯고 있다.
선생님:	맞습니다. 그것은 어디에서 뜯고 있습니까? (장소)
학생:	들판에서.
선생님:	들판 또는 초원. 둘 다 야외, 즉 풀이 자라는 평탄한 땅을 의미합니다. 풀을 뜯을 때 소는 어떤 기분이겠습니까? (느낌) 화가 나겠습니까? 행복하겠습니까? 또는 단지 평화롭고 만족스럽겠습니까?
학생:	풀을 뜯고 있는 동안 소는 평화롭습니다.
선생님:	맞아요, 그 소는 아무도 괴롭히지 않지요? 그것은 단지 평화롭게 풀을 뜯고 있습니다. 자, 개구리와 소에 대한 이야기를 합시다. 옛날에 - 이것은 과거 어느 때 일어난 이야기를 시작하는 방법입니다 - 소가 들판에서 평화롭게 풀을 뜯고 있었습니다. 소는 어떻게 생겼습니까? 말랐습니까?
학생:	소는 크고 뚱뚱합니다.
선생님:	색깔은? (모양)
학생:	갈색.
선생님:	좋아요. 큰 갈색 소가 들판에서 평화롭게 풀을 뜯고 있습니다. 몇 시쯤일 것으로 생각합니까?
학생:	아침이었습니다.

선생님: 그날 아침 비가 오고 있었습니까?

학생: 아니요, 매우 더웠습니다.

선생님: 무슨 요일이었을까요? (날짜)

학생: 어느 토요일이었습니다.

선생님: 자, 그러면, 어느 더운 토요일 아침 큰 갈색 소가 들판에서 평화롭게 풀을 뜯고 있었습니다. 어떤 종류의 풀을 뜯고 있었습니까? (대상) 풀은 딱딱하고 말랐습니까?

학생: 아니요, 부드럽고 달콤했습니다.

선생님: 좋아요. 그러면 오렌지와 같이 수분, 달콤한 수분이 가득하다는 것은 어떻게 말합니까?

학생: 즙이 많은.

선생님: 그래요, '즙이 많은'. 다른 말로 '수분이 많은'입니다. 풀은 수분이 많거나 즙이 많았습니다.

학생: 그러면 소는 즙이 많은 풀을 뜯고 있었습니다.

선생님: 예, 즙이 많은 푸른 풀. 그래요, 소가 즙이 많은 녹색 풀을 먹고 있을 때, 갑자기 사건이 발생했습니다. 개구리 한 마리가 왔습니다. 그것은 어디에서 왔습니까? (장소)

학생: 강에서.

선생님: 강에서. 개구리는 어떻게 움직입니까? (방법)

학생: 뜁니다.

선생님: 또는 팔짝 뜁니다. 왜 거기에 왔습니까? (이유)

학생: 소를 구경하려고요.

선생님: 이제 다음과 같습니다 - 소가 즙이 많은 녹색 풀을 먹고 있을 때 개구리가 소를 보기 위해 뛰어왔습니다.

학생: 왜 개구리는 소를 보고 싶어 했습니까?

선생님: 글쎄. 전에 그렇게 큰 동물을 본 적이 없기 때문이 아닐까?

학생: 아니요, 개구리가 평화롭게 자고 있는데, 소의 씹는 소리가 개구리를 거슬리게 했습니다.

선생님: 그거 좋은 생각이야! 소가 씹는 소리가 개구리를 성가시게 했다. 때로 '씹는다'는 말 대신에 '우적우적 먹다'라고 합니다. 파삭파삭하고 즙이 많은 것을 오랫동안 씹을 때, 우적우적 먹는다고 합니다.

자 이제 우리가 한 것을 정리해 봅시다: 어느 더운 토요일 아침 큰 갈색 소가 평화롭게 들판에서 풀을 뜯고 있었습니다. 소가 즙이 많은 푸른 풀을 먹고 있을 때, 갑자기 개구리 한 마리가 뛰어왔습니다. 개구리는 강가의 풀 속에서 자고 있었지만, 소가 씹는 소리 때문에 깨어났습니다.

2. 기본구문

여기에서는 판서에 대한 지시, 학생의 쓰기 내용에 대한 평가, 우리말 번역 또는 영작문 등 쓰기와 연관된 표현을 다음과 같이 정리하였다: A. 판서 및 필기 B. 작문 및 번역 C. 문제풀이

A. 판서 및 필기

> ① **Take out your pens.** Write this down in your notebook.

해설 펜을 꺼내세요. 이것을 공책에 적으세요.

syn You'll need your pens.
  Would you take your pens out?
  You need your pens.
  Pick up your pens.

어휘 write down=jot down, put down, take down, note

  cf. 필기에 대한 지시문
  Write it in the empty space at the top. (위쪽의 여백에 그것을 쓰세요.)
  Write this exercise out neatly in your notebooks.
  (공책에 이 연습문제를 반듯하게 쓰세요.)
  Make a note of the last two sentences. (마지막 두 문장을 적으세요.)
  Match these sentences, then copy them neatly.
  (이 문장들을 연결하고, 그것을 반듯하게 적으세요.)

② S: Why was what I wrote wrong?

해설   내가 쓴 것이 왜 [어디가] 틀렸습니까?

syn   Why did you mark this wrong?
        What's wrong with this? *(casual)*

   cf. Why did you put a line under this word?
      (이 단어 아래에 왜 줄을 그었습니까?)

③ I can't read your handwriting.

해설   너의 글을 알아볼 수가 없다.
        : 글씨체가 성의가 없거나, 아주 나쁠 때 사용하는 표현이다.

syn   I can't read [make out] your writing.
        Your handwriting is illegible.
        Your handwriting leaves much to be desired. *(rare)*
        You have horrible penmanship. *(rude)*

④ That's much better, but **there's something still missing in this phrase.**

해설   훨씬 좋아졌지만, 이 글에는 아직 빠진 것이 있다.

syn   …, but you've forgotten something here.

   cf. 문장의 오류 및 수정에 대한 지적
      That's quite good, but what's wrong in this line?

(꽤 좋지만, 이 줄에 틀린 곳이 어디냐?)

Is that a true sentence? Could you read what you have written please?

(그것이 맞는 문장이니? 네가 쓴 것을 읽어 보겠니?)

Think what that means! Does it make sense, or is it silly?

(그 말이 무슨 뜻이라 생각하니. 말이 되느냐, 아니면 틀렸느냐?)

If you omit the bracketed material and put a comma after "fractures,"
you can combine these two sentences.

((이 작문에서) 괄호 친 부분을 생략하고, 'fractures' 뒤에 쉼표를 넣으면, 이 두
개의 문장을 결합할 수 있다.)

---

⑤ **Would someone write his answers on the board?**

해설   답을 칠판에 써 볼 사람 있습니까?

syn   Would someone put his solutions on the board?
Would someone care to write his [their] answers on the board?
Would anyone[someone] volunteer to write their answers on the
board?

cf. Alright. Let's check [go over] your answers... Good. You've got some of
the information I asked for.

(좋아요. 답을 검토해 봅시다. ⋯ 좋습니다. 내가 물은 몇 가지 정보를 썼습니다.)

---

⑥ **Have you done that?** Can you tell me what you've got? I'll
write it on the board.

해설   너는 했니? 너의 답을 말해 볼래? 내가 그 답을 칠판에 적겠다.

syn   Are you done [finished] with that?

Done? *(casual)*
Finished? *(casual)*
Through? *(casual)*

어휘   get (이해하다)=understand, catch the meaning or import of

참고   **'Get'의 의미**

'Get'은 영어에서 가장 널리 사용되는 동사이다. 이것은 너무도 다양한 의미를 지니므로 'get'만을 사용하여 긴 이야기를 할 수도 있다. 다음 예문을 보자.

When it get [became] light, he get up [rose] and get dressed [put on his clothes] quickly. He get [prepared] himself some breakfast, get [organized] his papers together and get [was] ready for work. He get [bought] a newspaper at the corner, get [rode] the 7:20 bus to town and get [arrived] to his office by 7:50. After getting [riding] the elevator to the sixth floor he get [arrived] to his desk by his usual time and get down to [began] the job at once.

(날이 밝아지자 그는 일어나 재빨리 옷을 입었다. 그는 아침을 먹고 서류를 정리한 다음에, 출근할 준비를 했다. 그는 모퉁이에서 신문을 사서 시내로 가는 7시 20분 버스를 타고 7시 50분에 사무실에 도착했다. 6층으로 가는 엘리베이터를 탄 다음에, 그는 정상 시간에 그의 사무실에 도착하여 즉시 업무를 시작했다.)

B. 작문 및 번역

① What's this word [phrase, sentence] in Korean?

해설　이 단어[어구, 문장]는 우리말로 무엇이라고 합니까?

syn　Please translate this word [phrase, sentence] into Korean.
How would you translate this word [phrase, sentence] into Korean?
How do you say this word [phrase, sentence] in Korean?
What do you call this in Korean?

② How do you say 'doll' in Korean?

해설　'Doll'을 우리말로 무엇이라고 합니까?

syn　What's 'doll' in Korean?
What is the Korean equivalent of the word 'doll'?
What's the Korean (word) for 'doll'? *(informal)*

cf. What is the English equivalent of the Korean word, '인형'?
(우리말, '인형'을 영어로 무엇이라 합니까?)
= How do you say the Korean word, '인형', in English?

③ It would be more natural to begin with 'Who did...'

해설　'Who did...'로 시작하는 것이 더 자연스러울 것입니다.
: '올바른 영어' 또는 '영어다운 표현'은 'better [proper, correct]

400　　누구나 영어로 가르칠 수 있다

English'라고 표현한다.

It would sound better if you began with 'Who did...'
It would be better [proper, correct] English to begin with 'Who did...'
It would be better [proper, correct] English if you used 'Who did...'

It would be more English if you used 'Who did...' *(B.E.)*
It would be more English to begin with 'Who did...' *(B.E.)*
('좀 더 영어 같다'는 의미로 'more English'는 미국영어에서는 사용하지 않는다.)

④ **Before you write,** I want you to read this paragraph first. It's similar to the one you're going to write.

해설 쓰기 전에, 이 글을 먼저 읽으세요. 이 글은 여러분이 쓸 것과 유사합니다.

syn Before you begin to write, ...
Before you do any writing, ...
Before writing, ...

어휘 similar to=like, nearly the same as

cf. 작문에 대한 지시문
Write an essay of about 250 words on one of the following subjects. (다음 주제 중 하나를 택하여 약 250단어로 된 글을 쓰세요.)
Summarize the passage in not more than 100 words.
(그 글을 100단 이내로 요약하세요.)

Don't translate word for word. (단어를 하나하나 번역하지 마세요.)

⑤ Let's work out how this author planned his text. What does he do first? Think of our main points.

해설 저자가 본문을 어떤 방식으로 구성하였는지 알아봅시다. 먼저 그는 무엇을 하였습니까? 요점을 생각해 보세요.

어휘 work out(알다, 이해하다, 풀다)=figure out, discover, investigate, look at, find an answer to

C. 문제풀이

① Fill in the blanks of these sentences, then rewrite them, correcting all spelling errors.

해설 이 문장의 빈칸을 채우고, 틀린 철자를 고쳐서 다시 쓰시오.

syn Fill the blanks in these sentences, then write them, taking care with spelling. *(rare)*

② Now read it again and pick out the main points. Write them down.

해설 그것을 다시 읽고 요점을 찾아서 적으세요.

어휘 'Pick out' 대신 'identify', 'point out', 'underline', 'highlight' 등으

로 대체할 수 있다.

cf. **본문의 내용파악에 대한 지시문**

Now study it and underline the phrases which introduce new ideas.
(이제 그것을 읽고, 새로운 견해를 도입하는 것에 밑줄을 치세요.)

The first part of this essay is done for you. Read it, then write the rest.
(이 글의 처음 부분은 적어 놓았습니다. 그것을 읽고, 나머지를 쓰세요.)

What type of organization would be appropriate for this topic? Jot some ideas down.
(이 주제에 대해서는 어떤 방식으로 글을 구성해야 되겠습니까? 자신의 생각을 적으세요.) ,

Read the title carefully. What form of writing is it? Descriptive? Explanatory?
(제목을 주의 깊게 읽으세요. 어떤 형태의 글입니까? 묘사문? 설명문?)

---

③ How can you combine these 2 sentences into one longer one?

해설   두 문장을 결합하여 하나의 긴 문장으로 만드세요.

syn   How can you join these 2 sentences to make one longer sentence?

어휘   combine(결합하다)=blend, conjoin, fuse, join, merge, marry, synthesize, unify, unite, web

참고   결과의 부정사 (infinitive of result)
        결과의 부정사는 결과적으로 또 다른 사건이 야기된다는 것을 의미하므로, Jespersen은 이를 제3의 부정사 (infinitives of tertiaries)라고도 했다. 다음 예문에서도 'to 부정사'는 또 다른 사건을 담고 있다.

e.g.   The pilot returned to find his aircraft all ablaze. (제3의 사건)
(조종사는 돌아와서, 자신의 비행기가 불타고 있는 것을 보았다.)
He then left England never to return. (운명)
(그는 영국을 떠나서 영원히 돌아오지 않았다.)

④ What other changes will you need to make it sound better?

해설   보다 정확하게 나타내려면 어떻게 수정해야 되겠습니까?
: 이미 주어진 표현이 정확하지 않을 때 사용한다.

syn   What other changes will you need to make to make it sound
better?
What other changes are required to improve [enhance] the
sound of it?
What other changes will you need so that it sounds better?

⑤ I want you to write out the sentences to form a paragraph.

해설   그 문장들을 정리하여 하나의 글을 만드세요.

syn   Write out the sentences. Put them in order to make a paragraph.
Write out these sentences in paragraph form.

어휘   write out (모두 적다)=write in full

⑥ Now that you've answered all the questions (in full), you need to expand **on them.**

해설 이 모든 질문에 답한 다음에, 이 글을 전개[발전]시켜 보세요.

syn ... you need to write a little (bit) more about them.
... you need to develop [elaborate on] these answers.

어휘 in full (생략하지 않고, 완전히)=not abbreviated or condensed

먼저 모든 종류의 글에 적용될 수 있는 일반적인 논평을 제시하고, 다음에는 구체적인 논평에 대한 예문을 제시하기로 한다. 학생들의 영작에 대한 논평을 쓸 때 참고가될 것이다.

1 일반적인 논평

주제와의 일치, 글의 구성, 표현 방법, 전체적 균형 등에 대한 일반적인 평가로 모든 종류의 작문에 공통적으로 적용될 수 있는 평가이다.

1) 제목 및 주제

① Getting away from topic. (주제와 벗어나서 전개되고 있다.)

② What are your subtopics? Make them explicit in your introduction and make sure your paragraph elaborates on them.
(소제목은 무엇이냐? 서론에서 이 점을 명시하고, 글 전체가 이 소제목을 중심으로 전개되도록 하여라.)

③ Organization O.K. However, you didn't understand the topic you were assigned. I cannot understand a lot of what you are saying.
(글의 구성은 좋지만 주제를 잘 이해하지 못하고 있다. 글의 많은 부분이 이해하기 어렵다.)

④ Although you have an introduction, developing sentences and conclusion, there's no clear T.S., nor do individual sentences clearly relate. (T.S.=Topic Sentence or Thesis Statement)
(서론, 전개, 결론으로 구성되어 있지만 분명한 주제문이 없으며, 각각의 문장의 연관성이 결여되어 있다.)

⑤ Does the second paragraph deal with [relate to] the thesis you've announced in your opening paragraph?
(두 번째 단락은 첫째 단락에서 언급한 논제와 연관되어 있느냐?)

2) 구성 및 짜임새

① I'd like to see a general introduction, something to interest your reader.

(독자의 흥미를 끌 수 있는 일반적인 서문을 써야 한다.)

② This is well-organized, but some of your paragraphs need developing.

(글의 짜임새는 좋으나, 몇몇 단락의 내용이 좀 더 전개되어야 한다.)

③ Well-organized and well-developed in most cases, but the last point isn't well discussed.

(전반적으로 글의 짜임과 전개가 뛰어나지만, 마지막 요점에 대한 토의가 부족하다.)

④ Very well thought out and well-written although the first body paragraph is better than the other two.

(사고가 정연하고, 표현도 잘 되어 있지만, 본문의 나머지 두 단락은 첫 번째 단락보다 잘 쓰여져 있지 않다.)

3) 내용

① A few confusing parts. (몇 가지 사항이 혼돈되어 있다.)

② The argument remains a little superficial.

(논지가 다소 피상적이다.)

③ Some of your statements are so general that I don't know what you mean.

(표현이 지나치게 일반적이어서 글의 의도를 파악할 수 없다.)

④ You show a deep theoretical understanding of the problem but you need more detail.

(그 문제에 대해 이론적 지식은 해박하나, 상세한 설명이 결여되어 있다.)

⑤ Interesting examples and observations about people. A few unclear ideas and references, however.

(사람들에 대한 여러 가지 사례와 관찰이 흥미롭다. 다만 몇 가지 사고와 지시 관계가 명쾌하지 않다.)

⑥ You need to support your opinion by giving details and you need to organize your thoughts a little better.

(의견에 대한 상세한 설명이 필요하며, 사고를 좀 더 짜임새 있게 표현할 필요가 있다.)

⑦ You explain this quite nicely. It's clear why you liked it although you could have analyzed its appeal more deeply.

(너는 이것을 잘 설명하고 있다. 네가 왜 그것을 좋아하는지도 분명하지만, 그것의 좋은 점을 좀 더 깊이 분석했으면 좋겠다.)

⑧ This is a really excellent narrative but I do not really see any description here. You also have some other compositional changes to make in sentences and paragraph formation.

(이 글은 서술이 뛰어나지만 구체적인 설명이 결여되어 있다. 문장과 단락의 구성에서 약간의 변화가 필요하다.)

2 구체적인 논평

다음은 학생 개개인의 글에 대해 선생님이 구체적으로 평가한 사례에 대한 예문이다. 주제, 구성, 내용에 대한 다양한 평가가 이루어지며, 실제 우리 선생님이 학생의 글에 대해 자세히 평가를 할 경우에 참고가 될 것이다.

1) 에너지 위기(Energy Crisis)에 대한 글이 주제를 벗어났을 때.

The question is not "Are these energy sources decreasing?" but "How will the energy crisis change our modern lifestyle?" You will need to be a lot more specific in your composition. See if you can answer the following question: How will the energy crisis affect agricultural production, industry and personal comfort?

(주제는 "에너지 자원이 감소하고 있느냐?"가 아니고 "에너지 위기가 현대인의 생활양식을 어떻게 변화시킬 것인가?"하는 것이다. 작문이 훨씬 더 구체적이어야 한다. 다음 질문에 답을 할 수 있는가를 검토해 보라: 에너지 위기가 농업생산, 산업, 개인의 편리성에 어떤 영향을 미칠 것인가?)

2) 미국의 가족 구조의 변화(Changing American Family)에 대한 글에서 변화의 원인에 대한 구체적인 설명이 결여된 경우.

So far you have only told me your opinion ; you haven't told me why you believe what you do. You need to tell me what social, political and economic factors are putting pressure on the family to change. You stop just when it's getting interesting!

(이 글은 단지 너의 의견만 말했다 ; 너는 네가 무엇을 해야 하는가에 대한 이유를 말하지 않았다. 어떤 사회적, 정치적, 경제적 요인이 가족이 변화하도록 영향을 미치는가를 말해야 한다. 내용이 흥미를 유발할 부분에서 중단되었다.)

3) 학생의 영작이 내용은 충실하나 문법적인 오류가 많아서 이해하기 어려운 경우.

If people can't understand you, it doesn't help to have some very intelligent or interesting ideas. I am not saying that you do not work hard enough - I know that you do - but rather to let you know you have a problem. When you rewrite this, I want you to concentrate on the language only. Don't even try to change or improve the content. Try to learn from rewriting how you should express your ideas in clearer and more correct language.

(사람들이 문장을 이해하지 못한다면 아주 지적이거나 재미있는 견해를 가진 것도 도움이 되지 않는다. 열심히 연구하였다는 것은 알지만, 문제점이 있다는 것을 지적하고 싶다. 이 글을 다시 쓸 때에는 언어 표현에만 신경을 써라. 내용을 변화시키거나 다듬으려고 하지 마라. 다시 쓰면서 너의 사고를 보다 분명히 그리고 올바른 언어로 표현하는 방법을 배우도록 하여라.)

1. 현장예문 (Real-life Situation)

Correcting Oral Errors

(adapted from Glenn T. Gainer (1989))

선생님이 문제를 구두로 말하고, 다음으로 학생들이 주어진 문제에 대한 답을 테이프를 들으면서 찾아내는 방식이다. 이 방법은 Part III, Unit 2의 방법과 더불어 듣기 시험에서 가장 일반적으로 시행되는 방법의 하나이다. 구체적으로 예를 들어 살펴보자. 먼저 선생님은 영화배우 Bruce Lee,의 생애에 대해 다음과 같이 문제를 미리 읽어준다.

〈문제〉 ① Where was Bruce Lee born?

② What kind of work did his father do?

③ When was he born?

④ How many brothers and sisters [siblings] did he have?

다음으로 선생님은 위의 질문에 대한 답을 찾아내도록 테이프를 들려준다. 학생들은 선생님이 들려주는 Bruce Lee의 생애에 대한 이야기를 테이프로 들으면서, 위의 문제에 대한 답을 적는다. 학생들이 테이프를 통해 답을 적은 뒤에, 선생님은 학생들이 쓴 답을 확인하기 위해 다음과 같이 학생들에게 질문을 한다.

When correcting oral errors in the classroom a teacher must be careful not to be overly critical so as not to discourage students from speaking in class. Yet, teachers will certainly find occasion to correct oral errors in almost every class. This unit provides the teacher with some of the basic language needed to address students oral errors. In particular, the unit covers checking student comprehension of their own spoken answers, correcting student pronunciation, and checking for vocabulary comprehension. Aside from correcting oral errors, the unit also touches on correcting spelling mistakes and written grammatical mistakes.

Now listen to the dialogue.

T: Miss Kim. What is your answer to the first question?[1]

Kim: San Francisco.

T: Correct. Now do you remember the question?[2]

(Students look a bit puzzled.)

T: Do you remember the first question I asked you?[3]

Kim: Where did Bruce Lee born?

T: Very close.

(Teacher writes correctly produced words on the blackboard with a blank in the second spot as follows: 'Where _____ Bruce Lee born?')

Kim: *(She consults with a classmate)* Was.

T: Correct.

T: *(To another student who answered the second question.) Do you remember the question you just answered?)*

Kim: What kind work his father do?

T: Almost.[4]

(Teacher writes correctly produced words on the blackboard with blanks in the third and fifth spots as follows and points to the first blank: 'What kind _____ work _____ his father do?')

Kim: Of.

T: Right.[5]

(Teacher writes 'of' in the first blank and points to the second blank).

Kim: Did.

T: Correct.[6] *(Teacher writes 'did' in the second blank.)*

1 (1번 문제의 답은 무엇입니까?) 이 문장에서 명사 'answer' 다음에 전치사는 'to' 또는
   'for' 둘 다 가능하지만, 미국영어에서는 주로 'to'를 사용한다.
   What is your answer for the first question? ; What do you have for number 1?
   ; What's your answer for number 1?
2 (질문을 기억하고 있습니까?)
   Now, can you remember the question? ;
   Now, do you recall the question?
3 (내가 물은 첫 번째 질문을 기억하고 있습니까?)
   Do you remember question number one?
   Do you remember my first question?
4 (거의 비슷합니다.)
   Not quite ; Just about; You're almost there; You've almost got it.
5 (맞습니다.)
   Yes; Good ; That's right.
6 (맞았습니다.)
   Bingo ; you got it.

해석

선생님: 김양. 1번 문제의 답이 무엇이지요?
김양: 샌프란시스코.
선생님: 맞습니다. 그런데 문제가 기억납니까?
        (학생들이 조금 당황한다.)
선생님: 내가 물은 첫 번째 질문을 기억합니까?
김양: Where did Bruce Lee born?
선생님: 매우 비슷합니다. (선생님은 올바르게 발음한 단어를 칠판 위에 적고 두 번째
        칸은 빈칸으로 남겨둔다:'Where _____ Bruce Lee born?')
김양: (급우들과 상의한다.) Was.
선생님: 맞습니다….
선생님: (두 번째 질문에 답을 한 학생에게) 내가 물은 질문을 기억합니까?
이양: What kind work his father do?
선생님: 거의 비슷해요. (선생님은 올바르게 발음한 단어를 칠판에 적고 셋째 단어와 다

섯째 단어가 들어갈 지점을 빈칸으로 처리한다. 그리고 첫 번째 빈칸을 가리킨다.:'What kind ___ work ___ his father do?)

이양: Of.

선생님: 맞습니다. (첫 번째 빈칸에 'of'라 적고, 두 번째 빈칸을 가리킨다.)

이양: Did.

선생님: 맞습니다. (선생님은 두 번째 빈칸에 'did'를 적는다.)

2. 기본구문

여기에서는 어휘와 문장의 발음과 의미, 철자와 숫자, 문장에 대한 문법적 설명과 관계된 표현을 다음과 같이 정리하였다: A. 발음 B. 의미와 형태 C. 철자와 숫자 D. 문법 및 대체연습

A. 발음

---

① Your pronunciation is very good. Say it out loud.

해설   발음이 좋습니다. 크게 말해 보세요.

syn   You sound great.
You sound like a native speaker. (이 경우 'like a native speaker' 가 'like a native'보다 널리 사용된다.)
You have very good pronunciation.
You sound very American. *(informal)*
You sound English. *(informal)*

   cf. You speak quite well [very fluently]. (말을 유창하게 하는군요.)
     You speak without an accent. (너의 표현에는 강세가 없다.)

어휘   out loud=aloud, loudly *(A.E.)*, loud *(B.E.)*

---

② How do you pronounce this word [the next word]?

해설   이 단어[다음 단어]를 어떻게 발음합니까?

syn　　How is this word pronounced?

What's the correct pronunciation of this word?

I'm not sure how to say this word.

I'm not sure how this word is pronounced.

　　cf. What's the next word? (다음 단어는 무엇입니까?)

　　　: 단어의 발음 또는 의미를 모를 때 사용한다.

---

③ **Which is the strongest syllable?**

해설　　가장 강한 음절은 어느 것입니까?

syn　　Which syllable is the strongest?

Mark the strongest syllable.

---

④ **Listen to how I say it.**

해설　　내가 말하는 방법[발음하는 방법]을 잘 들으세요.

syn　　Listen to the way I say it.

Listen to me saying it.

Try to mimic my pronunciation.

Try to copy my pronunciation.

---

⑤ **Listen to the way my voice goes up.**

해설　　내 목소리의 어조를 잘 들으세요.

syn   Listen for the change in my voice.

        Listen to the inflection in my voice.

        Now listen again and notice how my voice changes.

cf. **발음·억양과 관련된 표현들**

Remember last week we learned about different intonation patterns. (지난주 우리가 여러 종류의 억양의 유형에 대해 학습한 것을 기억하세요.)

Where's the accent in this word? (이 단어의 강세는 어디에 있습니까?)

Watch my mouth closely. (내 입을 잘 보세요.)

Notice how my tongue touches my teeth.
(내 혀가 이빨에 접촉하는 방법을 보세요.)

Be careful with the 'th' sound. ('th'음에 유의하세요.)

The first sound is [], as in 'this'. (처음 소리는 'this'와 같이 []입니다.)

You must let your voice fall [rise] at the end of the sentence.
(문장 끝에서는 목소리가 내려[올라]가게 해야 합니다.)

---

⑥ **Check the new vocabulary from the list at the back.**

해설   교재 뒤에 있는 목록에서 새 단어를 확인하세요.

syn   Take a look [a peek, a gander] at the new vocab in the back of the book.

        Check out [Look over] the new vocabulary (list) in the back of the book.

        Review the new vocabulary from the list at the back.

어휘   review(살펴보다, 훑어보다)=make or give a survey of

cf. **새로 나온 단어의 학습과 관련된 표현**

This is a new word. Listen to how I pronounce [read] it.

(이것은 새 단어입니다. 그것을 발음하는[읽는] 법을 들어 보세요.)

I want to teach you a few words that we will need for a dialogue.
(대화 학습에 필요한 몇 가지 단어를 가르쳐 주겠습니다.)

---

⑦ You don't seem to know the vocabulary. *(formal)*

해설 너는 그 어휘를 모르구나. [너는 그 어휘를 공부하지 않았구나.]
: '어휘'는 'vocabulary' 또는 'vocab.'라고 하며, '*voca'라고는 하지
않는다.

syn You didn't care to study the vocab. *(impolite)*
You don't seem to have paid any attention to the vocabulary.
You don't seem to have bothered to learn the vocabulary. *(very formal)*
You didn't familiarize yourself with the vocab.
You don't appear to have familiarized yourself with the vocabulary.

B. 의미와 형태

---

① Do you understand every word?

해설 모든 단어를 알겠습니까?

syn Do you have an understanding of it?
Is there something [anything] you don't understand?
Are you comfortable with it?

If there are any words you don't know, please ask.

If you're not entirely clear, just ask.

If you don't get [grasp] it, please ask.

cf. 본문에 앞서 단어 학습 확인을 위한 지시문

Are there any words you don't know the Korean words for?

(우리말로 의미를 모르는 단어가 있습니까?)

Before we begin [proceed, commence, start], I want to make sure (that)
you know the meaning of a few words.

(시작하기 전에, 단어의 의미를 아는지 확인해 보겠습니다.)

Can you say this number aloud in English?

(이 숫자를 영어로 읽으세요.)

---

② T: Do you know the meaning of all the words [phrases]?
 S: I don't understand the second word in line 1.

해설 T: 모든 단어의 의미를 압니까?
 S: 첫째 줄 두 번째 단어를 모릅니다.

syn T: Are there any words [phrases] you don't know (the meaning
 of)?
 Are there any words [phrases] you are unfamiliar with?
 Do any words cause you difficulty?
 May I help you with any words or phrases?
 Are any words unfamiliar to you?
 Are there any strange words [phrases]? *(informal)*
 S: What does the second word in line 1 mean?

③ What does the word, 'cute', mean?

해설 단어 'cute'의 의미는 무엇입니까?

syn What is 'cute'?
What does 'cute' mean?
What's the meaning of (the word) 'cute'?
Does anyone know what the word 'cute' means?
Can anyone tell me what the word 'cute' means?
Do you know the meaning of the word 'cute'?
Who knows what this word means:'cute'?

What could this word, 'cute', mean? *(rare)*

활용 상황에 따라 'the word, 'cute"(단어, cute), 대신 'the idiom, 'look after"(관용어, look after), 'the expression 'at a loss"(at a loss 란 표현), 'words in italics'(이탤릭체로 쓰여진 표현), 'words underlined'(밑줄 친 단어), 'letters 'UNESCO"(UNESCO라는 문자), 'abbreviation 'am"(축약어 'am'), 'initials AM'(두음자 'AM') 등으로 대체할 수 있다.

cf. What's Korean for this word? (이 단어는 우리말로 무엇이라고 합니까?)
:'Korean' 앞에 정관사 'the'를 붙이지 말 것.

④ Who knows what this is in English?

해설 자! 이것은 영어로 무엇입니까?

syn Does anyone know what this is in English?
What's this in English?

What does the word mean? *(informal)*

해설 그 단어의 의미는 무엇입니까?

syn What's the meaning of the word? *(formal)*
Do any of you know the meaning of the word?
Could you explain the meaning of the word? *(polite)*
I don't understand the meaning of the word. *(very polite)*
Could you clarify the word's meaning?

cf. 단어카드를 가지고 어휘 학습을 하기 위한 지시문
We'll use some flash cards with words and pictures on them. Look.
(단어와 그림이 있는 단어카드를 사용하겠습니다. 보세요.)
Pick out the card which goes with this word [sentence].
(이 단어[문장]와 어울리는 카드를 고르세요.)
Match the words to the right pictures. Like this.
(단어와 그림을 짝지으세요. 이런 방식으로.)
I want you to read the cards out loud to [for] me.
(카드를 큰 소리로 읽어 보세요.)

⑥ What does the word 'blue' mean here?

해설 이 문장에서 'blue'의 의미는 무엇입니까?

syn How is (the word) 'blue' being used here?
In what sense [way] is the word 'blue' used here?
What does the word 'blue' mean in this context?
What does the word 'blue' refer to in this context?

어휘 위의 의문문에서는 단어나 구를 직접 말하지 않고, 앞에 'the word'

누구나 영어로 가르칠 수 있다

또는 'the phrase'라는 말을 부가하는 것이 분명하고 자연스럽다.

cf. 본문 속의 단어의 의미 또는 차이와 관련된 질문 또는 설명

Does it refer to _____? (그것은 _____을 의미합니까?)

In line 8, what does the word 'however' tell you about what follows?

(여덟째 줄에서 단어 'however'는 어떤 내용이 이어지는 것을 나타냅니까?)

You're right. It does mean 'crazy' usually, but it means 'angry' in this particular context.

(맞습니다. 그것은 일반적으로 'crazy'라는 의미이지만, 이 문맥에서는 'angry' 라는 의미입니다.)

What's the difference between 'sick' and 'ill'?

('sick'과 'ill'의 차이는 무엇입니까?)

---

⑦ **Does anyone know when you would use the word, 'cute'?**
I'll give you a clue. It has something to do with 'a baby'.

해설   'Cute'라는 단어를 언제 사용하는지 압니까? 힌트를 주겠습니다. 그것은 어린이와 관계가 있습니다.

syn   Can anyone tell me when you would use the word, 'cute'?
When can I use the word 'cute' in a sentence?
When can the word 'cute' be used?

주의   'Has'가 본동사일 경우 'It has'를 'It's'로 축약하지 말 것.

---

⑧ **What's a synonym for 'huge'?**

해설   'Huge'의 동의어는 무엇입니까?

syn   Give me a synonym for 'huge'.

       What's another word that means the same (thing) as 'huge'?

    cf. 동의문에 대한 질문

    What's another word for it? (그것을 다른 말로 표현하면?)

    What's another way of saying 'he stumbled'?

    ('He stumbled'를 달리 표현하면?)

    What's a shorter way of saying 'he went by plane'?

    ('He went by plane.'을 간단히 표현하면?)

    What are two words that mean the same (thing) as 'tripped' (in the paragraph)?

    = Can you give me two words that mean the same (thing) as 'tripped' (in the paragraph)?

    ((이 글에서) 'tripped'와 같은 의미를 가진 두 단어는 무엇입니까?)

어휘   trip (헛디디다)=make stumble

> ⑨ Well, what's the opposite of it?

해설   그것의 반대말은 무엇입니까?

syn   What's its opposite?

       Do you know its opposite form?

       Can you tell me what the opposite form is?

> ⑩ Point to a word in the passage which means the same as 'press'.

해설   이 단락에서 'press'와 같은 의미를 가진 단어를 찾으세요.

syn   What words mean the same as 'press'?

What word is a synonym of 'press'?

Show me a word with the same meaning as 'press'.

Are there any synonyms of 'press' in this passage?

cf. 지시하는 것을 찾기

Show me a phrase in the passage which describes a...

(글에서 …를 묘사하는 구를 찾으세요.)

Find the person in the picture who is...

(그림에서… 한 사람을 찾으세요.)

---

⑪ What's the noun that corresponds to this verb?

해설 이 동사의 명사형은 무엇입니까?

syn Can anyone tell me the corresponding noun?

Form the noun from this verb.

cf. 파생어에 대한 질문 및 설명

What's the noun form of it? (그것의 명사형은 무엇입니까?)

What's a prefix that means 'not'?

('Not'을 의미하는 접두어는 무엇입니까?)

What's the adjective derived from this word?

(이 단어의 형용사형은 무엇입니까?)

Look. The word ends in 'ness', so it must be a noun.

(자, 그 단어는 'ness'로 끝나므로 명사임에 틀림없다.)

---

⑫ What's the noun derived from the word 'luxurious'?

해설 'Luxurious'의 명사형은 무엇입니까?

What's the noun that comes from the word 'luxurious'?
What noun is derived from 'luxurious'?

참고 **'Luxury hotel'과 'luxurious hotel'의 차이점**
위의 두 단어는 의미상으로는 유사하지만 실용적인 면에서는 차
이가 있다. 먼저 'luxurious hotel'은 호텔에 대한 개인적인 판단으
로, 우리말로 '화려한 호텔'의 의미를 지닌다.
e.g. We had good time at that hotel. The accomodation was
luxurious.

반면 'luxury hotel'은 숙박업계에서 공식적으로 분류된 호텔로,
우리의 경우 무궁화가 표시된 '일급호텔'을 일컫는다.

---

⑬ What's a man who teaches students called?

해설 학생을 가르치는 사람을 무엇이라 합니까?

syn What do you call a person who teaches students?
A man who teaches students is called (a) what?

---

⑭ It is something to do with 'World Cup'. What could it be?

해설 그것은 'World Cup'과 관계가 있습니다. 그것은 무엇입니까?

syn It's related to 'World Cup'. What is it?
It has something to do with 'World Cup.' What is it?

cf. **단어 알아맞히기와 관련된 표현**
It begins with A. It's similar to '_____'. Take a guess.

(그것은 A로 시작합니다. 그것은 '_____'와 유사합니다. 알아맞혀 보세요.)

It begins with A. It rhymes with '_____'. Take a guess.

(그것은 A로 시작합니다. 그것은 '_____'와 같은 음을 가집니다. 맞추어 보세요.)

⑮ Explain the meaning of the following words in English.

해설   다음 단어의 의미를 영어로 설명하세요.

syn   Explain in English the meaning of the following words.
Explain the meaning in English of the following words.
(incorrect)

어법   일반적으로 영어는 '동사+목적어+부사구'의 어순을 가진다. 그러나 일상적인 표현에서 간혹 동사의 목적어가 길 경우, '부사구가 목적어 앞에 위치할 수도 있다. 그러나 위와 같이 목적어구 내부에 부사구가 위치할 수는 없다.

cf. 어휘에 대한 설명

e.g. 'Need'

The word 'need' spelled N-E-E-D means something you require, something you must have. The word 'want' spelled W-A-N-T means something you would like to have. Sometimes in informal conversation these words have the same meaning.

(단어 'need'는 철자가 'N, E, E, D'이며, 요구하거나, 가져야 하는 것을 의미한다. 단어 'want'는 철자가 'W, A, N, T'이며 가지고 싶은 것을 의미한다. 때로 일상영어에서 이 두 단어는 같은 의미를 가진다.)

'Too hard'

The expression 'too hard' and the word 'impossible' used in today's conversation have similar meaning. The word 'hard' spelled

H-A-R-D means difficult, the opposite of 'easy.' The word I-M-P-O-S-S-I-B-L-E means too hard, so difficult that it can't be done.

(오늘날 회화에서 'Too hard'라는 표현과 'impossible'이라는 단어는 유사한 의미를 가진다. 단어 'hard'는 철자가 'h, a, r, d'이며 어렵다는 말로, 'easy'의 반대말이다. 단어 'impossible'은 너무 어렵거나 난해해서 할 수 없다는 의미이다.)

'Used to'
The expression used, U-S-E-D plus 'to', T-O means something that was done in the past but not now. The expression 'used to be' has the meaning of 'was.'

('Used'와 'to'로 된 표현은, 과거에는 행해졌으나 지금은 행해지지 않는 것을 의미한다. 'Used to be'라는 표현은 'was'라는 의미를 지닌다.)

---

⑯ You'll need to practice these words.

해설   이 단어들을 연습[공부]하세요.

syn   You need some more practice with these words.
You'll have to spend more time practicing these words.

---

⑰ S: What's the difference between A and B?

해설   A와 B는 어떤 차이가 있습니까?

syn   How do A and B differ?
How are they [A and B] different?
Is A the same as B? *(casual)*

그리스 신화에 나오는 신의 별칭

유럽 문화와 문학에 커다란 영향을 미친 그리스 신화에 나오는 여러 신과 괴물은 라틴어에서 이름만 다르게 불리는 경우가 많다. 이들은 미국 초등학교 사회과목에서 자세히 다루므로 알아둘 필요가 있다. 여기에 대표적으로 몇 가지만 열거하면 다음과 같다.

Greek Name	Roman Name	
Zeus	Jupiter [Jove]	King of the Gods (신의 왕: 천둥과 하늘의 신)
Hera	Juno	Wife of Zeus (제우스의 아내, 여자와 결혼의 여신)
Poseidon	Neptune	God of the sea (바다의 신)
Apollo	Apollo	God of light (제우스의 아들: 태양의 신)
Artemis	Diana	Goddess of the moon and hunting(아폴로의 쌍둥이 누이: 달과 사냥의 여신)
Aphrodite	Venus	Goddess of love and beauty (사랑과 미의 여신)
Eros	Cupid	God of Love (son of Aphrodite, 사랑의 신)
Athena	Minerva	Goddess of wisdom (지혜의 여신)
Ares	Mars	God of war (제우스의 아들: 전쟁의 신)
Hermes	Mercury	God of commerce, science, eloquence, cleverness, travel, and thievery (상업, 과학, 변론, 교활, 여행, 절도의 신, 신들의 사자)
Hephaestus	Vulcan	God of fire and the forge(제우스의 아들: 불과 대장일의 신)
Hades	Pluto	God of the underworld (명부의 신)
Dionysus	Bacchus	God of wine (술의 신)
Demeter	Ceres	Goddess of grain and of the harvest(곡물과 수확의 여신)
Pan	Silvanus	A creature with goat horns and goat hooves(목동, 산야의 괴물)

C. 철자와 숫자

---

① How do you spell the word, 'boxes'? Spell it out loud.

해설　'Boxes'의 철자가 무엇입니까? 크게 말해 보세요.

syn　How is the word 'boxes' spelled?
　　　What is the correct spelling of the word, 'boxes'?
　　　The correct spelling of the word 'boxes' is what?
　　　Now, tell me how to spell 'boxes'.

　　　*How spell 'boxes'? *(incorrect)*

주의　한국인에게 영어를 가르치는 외국인 강사들의 지적에 의하면, 위의 경우와 같이 우리나라 학생들이 'How do you spell it?'을 'How spell it?' 또는 'How spell?'로 주어 부분인 "Do you"를 생략하는 경우가 많다고 하는데, 이는 잘못이다. 이런 현상은 아마 우리말의 주어를 생략하는 표현방식에서 영향을 받은 것 같다.

cf. 철자에 대한 표현들
Are there two 'l's or only one? ('l'이 두 개입니까? 하나입니까?)
Do I need a hyphen [comma, period]?
(하이픈[쉼표, 마침표]이 필요합니까?)
: period = full stop
What's the preposition after 'to rely'?
('To rely' 다음에는 어떤 전치사가 옵니까?)

　　　　　　　　　　　　　　　누구나 영어로 가르칠 수 있다

② Have you spelled it right?

해설   철자가 맞습니까?

syn   Did you spell it right? *(casual)*
Is it spelled correctly?
Is there a problem with the spelling?
Is it right?
Did you get it right?
Do you have it right?
I wonder if you've spelled it right.
Let's see if you spelled it right [correctly].
Is there anything wrong with the spelling?
Is this letter right [correct]?

③ I'm afraid this is spelled wrong.

해설   이 단어의 철자가 틀렸다.

syn   There's a spelling error here.
This is spelled incorrectly.
You've made a spelling mistake.
You've botched the spelling. *(rude, rare)*

cf. You still have some trouble with your spelling.
(아직 철자를 잘 못쓰는 것 같다.)

④ There are two words you've spelled wrong.

해설   두 단어의 철자가 틀렸다.

syn   You've spelled 2 words incorrectly.
       There are two errors [slip ups].
       You've made 2 spelling mistakes.
       You made 2 mistakes.
       You've slipped up on two words.

⑤ Make sure you put spaces between the words.

해설   단어 사이에 간격을 두세요.

syn   Make sure your spaces between the words are clear.
       See that your spaces between the words are clear. *(rare)*

   cf. **철자와 의미와 관련된 표현**
       The word begins with 'un', so it means 'not' something.
       (그 단어는 'un'으로 시작되므로, 'not'과 같은 의미로 사용됩니다.)
       They're spelled the same, but pronounced differently.
       (그것들은 철자는 같으나, 발음이 다릅니다.)

⑥ T: What letter is missing?
   S: There's a 'g' missing.

해설   T: 무슨 자가 빠졌습니까?
       S: 'G'가 없습니다.

syn You're missing a 'g'.
  A 'g' is missing [is needed].
  You need a 'g'.
  (The letter) 'g' is missing.

> ⑦ Make sure your 'g's, 'y's, and so on have tails which hang down.

해설 'G'와 'y'의 꼬리가 내려오도록 쓰세요.

syn Take care to include tails which hang down on your 'g's and 'y's.
  Be sure to put tails on your 'g's and 'y's.

어휘 make sure(확실히 하다, 명심하다)=see that, don't forget, be sure that, see to it that

cf. 철자와 관련된 지시문

See that your 'k's, 'l's and so on go straight up.
: 영국영어에서는 '똑바로'를 'right'라고도 한다.
Don't forget to cross your 't's and dot your 'i's.
('T'에 줄긋고, 'i'에 점찍는 것을 잊지 마라.)
Check your spelling of '____'. ('____'의 철자를 확인해라.)
Write it separately [together]. (그것을 떼어 써라.)
Put a comma after this word. (이 단어 뒤에 쉼표를 붙여라.)
Don't forget to put capital letters where needed.
(필요한 때에는 반드시 대문자를 써라.)
Don't forget to spell correctly and write neatly.
(단어는 반드시 바르게 적고, 깨끗이 써라.)
There should be an 'o' instead of a 'u'. ('U' 대신에 'o'이어야 합니다.)

D. 문법 및 대체연습

> ① Put the sentences into the passive voice.
> How many different sentences can you make [say]?

해설   다음 문장을 수동태로 바꾸세요.
: 말로 표현할 때는 'make' 대신 'say'를 사용한다.

syn   Rewrite the sentences, using the passive voice.
Make the sentences passive. *(casual)*

    cf. 문장 만들기에 대한 지시문
    Now I'm going to erase some words. Can you make a new sentence?
    (몇몇 단어를 지우겠습니다. 새로운 문장을 만들 수 있습니까?)
    Remember, in this exercise you have to ask [make] the questions. The
    answers will be on the tape.
    (이 연습문제에서는 질문을 만들어야 합니다. 답은 테이프에 있습니다.)

> ② Can anybody correct this sentence?

해설   이 문장을 고칠 수 있습니까? [이 문장의 틀린 부분은 어디입니까?]

syn   Can anyone find the mistake in this sentence?
What is the mistake in this sentence?
Can any of you pinpoint the error in this sentence?
Who can identify the mistake in this sentence?

    cf. Can anyone put a finger on the mistake in this sentence?

(이 문장의 내용상 잘못은 무엇입니까?)

: 'Put a finger on'은 '내용상 잘못은 무엇입니까?'라는 의미로, 문법적인 잘못이 아니라 추상적인 사고나 생각 (abstract thought or idea)에 대한 (내용의) 잘못을 지적할 때 주로 사용한다.

③ Now say it with 'shopping' instead of 'to school'.

해설   'To school' 대신 'shopping'으로 대체하세요.

syn   Now change it, using 'shopping' instead of 'to school'.

Now say it with the word 'shopping' instead of the words 'to school'.

Now replace 'to school' with 'shopping'.

Now, instead of 'to school' use 'shopping'.

Now change it, say 'shopping' instead of 'to school'. *(rare)*

cf. **어휘 대체 및 문법연습에 연관된 표현**

Listen to the cue and use the cue word.

(제시어를 듣고 제시어를 사용하세요.)

We're going to do a conversation drill with (the word) 'need'.

(단어 'need'를 가지고 대화연습을 하겠습니다.)

I'm going to read some sentences which are in either the past or the present tense.

(과거 또는 현재시제로 된 몇 가지 문장을 읽겠습니다.)

Listen. I'll do the first two for you so you will understand.

(잘 들으세요. 이해를 돕기 위해 처음 두 문제는 내가 하겠습니다.)

④ Substitute (the words) 'too' and 'enough' for 'so' in these sentences.

해설   이 문장 속의 'so' 대신에 'too'와 'enough'로 대체하시오.

syn   Replace 'so' with 'too' and 'enough' in these sentences.

    cf. What's the rule about using 'few' and 'little'?
      : 이 경우 'using'을 생략하지 않는 것이 의미를 명확하게 한다.

⑤ What's the past tense of 'to sing'?

해설   'To sing'의 과거 시제는 무엇입니까?

syn   Do you know the past tense of 'to sing'?

    cf. 시제 또는 조건절에 관한 표현
      Which tense do we use after 'if'?
      ('If' 다음에는 무슨 시제를 사용합니까?)
      You've forgotten everything I ever taught you about the conditional. (조건법에 대해 가르쳐 준 모든 사항을 잊었구나.)
      Today we have practiced the past tense and you've learned how and when to use the past tense.
      (오늘은 과거시제를 학습했으며, 과거시제를 어떻게 언제 사용하는가를 배웠습니다.)

⑥ Write the verbs in brackets in their correct form.

해설   괄호 속의 동사를 올바른 형태로 고치세요.

syn   Place the correct form of the verb in the brackets.

Insert the correct form of the verb in the brackets.

cf. 문법문제의 풀이에 흔히 사용되는 지시문

Use appropriate forms of 'to be' to complete the sentences.

('to be'를 적절히 고쳐서 문장을 완성하세요.)

Change these sentences in the same way as the example.

(보기와 같이 문장을 바꾸세요.)

Change all the nouns into pronouns.

(모든 명사를 대명사로 바꾸세요.)

⑦ Insert the words given in brackets into the sentences.

해설   괄호 속에 주어진 동사를 문장 속에 삽입하세요.

syn   Fill in the blanks, using the words given.

Complete the sentences with the words given (in brackets).

⑧ Complete the sentences by adding an article.

해설   관사를 넣어서 문장을 완성하세요.

syn   Fill in 'a(n)' or 'the' where necessary.

Complete the sentences, using an article.

Use an article to complete the sentences.

⑨ You left out the preposition.
Which preposition follows 'to be proud'?

해설   전치사가 빠졌습니다. 'to be proud' 다음에는 어떤 전치사가 옵니까?

syn   You forgot (to include) the preposition.
You didn't include the preposition.
You failed to [neglected to] include the preposition.
You left the preposition out.

Which preposition can 'to be proud' use [take]?
Which preposition comes after 'to be proud'?
Which preposition can be used with [couple with, connected to, linked to, linked up with] 'to be proud'?

⑩ **Is a relative pronoun necessary here?**
I suggest (that) you omit the relative pronoun.

해설   여기에 관계대명사가 필요합니까? 관계대명사를 생략하세요.

syn   Do we need a relative pronoun here?
Do we need to include a relative pronoun?
Is a relative pronoun required here?
Is a relative pronoun mandatory here?
Is this sentence OK without a relative pronoun?
Are we in need of a relative pronoun here?

⑪ Is the word order right?

해설 어순이 맞습니까?

syn Are the words in the correct order?
Do I have the words in the right order?

> **cf. 어순(word order)문제와 관련된 표현들**
> What if we change(d) the word order? (어순을 바꾸어 보세요.)
> Rearrange the words in the correct order.
> (다음 단어를 올바른 순서로 재배열하세요.)
> Put the adverb at the end. (부사를 마지막에 두세요.)
>
> What if you start(ed) with the adverb?
> How about if you start(ed) with the adverb? (not clear)
> : 문장의 형태를 의미하는지, 내용을 의미하는지가 분명하지 않다.

⑫ S: That word is new to me.

해설 나는 그 단어를 모릅니다.

syn I've never heard that word before.
I've just learned a new word.

> **cf.** I don't understand the last word on line 7.

⑬ S: I don't understand what this means.

해설 (이것이) 무슨 뜻인지 모르겠습니다.

syn   It still isn't clear to me what this means.

I still don't get it.

It's still confusing to me.

The meaning is still hard to pin down.

*I didn't understand what this means. (incorrect ; 시제의 일치를
어김)

---

⑭ S: Which tense should I use?

해설   어떤 시제를 써야 합니까? [시제는 무엇입니까?]

syn   Which tense is required?

Which tense do I need? *(rare)*

cf. Could you use the future [past] tense here?
(여기에 미래 [과거] 시제를 쓸 수 있습니까?)

---

⑮ S: Why do you need the article?

해설   왜 관사가 필요합니까?

syn   Why is the article required?

Is an article necessary?

Why is it important to have an article?

Do I [you] have to have an article?

◆ 어휘 교수법

먼저 어휘 학습의 유의사항을 정리하고, 다음으로 어휘교수 방법에 대해 살펴보기로 한다.

어휘 학습에서 교사가 유의해야 할 사항은 다음 몇 가지로 요약할 수 있다.

첫째, 새로 나온 어휘를 처음 학습할 때에는 교사는 의미를 명확하고 간단하게 설명해야 한다. 간단하게 학습자의 모국어를 사용하는 것도 가능하다(Laufer & Shmueli, 1997). 예를 들어 초급영어 학습에서 처음 나온 단어, 'hopothesis(가설)'의 경우를 보자.

hypothesis; unproved idea (가설: 증명되지 않은 생각)

위의 단어는 초급과정에서는 빈도가 적고 필수적인 단어가 아니므로 설명이 매우 짧다. 이 단어는 간단히 정의하거나 모국어로 해석한 뒤 교과 활동을 진행해도 충분하다.

둘째, 학습자는 단어가 가진 기저 의미를 명확히 이해한 뒤, 파생된 의미와 어떤 연관이 있는지를 배워야 한다. Nation(2001)의 다음 예를 보자.

head; the top or most important part, for example, head of your body, head of a match, head of the organization
(꼭대기 또는 가장 중요한 부분, 예를 들면, 신체의 머리, 성냥 꼭지, 조직의 수장)

위의 규정은 기저 의미에 대한 간단할 설명에 이어 예문이 제시되어 있다. 실제 사전에는 'head'에 대한 20가지 이상의 항목이 있지만, 대부분이 이 기저 의미에서 파생된 것이다.

셋째, 어휘는 반복하여 학습해야 한다. 어휘에 대한 접촉이 반복되면 이전의 지식이 강화되고 다양해지는 효과가 있다. 어휘 학습은 누적적이므로 교사는 필요할 경우 그 어휘의 지식을 강화하고 풍부히 하기 위해 다양한 방법으로 복구해 볼 필요가 있다.

넷째, 학습자가 어휘의 정의를 명확히 인지하게 도와주어야 한다. 어휘의 정의에 대한 학습자의 인지 정도를 진단하기 위해서 시험을 보거나, 교재나 문제풀이를 통해 단어의 정의를 인식하는 훈련을 시킬 수도 있다. 그 다음에는 학생이 직접 예문을 표현하게 하고 교사는 점차로 설명을 줄여 나가야 한다.

다섯째, 어휘의 개념에서 어떤 부분이 먼저 설명되어야 하는지 우선순위를 정해야 한다. 어휘는 다양한 의미를 지니고 있으므로 어휘에 대한 지식의 정도에 따라 사용 능력도 달라진다(Nist & Olejnik, 1995). 단어는 대개 의미에 중점을 두지만, 때로는 철자, 발음, 연어 관계, 문법적 특성, 공손의 정도, 공식성, 방언 또는 전달 매체까지도 고려해야 한다.

여섯째, 교사는 학습자가 학습한 어휘를 암기하도록 도와야 한다. 교사가 어휘를 설명하는 방법은 학생의 이해와 암기 또는 기억 둘 다에 영향을 줄 수 있으므로 교사는 어휘에 대한 정보를 신중하고 철저히 처리해야 한다. 교사는 기억을 돕기 위해서 단어의 각 부분(어근과 어미)이 단어의 의미와 어떤 연관이 있는지 설명할 수도 있고, 과거의 경험, 철자, 문법적 유형, 연어 관계를 언급할 수도 있다. 다음 예문을 보자.

compound; a thing consisting of two or more separate things
(복합체)　　　(두 개 이상의 별개의 것들로 구성된 것)

위의 규정은 접두어, 'com'의 의미에 초점을 두어 기억에 도움을 준 것이다. 이런 규정은 단어가 발생하는 문맥과 연관이 있어야 한다.

끝으로 연관된 단어에 의한 간섭을 피해야 한다. 어휘설명에서 형태나 의미가 유사한 단어는 함께 학습하지 말고 별도로 학습해야 한다. 연관된 단어들은 혼란을 가중시켜 학습자의 기억을 어렵게 할 수 있으므로, 어휘 학습의 초기 단계에서는 연관된 단어를 가르치는 것은 도움이 되지 않는다.

이제 위의 유의 사항을 바탕으로 구체적인 어휘 교수방법을 살펴보자.
Haynes & Baker(1993)와 Nation(2001)의 구분에 따르면 어휘 교수 방식은 여덟 가지 유형 — 즉, 설명, 정의, 규정, 예시, 동의어/반의어, 비언어적 설명, 복합적 규정, 모국어번역 — 으로 구분할 수 있다. 이를 구체적으로 살펴보면 다음과 같다.

① 설명: 어휘의 의미를 사전적으로 규정하지 않고, 담화체로 풀어서 설명한다.
② 정의: 사전적 의미나 문법적인 규정 또는 어원을 이용하는 것이다.
③ 규정: 주로 화용적인 면에서 어휘나 표현의 용법을 제한하는 것이다.
④ 동의어/반의어: 동의어, 반의어를 제시하는 것이다.

⑤ 예시: 어휘의 의미를 상위어 또는 (상호) 하위어를 통한 포함관계를 이용하여 설명한다.

⑥ 비언어적 설명: 그림, 도표, 또는 행위를 이용하여 설명하는 것이다.

⑦ 복합적 규정: 위의 설명 방식을 두 개 이상 동시에 이용하여 설명하는 것이다.

⑧ 모국어 번역: 의미상 대응되는 모국어를 사용하는 것이다.

위의 분류방식을 기준으로 원어민의 어휘교수법의 특징을 살펴보면 다음 몇 가지로 요약될 수 있다.

첫째, 원어민의 어휘에 대한 설명은 '어휘의 의미를 명확하고 간단히 설명해야' 한다는 어휘교수법의 원칙에 부합하고 있다. 구체적으로 각각의 유형에 대한 예문을 살펴보자.

설명 'Obsessive' means when you do something you can't stop. You concentrate on one thing.
('집착하는' '여러분이 어떤 일을 중단하지 못하고 할 때'를 의미한다. 당신은 한 가지에 집중합니다.)

정의 'Statuo quo' means nothing bad nor nothing good has happened.
('그저 그래'는 '나쁜 일도 좋은 일도 일어나지 않았다'는 의미이다.)

규정 'Lover' usually means sexual partner.
('연인'은 '성적 상대'를 의미한다.)

예시 'Articles' are the words, 'a, an, the'.
('관사'는 'a', 'an', 'the'이다.)

동의어 'Tranquility' means calmness, peace, and quiet.
('고요'는 '평온, 평화, 조용함'을 의미한다.)

위의 예에서 보는 바와 같이 원어민은 어떤 방식을 택하든 간에 모든 어휘를 가능한 쉽고 구어적인 방식으로 설명한다는 것을 알 수 있다. 이런 교수방식은 비록 어휘의 정확한 의미를 전달하지는 못하더라도, 의미를 간결하게 설명해야 한다는 어휘교수법의 원칙에는 부합된다고 본다.

둘째, 어휘 교수 활동이 다양한 학습 환경에서 이루어지고 있다: 어휘학습은 주로 교과활동 중에 이루어지지만, 때로 학습자 질의, 학습자 오류, 교사가 유발하는 방식도 이용한다. 예를 들어 교과 학습과정에서 어휘에 대한 최초의 인지 활동은 아래와 같이 대부분 교사의 질의를 통해 시작된다.

> T: Today, we will be looking at a real military briefing. So, who knows what Missilex means?
> (이번에는 간단한 군사브리핑을 살펴보겠습니다. 그래, '미사일연습'이 무슨 뜻인지 아는 사람?)

위의 발화에서 교사는 먼저 화제를 도입하고, 그 다음 화제에 연관된 어휘의 의미를 학습자에게 질문하는 방식으로 어휘학습을 진행하는 것이다. 다음으로 학습자의 응답에 오류가 발생할 때 교사가 수정하는 방식이나, 모르는 어휘에 대한 학습자의 질의를 이용하여 어휘학습을 진행한다. 그리고 아래와 같이 교사가 의도적 유발하여 어휘학습을 수행하기도 한다.

> S: Do you have any special plan for the vacation?
> (방학 때 특별한 계획이 있습니까?)
> T: *Beats me*. I haven't thought about it yet.
> (몰라. 나는 아직 생각해 보지 않았어.)
> Ss: Beats me? What do you mean? We didn't beat you.
> (몰라? 무슨 뜻이죠? 우리 당신을 때리지 않았어요.)

위의 담화에서 교사는 의도적으로 학습자에게 생소한 관용어구를 사용하여 응답함으로써 학습자의 질문을 유도하는 것이다. 이런 방식은 주로, 'have butterflies in stomach', 'get down to', 'status quo'와 같은 일상에서 흔히 사용되는 관용구나, 'brother and sister', 'relative'와 같은 문화적 차이를 설명하기 위한 어휘 학습에 이용되었다. 이와 같은 어휘학습방식은 '어휘학습은 수시로 반복하여 주지시켜야 하며, 다양한 방식으로 진행되어야 한다'는 어휘학습의 원칙에도 부합한다고 볼 수 있다.

셋째, 동의어/반의어 또는 예시를 이용한 어휘학습과 달리, 사전적 정의는 학습자의 이해에 도움이 되지 않는 경우가 빈번하였다. 다음 예문을 보자.

S: What is photosynthesis?

   (광합성은 무엇입니까?)

T: Photosynthesis is the process of plants using sunlight as the source of energy.

   (광합성은 식물이 에너지의 원천으로 태양을 이용하는 과정입니다.)

Ss: *(students talk)* What's the word in Korean?

   (*(학생들이 중얼거린다)* 우리말로 무엇이라고 하지요?)

위의 광합성에 대한 교사의 사전적 정의는 정확하지만, 학습자의 이해 또는 인지에는 도움이 되지 않았다. 오히려 간단한 모국어 해석이 도움이 되었다.

넷째, 어휘 자체의 설명이 어려울 경우 교사는 정의 대신 예시를 사용하였다. 이 방식은 단어의 의미는 반복된 예시를 통해 효과적으로 이해시킬 수 있다는 어휘교수법에도 부합된다고 본다(Nation 2001).

T: Innovations. What does that mean?

   (혁신(제품). 그게 무슨 뜻이지요?)

S: Improve...

   (개선하다...)

T: Yes, you can improve the world. Think about new innovations. Can you give examples?

   (예, 여러분을 세상을 개선할 수 있어요. 혁신제품에 대해 생각해 보세요. 예를 들어보세요.)

S: Fax machines, cell phones, microwaves, etc.

   (팩스기, 휴대폰, 전자레인지 등.)

설명이 어려운 'innovation'에 대한 정의 대신 혁신과 연관된 제품을 나열하게 함으로써 초급회화 수준의 학생들의 이해를 돕고, 응답을 용이하게 하였다.

다섯째, 복합어의 경우에는 단어의 각 부분의 의미를 해체하여 설명함으로써 학습자가 이해하고 기억하기 쉽게 하였다.

T: Do you guys know what 'double standard' means?

   ('이중 기준'이 무슨 뜻인지 알아요?)

S: Umm...
   (음...)
T: What's 'double' mean?
   ('배'는 무슨 뜻이지요?)
Ss: Umm, two.
   (음... 두 개.)
T: Yeah! And what about standard? (pause) It's a rule. So, 'double standard' means two rules. Now, let's think about this...
   (그래! 그리고 '기준'이 무엇이지요. (멈춤) 그건 규칙입니다. 그래서 '이중 기준'은 두 개의 규칙을 의미합니다. 자, 여기에 대해 생각해 봅시다.)

즉 어휘를 해체하여 각각의 어휘성분에 대한 설명을 한 뒤, 다음에는 예문을 통한 구체적인 설명이 이어지고 있다.

마지막으로 어휘학습의 심리적 단계면에서 원어민의 어휘교육의 효과를 살펴보자: 즉, 어휘학습은 새로운 어휘에 대한 인지⇒ 과제수행 또는 복습을 통한 복구⇒ 학습한 어휘를 학습자가 직접 새로운 문장의 생성 또는 사고의 표현에 이용하는 어휘 생성이라는 삼 단계를 통해 완성된다. 이 기준에서 보면 원어민의 어휘교수법은 학습자가 어휘를 지각하고, 이해하는 활동이 과반수를 차지하고, 그 다음에는 학습한 어휘를 복습하고, 설명을 덧붙이는 활동이 삼분의 일 이상을 차지한다. 즉, 원어민 어휘교육의 90% 이상이 단순히 어휘를 지각하고 복구하는 데 편중되어 있으며, 현대 영어교육에서 점점 중시되는(Nation 2001, Ellis 2008) 어휘에 대한 학습자의 창조적 생성활동 단계에까지는 도달하지 못하고 있다. 학습자가 마지막 창조적 생성의 단계까지 도달한 경우를 살펴보자.

T: Do you all know what it means to be greedy? How about being arrogant?
   ('탐욕스러운'은 무슨 뜻인지 모두 압니까? 오만하다는 것은?)
S: Being greedy is to be selfish and not to share with other people. For example, *Mr. Kim is greedy.* He never shares food with cadets. Also, being arrogant is to be showing bad attitude. It is ignoring other people.

(탐욕스럽다는 것은 이기적이고 타인과 나누지 않는다는 것입니다. 예를 들면, *김군은 탐욕스럽다.* 그는 생도와 음식을 나누어 먹지 않는다. 또한, 오만한 것은 나쁜 태도를 드러내는 것입니다. 그것은 타인을 무시하는 것이다.)

위의 예문은 어휘에 대한 복습과정에서 발생한 대화이다. 원어민의 질문에, 학습자는 어휘의 의미를 비교적 정확히 설명하고, 동시에 이탤릭 부분에서 보는 바와 같이 간단하지만 'greedy'를 이용한 낮은 수준의 문장 생성활동까지 발전하고 있다. 이와 같은 생성활동은 학습자가 추후 언제든지 그 어휘를 자신의 문장 속에서 생성해 낼 수 있다는 것을 보여 주는 것이다. 이와 같은 생성행위는 심리적 학습의 최종단계로 매우 바람직 하지만 아쉽게도 매우 적은 분포를 보이고 있다.

1. 현장예문 (Real-life Situation)

Using Pictures to Study English
(adapted from C.J. Kennedy (1974))

삽화를 가지고 하는 수업에는 대개 1~6개 정도의 장면이 적당하다. 삽화 한 장의 크기는 50×70cm 정도가 적당하다. 학습방법은 대개 4단계 — 제시(Presentation), 반복 연습(Repetition), 질의응답(Question and Answer), 연습(Practice) — 으로 나누어진다. 교실 상황 및 필요에 따라 어느 단계를 생략하거나, 변형하여 사용할 수도 있다.

Teachers frequently ask their students to comment on what they see in a picture, whether from a textbook, magazine, or other picture types. The language covered in this unit includes how to introduce a picture to the class, questioning the class on a picture, asking the students to look carefully at the picture, handing out pictures to the class, describing a picture, engaging the students in exercises related to the picture, and playing games using pictures.

Now listen to the description of the following pictures and dialogue.

1. 제시단계(Presentation)
a) 먼저 학생들에게 삽화를 보여주고, 각각의 삽화를 설명해 준다.
b) 삽화에 대한 설명에서, 시제를 한정 — 과거(진행)시제, 또는 현재(진행)시제 등 — 시켜야 한다.
c) 어휘는 이미 학습한 어휘를 이용하며, 새로운 어휘는 최소한으로 사용해야 한다. 삽화에 대한 설명에 사용되는 새로 나온 어휘는 먼저 적어주고 설명한 다음에 시작한다.

cf. 여러 장의 삽화로 구성된 경우 첫 번째 삽화를 학생과 함께 풀이한 후, 나머지 삽화는 학생들을 그룹으로 나누어 상황에 맞게 이야기를 직접 작성하여 발표하게 할 수도 있다.

2. 반복 연습(Repetition)

제시단계에서 선생님이 말한 문장을 학생은 처음부터 차례로 반복 연습해야 한다. 이때 한 문장씩 반복할 수도 있고, 첫 번째 학생이 한 문장을 반복하면, 다음 학생이 그 문장과 그 다음 문장을 반복하는 방식을 택할 수도 있다.

(예)   Pupil 1 - Sentence 1

         Pupil 2 - Sentence 1 + S. 2

         Pupil 3 - Sentence 1 + S. 2 + S. 3

3. 질의응답(Question and Answer)

삽화에 관하여 선생님이 질문을 하면, 학생은 답을 해야 한다.

4. 연습(Practice)

상황에 따라 선생님은 최소한의 조언 및 질문에 응답한다.

a) 재생산(Reproduction): 각 그룹별로 나누어 삽화를 보고, 적절한 이야기를 창작한다.

b) 질문(Questions): 삽화를 보고, 학생들 간에 질의응답을 한다.

c) 대화(Dialogue): 삽화를 보고, 학생들 간에 적절한 대화를 만들어낸다.

d) 단막극(the Playlet): 그룹으로 나누어, 학생들 간에 간단한 연극을 만들어 실습한다.

위의 학습 방법을 실제 수업 진행에 구체적으로 적용해 보자. 먼저 다음 삽화를 보자.

1. 제시단계(Presentation)

다음은 위의 삽화에 대하여 선생님이 학생들에게 제시할 수 있는 한 가지 예문이다.

Picture 1

It was a lovely day yesterday. The sun was shining. At ten o'clock everybody in the office was working hard. Mr Smith, the boss, was writing lots of letters, and Sue, his secretary, was typing lots of letters. However James wasn't working hard. While his boss was writing and the secretary was typing, he was looking out of the window and dreaming of his girl friend, Ann.

〈해설〉 사무실의 전반적인 상황―시간(when)과 날씨(weather), 누가 (who), 무엇을(what) 하고 있는지―을 묘사하고 있다: 어제는 날씨가 좋았다. 햇살이 빛났다. 10시경, 사무실의 모든 사람은 열심히 일하고 있었다. 상관인 스미스 씨는 편지를 쓰고 있고, 비서인 수는 타이프를 치고 있었다. 그러나 제임스는 열심이지 않았다. 그의 상관이 편지를 쓰고, 비서가 타이프를 치는 동안, 그는 창밖을 보고 그의 여자친구 앤을 생각하고 있었다.

(Picture 2부터는 Picture 1을 참조하여 학생들을 그룹으로 직접 나누어 작성하게 할 수도 있다.)

Picture 2

James went to see the boss. When he entered the office, the boss was working hard. James held his head in his hands and groaned. The boss looked at him. James said, 'I'm ill, sir.' The boss said, 'You must take an aspirin and go to bed. Come back tomorrow.'

〈해설〉 제임스의 사무실 안에서의 행동을 묘사하고 있다: 제임스는 상관에게 갔다. 그가 사무실에 들어갔을 때 그의 상관은 열심히 일하고 있었다. 제임스는 그의 머리에 손을 얹고 신음을 하였다. 상관이 그를 보았다. 제임스가 '몸이 안 좋습니다.'라고 말하자 상관은 '아스피린 먹고 자라. 내일 출근해.'라고 말했다.

Picture 3

James left the office and ran to the park. He met his girl friend there. She was sitting on a bench when he arrived. A man was sitting beside her reading a paper and smoking a pipe. Some children were playing soccer. They talked in the sunshine for a long time.

〈해설〉 제임스의 사무실 밖에서의 행동을 묘사하고 있다: 제임스는 사무실을 나와 공원에 달려갔다. 거기에서 여자친구를 만났다. 그가 도착했을 때, 그녀는 벤치에 앉아 있었다. 한 남자가 그녀 옆에 앉아서 신문을 읽고 담배를 피우고 있었다. 몇몇의 아이들은 축구를 하고 있었다. 그들은 햇살 아래에서 오랫동안 이야기했다.

Picture 4

At one o'clock they went to a restaurant. A lot of people were talking, eating and drinking. They found a table and ordered a meal. At the table behind them a man was sitting. It was James's boss. James didn't notice the boss because he was talking to Ann but the boss noticed James.

〈해설〉 식당에서의 상황을 묘사하고 있다: 1시에 그들은 식당에 갔다. 많은 사람들이 떠들고, 먹고, 마시고 있었다. 그들은 자리를 잡고 식사를 주문했다. 그들 뒤의 식탁에는 한 남자가 앉아 있었다. 그는 제임스의 상관이었다. 앤과 이야기 하느라 제임스는 상관을 알아보지 못했지만, 상관은 제임스를 알아보았다.

Picture 5

After the meal James called the waiter and asked for his check. The waiter said, 'A gentleman was sitting at that table. He paid your check and then left.' James and Ann were very surprised.

〈해설〉 식당에서 일어난 사건을 묘사하고 있다: 식사 후 제임스는 종업원을 불러 계산서를 청구했다. 웨이터가 '식탁에 앉아 있던 어떤 신사분이 계산을 치르고 갔다.'고 말했다. 제임스와 앤은 매우 놀랐다.

Picture 6

The next day James went to work. When he arrived the secretary was typing letters but the boss was standing beside James's desk. He was angry. He gave James the check and gave him the sack as well.^{주)} The secretary was still typing letters when James left for the last time!

〈해설〉 사건의 결과를 묘사하고 있다: 다음 날 제임스는 출근을 했다. 그가 도착했을 때, 비서는 편지를 타이프치고 있었으나, 상관은 제임스의 책상 옆에 서 있었다. 그는 화가 나 있었다. 그는 제임스에게 계산서를 주고, 해고장도 동시에 주었다. 제임스가 마지막으로 떠날 때, 비서는 편지를 타이프치고 있었다.)

(주) He gave James the sack. (그를 제임스를 해고시켰다.)
= James get fired. (제임스는 해고되었다.)

2. 반복 연습(Repetition)
반복연습은 학생들의 흥미를 유지시키기 위해 다소 빠르게 진행하는 것이 좋다.

(그림 1의 경우)

Teacher:	It was a lovely day yesterday.
Pupil 1:	It was a lovely day yesterday.
Pupil 2:	It was a lovely day yesterday.
Teacher:	It was a lovely day yesterday. The sun was shining.
Pupil 3:	It was a lovely day yesterday. The sun was shining.
Pupil 4:	It was a lovely day yesterday. The sun was shining. and so on.

3. 질의응답(Question and Answer)
구문 연습과 이해력을 돕기 위해 선생님은 학생들에게 가능한 많은 'Yes / No' 의문문과 'Wh-의문사'로 이루어진 질문을 해야 한다. 또한 이 경우에는 그림에 따라 구체적인 질문, 추론적인 질문, 개인에 관계된 일반적인 질문 등을 할 수가 있다.

1) 구체적인 질문
① Yes / No question
Q: Was it raining?
A: No, it wasn't.
Q: Was the boss reading?
A: No, he was writing.

② Wh-question (From Picture 4)

    Q: Tell me where James and Ann went.

    A: They went to a restaurant.

    Q: Tell me what time it was.

    A: It was one o'clock.

2) 추론적인 질문(inferential questions)

    Q: (Picture 4) What did James order?

    Q: (Picture 3) What paper was the man reading?

3) 일반적인 질문 (general questions)

    Q: (Picture 1) Does your father work in an office?

    Q: (Picture 1) Do you dream of your girl friend?

4. 연습(Practice)

1) 재생(Reproduction)

학생들 자신들이 삽화를 보고 이야기를 한 문장씩 창작하는 것이다. 예를 들어 'Picture 3'을 보자.

Pupil 1: James ran to the park.

Pupil 2: James ran to the park. He met Ann there.

Pupil 3: James ran to the park. He met Ann there. She was sitting on a bench when he arrived.

2) 질문(Questions)

학생들 간에 'Wh-의문문' 등을 이용하여 삽화에 연관된 질문을 하도록 유도한다. 예문 생략.

3) 대화(Dialogues)

삽화를 이용하여, 학생들이 그룹으로 나뉘어서 적절한 대화문을 만들도록 하고 선생님은 조언을 해 준다. 다음 대화가 학생들이 만들 수 있는 한 가지 예문이다.

Picture 1

James:	What a lovely day, Mary!
Secretary:	I'm sorry, James, but I don't have time to talk. I'm busy.
James:	What are you doing?
Secretary:	Typing letters. Can't you see!^{주)}
James:	What time is it?
Secretary:	Look at the clock! Ten o'clock.
James:	Ten o'clock. Oh! I'm late.
Secretary:	Late? Where are you going?
James:	Sorry, Mary. I don't have time to talk. I'm very busy.

(주) 'Can't you see?' (보면 모르니?): 친한 사이에서는 흔히 사용하지만, 무례하게 들릴
수도 있으니 유의해야 한다.
  e.g. A: What are you doing now? (지금 뭐 하니?)
       B: Can't you see I'm working? Don't bother me.
       (보면 모르니, 공부하고 있어. 귀찮게 굴지 마.)

Picture 2

James:	Excuse me sir.
Boss:	…
James:	Sir!
Boss:	Yes?
James:	I have a terrible headache. I feel terrible.
Boss:	I see. Take an aspirin and go to bed.
James:	Thank you, sir. You're very kind.
Boss:	But you must be in the office tomorrow morning.
James:	Of course, sir.

Picture 3

James: Hello, Ann. I ran all the way.

Ann: Did your boss believe your story?

James: Yes, he's stupid. Now we have the whole day together.

Ann: Lovely. We can enjoy the sun. What shall we do?

James: Let's go for a walk and then go to a restaurant for lunch.
         Do you like Chinese food?

Ann: Not very much. But I like French food.

James: Let's go to a French restaurant then.

Picture 4

James: There are a lot of people here.

Ann: It's always busy at this time.

James: What will you have? I'll have a steak.

Ann: Good. I'll have some fish. I'm so glad your boss believed your
         story. Now we can enjoy ourselves.

James: What shall we do this afternoon?

Ann: Let's go to the movies.

James: What a good idea. Robert Ford is in 'Spring Song' at the 'Ritz.' 주)

(주) Robert Ford is in 'Spring Song' at the 'Ritz': 로버트 포드가 출연하는 'Spring
Song'(연극 이름)이 'Ritz' (극장 이름)에서 공연되고 있다.

Picture 5

Ann: What time does the movie begin?

James: Three o'clock, I think. I must pay the check, Waiter! Check,
         please.

Waiter: There is no check, sir. A gentleman was sitting behind you and
         he paid the check, and gave me a large tip. Was he a friend of
         yours?

James: I don't know. I didn't see him. How strange!

Picture 6

Boss: Ah, Brown. I have a present for you.

James: For me! Oh, it's a check.

Boss: It's your check! I paid it yesterday at the restaurant. Headache indeed. I heard everything. While I was working hard, you were talking about me and having a good time. Do you think I'm stupid? Well, I'm giving you the sack!

James: But what shall I do?

Boss: Take your girl friend to the movies. Goodbye!

4) 단막극(The Playlet)

책상, 의자 등을 배치하여 실제 연출을 함으로써 표현력을 높인다.

예문 생략.

2. 기본구문

여기에서는 영어학습의 흥미를 유발하고 학생들의 표현 능력을 향상시키기 위해 사용하는 여러 가지 학습 자료들과 퀴즈 및 게임에 연관된 표현을 다음과 같이 정리하였다: A. 그림과 자료 활용 B. 퀴즈와 게임

A. 그림과 자료 활용

① Let's look at [take a look at] some pictures.

해설   몇 가지 그림[사진]을 보여 주겠습니다.

syn   I'll show you some pictures.
I have some pictures. I'd like to show you.

Let me show you some shots [photographs].
('Shot'은 그림이 아니라 사진을 의미한다.)

② Look at this picture. Who do you think they are, these people?

해설   이 그림을 보세요. 이 사람들은 누구라고 생각합니까?

syn   Who do you think these people are?
Who are these people?

cf. 그림 속 대화의 주제와 표현 방법에 관련된 질문
What were they talking about?
= What were they discussing? (그들은 무엇에 대해서 이야기했습니까?)

Now, these people are good friends, so they speak informally to each other.
(자, 이 사람들은 친구입니다, 그래서 그들은 서로 격의 없이 말합니다.)
Now, these people have never met before, so they are very polite.
(자, 이 사람들은 전에 만난 적이 없습니다. 그래서 그들은 정중합니다.)
The people in this dialogue are going to introduce a friend to someone.
(이 대화 속의 사람들은 친구를 누군가에게 소개하려고 합니다.)

③ Can you make a sentence about each person in the picture?

해설   그림 속에 있는 각 개인에 대한 문장을 만드세요.

syn   I want you to make a sentence about each person in the picture.

cf. 그림과 관련된 지시문

Now, in twos, look at the picture and make up a short dialogue like this. (자, 짝을 지어서, 그림을 보고, 이와 같이 짧은 대화를 만드세요.)
Listen and tell me which picture [table] this refers to.
(잘 듣고, 이 말은 어느 그림[표]을 지칭하는지 말해 보세요.)

Look at the names of the people in the picture. They want to buy [purchase] one of these things.
(그림 속의 사람들의 이름을 보세요. 그들은 이 물건 중에 하나를 사려고 합니다.)

④ Would you please take [have] a good look at the picture?

해설   이 그림을 자세히 보세요.

syn   Please look carefully at this picture. *(formal)*

Please take a close [careful] look at this picture.
Look at the picture carefully.
Look closely at this picture.
Look over this picture.
Study this picture carefully.

---

⑤ Take a good [close] look at the man sitting in the boat.

해설   (그림 속에서) 보트에 앉아 있는 사람을 자세히 보세요.

syn   Fix your eyes on to the man sitting in the boat. *(slang, informal)*
Focus your attention on the man sitting in the boat.
Look closely at the man sitting in the boat.
Pay attention especially to the man sitting in the boat.
Pay close attention to the man sitting in the boat.
Study the man sitting in the boat.

어법   'Good look'은 널리 사용되지만 'good attention'은 사용되지 않는다.

---

⑥ Look at it and pass it on.

해설   그것을 보고, (다음 사람에게) 넘기세요.

syn   Look at it [Look it over] and pass it to the next person.
Take a look and then pass it on. *(casual)*
Take a peek and pass it around.
Take a look and hand it around.

어휘   take a look(보다)=take a gander, take a peek, have a glance, have a look (*B.E.*에서 주로 사용)

---

⑦ Look at the people on the left of the poster.

해설   포스터의 왼쪽에 있는 사람들을 보세요.

: 상황에 따라 'the people' 대신 'the surroundings', 'the scenery' 등으로 대체될 수 있다. 또한 'on the left [right]' 대신, 상황에 따라 'in the middle [centre] of', 'the top[bottom] of', 'in the bottom left hand corner (of the poster)', 'in the top right hand corner (of the poster)' 등으로 표현이 대체될 수 있다.

cf. 포스터의 위치에 대한 표현

Take a good look at the top part of the poster.
(포스터의 위쪽을 자세히 보세요.)
Please look carefully at the bottom of the poster.
(포스터의 아래쪽을 자세히 보세요.)
Focus your attention on the people at the bottom of the poster.
(포스터의 아래쪽에 있는 사람들을 자세히 보세요.)

---

⑧ This is a picture [a shot] of a bus station.
I'll ask you some questions about the picture.

해설   이것은 버스정거장 사진입니다. 이 사진에 대해 몇 가지 질문을 하겠습니다.

syn   This is a bus station. Now, let me ask you some questions.
This picture shows a bus station. I'll ask you some questions.
Take a look at this picture of a bus station, then I'll ask you

some questions.

Take a look at this picture of a bus station. Now, I'll ask you some questions.

---

⑨ Is there something strange about this picture?

해설 이 그림에 이상한 점은 없습니까?

syn Do you see anything unusual in [about] this picture?
: 이 경우 'in'이 'about'보다 널리 사용된다.
Do you notice anything odd about this picture?
Can you find anything different about this picture?

어휘 odd=strange, unusual, peculiar, out of the ordinary

---

⑩ When was this picture taken? How do you know?

해설 이 사진을 언제 찍었습니까? 어떻게 알 수 있습니까?

syn At what time of the day was this picture taken? How can you tell?
At what time of the day do you think this picture was taken? How do you know?
When did they take picture? How do you know?

---

⑪ Take out your colored pencils. Let's draw some pictures.

해설 색연필을 꺼내세요. 몇 가지 그림을 그립시다.

syn   I want you to draw some pictures.
       We're going to draw some pictures.
       Draw some pictures.

cf. 칠에 대한 지시문
       Color the bus red. (버스를 붉게 칠하세요.)
       (We're going to) Draw a bus and color it red.
       (버스를 그려 그것을 붉게 칠하세요.)

⑫ There are 8 objects in this picture.
Choose one object and don't tell anyone which one it is.
The rest of you have to ask questions to find out which one it is.

해설   이 그림에는 8개의 물건이 있습니다. 한 가지를 선택하되 그것이
       무엇인지 말하지 마세요. 나머지 여러분들은 질문을 통하여 그것
       이 무엇인지 알아내야 합니다.

syn   Choose one and don't tell the others which one it is.
       Choose one thing and don't tell anyone which it is.
       *Choose one thing and not tell anyone which it is. *(incorrect)*

⑬ There are 6 sets of pictures **which have five different things
in them.**
Ask each other questions to discover what the differences are.

해설   6조의 그림에는 다섯 가지의 차이점이 있습니다. 서로에게 질문
       을 하여 그 차이점을 찾아내세요: 이 경우 미국영어에서는 'thing'
       대신 'element', 'point' 등을 사용하지는 않는다.

3. 분야별 학습 | Unit 6 그림과 게임   **461**

syn   There are 6 sets of pictures with (only) five differences (in each picture).

There are 6 sets of pictures which (only) have five things different.

어휘   'Set'은 두 개 이상이 조를 이룰 경우, 'pair'는 두 개가 한 조를 이룰 경우에 사용한다. 카드 한 벌은 'a deck of cards'라고 한다.

B. 퀴즈와 게임

> ① Look, we've got three minutes left. **So, why don't we play a game?**

해설   자, 3분 남았으니, 게임 하나 할까요?

syn   Let's play a game. *(casual)*
What about a game?
Why don't we have a game? *(rare)*

cf. 노래와 관련된 지시문

Let's sing a song.
First we will sing, and then we will work.
(먼저 노래를 부르고 수업하겠습니다.)
Listen to the words of the song. (노래의 가사를 잘 들으세요.)
Here is a song by Miss Yang called 'Love'.
(이것은 양양의 '사랑'이라는 노래입니다.)
First, I'll explain the words to you. (먼저, 단어를 설명하겠습니다.)
Sing along with the children on the tape.

(테이프의 어린이를 따라 노래하세요.)

Don't worry if you don't know the tune. I'll accompany you on my guitar.

(곡은 몰라도 됩니다. 내가 기타로 반주하겠습니다.)

---

② Now we'll play a guessing [spelling, miming] game.

해설　자, 이제 알아맞히기 [철자, 무언극] 놀이를 하겠습니다.

syn　Let's play a guessing [spelling, miming] game.

  cf. 알아맞히기 게임과 관련된 지시문

  What am I holding behind my back? I'll give you three guesses.

  Guess what I'm holding.

---

③ I'll give you three chances to guess what is in the basket [under my desk].

해설　바구니에 있는 [책상 아래에 있는] 것이 무엇인지 알아맞히기 위해서 3번의 기회를 주겠습니다.

syn　You'll have three chances to guess what is in the basket [under my desk].

    You'll have 3 chances. What is in the basket [under my desk]?

    (informal)

---

④ Do it like this..

해설　이런 식으로 하시오.

: 방법을 설명할 때 사용하는 표현이다.

syn   Do it this way. *(casual)*
        Watch me doing it.
        Do what I am doing.
        Try to do it exactly (the same way) as I'm doing it.

   cf. Like this, not like that. (이런 방식으로, 그런 방식이 아니라.)

---

⑤ **We'll flip a coin to see which team starts.**
Heads or tails?... (Minsu throws the coin) Heads, your team starts.
[Tails, Minsu's team starts.]

해설   동전을 던져서 어느 팀이 먼저 시작할지를 결정하겠습니다. 앞쪽
        또는 뒤쪽? … (민수가 동전을 던진다.) 앞쪽이구나, 너희 팀이 먼
        저 시작하여라. [뒤쪽이구나, 민수 팀이 먼저 시작하여라.]
        : 운동경기에서 선공을 가릴 때 흔히 사용하는 표현이다. 동전을
        던질 때에는 'flip a coin'이라고 하고, 공을 던져 올릴 때는 'toss a
        ball'이라고 한다. 한편 가위, 바위, 보를 할 때 미국인들은 우리와
        는 달리 'rock(바위), scissors(가위), paper (보)'라고 한다.

syn   Let's decide which team starts by flipping a coin. We'll flip a
        coin.

참고   **동전의 앞면과 뒷면**
        '앞면 또는 뒷면'이라고 할 경우 'heads or tails'라고 표현하며, 동
        전에서 숫자가 적힌 면이 앞면이고 그림이 그려진 쪽이 뒷면이
        다. 원래 동전의 한 면에는 영국 여왕의 머리(Queen's head)가 각
        인되어 있었고, 다른 한 면에는 동물이 꼬리(tail)와 함께 각인되
        어 있었던 모양에서 이 표현이 유래되었다.

누구나 영어로 가르칠 수 있다

다음은 실제 현장에서의 상황이다.

e.g. Heads or tails? Heads this team starts, tails Tom's team starts. ... On your mark. Get set. Go!
(앞쪽 또는 뒤쪽(을 선택하시오). 앞쪽이면 이 팀이 시작하고, 뒤쪽이면 탐의 팀이 시작한다. ⋯ 너희 쪽이구나. 준비. 시작!)

---

⑥ The first one to answer will get a point.

해설 먼저 답한 편이 1점을 얻습니다.

syn The one who answers first will get a point.

cf. 점수 및 결과와 관련된 표현

It's a draw [a tie]. (비김, 무승부) ◦

Team A is the winner. (A팀이 이겼다.)

You lose a point if you answer wrong [incorrectly]. (틀리면 감점입니다.)

How many points do you have altogether? (합계 몇 점을 받았니?)
= How many points have you got [did you get] altogether?

You guessed right, so now you come out and ask.
(네가 맞았다. 이제 네가 나와서 질문하여라.)
= You guessed right, so now you get to ask the questions.

⑦ Someone else has to think of an object for 'Twenty Questions'.
Don't show the others! Keep it a secret.
Everyone else has to guess what it is by asking questions
which have Yes/No answers.
For example, 'Is it alive?'
Whoever guesses correctly first has the next turn. OK?

해설 누군가가 스무고개를 위한 대상을 생각하세요. 다른 사람들에게
보여 주지 말고, 비밀로 하세요. 모두가 Yes/No로 답할 수 있는
질문을 통하여 그것이 무엇인지 추측해야 합니다. 예를 들면, '그
것은 살아 있습니까?' 먼저 정확히 알아맞히는 사람이 다음 차례
가 됩니다. 알겠습니까?

cf. 다음은 '직업 알아맞히기'를 하기 위한 지시문이다.

Each team must write down a job or a career, like doctor, for 'What's
my line'. Don't show the others! Keep it a secret! The other teams have
to guess what job it is by asking questions beginning with 'do' or 'does'.
For example 'Do you work indoors?' Whichever team guesses first gets
a point. OK?

('나의 진로는?'이라는 질문에 대해 각 팀은 '의사' 등과 같이 직업 또는 경력을
적습니다. 다른 사람에게 보여 주지 마세요. 비밀로 하세요. 상대팀은 'do' 또는
'does'로 시작하는 질문을 통하여 그 직업이 무엇인지 추측해야 합니다. 예를
들면, '실내에서 일을 합니까?' 먼저 알아맞히는 팀이 점수를 얻습니다. 알겠습
니까?)

◆ 의사소통을 위한 전략적 능력

Hymes(1972)는 효과적인 의사소통을 위해서는 Chomsky(1965)가 주장하는 언어 자체에 대한 문법적 능력만으로는 부족하며 언어사용에 대한 능력까지 갖추어야 한다고 주장하였다. 이로 인하여 외국어 교육이 문법 중심교육에서 의사소통 능력을 배양하는 교육으로 전환되는 중대한 계기가 되었으며, 또한 외국어 교육이 종래의 단순하고 지루한 문법중심에서 사회 문화적 환경에 맞는 적절한 표현능력을 신장하는 방향으로 전환되게 되었다(Tarone & Yule 1989).

외국어를 이용한 효과적인 의사소통을 위해서는 담화 참가자는 세 가지 능력 — 즉, 문법적 능력(grammatical competence), 사회언어학적 능력(sociolinguistic competence), 전략적 능력(strategic competence) — 을 구비하고 있어야 한다. 이 중에서 외국인이 담화에서 부족한 어휘나 관용구에 대한 지식의 한계를 극복하고 효과적으로 자신의 의사를 성공적으로 전달할 수 있는 능력을 전략적 능력이라 한다. Dörnyei & Thurrel(1991)에 따르면, 전략적 능력은 언어능력이 한계에 부딪칠 때 사용하는 전략이므로 외국어 학습자에게는 보다 더 결정적인 역할을 하는 것이다. 전략적 능력이 부족하면 문법적 지식과 풍부한 어휘능력을 지닌 학생도 구두시험에 미달하는 반면, 전략적 능력이 뛰어난 학생은 단지 자신이 아는 수백 개의 단어만으로도 효과적으로 자신의 의사를 전달하여 구두시험에 성공할 수 있는 것이다.

의사소통능력의 일부인 전략적 능력에 대해 널리 인정되는 Canale & Swain (1980:30)의 규정은 다음과 같다:

Verbal and nonverbal strategies that may be called into action to compensate for breakdowns in communication due to performance variables or to insufficient competence.
(수행상의 변수 또는 불충분한 능력으로 인한 의사소통의 단절을 상쇄하기 위해 활용되는 언어적 비언어적 전략)

즉 화자가 언어수행상의 변수 또는 부족한 언어능력을 극복하고 효과적으로 의사소통을 하기 위한 언어적 또는 비언어적 전략이라고 규정한 것이다.

한편 Bialystok(1990:35)은 다음과 같이 규정하였다.

Communication strategies overcome obstacles to communication by providing the speaker with an alternative form of expression for the intended meaning.

(의사소통전략은 화자에게 의도하는 의미를 나타내는 대안이 되는 표현 형태를 제공함으로써 의사소통의 장애를 극복한다.)

즉, 화자가 부족한 언어능력으로 인하여 자신의 의도를 표현하기 어려울 때, 대체 가능한 표현 형태를 이용하여 의사소통의 장애를 극복하는 전략이다.

다양한 연구를 종합하여 의사소통전략에 대한 이론을 체계화한 Dörnyei(1995)는 의사소통전략을 세 가지 전략 — 회피 및 축소전략(avoidance or reduction strategies), 성취 또는 보상전략(achievement or compensatory strategies), 지연 및 시간 연장 전략(stalling or time-gaining strategies) — 으로 구분하였다. 여기에서 두 번째인 성취 또는 보상전략은 언어를 사용한 적극적 성취전략으로 외국어 교육에 대한 연구의 중심이 된다. 그는 이 전략을 아래 일곱 가지로 구분하였다:

첫째, 우회적 표현(circumlocution)은 표적이 되는 대상이나 행동을 묘사하거나 설명하는 것으로, 예를 들면 'pottery'를 'the thing you put something in'으로 설명하는 것이다.

둘째, 근사어(approximation)는 표적이 되는 어휘의 의미와 가장 가까운 대용어를 사용하는 전략으로 'sparrow'를 상위어인 'bird'로 표현하는 것이다.

셋째, 다목적용 어휘 사용(use of all-purpose word) 전략으로, 특정 어휘를 모를 경우 일반적이고 의미가 막연한 어휘를 사용하는 것으로, 예를 들연 'corkscrew'를 'a thing[stuff, tool] for bottles' 또는 'what-do-you-call-it'과 같은 극히 일반적인 표현 또는 단어를 사용하는 것이다.

넷째, 조어(word-coinage)를 사용하는 전략으로 가상 규칙을 기초로 존재하지 않는 L2를 만드는 것으로, 예를 들연 'vegetarian'에서 'vegetarianist'를 조작해 내는 것이다.

다섯째, 축어적 번역(literal translation) 전략은 L1(모국어)의 어휘, 관용구, 복합어 또는 구를 L2(대상언어)에 적용하여 번역하는 것으로, '주택관리인'을 'caretaker'이라 하지 않고, 우리말식으로 'house controller'이라고 하는 것이다.

여섯째, 부호전환(code switching)은 모국어 어법사용 전략으로, 음운 또는 형태적으로 L1(모국어)의 단어 또는 구문을 L2(대상언어)에 적용하는 것이다. 예를 들면 독일학생이 'Shut the door.'라고 하지 않고, 독일어의 문장구조를 이용하여 'Make the door shut.'이라고 표현하는 것이다.

마지막으로 외래어화(foreignizing)는 L2 대신에 L1 또는 L3의 발음 또는 어휘를 사용하는 것으로, 예를 들면 'selfie(셀프카메라)'를 'selca(셀카)'라고 하는 것이다.

이상의 모든 전략은 화자가 대상 어휘 또는 구문을 정확히 모를 경우 사용하는 대안으로, 이용 가능한 언어를 활용 또는 조작하여 원래의 의사소통의 목적을 달성하려고 시도하므로, 성취 또는 보상전략이라고 하는 것이다.

한편 Gilmore(2005)는 단어에 대한 일본 학생들의 전략을 파악하기 위해 '병따개(bottle opener/corkscrew)'를 집어 들고 상점에서 이 물건을 사기 위해 어떻게 표현할 것인지를 간단히 묘사하게 하였다. 그 결과 일본 학생들은 다음 여섯 가지 유형의 표현을 주로 사용하였다.

a. I'd like to buy a "wain oupunaa."
   (와인 오프너를 사고 싶습니다.)
b. It's used for opening [used to open] wine bottles.
   (그것은 포도주병을 여는 데 이용됩니다.)
c. It looks (a bit) like a screw with handles.
   (그것은 손잡이가 있는 나사와 (약간) 같습니다.)
d. It's about XX cm long/wide/tall. It's made of metal or plastic.
   (그것은 xx센티 길이/넓이/크기입니다. 그것은 금속이나 플라스틱으로 만듭니다.)
e. lt's like a big screw./ lt's a kind of kitchen equipment.
   (그것은 큰 나사처럼 보입니다. 그것은 일종의 주방 기구입니다.)
f. I'd like a cork puller.
   (코르크 따개가 필요합니다.)

(a)는 외래어화 전략으로 '병따개'에 대한 일본식 어법과 발음을 사용하여 표현한 것이다. (b), (c), (d)는 우회적 표현 전략으로 사물의 용도, 모양, 재질 또는 일반적인 특성을 기술한 것이다. (e)는 근사어 사용 전략으로, 'screw' 또는 'equipment'와

같은 상위어를 사용한 것이다. (f)는 조어사용 전략으로 L2의 표현 방법을 이용하여 새로운 단어를 창조한 것이다. 이와 같이 일본 학생들도 생소한 어휘를 표현하기 위해 다양한 전략을 사용하였다.

부록: 원어민 영어교수들의
상용 교실영어표현 500선

여기에 수록한 자료는 2005년부터 2007년까지 국내에서 영어를 가르치는 Native speakers(미국인 3명, 캐나다인 3명)가 수업 중 가장 빈번하게 사용한 교실영어 표현을 분야별로 정리한 것이다. 초급에서 중급 정도의 영어회화 능력을 가진 학생들을 대상으로 한 수업에서 사용된 표현이다.

실재 Native Speakers의 수업을 참관할 기회가 많지 않는 우리 선생님들의 경우에는 이 표현들을 읽어보면 단 시간에 이들의 수업을 다양하게 경험하는 효과가 있을 것이다. 또한 이 표현들은 저자가 직접 참관 기록한 자료와 평가를 위해 수집된 자료들을 바탕으로 작성되었으므로 현장감을 느낄 수 있으며, 언제든지 영어강의에서 활용할 수 있는 유용한 표현들이다.

자료에 대한 분류방식은 교실영어 분석의 고전인 Sinclair and Coulthard(1975)와 Bowers(1980) 그리고 최근의 담화분석에 대한 연구 자료를 응용하였다.

자료을 수정한 Gregory Goguts 선생님 및 수집에 도움을 준 분들에게 사의를 표합니다.

Contents

1. Greetings

(Greetings)
Hello, everyone.
Good morning.
How are you today?
Good morning, folks. You guys look lively today.
How's it going?
How are you (guys) feeling this morning?

(First class)
Hello, ladies and gentlemen. Welcome to our English class.
Today is the first day of the class! Nice to meet [see] all of you [you all].
It's been a while. How's everything?
Wooo, I am back again!
That's good. All of you back again?

(Inquiries)
What happened?
Tell me about what happened.
What's up, guys?
What's the problem?
What's going on?
Anything new [special], guys ?
Is anything [special] happening?
Tired? What happened (to you)?
You look very tired. Is everything all right?
Are you sleepy today?
Hey! Tell me what's eating[bothering] you.
Oh really? I didn'know that.
Good god.

That's too bad. Jeez. Are you alright?

Oh please take care.

I'm sorry to hear that.

I am sure it will get better.

Oh my God [my goodness]! You guys have very tight schedule.

It seems to me that everyone's very busy these days.

2. Small Talk and Checking Attendance

(Weather)

Lovely day, isn't it?

Nice weather, right?

It's very hot today. But the air conditioner is not working.

What do you call this kind of weather?

Cheer up, (everybody)! Don't let the weather affect your mood.

T: How is the weather today? What do you call this kind of weather?

S: Humid.

T: Humid or another word?

S: Wet.

T: Muggy. It's really sticky and muggy. But the air conditioner is not working.

(Small talk)

It's Monday. What did you do over the weekend?

So, how was your weekend?

What did you do over the weekend?

What's your favourite food?

Where are you from?

Where do you live?

누구나 영어로 가르칠 수 있다

How much was that?

(Encouraging)
I know you guys are excited but please settle down [calm down].
The term is almost over and you can finally go home. Get excited!
I see that you guys have a very tough schedule but please don't be stressed.
Hmmm. Let me guess that you guys are tired since you all look worn-out.

(Checking attendance)
Is everyone here?
Who is absent today?
Who's missing?
Is he[she] coming?

3. Direction, Distraction and Discipline

(Direction)
Settle down, everyone.
Pay attention, please.
Look!
Look straight ahead.
Face the front.
Eyes to the front.
Can I get the groups' attention?
Everyone's attention, please?
Stay seated.
Stay in your seat.
(Distraction)

(Be) quiet, please.

Calm down (now)!

Hush!

Chill out, (now)!

It's too noisy. Settle down, everyone.

You guys are getting [speaking] too loud.

Sheeeeeee.

Keep silent please.

Stop talking.

Stop talking and look at me.

Why are you talking?

Ask me!

Are we allowed to talk?

(Attitude)

Be more polite.

Be a good boy.

Do not sleep in class. If you are tired please stand up!

In order to improve your English, everybody should at least have an interest in learning English.

Thank you for being well-mannered.

(Discipline)

Shame on you!

I'm disappointed in you.

Don't do that.

Stop it now!

Be professional.

Behave!

That's very mean of you.

You naughty!

How many times did I say that ? I am going to punish you if you do it one more time.

Don't make phone call unless it's your parents or in case of an emergency.

4. Starter and Preparation

(Starter)
Okay!
Now, ⋯
Anyway, ⋯
Ready?
Ready to begin?
Let's begin.
(Are you) ready for class [it]?
Let's get going.
Time is running out. Let's get started.
Let's start.
It's time for English.
Kick off.
Before we move on, ⋯
Let's review.
Now a little bit of review.
Revise for the past class. Close your books.

(Preparation)
Prepare for the class.
Take your books out, please.
Open your grammar book. We are going to study grammar today.
Open your idiom books, page 33.

Did you read?

Have you studied for it?

Why aren't you prepared?

I am worried that you can't follow the text.

Where is the book [thesaurus]?

Do you have the book [thesaurus]?

Who has not brought their book?

Why don't you have the book?

Everyone should at least bring your book and dictionary.

T: *Did you prepare your project?*

Ss: *Two weeks later.*

T: *No, two weeks from now [In two weeks]. Half of the time already has passed.*

5. Presenting topics

(Presenting topics)

Today we are going to talk about the importance of mood in the poem.

Today we will discuss English American short stories.

We're going to continue to study idioms [grammar] and practice them until the end of the semester.

Now, let's practice conditional clauses with 'if' clauses.

6. Indicating pages and Nomination

(Indicating pages or parts)

Next page!

Turn to the next page.

Turn to page 52

Open your book, page 52.

Now, open your books to page 52.

Let's look at page 52. Minsu, can you read that, please?

Turn back to page 51.

The top of page 51 ···

Page 58, exercise 9.

Let's take a look at the first paragraph.

Let's go to the next chapter.

Have a quick look at the graph [table] on page 62.

Now look at the picture. Can you see the picture?

Where were [are] we?

What's our next subject?

(Nomination)

Who's next?

Come on. Isn't it your turn?

Your turn.

You're next.

It is time for you to speak.

I'll just point.

I want to start with Sumi first today.

If you know the answer, raise the hands.

Everyone can try, but one at a time.

Will you try?

One by one.

Now, we'll begin with Mr. Kim and we'll go around.

Back to your seats. You'll come back at the end.

(when a group is not prepared for presentation)

Can you read the next one?

Let's read Minsu's sentence.

Can you please read the sentence?

Read it with emotion!

Read number nine [question number nine] please.

7. Activities, Comment and Checking Comprehension

(Activities)

Close your books.

You, come up here.

Come up here and draw _____ (on the board).

What I'd like you to do is to···.

Do as I say.

Do what I'm doing.

Do it like this.

Look at me doing this.

Can you do that?

Can you demonstrate?

All right, you can do it now.

Practice[Memorize] this.

S: I went kayaking last week.

T: How did you go kayaking? Can you demonstrate? Show me.

(Comment and Explanation)

It is (very) important. Learning the differences is very important.

You have to know what to use.

This is a very common mistake for students.

Some of you look confused.

Some people are confused. We'll go over it again.

For example, ···

누구나 영어로 가르칠 수 있다

This is an example to help you.

I'll talk more about it later.

A while ago [A few moments ago] we talked about it.

Remember, I use that often.

I used [showed] an example in class.

Details aren't important right now.

I have no time to go into details.

In this case, we don't use this word [expression].

It's more of a polite answer. [It's a more polite answer.]

Common expressions are used everyday.

They're very common expressions.

Try to remember those expressions.

It is "be going to" when you've already planned it.

Here we see some abnormal change. But in the second one[paragraph], it flows smoothly.

Stanza and rhythm are important aspectsof the poem. Make sure you know this. [= You should keep this in mind.]

When you say "I'm not at home", it means I am out of the house.

"Innovation", what does that mean?

T: Does it make (any) sense?

S: A little bit but it's still confusing.

(Checking Comprehension)

See?

Everything okay?

You got it.

You understand [know] what I'm saying.

I am not saying this twice.

Did you understand the instructions?

This is a very important lesson. Everybody understood?

Did you understand everything perfectly? Does everybody understand?
Everybody knew it already, right?

8. Questions and Response

(Questions)
When [Where, Why] did this happen?
Got it?
Understood?
All right?
Can you understand this?
What would you like to tell me?
Ask questions.
Any questions (on dialogue 2)?
Any further questions?
Anything special?
Would anyone like to ask me a question?
What other questions?
Do you have any more questions?
What else?
Next one. What's your next question?
Who has any questions about number 6?
Who would like to answer this question?
Do you know what _____ is?
So why is it incorrect?
What's the difference?
Give me an example.
What are the main similarities and differences between the two?
What do you mean?
Do you agree?

Does every one of you agree?

Is that true?

Is that believable?

This is a very fascinating fact. Do you guys know this?

Who wants to explain to me what you do in Chuseok?

If not now, when?

(when the student says that he is not prepared in 3 minutes)

What are you doing?

I want you to make a sentence [a paragraph] with[using]⋯.

Don't just call out [yell out] the answer. Raise your hands.

If you think you are right raise your hands.

Raise your hand if you don't understand what I just said.

Take time and think for a minute.

(Response)

Good job.

Got it. Okay, I understand.

Why not? That doesn't matter. That's Okay.

They are the same.

They have no difference.

We've talked about it many times!

See the rhythm.

Let me see.

No way! [No!]

Wrong!

S: *I don't know when to use this saying.*

T: *We'll go over in the class.*

S: *I didn't know.*

T: *What did I emphasize in class? How many times did I say?*

You have to know what to use.

(Positive Response)
Lovely!
Good!
Nice (job)!
Good answer.
Yes, that's a good answer.
There you go. [You did it right.]
Thank you for giving me the right answer.
You make me smile. You made my day!

9. Listening and Repetition

(Listening)
Listen, (lads).
Listen up!
Listen carefully.
Listen to the tape.
Listen (again) and repeat (after me).
Please listen carefully; I am not going to say this twice.
(Repetition)
Sorry?
Pardon? I didn't hear you.
Excuse me?
Can you repeat that again?
You what? What did you say, again? I couldn't hear you clearly.
I don't get [understand] you. Can you speak a little bit louder please?
Repeat after me, please.
Please, say what I'm saying.

Keep practicing!

10. Solving problems and Checking answers

(Solving problems)
Take 2 minutes [a few moments] to do the exercises.
I'll give you 10 minutes to get ready (for the presentation).
You (should) follow the instructions.
You should use your own imagination.
Find out the meaning.
Please continue to work on it.
Don't give up. You can do it.
Keep working on it and if you still don't get it, let me know, so I can help.
OK guys, time is up!
Are you ready for the presentation?
Work by yourself.
Work in pairs.
There is the possibility of losing marks [points] if you don't do these correctly.
You may lose points if you don't do it.

(Checking the result)
All right. Next one.
What would you do with (question) number two?
Who got that right?
Who did it right?
Is it hard [difficult]?
Both are possible.
The answer will be the same (as before).

That was an easy one [question].

Everyone should get that one right.

You skipped one question.

You skipped the third question.

Who doesn't understand their mistakes?

Because you put this word [phrase] in the wrong place.

Because you put this word [phrase] somewhere else.

Check that out.

Fix it if it is wrong.

Check this. [Refer to this.]

Check if it's right.

S: *Which one is right?*

T: *Both can be right.*

S: *Can we take a rest for a few minutes?*

T: *If you got that right.*

11. Speaking : Asking, Discussion, Prompt, Correction and Evaluation

(Asking)

How do you say this in English?

Would you speak more clearly?

Be more specific. I don't get [understand] you.

Could you repeat that again? I didn't catch you fully.

Would you spell it for me, please?

Nice and loudly. Speak loudly.

Hey you are speaking too soft. Please speak up

In English, please.

누구나 영어로 가르칠 수 있다

In English. No writing.

Hey, hey in English please! I can't understand you guys if you talk in Korean.

In America, we call this _____. How do you say that in Korean?

Well, think about it one more time and let me know.

Don't speak until I say so.

Can I talk?

T: What does this mean, "screen calls"?

S: (Nobody answers.)

T: When would you use "screen calls"?

S: (Nobody answers.)

T: OK. If you have an answering machine, what would your message say?

(Discussion)

Look at [See] that from a different point of view.

Why is this better than the first one [item, sentence]?

What are the pros and cons of the machines?

What's going on? (when a group is arguing about something.)

Now choose two topics. And make conditional clauses.

Don't worry about your grammar. Just speak.

T: (We'll) Begin with 10 minutes discussion. You should give a discussion in 10 minutes. Choose two topics, two free topics and describe them in 10 minutes. It is about "what will be going on in Korea in the next 15 years or to you?" You can choose any topic... Group A, Captain Jung, what are your two topics?

T: When you talk about something bad or disadvantages, (for example, of cellular phones or cloning), you must give a solution. You offer a

solution. For example, if you are talking on the phone while driving,
you can cause an accident and it is very dangerous. So, we made or
invented something. What is it? So, what do we use when we drive?

S: *Hands free.*

T: *OK. You use hands free. Why is hands free good?*

S: *You can drive while talking.*

(Prompt)

Come on.

Be brave!

Speak out!

Get (it) out!

Don't be shy.

Shoot!

No chicken. No coldfeet.

Take charge!

Take initiative!

Concentrate!

Keep going.

Please hurry up!

Now you are talking!

Relax!

There is no need to rush. [=Don't hurry]. Please take your time.

Don't be afraid of making mistakes. I am here to correct them.

When you speak in front of the classroom, speak up and please don't be shy.

You have not said anything today. You have been very quiet.

Try to speak as much English as possible.

Try to speak in English as much as possible.

T: *Group B. What will change in the future?*

Minsu (captain of group B) : Lifestyle will change.
T: Lifestyle. And? ...Keep going, Minsu.

(Corrections)
No, we don't say⋯.
Not "I'm so hard.", "it's so hard".
Please don't say [use] the word, "shit".
You should say "yes" instead of "yeap" when you talk to your senior.
It's not polite.
What's better than the word?
In this case[situation]⋯.
No, we are not talking about⋯.
Pardon me, I didn't mean to hit you like that. I mean⋯.
I'm sorry but I didn't intend to⋯.

S: Last week, I played canoeing.
T: We don't say "play canoeing." We went canoeing.

(Positive Evaluation)
Good attempt [try, job].
Nice work!
Cool.
There you go.
Perfect.
Well done.
That is great English!
You speak English well.
Hold it there; what you just said was really good. I respect your idea.
Do you remember the first day of the class when you guys were all afraid to speak in English?

12. Taking notes and Writing

(Taking Notes)

Take a look at the board. Please write it down.

(Is) everyone writing this down?

Write the notes down in your notebook.

Keep notes.

This is very important, so make sure you have all this written down in your notebook.

Everybody, check out the board. [Look at the board.]

What did your just write?

Please make sure you get the rest of the notes from your classmates.

(when a student comes back from an absence.)

(Writing)

Write down the definition.

Write your answer(s) down.

Don't just say them. Write your answers correctly.

Make your own sentence.

What's another way we can begin this paper?

Everybody is doing the same thing [topic].

In English composition, it is important to have proper [right] punctuation.

This doesn't look like your own work. Did you copy and paste?

Do not copy and paste or plagiarize works of the others.

You should use your own imagination on the writing.

I can tell whether you guys copied directly from the Internet. So I will say this again; Don't plagiarize!

Well, if you keep on practicing and if you continue writing on your own, I am sure it will get better.

Everybody made mistakes. Revise after class.

This is very good writing.

You are improving rapidly.

T: Use your own ideas. I want you to think of your own idea. Take 3 minutes. Now take 3 minutes. Write your own idea. I'll look at your grammar. (In 3 minutes) Ready? Read your sentence, Minsu.

S: If you are unmarried, you'll save much money.

T: If you remain single, you'll save a lot of money. Repeat.

S: If you remain single, you'll save a lot of money.

T: Good job! Good! Now, Sumi, how about your answer?

13. Vocabulary and Grammar

(Vocabulary)

How do you pronounce it?

How do you read this word?

Difficult to pronounce it, isn't it?

Does anyone know this word, "induction", in English?

Do you know "refurbish"?

What does it mean to "refurbish"?

What is the opposite of "the word"?

The difference between dinner and supper is⋯.

"Beautiful" comes from "beauty".

We'll go over the words in class.

"No, I don't" or "Yes I do". Either one is OK.

"In 3 years" or "3 years from now". Both are OK.

"Where do you come from?" or "Where are you from?" "Where are you from?" is more common [better].

"Later" is OK. "These days" is better.

There's no mistake, here.

T: (while correcting mistakes in the dialogue) There is one mistake here. What happens to "so-so"?

S: (No answer.)

T: Just erase (it).

S: What's the difference between "study" and "research"?

T: Can't really tell. [There is little difference.]

S: How does she look like?

T: What does she look like? Not how does she look like?

T: What is "well-being" to Koreans? What does well-being mean to Koreans? A little bit of Korean is OK (when you discuss). Now write the sentences.

T: (reviewing idioms) I'm going to do something difficult or dangerous. What do you say for encouragement?

S: Good luck.

T: Good.

(Grammar)

Perfect sentence.

Yeap, grammatically it's correct.

What's wrong with this sentence [message]?

S: If you don's sleep at night, we can't go on weekend.

T: Be careful of your grammar. We won't be able to go out on the weekend or go out this weekend.

14. Assignment and Examination

(Assignment)

For your homework, I want you to do this···.

I am going to give you guys homework now.

For this week, ···

I will give you some time to complete your report.

You have until next week to finish.

One copy for each person.

This assignment is an individual task. Do it on your own.

Okay guys, pass down the homework now.

You guys should review and preview in order to get good grades.

Who forgot their homework?

Did you do your homework?

Who did their homework?

Who has done [didn't do] their homework?

Some people didn't do their work!

Do you have a persuasive reason so?

Do you have a good[valid] reason for not doing it?

I don't care what your excuses are.

Not doing homework is unacceptable.

No excuses.

Alright but do finish it by next class.

Good, good. I am very satisfied with all of your efforts.

T: *Now, homework. Choose one innovation. I don't care about any*
    machines. What are the pros and cons of the machine? Do you know
    pros and cons? Pros means positive things and cons the negative
    things. And preview Unit 3, Streamline. Just look through it and the
    vocabulary. Good job today. Have a good week.

(Examination)

Today we have our debate contest.

Are you guys all prepared for it?

Put your papers[books] away.

No cheating. Don't cheat.

This is not an easy task, so be sure to go over it once more before you give it to me.

Take one and pass them on.

Take one and pass the rest of them back.

One for each person. Pass out the copies.

Please write your name (on top right).

Get another piece of paper.

Time's up!

Put your pencils down.

Time is up. Are you ready to present [speak out]?

(Hey,) pencils down.

And we are going to check the answers.

What did you put [write]?

Next week is the mid-term exam. Have you studied for it?

T: *Everybody remember that we have a quiz today. Please put everything away. Sumi and Minsu, put your books away. Put your names on the paper. You will have about 20 minutes for this quiz... (after 20 minutes) Pencils down. And we are going to check the answers. Change the papers. Have the red pencils in the middle... (after scoring) Count the total number correct. My goal for this quiz is 60. I know this material is not easy. Please give them back to me.*

15. Checking the Result and Evaluation

(Checking the Result)
What have you got?
Who got it perfect?
Who got perfect points?
Who got everything right?
It's an easy A. Everyone should get that one.
Give it to me. Let me see.
What is your worst grade?
It's a great job, but you should concentrate more on the vocabulary.
Who doesn't understand their mistakes?

S: *Can you look over my grade?*
T: *I've already checked it.*
S: *You corrected this wrong.*
T: *Oh, I'm sorry about that.*

(Positive Evaluation)
Wow, good [great] job!
Great work!
Good effort!
Oh good stuff!
You got a perfect score. Good for you.
You deserve it!
Wow you surely did a superb job. Let's give him a round of applause.
This is incredible.
Amazing!
Perfect!
Brilliant work!
Keep it up!

Keep up good work!
Fantastic! I'm impressed.
Everybody gets 2 points.

(Negative Evaluation)
I'm extremely disappointed.
It will be a laugh [ridiculous].
I can tell you did not put effort in this.
You all did a decent job on your work. But you guys should be more
enthusiastic about making presentations.

16. Games

Okay, let's have some fun today.
We are going to do an activity today.
Work in groups of six.
Get yourself into groups of six.
You have to know what (word) to use. *(in vocabulary game)*
What's your next word going to be?
Would you be able to guess the word?
True or false?
It's so much fun!
It's a lot of fun.

17. Closing and Ending

(Closing)
It's time to wrap up.
Class is finished. You can go.

Classes are adjourned.

You are dismissed. See you.

You are free to go.

You can go now.

Ok, that's it for the day.

You guys are done. See you tomorrow.

Already? OK guys, get out of here.

Do you want a break or leave early?

Do you need a break or do you want to end early?

No break time!

OK. Would you like a short break?

Now, take a break.

Take 10 minutes. [10 minutes' break.]

(Ending)

(Very) good afternoon to all of you.

Have a nice week!

Have a great weekend!

It is the weekend. See you next week.

Thank you for being a great [good] class.

Awesome! [Very Good!] Have fun and enjoy your holiday.

You guys have been so great throughout the semester. This was my best class.

18. Notice

There is one important thing I'm trying to tell you. Jot this down.

Please jot down a memo.

I also have a couple of other things that I want to tell you.

We have no class tomorrow.

Never mind; please ignore what I said earlier.

Don't forget to fill out [fill in] the survey before you leave the class.

Don't forget to bring your calculators next time.

Don't just go. Hand in your homework.

Don't forget to do your homework.

Mid-semester exam is coming.

The exam will be next week.

19. Counseling

Come to my office anytime.

Call me after school; I will help you if I am around.

If you need extra help or any assistance, come to my office whenever.

Whenever you need my help, I am always available.

If you want to talk with me, please do not hesitate to come to my office at any time.

Email me if you have any questions.

Oh please come in and be my guest.

Please feel free to help yourself to coffee or tea. (in the office)

Anybody want some thing to drink?

Anyone care for coffee or tea?

S: *May I visit your office to go over the assignment?*

T: *Absolutely ! [Definitely! Surely!]*

S: *Could you join us for lunch today?*

T: *Cool, I will be there./*

   Well well, I will check my schedule first and then decide whether I will do that or not.

20. Aside

Booyah!

Hurrah!

Oops!

Hokey-dokey.

Blah blah blah. Whatever.

Bless you! (when someone sneezes)

Watch out! [Watch it!]

Aww, it is cute. (when a student showed a picture of his kitten.)

Never mind.

Alright.

No problem.

My pleasure.

That's very nice [honest] of you.

Oh, I see. That's why I had a hard time understanding that.

Sometimes we make mistakes.

Do you regret that you chose English as major?

I believe that….

〈End〉

참고문헌

- Abbs. B. & I. Freebairn (1996) *Blueprint.* Longman.
- Alexander, L. G. (1994) *Right Word Wrong Word.* Longman.
- Allwright, D. (1988) Observation in the Language Classroom. Longman.
- Aslanian, Y. (1985) Investigating the reading problems of ESL students : an alternative, *ELT Journal.* Oxford University Press.
- Bardovi-Harlig, K. et al (1991). Developing pragmatic awareness : closing the conversation, *ELT Journal.* Oxford University Press.
- Black C. et al (1977) Classroom English : Materials for Communicative Language Teaching, *ELT Journal.* Oxford University Press.
- Boatner, M. T. & J. E. Gates (1975) *A Dictionary of American Idioms.* Barron's Educational Series, Inc.
- Bowers, R. G. (1980) *VERBAL BEHAVIOUR IN THE LANGUAGE TEACHING CLASSROOM.* University of Reading.
- Buckingham A. & Whitney N. (1997) *Open Ticket.* Oxford University Press.
- Case, D. (1977) Drilling in Advanced Levels, *ELT Journal.* Oxford University Press.
- Christopher Sion (1985) *Recipes for Tired Teachers.* Addison-Wesley Publishing Company. Dornyei Z. et al (1991) Strategic competence and how to teach it, ELT Journal. Oxford University Press.
- Douglas, L. Drewry (1984) *Enlisted Eval and Officer Fitrap Writing Guide.* Professional Management Spectrum, Inc.
- Edge, J. 'Acquisition disappears in adultery' : interaction in the translation class, *ELT Journal.* Oxford University Press.
- Ernst, G. (1992) "Talking Circle" : Conversation and Negotiation in the ESL Classroom, *TESOL quarterly.*
- Ferrer-Hanreddy, J. et al (1996) *Mosaic.* The McGraw-Hill Companies, Inc.
- Fulcher, G. (1987) Tests of Oral Performance ; the need for data-based criteris, *ELT Journal.* Oxford University Press.
- Gainer. G. T. (1989) Closing in on oral errors, *ELT Journal.* Oxford Univeristy

Press.

- Gerber U. (1990) Literary role play, *ELT Journal*. Oxford University Press.
- Gilbert, J. B. (1984) *Clear Speech*. Cambridge University Press.
- Hall, P. (1991) *Handbook for Writers*. Prentice Hall.
- Harbord, J. (1992). The use of the mother tongue in the classroom, *ELT Jouranl*.
- Heaton, J. B. (1990) Classroom *Testing*. Longman.
- Heffernan, I. A. W. et al (1986) *Writing : A College Handbook*. W. W. Norton and Company.
- Helgesen et al (1996) *Active Listening*. Cambridge University Press.
- Higgins, John (1983) Silent English. *ELJ Journal*. Oxford University Press.
- Hoekje B. et al (1993) *Authenticity in Language Testing : Evaluating Spoken Language Tests for International Teaching Assistants*.
- Hornsey, A. W. (1971) Mr Best's Ladder : Question-and-Answer Work in Foreign-Language Teaching, *ELJ Journal*. Oxford University Press.
- Hughes, Glyn S. (1981) *A Handbook of Classroom English*. Oxford University Press.
- Jones, C. and S. Fortescue (1987) *Using Computers in the Language Classroom*.
- Jones, L. (1984) *Ideas*. Cambridge University Press.
- Jones L. & Baeyer C. von (1983). *Functions of American English*. Cambridge University Press.
- Jordan, R. R. (1990) Pyramid discussions, *ELT Journal*. Oxford University Press.
- Kennedy, C. J. (1974) Story-Telling Wall-Pictures, *ELT Journal*. Oxford University Press.
- Kraus-srebic, Eva (1976) Classroom Games in Compulsory School, *ELT Journal*. Oxford University Press.
- Kumaravadivelu, B. (1991) Language learning tasks: teacher intention and learner interpretation, *ELT Journal*. Oxford University Press.
- Ladousse G. P. (1983) *Speaking Personally*. Cambridge University Press.
- Lee, L. (1998) *Transitions*. Oxford University Press.
- Lee, W. R. (1979) *Language Teaching Games and Contents*. Oxford University Press.

- Leggett, G. et al (1991) *Handbook for Writers*. Prentice-Hal, INC.1
- Lier, L. V. (1984) Analyzing interaction in second language classrooms, *ELT Journal*. Oxford University Press.
- Losey, K. M. (1989) Gender and Ethnicity in the Development of Verbal Skills, *TESOL Quarterly*.
- Lynch T. (1991) Questioning roles in the classroom, *ELT Jouranl*. Oxford University Press.
- Lyons, J. (1977) *Semantics*. Cambridge University Press.
- Mackay, R. (1993) Embarrassment and hygiene in the classroom, *ELT Journal*. Oxford University Press.
- Malamah-Thomas, Ann (1987) *Classroom Interaction*. Oxford University Press.
- Meloni C. F., Shirley Thompson, & Andres Beley (1982) *Say The Right Thing*. Addison-Wesley Publishing Company.
- Mendonca O. C. et al (1993) Peer Review Negotiations: Revision Activities in ESL Writing Instruction, *TESOL Quarterly*.
- McCrimmon J. M. (1973). *Writing with a Purpose*. Houghton Mifflin Company.
- Mouat L. H. & C. Deneus (1966) *To Make a Speech*. Pacific Books, Publishers.
- Nunan, D. (1987) Communicative language teaching: Making it work, *ELT Journal*. Oxford University Press.
- Nunan, D. (1995) *Atlas*. Heinle & Heinle Publishers.
- Ohashi Y. (1978) *English Style*. Newbury House Publishers, INC.
- Oller, J. W. Jr (1982) Story Writing Principles and ESL Teaching, *TESOL Quarterly*. Georgetown University.
- Peccei J. S. (1999). *Pragmatics*. TJ international Ltd, Padstow, Cornwall.
- Potter, Simeon (1976?). Question Box. *ELT Journal*. Oxford University Press.
- Ramani. E. (1987) Theorizing from the classroom, *ELT Journal*. Oxford University Press.
- Retter, C. & Valls N. (1984) *Bonanza*. Longman.
- Richard J. C. (1998) *Springboard*. Oxford University Press.
- Richards J. C. with Hull H. and Proctor S. (1990) *Interchange: English for international communication*. Cambridge University Press.

- Roberts, J. (1983) Teaching with Functional Materials; the problem of stress and intonation, *ELT Journal*. Oxford University Press.
- Rodman, R. et al (1993) *An Introduction to Language*. Harcourt Brace College Publishers.
- Salama, N. (1973) *Let them Speak*, ELT Journal. Oxford University Press.
- Salt, M. J. (1975) Vocabulary Acquisition with the Help of Photographic Transparencies, *ELT Journal*. Oxford University Press.
- Sarkar, S. (1977) The Use of Pictures in Teaching English as a Second Language, *ELT Journal*. Oxford University Press.
- Schultz M. & Fisher A. (1988) *Games For All Reasons*. Addison-Wesley Publishing Company.
- Short D. J. (1993) Assesssing Integrated Language and Content Instruction, *TESOL Quarterly*.
- Siegrist, Ottmar K. (1985) A complete silent alphabet for English. *ELT Journal*. Oxford University Press.
- Sinclair, J. and Coulthard, M. (1975) *Towards an Analysis of Discourse*. Oxford: Oxford University Press.
- Sion, C. (1985) *Recipes for Tired Teachers*. Addison-Wesley Publishing Co.
- Solorzano, H. S. et al (1995) *Introductory Topics*. Longman.
- Spriggs R. ed. (1975) *The Fables of Aesop*. Rand Mcnally & Company.
- Taylor, H. M. et al (1977) *Michigan Action English*. The University of Michigan.
- Tillitt B. & Bruder M. N. (1985). *Speaking Naturally*. Cambridge University Press.
- Thompson, G. (1997) Training teachers to ask questions, *ELT Journal*. Oxford University Press.
- Thornbury, S. (1996) Teachers research teacher talk, *ELT Journal*. Oxford University Press.
- Todd, L. & Ian Hancock (1986) *International English Usage*. Croom Helm Ltd.
- Underhill, A. (1989) Process in Humanistic education, *ELT Journal*. Oxford University Press.
- Viney, P. & Viney, K. (1996) *Handshake: a course in communication*. Oxford

University Press.

- Williams, R. (1986) 'Top ten' principles for teaching reading, *ELT Journal*. Oxford University Press.

- Willis, J. (1981) *Teaching English through English*. Longman.

- Woodman, J. & Thomas P. Adler (1985) *The Writer's Choices*. Scott, Foresman and Company.

- Wrigley H. P. (1987) *May I help you?* Addison-Wesley Publishing Company.

- Young, R. (1983) The negotiation of meaning in children's foreign language acquisition. *ELT Journal*. Oxford University press.

- Yule, J. and Gregory W. (1989) Survey Interviews for interactive English language learning, *ELT journal*. Oxford University Press.

- Zamel. V. (1984) Responding to Student Writing, *TESOL Quarterly*. Georgetown University.

- 황기동(2014), 현대교실영어와 교수법, 한국문화사.

〈삽화 및 그림〉

- Mouat L. H. & C. Deneus (1966) *To make a speech*. Pacific Books publishers.

- Archie Digest Library (1994) Archie Comic publications, Inc.

- Defense Language Institute, *American Language Course*.

Anyone Can Teach In English

누구나 영어로 가르칠 수 있다

개정증보판 1쇄 발행일 2020년 7월 21일

지은이 황기동
해 설 Gerry Gibson, Gregory Goguts, Diane. B. Hertberg, Katherine Spinney
펴낸이 박영희
편 집 박은지
디자인 최소영
마케팅 김유미
인쇄·제본 AP프린팅
펴낸곳 도서출판 어문학사
　　　　서울특별시 도봉구 해등로 357 나너울카운티 1층
　　　　대표전화: 02-998-0094/편집부1: 02-998-2267, 편집부2: 02-998-2269
　　　　홈페이지: www.amhbook.com
　　　　트위터: @with_amhbook
　　　　페이스북: www.facebook.com/amhbook
　　　　블로그: 네이버 http://blog.naver.com/amhbook
　　　　　　　다음 http://blog.daum.net/amhbook
　　　　e-mail: am@amhbook.com
　　　　등록: 2004년 7월 26일 제2009-2호
ISBN 978-89-6184-953-1 03740
정가 20,000원

이 도서의 국립중앙도서관 출판예정도서목록(CIP)은 서지정보유통지원시스템 홈페이지
(http://seoji.nl.go.kr)와 국가자료종합목록 구축시스템(http://kolis-net.nl.go.kr)에서
이용하실 수 있습니다. (CIP제어번호 : CIP2020026244)

※잘못 만들어진 책은 교환해 드립니다.

Anyone
Can Teach
In English

누구나 영어로 가르칠 수 있다